ARNHEIM FOR FILM
AND
MEDIA STUDIES

Rudolf Arnheim (1904–2007) was a pioneering figure in film studies, best known for his landmark book on silent cinema *Film as Art*. He ultimately became more famous as a scholar in the fields of art and art history, largely abandoning his theoretical work on cinema. However, his later aesthetic theories on form, perception, and emotion should play an important role in contemporary film and media studies.

In this enlightening new volume in the AFI Film Readers series, an international group of leading scholars revisits Arnheim's legacy for film and media studies. In fourteen essays, the contributors bring Arnheim's later work on the visual arts to bear on film and media, while also reassessing the implications of his film theory to help refine our grasp of *Film as Art* and related texts. The contributors discuss a broad range of topics including Arnheim's film writings in relation to modernism, his antipathy to sound as well as color in film, the formation of his early ideas on film against the social and political backdrop of the day, the wider uses of his methodology, and the implications of his work for digital media.

This is essential reading for any film and media student or scholar seeking to understand the meaning and contemporary impact of Arnheim's foundational work in film theory and aesthetics.

Scott Higgins is Associate Professor of Film Studies at Wesleyan University. He is author of *Harnessing the Technicolor Rainbow: Color Design in the 1930s.*

Previously published in the AFI Film Readers series
Edited by Edward Branigan and Charles Wolfe

ARNHEIM FOR FILM
AND
MEDIA STUDIES

EDITED BY

SCOTT HIGGINS

Routledge
Taylor & Francis Group

NEW YORK AND LONDON

First published 2011
by Routledge
270 Madison Avenue,
New York, NY 10016

Simultaneously published in the UK
by Routledge
2 Park Square,
Milton Park, Abingdon,
Oxon OX14 4RN

Routledge is an imprint of the Taylor & Francis Group, an informa business

© 2011 Taylor & Francis

Typeset in Spectrum
by Keystroke, Tettenhall, Wolverhampton
Printed and bound in the United States of America on acid-free paper
by Walsworth Publishing Company, Marceline, MO

Library of Congress Cataloging in Publication Data

Arnheim for film and media studies / edited by Scott Higgins.
p. cm.
Includes bibliographical references.
1. Arnheim, Rudolf—Criticism and interpretation. 2. Motion
pictures—Philosophy. 3. Motion pictures—Aesthetics.
PN1998.3.A7557A75 2013
791.4301—dc22
2010024136

ISBN 13: 978–0–415–80107–2 (hbk)
ISBN 13: 978–0–415–80108–9 (pbk)
ISBN 13: 978–0–203–87691–6 (ebk)

contents

contents

vi

illustrations

illustrations

rudolf arnheim

in retrospect

d u d l e y   a n d r e w

The Rudolf Arnheim chapter of *The Major Film Theories* was composed in Paris in Fall 1973, where I had gone—my first trip abroad—to research André Bazin's life, having recently defended my dissertation on his ideas in light of French philosophy. You can imagine why Arnheim appears in that book mainly as a foil to Bazin, for he had laid out an aesthetics of the silent cinema based on principles of "classical" art, whereas Bazin, as has become increasingly clear, assumed sound cinema to be a natural development of an artform whose "modern" phase he felt himself privileged to witness in its *prise de pouvoir*. Arnheim wrote defensively and often nostalgically, anxious over the coming collapse of everything he held dear, while Bazin radiates optimism, expectant about the technology and the films to come.

Just a couple months after completing that chapter, Arnheim appeared to me in a better light. I was lucky enough to be among the dozen participants in Christian Metz's annual seminar at the École Pratique des Hautes Études. One week he announced a break in his suite of presentations that would later appear as "The Imaginary Signifier," for he wanted to talk about Arnheim whose writings he had just encountered, seemingly for the first time. *Toward a Psychology of Art* had appeared in French translation late in 1973; so too had a small section from *Film as Art* in a special "cinema issue" of *Revue d'Esthétique*. Perhaps these translations sent Metz to locate *Film als Kunst*, fluent as he was in German. In any case, he laid out Arnheim's abstract aesthetics and insisted on their pertinence for any film theory that, like his own, aimed both at technological limits and at the spectator's experience. He speculated on what Arnheim might have to say about holography and he pressed me—as an American and thus supposedly technophilic—to develop a presentation on the topic, something I did miserably a week later. I believe Metz looked at Arnheim as the luminous side of the lunar landscape of film perception, while Freud represented the hidden side that he was assiduously pursuing in his own theory. This taught me a lesson: in Paris in 1974 Arnheim was thought to belong to the spectacular rise of the discipline of film theory, while Bazin, undisciplined, was clearly retrograde.

I never heard Metz refer to Arnheim again; had he pursued his brief enthusiasm he would have come across a volume at the Bibliothèque Nationale, published originally in French in 1937, *Le rôle intellectuel du cinéma*. Arnheim is listed as first author in what is an anthology commissioned by the League of Nations, the organization for which he worked at the time in Rome. Arnheim was preparing just then his "New Laocoön," where he expresses outright in the first paragraph "the feeling of extreme uneasiness that every talking film arouses in the author and that is not appeased by increased acquaintance with the new medium."[1] Just a year before, Roger Leenhardt had proclaimed the opposite in his "Little School of the Spectator" in *Esprit*.[2] Film is not based on the "image," he argued, contradicting Arnheim, but on "the shot," a morsel of space–time. Panchromatic stock had already begun to de-sublimate the "diaphanous image" of 1920s art cinema; sound completed this task, tying down every picture to its material source. Bazin took over this position from his friend, pushing not only beyond the image to "the shot" but beyond the shot to "the fact," which he declared to be the atomic unit of Rossellini's films and by extension of modernist cinema overall.[3]

In 1977, the year after *Major Film Theories* was published, an anthology of Arnheim's Weimar criticism came out in German, finding its way into English twenty years later. Suddenly the man whom I had taken to be the dispassionate philosopher and analyst of the visual image appeared as a participant in a crowded and noisy cultural field. And what a culture! The Weimar period that followed World War I was even noisier than the existentialist era Bazin thrived in after the following world war. Both Arnheim and Bazin had graduated from top universities only to find themselves writing regular film criticism for weekly and monthly journals, where they applied principles learned in their studies of art history and literature, respectively, to the movie culture around them. Like the Frankfurt school intellectuals writing at the same time, Arnheim took up contemporary media with gusto, including radio; for this is where money and attention gravitated and this is what people argued over. Magazines and scholarly reviews were full of the subject. It is easy to imagine Arnheim (and Bazin) in the thick of our discussions today concerning computer culture and new media; no doubt they would still be taking opposed positions.

This natural rapport that Weimar intellectuals like Arnheim could maintain with their culture, one where they felt their words really did make a difference, was poisoned at Hitler's ascendency just after *Film as Art* came out. Arnheim would never regain it, moving for some years to Italy, then briefly to the UK, before landing in New York where he found himself, like it or not, walled inside academia. He may have monitored this new world and its energetic popular expressions like any immigrant, but his continuous rapport with the cinema, always troubled, was broken. No longer included in the public sphere, he could consecrate himself to more timeless properties of visual perception and to the principles of art. Everyone admires what he produced decade after decade in the USA: *Art and Visual Perception* (1954), *Toward a Psychology of Art* (1966), *Visual Thinking* (1969), *Art and Entropy* (1971), *The Power of the Center* (1982). I would read each of these expecting to learn something utterly new, while knowing I could relay some of this to my film students so as to turn them, if only intermittently, toward the purely visual dimension of an art form we otherwise invariably tended to discuss in narrative terms.

Arnheim visited Iowa in the Spring of 1975 as part of a symposium on photography and video.[4] I was on a panel keyed to his well-known essay, "The Nature of Photography," which had appeared in the inaugural issue of *Critical Inquiry* just the year before. Naturally I (and many of our graduate students) wanted to skip the advertised topic so as to find out if he still maintained the positions so boldly laid out in *Film as Art*. He seemed fatigued by the question, understanding our concerns in advance; he told us that the field was ours to cultivate as we wished. He was working in other terrain. I drove him to a party that night at the home of Maurice Van Allen, a noted professor of neurology and brother of astronomer James Van Allen, Iowa's Nobel laureate. There Arnheim was introduced to famed literary theorist René Wellek, who by coincidence was giving a short course for Comparative Literature that week. Both men remembered having traversed the Atlantic aboard ship from London to New York, just before German submarines disrupted such service. What impressed me—aside from being in a room with such legendary figures—was that Arnheim and Wellek rather quickly moved beyond the pleasures of catching up on four decades' worth of mutual friends and subsequent experiences; it was aesthetics they wanted to discuss. Where was my tape recorder?

And why did I not prepare for his visit, or ask him back, or seek him out when I would find myself going to Ann Arbor? The essays in this anthology you are holding raise many questions he ought to have been pressed to answer more thoroughly when we had him alive before us. As Patrick Keating so neatly demonstrates, already in 1957 he understood the lure and the problem of contingency in art, a problem his encounter with Kracauer's *Theory of Film* would force him to think through in relation to cinema. Evidently he was taken with neorealism's strategic use of apparently haphazard details of life; he could sense the energy that contingency brings to a work if it can be contained somehow . . . if it can be made art. Like many in the early sixties, he was sure that Antonioni had misinterpreted neorealism's lesson and had allowed the haphazard to take control of his films rather than the reverse. Arnheim struggled with the shift toward modernist cinema that he like so many others could sense occurring between 1957 and 1966. But the very fact that cinema once again caught his attention validates the medium's pretensions to maturity at the rise of the nouvelle vague. Evidently European cinema was worthy of at least the oblique scrutiny of this aesthetician who at the time was hard at work on weighty topics and artistic masterpieces. His *Genesis of a Painting, Picasso's Guernica* came out in 1962.

As this anthology makes abundantly evident, experimental film and animation were modes Arnheim felt no qualms about. Hence we can confidently think through his ideas in coming to grips with so much contemporary audiovisual expression, including mass-market movies that take advantage of computer effects. *Curse of the Golden Flowers* or *Spirited Away* invite Arnheim's studies of color and of composition, just as museum installations using video and film are anticipated by his reflections on "compound arts." The sticking point remains realist cinema. Even when he edges close to Kracauer in his appreciation of ephemera, it is only so as to bring the congenitally commercial aspects of cinema (crass reproduction of the world) under the regime and discipline of the plastic arts (creation, through form, of an alternate world).

And yet when you scan the films he took time to single out, Arnheim's tastes often run parallel to those of Bazin. De Sica has already been mentioned. But there was also Von Stroheim, Flaherty, and Chaplin. (*The Great Dictator* triggered brilliant essays by both men.) Perhaps because the fame of all three directors dates from the silent era, Arnheim expected something special from their sound films. Then there was Jacques Cousteau's *Le monde du silence*, where the enthusiasm of these two critics ran wild and closely converged. Its title alone must have attracted Arnheim. In a phrase redolent of Bazin's rhetoric, Arnheim claims he "would find it hard to argue with somebody who maintained that he would be willing to give the entire film production of the last few years for" this one film.

> [Its] authentically realistic pictures reveal a world of
> profound mystery, a darkness momentarily lifted by flashes
> of unnatural light, a complete suspension of the familiar

vertical and horizontal coordinates of space. Spatial orientation is upset also by the weightlessness of these animals and dehumanized humans, floating up and down without effort, emerging from nowhere and disappearing into nothingness, constantly in motion without any recognizable purpose, and totally indifferent to each other.[5]

Employing different principles Bazin would come to the same conclusion in one of his most beautiful and important essays, one he made sure would survive by including it in the first volume of *Qu'est-ce que le cinéma?* Characteristically, he thought least highly of the most clearly "poetic" sequences of *Le monde du silence*, preferring the moments when, if you'll permit my slightly modified translation, "without losing control of the event, the filmmakers at the same time let its grandeur outshine them, for the poetry of the image is always stronger and richer in interpretation than anything that they could lend it."[6] You may want to know that he singles out as the greatest such moment the one in which suddenly the little whale, wounded by the propeller of the filmmaker's vessel, is devoured by sharks. As so often, Bazin follows cinema to the edge of the human where we can look into the inhuman, into death. But Arnheim this time seems to follow this film to the same scary spot. *Le monde du silence*, he writes, "is a most successful although surely unintentional display of what the most important films of the last few years have been trying to do—namely to interpret the ghostliness of the visible world by means of authentic appearances drawn directly from that world. Cinema has been . . . using imagery to describe reality as a ghostly figment."[7]

Rudolf Arnheim is the ghostly figment described, probe after probe, in this anthology. He treasured clarity, yet has ended up, for me at least, a mystery.

notes

1. Rudolf Arnheim, *Film as Art*, Berkeley: University of California Press, 1957, p. 199.
2. Roger Leenhardt, "Cinematic Rhythm," in Richard Abel, *French Film Theory and Criticism II 1929–1939*, Princeton: Princeton University Press, 1988, pp. 200–204. Originally published in *Esprit* 40 (January 1936).
3. See André Bazin, inter alia, "Defense of Rossellini," in *What is Cinema?, Vol. 2*, Berkeley, University of California Press, 1971, p. 100.
4. David Van Allen, organizer of the 1975 "Refocus" event, supplied me with its program brochure.
5. Arnheim, "Art Today and Film," in *Film Essays and Criticism*, Madison: University of Wisconsin Press, 1997, pp. 26–27.
6. André Bazin, "Le monde du silence," in *Qu'est-ce que le cinéma?*, Paris: Cerf, "édition définitive," 1975, p. 38.
7. Arnheim, "Art Today and Film," p. 27.

acknowledgements

I wish to acknowledge the terrific work of the contributors who have put so many long hours into thinking about Arnheim, responded swiftly to requests for revisions, and who, in the final hour, undertook cuts for length. I also want to express thanks to series editors Edward Branigan and Charles Wolfe who supported this book from its very inception and provided sage guidance at every step. The team at Routledge was remarkably quick and skillful in handling this project, and Matthew Byrnie deserves special gratitude for patiently shepherding this anthology.

Several people made important contributions to this anthology, although their names do not appear on the contents page. David Rodowick organized and hosted the symposium *Rudolf Arnheim and the Moving Image* at Harvard, which brought many of our authors into productive and stimulating conversation. Emily Amendola provided vital support for that meeting, and directed me to Justin Ide of the Harvard University news office who provided our cover photo. The members of the Filmies list took up the cause of this anthology early on and spread word to the scholarly community. Closer to home, my colleagues at Wesleyan University, Jeanine Basinger, Lea Carlson, and Lisa Dombrowski, showed their customarily extraordinary encouragement and wisdom.

The photograph of Arnheim on this book's cover is used with permission of Harvard University. Illustrations for David Bordwell's essay are reproduced with permission from University of California Press. The "Blueberry" photograph for Vince Bohlinger's essay is courtesy of the United States Holocaust Memorial Museum.

I would like to dedicate this book to Sally Ross who graciously shared all the burdens (and joys) of balancing this work with the demands of our three children and our full house, and who deserves equal credit for any good ideas that I've managed to express.

introduction

s c o t t   h i g g i n s

Rudolf Arnheim was one of the most significant and prolific theorists of visual media in the twentieth century. During his lifetime, Arnheim published over twenty books and more than 300 articles, and he left a profound legacy of thought about art, perception, and the process of creation. This anthology is devoted to exploring the value of that legacy for the study of film and associated media. Arnheim is best known in film studies for his pioneering theoretical text on silent cinema *Film as Art*, originally published in 1932 as *Film als Kunst* and rewritten in the late 1950s. It was in the fields of art and art history, however, that Arnheim made his mark, beginning with the publication of *Art and Visual Perception* (1954) and continuing through the 1990s. Writing from the perspective of gestalt psychology, Arnheim devoted his life to understanding the power of form in organizing perception, expressing ideas, and conveying emotion. His chief concern was how architectures of composition, contour, line, and color interacted with a creative perceptual system. In 1974 he wrote "all observation is also invention."[1]

The breadth of Arnheim's interests was remarkable; as *The New York Times* obituary remarked, he "was practicing media studies long before the term was coined."[2] In a career that spanned seven decades and two continents, he explored television, radio, still photography, and film while breaking ground for the field of the psychology of art. Arnheim was born in Berlin in 1904, the son of a piano factory owner. By 1928 he had completed a PhD at the Psychological Institute at the University of Berlin under the tutelage of Max Wertheimer and Wolfgang Kohler, founders of gestalt psychology. At the same time, Arnheim also worked as a journalist, testing his ideas in the popular press. Writing in 1997, he recalled "it was really film that hijacked me into writing for the daily papers."[3] He reviewed films for newspapers including *Berliner Tageblatt* and journals including the satirical *Das Stachelschwein* (*The Porcupine*), and from 1928 to 1933 he served as a junior editor for the progressive journal *Die Weltbühne* where he contributed articles on film, psychology, literature, and art. Throughout the early 1930s Arnheim's interests in cinema and perceptual psychology were in productive conversation. Film offered "novel examples" in his exploration of art theory "as a proving ground for the principles of visual perception."[4] These twin fascinations drove his first book-length study, *Film als Kunst*, published in 1932 and translated into English as *Film* in 1933.[5]

Sale of *Film als Kunst* was prohibited by the Nazis in 1933 because of Arnheim's Jewish ancestry. That year Arnheim emigrated to Italy where he worked for the International Institute for Educational Films under the auspices of the League of Nations in Rome. There, he continued to focus on cinema and modern media, contributing to and editing the journals *Intercine* and *Cinema*, collaborating on an encyclopedia of film, and seeking publication of his manuscript *Radio*, which appeared in English in 1936. With the onset of racial laws in 1938 and the start of World War II the following year, Arnheim fled Italy. He worked briefly as a translator in London and arrived in New York in 1940. Max Wertheimer had already established himself in the city, and with his mentor's aid Arnheim secured a position at the New School for Social Research. He also received a Rockefeller Foundation fellowship to work with the Office of Radio Research at Columbia University. Arnheim's study of radio produced essays on foreign language broadcast in the U.S. and on daytime serials, but soon he turned his attention almost exclusively to the high arts.

In 1942 he was awarded a Guggenheim Foundation fellowship to study perceptual psychology and the visual arts, and the following year Arnheim joined the faculty of the psychology department at Sarah Lawrence College, where he would remain for twenty-five years. In 1954, Arnheim published his pioneering volume *Art and Visual Perception*, which solidified his position as a leader in the field of art theory. From the early 1960s he published major works with remarkably rapid succession, including *Picasso's Guernica* (1962), *Toward a Psychology of Art* (1966), *Visual Thinking* (1969) and *Entropy and Art* (1971).

He joined the Department of Visual and Environmental Studies at Harvard University as Professor of the Psychology of Art in 1969 and retired from teaching in 1974. For the next thirty-seven years Arnheim lived in Ann Arbor where he was a visiting Professor and then Emeritus Professor at University of Michigan. In retirement Arnheim continued to research and write; his final book, *The Split and the Structure* was published in 1996.[6] He died at the age of 102 in June of 2007.

This book takes up both Arnheim's explicit engagements with film and media, and the implications of his more strictly art-historical work. *Film as Art*, though, merits special attention here because of its importance to many of the essays that follow and to film studies in general. In Anglo/American film studies, the most familiar, canonical, version of the book is University of California Press's 1957 reissue. This is, in fact, a considerably shortened version featuring "selections adapted from *Film*," the 1933 English translation of *Film als Kunst*. When it appeared, *Film als Kunst* featured six chapters and ran to nearly 300 pages. Eliminated for the 1957 version was an extended discussion of sound film, which is taken up by Nora M. Alter in her essay "Screening Out Sound" in this anthology, and a discourse on film content. Sabine Hake argues that Arnheim also removed discussion of ideology and cultural politics in his rewrite: "a work marked by history—was transformed into a canonized text of the formalist tradition."[7] Several essays in this volume explore the cultural and historical underpinnings of Arnheim's work which have perhaps been underappreciated in the wake of the 1957 *Film as Art*. Yet, in his preface to the revised edition Arnheim still signaled a social mission for his theory and the strong bond between artistic form and culture:

> Shape and color, sound and words are the means by which man defines the nature and intention of his life. In a functioning culture, his ideas reverberate from his buildings, statues, songs, and plays. But a population constantly exposed to chaotic sights and sounds is gravely handicapped in finding its way. When the eyes and ears are prevented from perceiving meaningful order, they can only react to the brutal signals of immediate satisfaction.[8]

Sharp, meaningful forms, and viewers who could discern order in artworks, were for Arnheim culturally important. One senses in his work the belief that thoughtful form could be a bulwark against Fascist bombast. For better or worse, the 1957 edition has become the major touchstone for students and scholars of cinema and it is this version that forms a backdrop for the volume you are reading.

Arnheim famously declined to update his revision of *Film as Art* with reference to the history of cinema since 1932. Instead, he held that "film is, to me, a unique experiment in the visual arts which took place in the first three decades of this century."[9] As Noël Carroll points out, rather than persuading him to recant, "the passage of time radicalized Arnheim's position as a silent-film advocate during a period when that species was—and is—effectively extinct."[10] As a young intellectual and cinephile of the 1920s and 1930s, Arnheim was eager to make the case for film as an art form on the grounds established for respected arts like painting. Carroll views this as a quality of silent film theory in general, noting that it "can be seen as a reflection and codification of the principles underlying the ambitious and aspiring society of filmmakers who were seeking to turn their medium into an art on the terms set by the culture and art world of their day."[11] Those terms stipulated that an art form distinguished itself by the specific means it had to manipulate rather than imitate reality. Influenced by G. E. Lessing, Arnheim would argue that cinema's claim to the throne of art depended on particular material limitations that distinguished it from other arts and from simple reproduction. Arnheim crystallizes this position in his justly renowned pronouncement: "art begins where mechanical reproduction leaves off, where the conditions of representation serve in some way to mold the object."[12] The basis of his argument in *Film as Art* is his systematic accounting of the form's limitations, the aspects that blocked easy mimesis or exact reproduction. Arnheim used the term "*Materialtheorie*" to encapsulate his view that "artistic and scientific descriptions of reality are cast in molds that derive not so much from the subject matter itself as from the properties of the medium—or *Material*—employed."[13] This critical premise, that to understand film art one must attend to the materials of its making, was widely shared by aesthetic theorists of the silent era, and it accorded well with the tenets of modernism more generally.[14]

Arnheim's most recognized innovation in *Film as Art* is his grounding of silent film theory in the concepts of gestalt psychology, which had been developed by Wertheimer and Kohler, his teachers at the University of Berlin. Gestalt's universal principles of visual perception and cognition underwrite most of Arnheim's aesthetic doctrine, in essence granting the theory scope and systematicity while elevating cinema as an exemplary art. In positing perception as a creative act in which the mind organizes the material of the world, gestalt psychology gave Arnheim insight into the work of the artist. Art translates the stuff of the world into the materials of its medium in much the way that the act of perception creatively transforms raw sensory input. The basic schemata active during perception (the striving for balance, simplicity, clarity, expressiveness) should then inform successful art. In this model, art becomes an exalted form of perception. Artists do not strictly derive work from reality, but shape an equivalent that is sharper, cleaner, and more meaningful. Art itself could function as an exercise for viewers, helping them to appreciate and focus their perceptual powers as they work through the artist's materials to unlock an expressive representation.

Film, in this model, presented a "test case" for Arnheim. In his 1957 preface, he writes:

> if a mechanical reproduction of reality, made by machine, could be art, then the theory was wrong . . . I undertook to show in detail how the very properties that make photography and film fall short of perfect reproduction could act as the necessary molds of an artistic medium.[15]

The book is divided into two parts: the first lays out his taxonomy of ways that film diverges from mechanical reproduction; the second describes (and prescribes) how these divergences can be used artfully. As summary, Arnheim condenses his argument into a list of twenty "characteristics of the film medium" and a set of "applications" for each trait. For instance, his first characteristic is that "every object must be photographed from one particular vantage point" which renders the following applications:

> a) View that shows the shape of an object most characteristically; b) View that conveys a particular conception of the object (e.g., worm's-eye-view, indicating weight and forcefulness); c) View that attracts the spectator's attention by being unusual: d) Surprise effect due to the concealment of the back side (Chaplin sobbing; no! mixing a cocktail!).[16]

One pleasure of the book is the absolute assuredness with which Arnheim builds his taxonomy, encompassing qualities of the moving image that we tend to take for granted. Where the medium diverges from normal perception by imposing a single view of an object at a time, by depicting a three-dimensional image in two dimensions, and by separating vision from other bodily sensations, Arnheim sees expressive possibilities. Noël Carroll is undoubtedly correct that "no one could mistake Arnheim's review of the articulatory processes of film as comprehensive," and yet he writes with such unflinching certainty about often-overlooked fundamentals of film form that his case becomes compelling.[17] This logic led Arnheim rather infamously to count qualities like silence and black-and-white reproduction among film's generative characteristics, locking his aesthetic recommendations to now obsolete technological traits. Especially when reduced to an inventory, characteristics such as "the absence of sound" and "arrangement of light and shade, absence of color" become barriers that few contemporary students of film are willing to cross. Yet this often-quoted and -taught list of characteristics does disservice to the complexities and insights of *Film as Art*.

In *Philosophical Problems in Classical Film Theory*, Noël Carroll persuasively argues that Arnheim rests his case on a series of logically faulty presuppositions about the nature of art. Art, for Arnheim *must* diverge from reproduction, *must* be expressive, and *must* emerge from unshared, specific, qualities of the medium.[18] In the end, *Film as Art* has been properly criticized

5

for presenting an essentialist argument, and for casting historically contingent characteristics as the medium's essence. Along the way, though, Arnheim's framework sensitizes him to significant aspects of film form. For example, consider his discussion of composition and framing derived from the fact that the static camera can view a subject from only a single vantage point in two dimensions. For Arnheim, the very choice of camera angle leads to the possibility of defamiliarization (what he calls "provocative unfamiliarity") and expression.[19] While a vantage point in a continuous three-dimensional space is one among many, cinema can grant a sense of determined order to the image: "what is visible and invisible, and what is hidden strike one as being definitely intentional; one is forced to seek for a reason."[20] The occlusion and obstruction of objects becomes, in Arnheim's model, a creative tool: "the film artist who makes a virtue of necessity in taking his shots from a definite angle arranges the objects as he wishes, puts what seems to him important in the foreground, hides other things, suggests relationships."[21] Thus he praises a shot in Eisenstein's *The General Line* (1929) in which a fat landowner stands in front of a poor peasant woman and "the whole picture is suddenly filled and dominated by this huge, elephantine back" to suggest "power obliterating helplessness."[22] His methods anticipate contemporary formalist tactics for understanding cinema's poetics. Arnheim analyzes formal choices by posing hypothetical alternatives, as when he suggests a variety of framings for a shot of a prisoner leaving his jail in Abram Room's *Ghost that Never Returns* (1929), to throw light on the particular power of a filmmaker's preference. He also poses the task of filmmaking as a weighing of various solutions to artistic problems, as when he discusses the various means for depicting conversations, concluding that in the case of Jacques Feyder's *Les Nouveaux Messieurs* (1929), where a woman's face is shadowed by a man's in the foreground, "one seems to see more by seeing less."[23] Throughout, Arnheim exhibits a remarkable grasp of the fine-grain of film style and speculates convincingly about the filmmakers' choice situations.

Arnheim's best-known example of the power of camera placement reveals how his approach wove together gestalt concepts with aesthetic judgment and beliefs about the function of art. Arnheim cites the opening of *The Immigrant* (1917) in which Chaplin, back to camera, bends over a ship's railing so that "everyone thinks the poor devil is paying his toll to the sea," only to turn around and reveal "that he has hooked a large fish with his walking stick."[24] The moment is compelling, partly because it draws attention to the limits of cinema's vantage point. The viewer accepts the hypothesis that Chaplin is seasick because of the seeming completeness of the initial view. Upon the reveal, however, Arnheim's spectator becomes aware both of Chaplin's deception, and of the camera placement:

> The idea underlying the scene is no longer "a man is doing
> such and such a thing, for example, he is fishing or being

sick," but "a man is doing this and that *and* at the same time the spectator is watching him from a particular station point."[25]

Arnheim is fond of this sort of sight gag, which, as Gertrud Koch points out, depends on a "Gestalt switch."[26] The effect is not unlike psychologist Edgar Rubin's cut-outs that could be read either as a vase or as two profiles. Having grasped the image as a whole, Chaplin's reveal requires the viewer to constitute an alternative gestalt, which has the salutary effect of highlighting the very capacity of film form to select views.

For Arnheim, this awareness *of* form is essential to aesthetic experience. He casts the issue in terms akin to the Russian formalist's notion of defamiliarization:

> It is a well-known fact that many married couples do not know the color of each other's eyes; that people are ignorant of the very pictures that hang on the walls of their dining rooms . . . It is indeed exceptional—apart from persons of aesthetic tastes and training—for anyone suddenly to lose himself in gratuitous contemplation, to watch his neighbor's hands, to examine the telephone for its shape, to observe the play of shadows on the pavement.[27]

It is this very contemplation, the power to "make the stone stony" as Victor Schlovsky observed, that art required and could foster for Arnheim. The creative choice of camera angle was one of a number of "artifices by which the spectator may be induced to assume such an attitude," a method of teaching aesthetic perception.[28] The momentary defamiliarization brought on by Chaplin's gestalt switch drives the viewer back to an awareness and appreciation of form that is essential "to understand a work of art."[29] In this example, Arnheim begins with an instance of filmmaking that he finds aesthetically worthy, and then proceeds to explain it in gestalt and formalist terms. Further, he suggests an effect of form on the spectator that helps soften the often-elitist tone of the book. Though he derides the viewer of mass culture as "lacking in proper understanding when he is satisfied to notice merely the content," in the case of Chaplin Arnheim holds out hope that some popular films have pedagogical potential. Art could be a training ground for formal awareness.[30]

Film as Art is rife with observations on the nature of filmmaking, which remain valuable despite the text's prescriptive essentialism. For instance, Arnheim conceives of the film frame as enabling compositional hierarchies, as he explains "there is no balance in the infinite."[31] We need not accept this as a requirement of the medium to see its value as an analytical or creative tool. For Arnheim, a stable and balanced composition feels complete to the spectator, which makes its alteration come as a "psychological shock." Thus he explicates the comedy of the moment when Buster Keaton reveals himself in an office corner we had thought unoccupied in *The Cameraman* (1928): "a complete whole is shown, and the spectator has been lulled to a false sense of security; suddenly the total structure of this whole is altered by an insignificant twist which seems incongruous with what has gone before."[32] Similarly, Arnheim's notion of "indirect representation" making an event sharper and more vivid seems worthwhile. By finding visual equivalents for sound, for instance, an artist achieves clever emphasis and meaning. When Sternberg cuts to a rising flock of birds to signal gunfire in *Docks of New York* (1928), "the fact that a pistol shot is sudden, explosive, startling, becomes doubly impressive by transposition into the visible because only these particular attributes and not the shot itself are given."[33] In finding novel translations of events, or "robbing the real" as Arnheim puts it, film can deliver an expressive charge with startling concreteness.[34] As a theorist, Arnheim tends to harden his observations into law. He writes "the creative power of the artist can *only* come into play where reality and the medium of representation do not coincide."[35] Yet, if we bracket off such essentializing from his insights about film form, *Film as Art* emerges as a remarkably precise and perceptive treatise on the formal possibilities of silent narrative cinema.

Exploring beyond Arnheim's summary list of film characteristics also reveals the extent to which *Film as Art* is informed by the reigning aesthetic norms of the time. Though his examples range between German, French, Soviet, and American films, his preferences seem to lie with the carefully unified and motivated works of classical Hollywood. Several of Arnheim's rules, for instance his insistence that dissolves occur between scenes rather than within them, or his dismissal of ellipsis within a continuous space as "unusable," derive directly from the conventions of Hollywood cinema. Indeed, films from movements that purposefully bent these norms, such as French impressionist cinema, or Soviet montage, tend to fail for Arnheim. The constructive editing in Carl Theodor Dreyer's *Passion of Jean d'arc* (1928), for instance, stands for "form for form's sake . . . the rock on which many film artists, especially the French, are shipwrecked."[36] Arnheim favored, and required, "significant form" from his films. The meaning of a formal device, however, must not appear thrust from outside the film's world, as does the image of a tractor crashing through fences in Eisenstein's *The General Line*. Rather, "any symbolic scene must be so planned that it not only makes this implicit meaning visible in a comprehensible manner, but also fits smoothly into the action and the world depicted in the film."[37]

Above all, Arnheim values cleverness, meaning, and subtlety: films that experiment with novel stylistics to achieve meaning without stretching diegesis. Consider, for instance, his criticism of a scene in G. W. Pabst's *Diary of a Lost Girl* (1929) in which two lovers are seen to kiss first from inside a pharmacy with a glass door beyond them, and then from the street, in silhouette through that door. Arnheim finds the shot change "wholly superficial and decorative." He explains, "It signifies nothing. And things which have no significance have no place in a work of art."[38] The shot might be stronger, Arnheim conjectures, if Pabst had offered sufficient motivation within the story world, such as a character "looking through the door and watching the scene from the outside." Yet the real test of artistic validity would be for the shot change to function not simply as "a clever visual interpretation" but to achieve "symbolic depth."[39] This vision of significance achieved in a motivated fashion, of meaning that appears to emerge without drawing attention to the device, found its highest expression, for Arnheim, in the work of Charlie Chaplin. Chaplin's dining on an old boot in *The Goldrush* (1925), for instance, exemplifies how a film artist can forcefully embody an abstract concept (the contrast between rich and poor) in concrete terms without breaking from the story world.

Throughout the book, what Arnheim calls the "naturalistic narrative film," the form to which he most often refers, tracks closely the ascendant classical Hollywood style. Arnheim's aesthetic judgments return us to his theory's historical context. Though he claims universality, Arnheim actually has developed a worthwhile account of a certain kind of virtuosity that was achievable within the specific confines of late 1920s and early 1930s mainstream filmmaking. Most films, Hollywood productions included, failed to achieve the rank of art because they aimed only to "tell the people stories" and because filmmakers and "audiences are not concerned with form but with content."[40] Indeed, it is something of a paradox that the kind of cinema Arnheim elevated was one that so carefully hid its formal manipulations in order to better narrate. Arguably, the very qualities of subtlety and cleverness that Arnheim so valued were encouraged by classical Hollywood's imperative to engage and entertain mass audiences. Nonetheless, time and again through its examples *Film as Art* reminds us of the virtuosity that could be attained, and it stands as a call for higher achievement of "what might be, what lies hidden and untapped" within that system.[41] Similarly, Arnheim held out hope that viewers might, through popular art, be brought to aesthetic awareness.

Arnheim's watchwords of subtlety and motivation, his dislike of overt artifice and "interfering with reality," and his overriding concern that art "interprets and molds material without doing violence to it" put him in an ambivalent position with regard to modernism.[42] His *Materialtheorie* anticipates Clement Greenberg's arguments for medium specificity, and yet Arnheim seems uncomfortable with abstraction. Ara H. Merjian notes that in its anti-mimetic stance Arnheim's theory "appropriates a distinctly modernist conception of art in its battle against filmic realism."[43] Moreover, Merjian profitably sees Arnheim's aesthetic rigidity as akin to a modernist manifesto: "it is precisely such unyielding parochialisms . . . that distinguish the theory both as an emblem of modernist dogma and a forerunner of Greenberg's peremptory purism."[44] Yet *Film as Art* repeatedly returns to meaningful significance as the sole purpose of visual distortion. Filmmakers must resist reproduction, but, Arnheim warns, "the character of the objects represented should not thereby be destroyed but rather strengthened, concentrated, and interpreted."[45] From this perspective, black-and-white cinematography clarifies faces, turning them into "stylized expressive masks" and the absence of sound shapes, interprets and concentrates gesture.[46] This tension between abstraction and meaning leads Merjian aptly to term Arnheim's theory "a definitively middlebrow modernism" which calls "for intelligibility in art above all else."[47] Arnheim's rejection of imitation, which may well have derived from his gestalt background, resembles aesthetic modernism, but the goal for him was always a sharper and clearer expression of meaning, not its questioning and dissolution.[48] Bound on one hand to notice form but on the other to seek narratively recuperable meanings, Arnheim, and his ideal spectator, are aesthetically aware connoisseurs of an art that rewards contemplation with significance.

This book aims, in part, to bring the ideas that Arnheim initiates in *Film as Art* to bear on the concerns of contemporary film and media scholars. By narrowing and historicizing its claims, Arnheim's theory and his observations on film form and viewer perception may yet serve us. Though the assumptions of gestalt psychology are open to question, Arnheim's ideas can help drive piecemeal theories about how filmmakers make compositions legible or expressive, how visual qualities guide the eye across a frame, how perceptual competences shape cognition and creation, and even how film styles develop and change over time. The essays that follow also revisit Arnheim's thoughts on associated mass arts such as photography, radio, and television. In each case, Arnheim tends to build upon the framework he developed in his first book. Radio, for instance, made a virtue of its limitations because "for the first time it makes use of the aural only, without the almost invariable accompaniment of the visual which we find in nature as well as in art."[49] If sound threatened cinema by loosening the form's generative restrictions so too might television impinge on radio's aesthetic potential.[50] Perhaps even more remarkably, the ideas of *Film as Art* remained central to Arnheim's more influential writing on painting. Even acknowledging that Arnheim revised *Film* in light of *Art and Visual Perception*, his mode of analysis is remarkably consistent from book to book. In introducing *The Power of the Center*, for example, Arnheim remarks: "My work is based on the assumption that the most powerful conveyer of meaning is in the immediate impact of perceptual form. And it is this impact that distinguishes art from other kinds of communication."[51] The connection of form to meaning, the value of immediate perceptual impact, and the notion that awareness of form distinguishes art from other kinds of cultural transmission, can all be traced back to Arnheim's theory of film. In bringing Arnheim back to considerations of the moving image and media, this volume returns to the theorist's foundations while partaking of the full evolution of his thought.

This volume opens with David Bordwell's expanded version of the piece that inspired this book. Bordwell frames Arnheim's contribution to the field of aesthetics in relation to E. H. Gombrich, the other titan of twentieth-century modern art theory. Both responded to scientific theories of perception in their accounting of aesthetics, but while Gombrich sought to explain the means of representation, Arnheim devoted himself to the question of how forms become expressive. Gestalt theory's emphasis on fundamental capacities over cultural learning put Arnheim at odds with Gombrich as well as with recent trends in aesthetic theory. Yet Arnheim's unyielding principles were also a source of progress, encouraging a provocative and expansive approach to how form works for artists and viewers. For Bordwell, Arnheim models rigorous and passionate scholarship that should be remembered and emulated.

The remainder of this anthology moves outward from essays that consider Arnheim's film writing to broader discussions of related media. In the second chapter, Malcolm Turvey takes up a fundamental question with regard to Arnheim's film theory: is it modernist? Several scholars, most notably Ara Merjian in his compelling essay "Middlebrow Modernism," have placed *Film as Art* in the tradition of modernist criticism exemplified by Clement Greenberg. Turvey, reconsidering his own ideas about Arnheim in his book *Doubting Vision*, now views the matter as more complex. Arnheim's gestalt-derived theories of expressive form and creative perception run counter to modernist assumptions about the inferiority of human vision, the purity of art forms, and the progress of a medium. While Arnheim shares the notion of medium specificity with the likes of Greenberg, Turvey argues that his belief in the creative eye and visual understanding through art made him a more innovative and original thinker. Arnheim resists criticisms that might be leveled at a simple modernist position, and Turvey reveals his theory to be more supple and varied than is commonly understood.

Eric Rentschler, in Chapter 3, also broadens our view of Arnheim's film theory by considering his work as a young critic in the 1920s and 1930s. Like Sabine Hake, noted above, Rentschler finds the 1957 rewrite of *Film as Art* to be devoid of the historical and political inflections that marked the 1932 original. Returning to Arnheim's earliest writing on film, Rentschler suggests that his ideas formed in conversation with social and political currents of the day. Indeed, Rentschler argues, Arnheim's perspective was remarkably close to Siegfried Kracauer's on cinema's sociological import. Arnheim's criticism also shows him to be a sharp, witty, and referential writer, qualities downplayed by the canonized academic view of *Film as Art*. The chapter presents an "unrecognized" Arnheim, and helps us appreciate the cultural and political foment from which his film theory emerged.

Nora M. Alter, in Chapter 4, confronts Arnheim's most notorious aesthetic judgment in *Film as Art*: his antipathy to sound. By parsing three versions of *Film* and Arnheim's critical writing, Alter reveals a theorist who wrestled with questions raised by the new medium and, ultimately, came to a tentative acceptance of it. The crisis of sound, for Alter, exposes Arnheim's prejudices against mass culture as well as his class, gender, and regional biases, but it also brings to light his process of thought. Initially it seemed that dialogue in film compromised the cinema's specificity, and that sound made the image more concrete, less prone to aesthetic vision. To a certain extent, Arnheim's intuition about sound was on track. Sound did build a realistic diegesis at the expense of abstraction as evidenced by the decline of associational montage and superimposition. Finally, he reasoned that sound montage, or the complex layering of sound, held aesthetic potential. In Walter Ruttman's imageless sound film *Weekend* (1930), Arnheim sensed the mixture of mimesis and strangeness that had enabled silent cinema's expressive power.

In Chapter 5, Meraj Dhir uncovers Arnheim's theory of expressive composition initiated in *Film as Art* and fully developed in his later work. For Dhir, Arnheim's observations provide a trove of analytical methods useful to film scholars. In particular, Dhir explores how Arnheim's gestalt framework leads him to view composition as a meaningful balance of interconnected forces. Using Hal Ashby's *Harold and Maude* (1971) as a test case, Dhir brings Arnheim's ideas about composition back to the moving image and argues that pictorial patterning guides the viewer to construct meaning. Because meaning is integral to form for Arnheim, Dhir believes that his analytical model speaks to debates about the role of interpretation in film aesthetics. Posing form as expressive might allow us to track thematic implications of composition in a "bottom-up" fashion.

In my essay, Chapter 6, I address another form that Arnheim famously rejected, color cinema. Though he originally denied color any artistic merit in the pages of *Film*, a few years later Arnheim was cautiously optimistic of its theoretical possibilities. He never pursued color cinema as a formal problem at any length, but his later work on painting and composition yielded powerful observations about the role of chroma in shaping perception. Color, for Arnheim, was a force for binding and segregating areas of the canvas. I adapt his ideas to cinema and suggest their utility for analyzing the unusually complex color designs of filmmakers like Vincente Minnelli. Through a close analysis of the "Skip to My Lou" number from *Meet Me in St. Louis* (1944), I consider how color can structure attention and I argue that Arnheim's color theory newly reveals the intricacies of Minnelli's masterpiece.

Jinhee Choi's Chapter 7, also begins from the apparent narrowness of Arnheim's formal preferences. She turns to Arnheim's argument about "The Complete Film," which originates in *Film as Art*, and extends its relevance to contemporary aesthetics. Arnheim's view that technological progress in filmic reproduction is a corrupting but inevitable process would seem to put his theory at odds with the digital revolution. However, Choi explores continuities between Arnheim's theory and current discussions of digital intermediate. She argues that by separating Arnheim's aesthetic principles from his ontological argument we can uncover a framework that still holds sway in contemporary debates about the digital media. In particular, ideas like the duality between mimetic and expressive functions of technology, and principles such as homogeneity and naturalism, continue to inform the way we think about the moving image.

The remaining essays reach beyond *Film as Art* in a variety of ways. Patrick Keating, in Chapter 8, pursues Arnheim's later film theory and finds a surprising congruence with Siegfried Kracauer on cinema's power to capture the contingent. Beginning with "Melancholy Unshaped," Arnheim's review of Kracauer's *Theory of Film,* Keating traces the evolution of thought that led him to qualify his anti-mimetic stance. The task of art continued to be the unveiling of meaningful structure, but Arnheim increasingly saw the quest for order as balanced against the search for complexity. The contingent and accidental qualities of modern experience posed a kind of complexity that art might seize and interpret. From this new perspective, film's mechanical basis, its lack of intentionality, became a positive potential in that it could help the artist address and thematize modernity. Keating develops Arnheim's comments on Vittorio De Sica's neorealist classic *Umberto D.* (1952) to illustrate how the theorist's attention to compositional strategies can help us grasp the nature of cinematic realism in that work. Once again, a careful reevaluation suggests that Arnheim's ambit is more expansive than the rigidity of *Film as Art* leads us to expect.

Like Keating, Maureen Turim brings Arnheim's theory to a kind of film he rarely addressed in writing. In Chapter 9 she returns to the subject of her first book *Abstraction in Avant-Garde Films* to ask how Arnheim's ideas about visual thinking might resonate with film artists such as Maya Deren, Hollis Frampton, and Larry Gottheim. She suggests that across his career Arnheim wrestled with and articulated problems of form and order that post-war avant-garde filmmakers were simultaneously engaging with. His exploration of film's material transformations of reality, for instance, drew him to appreciate Deren's combination of abstraction and mimesis. Though Arnheim tended to focus on balance and order in art, Turim identifies a countervailing fascination with discontinuity and entropy, which evolved in his later work and bears on film experimentation of the 1970s. The chapter places Arnheim in productive conversation with experimental cinema, and finds critical tools for elucidating difficult and challenging film practice.

Arnheim's interest in media reached beyond film and into the realm of broadcasting. In his analysis of Arnheim's writing on radio in Chapter 10, Shawn VanCour examines how the theorist interwove formal, economic, and cultural contexts to make sense of the new medium. In taking up extratextual issues like regulatory practice, the reception of radio narratives, and ideology, Arnheim engaged in a complex mode of media analysis. *Materialtheorie* offered a basis for defining the artistic, formal possibilities of the medium in much the way it had enabled *Film as Art*. Arnheim celebrated radio's potential for direct expressive power, made possible because sound was freed from the mimetic image. Yet Arnheim was also attuned to the sociological aspects of the mass medium. He was concerned that programmers balance mass appeal with meaningful cultural content and, in his work on American soap opera in the early 1940s, Arnheim argued that female audiences would be better served by a form that located problems in social institutions rather than individual villainy. The case of radio, VanCour argues, shows how Arnheim blended formal and sociological concerns in a manner that serves as a model for contemporary media studies.

Doron Galili, in Chapter 11, extends this line of thought in his detailed analysis of Arnheim's discussions of television. Writing after television's innovation but before its dissemination as a mass medium, Arnheim speculated on its potentials and dangers. By turns utopian and alarmist, Arnheim's view of television celebrated the unifying effects of simultaneous transmission of live events and warned of the medium's tendency to produce passive, isolated viewers. Television also provided a spur to Arnheim's thought about media specificity. As a delivery technology, it separated the arts of theater and film from their material bases, which encouraged Arnheim to refine his ideas about each art's distinctive characteristics. For Galili, Arnheim modeled an "intermedial" approach to television, envisioning arts and media as a set of related cores and peripheries. Arnheim's ability to countenance the new medium in relation to his paradigms for film and radio may hold lessons for contemporary scholars of digital media. He responded to the new media of the 1930s by parsing existing forms, remaining sensitive to distinctions between them, and attending to continuities, all strategies that Galili suggests might help us better grasp our own digital revolution.

Arnheim examined the processes of perception in order to understand art, an approach that need not be limited to film and painting. In Chapter 12 Greg M. Smith takes what he calls a "neo-Arnheimian" view of comics, a form that the theorist barely acknowledged. Smith argues that by bracketing off the prescriptive aspects of Arnheim's theory and taking up its "processual" concepts, we can open up the complex workings of "sequential art" like comic strips, comic books, and graphic novels. The great defender of silent cinema would almost certainly disapprove of comics as a hybrid medium. Yet, Smith illustrates how Arnheim's frameworks for understanding painting and film can shed light on the nature of comics. The form's mandate to represent movement through a series of static images, for instance, provides the kind of artistic problem, the blockage of representation, that Arnheim saw as generative. In bringing Arnheim's ideas to Alan Moore's and Brian Bolland's *Batman: The Killing Joke*, Smith makes a convincing case for the continued expansion and deepening of Arnheim's approach.

In Chapter 13 Colin Burnett, too, brings Arnheim's thought to new ground: in this case, the question of how film scholars define and utilize the concept of "style." In Arnheim's essay "Style as a Gestalt Problem," Burnett finds a convincing solution to problems and confusions endemic to scholarly discussions of film style. As commonly used in film studies, style remains an ill-defined and under-theorized concept that tends to blur the historically distinct issues relating to classes of art and to the devices within specific artworks. Arnheim distinguishes between "style," referring to historical classes of art and "composition," referring to techniques within an artwork. In his model, styles are not monoliths, but weavings of impulses. Style is identifiable as a "way of making" rather than as a collection of formal techniques. Burnett shows how a film style, like classical Hollywood cinema, which appears unified at one level of analysis, will probably appear more eclectic at a higher magnification that reveals its weave of disparate techniques and functions. Arnheim promotes a philosophically robust conception of style that helps account for the diverse field of forces at work in any film, movement, or historical period. For Burnett, this approach allows us to acknowledge the stakes in talking about film style, to pose questions about it more sharply and to be conceptually more precise in parsing trends of filmmaking.

In the final chapter of this volume, Vincent Bohlinger turns his attention to Arnheim's last major essay on film and photography, "Two Authenticities of the Photographic Media," first published in 1993. Prompted by controversy surrounding the use of video evidence in the Rodney King trial, Arnheim revisits his ontological arguments from *Film as Art*. The case of digital video manipulation leads him to identify a tension between the authenticity of realistic representation and the authenticity of human experience and expression: two authenticities that have shaped the history of representational art. In this model, mechanical reproduction is no longer the antithesis of art, but one aspect of a duality between depiction and expression that defines the arts. For Bohlinger, this reformulation is an opportunity to revisit the oft-studied opposition between André Bazin's and Arnheim's theories. The comparison sheds new light on the nature of Arnheim's conceptions of ambiguity, reality, and form. The two authenticities also provide Bohlinger with a theoretical vantage point on troubling visual documents like the Rodney King tape or the infamous Abu Ghraib photos. The strong emotion elicited in these cases stems from tension between authenticities and points up photography's special balance between depiction and form. "Two Authenticities of the Photographic Media" offers a telling glimpse of Arnheim's encounter with the digital age, and it provides a final example of how Arnheim's thought can continue to stimulate contemporary theorizing.

Together, the essays in this volume make a case for the continued relevance of Arnheim's work. The authors here sift Arnheim's valuable insights from his narrow prescriptions and trace the cultural and ideological threads in his formalist writing. They broaden the range of media and film practice that Arnheim's theory can speak to, and acknowledge the complexity of his argument with regard to works that don't fit the tightly defined ambit of *Film as Art*. Ultimately, I hope that this book testifies to the richness of Arnheim's body of thought as a force for directing and shaping the way we study, observe, and invent film and media.

notes

1. Rudolf Arnheim, *Art and Visual Perception*, The New Version, Berkeley: University of California Press, 1974, p. 5.
2. Margalit Fox, "Rudolf Arnheim, 102, Psychologist and Scholar of Art and Ideas, Dies," *The New York Times*, 14 June, 2007. Available online at http://www.nytimes.com/2007/06/14/obituaries/14arnheim.html (accessed 12 August, 2008).
3. Rudolf Arnheim, *Film Essays and Criticism*, trans. Brenda Benthien, Madison: University of Wisconsin Press, 1997, p. 4.
4. Ibid.
5. Arnheim's first published book was an anthology of twenty-five essays and reviews including a number of film reviews from *Das Stachelschwein* entitled *Stimme von der Galerie: 25 kleine Aufsätze zur Kulter der Zeit*, Berlin: W. Benary, 1928.
6. The 1997 book *Film Essays and Criticism* is an anthology of early film writings, translated from a German collection published in 1977.
7. Sabine Hake, *The Cinema's Third Machine: Writing on Film in Germany 1907–1933*, Lincoln: University of Nebraska Press, 1993, p. 289.
8. Rudolf Arnheim, *Film as Art*, Berkeley: University of California Press, 1957, pp. 6–7. Tom Gunning first brought my attention to this aspect of *Film as Art*.
9. Ibid., p. 1.
10. Noël Carroll, *Philosophical Problems of Classical Film Theory*, Princeton: Princeton University Press, 1988, p. 19.
11. Ibid., p. 29.
12. Arnheim, *Film as Art*, p. 57.
13. Ibid., p. 2.
14. Carroll notes an important distinction between Lessing and Arnheim: "Lessing is concerned to find where a medium excels in representation, whereas Arnheim is most interested in where a medium falters in terms of perfect representation." Carroll also suggests that because Arnheim is not interested in using the medium reflexively, his appeal to film's specificity is not strictly modernist. Arnheim's relationship to modernism is further discussed below. Carroll, *Philosophical Problems*, pp. 35–36, 81–83.
15. Arnheim, *Film as Art*, p. 3.
16. Ibid., pp. 127, 128.
17. Carroll, *Philosophical Problems*, p. 58.

18. Ibid., p. 91. Carroll builds this case carefully across the entire chapter, but summarizes his points here.
19. Arnheim, *Film as Art*, p. 45.
20. Ibid., p. 59.
21. Ibid., p. 49.
22. Ibid., p. 53.
23. Ibid., p. 56.
24. Ibid., p. 36.
25. Ibid.
26. Gertrud Koch, "Rudolf Arnheim: The Materialist of Aesthetic of Illusion," *New German Critique* 51, Fall 1990, p. 173.
27. Arnheim, *Film as Art*, p. 43.
28. Ibid.
29. Ibid.
30. Ibid., p. 57.
31. Ibid., p. 74.
32. Ibid., pp. 77–78.
33. Ibid., p. 109.
34. Ibid., p. 111.
35. Ibid., p. 110, emphasis added.
36. Ibid., p. 41.
37. Ibid., p. 151.
38. Ibid., p. 30.
39. Ibid.
40. Ibid., p. 133.
41. Ibid.
42. Ibid., pp. 81, 121.
43. Ara H. Merjian, "Middlebrow Modernism: Rudolf Arnheim at the Crossroads of Film Theory and the Psychology of Art," in Angela Dalle Vacche ed., *The Visual Turn: Classical Film Theory and Art*, New Brunswick, NJ: Rutgers University Press, 2003, p. 167.
44. Ibid., p. 172.
45. Arnheim, *Film as Art*, p. 35.
46. Ibid., pp. 68, 109.
47. Merjian, "Middlebrow Modernism," p. 178.
48. On the relationship between gestalt theory and modernism, see Koch, "Rudolf Arnheim: The Materialist Aesthetic of Illusion," pp. 170–173.
49. Rudolf Arnheim, *Radio*, New York, Ayer, 1986, p. 14. See Shawn VanCour's chapter in this volume.
50. See Doron Galili's chapter in this volume.
51. Rudolf Arnheim, *The Power of the Center: A Study of Composition in the Visual Arts*, The New Version, Berkeley: University of California Press, 1988, p. xi.

rudolf arnheim

clarity, simplicity, balance[1]

o n e

d a v i d   b o r d w e l l

"Progress in any field of knowledge," wrote Rudolf Arnheim, "tends to come from one-sided theses."[2] He was referring to the arguments of E. H. Gombrich, but he could easily have been writing of himself. For seventy years, he maintained that sound cinema was an aesthetic mistake. He adhered to gestalt psychology in an era celebrating psychoanalysis and information-processing models of the mind. He championed art appreciation at a time when humanists began to suspect the very idea of art. Yet despite his intellectual obstinacy, he became one of his century's most famous thinkers about how we make, use, and respond to images.

a good gestalt

Arnheim and Gombrich, both refugees from the Third Reich, virtually created modern art theory. In the early twentieth century, the term referred principally to the systematic knowledge that undergirded artists' practices: the underlying precepts of chiaroscuro or color blending or central perspective. Art theory amounted to the principles of craftsmanship.

Arnheim and Gombrich undertook more basic conceptual work. Why, Gombrich asked in *Art and Illusion* (1960),[3] does representational art have a history? Why couldn't people in ancient Egypt or medieval Europe immediately and accurately draw what they saw? Arnheim approached images from a different angle. Why do certain forms have emotional energy? Why do some visual strategies engage our eyes and minds, while others don't?

In trying to answer such questions, Arnheim and Gombrich anticipated E. O. Wilson's call for "consilience"—the reconciliation of modern scientific research and humanistic studies, both in their methods and their findings. Granted, thinkers about the visual arts had long based their ideas on philosophical and psychological thinking.[4] In the Germanic tradition which nurtured both Gombrich and Arnheim, perceptual psychology was seen as highly relevant to understanding pictures. But with the rise of the humanities as a distinct field of endeavor in the twentieth century, the allegiance of art and science was strained to the breaking point. Influential modernists of many schools tended to see scientific theorizing, with its principles of analysis and measurement, as opposed to the ineffable creativity of the artistic imagination. Science was something to be castigated (as positivism), ignored, or mocked, as in Duchamp's *Three Standard Stoppages*, strips of canvas trimmed to the random curves of three pieces of string.

In a climate in which art theorists suspected science, Gombrich and Arnheim eagerly sought lessons from psychology. But the two men followed different paths of study. Gombrich, younger by five years and trained in Renaissance studies, saw his early academic career interrupted by war service monitoring German radio broadcasts. The experience of deciphering cryptic messages oriented him toward seeing artworks as information-bearing artifacts. He was accordingly alert to the emergence of cognitive psychology in the 1950s, becoming friends with Richard Gregory and James J. Gibson. *Art and Illusion* bears the influence of "new look" psychology in its effort to show how art-making develops out of the interaction of historical traditions with innate mental tendencies toward information pick-up. Still, for Gombrich theory came second to historical research and criticism; he drew on the sciences to illuminate problems of artistic continuity and change.

Arnheim invoked theory as an aid to understanding creativity and appreciation. He sought to explain the traditional concerns of visual design through the gestalt account of perception. He believed that the perceptual laws discovered in the psychological laboratories of Berlin had been intuitively applied by artists around the world. The key insight came to him during his university studies when he was about twenty years old.

> My teachers Max Wertheimer and Wolfgang Köhler were
> laying the theoretical and practical foundations of gestalt

theory at the Psychological Institute of the University of Berlin, and I found myself fastening on to what may be called a Kantian turn of the new doctrine, according to which even the most elementary processes of vision do not produce mechanical recordings of the outer world but organize the sensory raw material according to principles of simplicity, regularity, and balance, which govern the receptor mechanism.

This discovery of the gestalt school fitted the notion that the work of art, too, is not simply an imitation or selective duplication of reality but a translation of observed characteristics into the forms of a given medium.[5]

Although art history was one of his doctoral areas, Arnheim's thesis research involved testing people's "physiognomic perception" of faces and hand-writing, an early indication of his interest in art as expression.[6]

The gestaltists thought that empiricism, which tended to treat perception as the accumulation of discrete sensations, did not acknowledge that the whole was greater than the sum of its parts. Experiments displaying partial figures or pulsating lights showed that complete forms emerged from incomplete or degraded stimuli. Certain principles—geometrical simplicity, figure–ground differences, completeness, good continuation, and the like—were fundamental to all human perception, across times and cultures. *Art and Visual Perception* (first published in 1954 and wholly revised in 1974) makes a powerful case for gestalt universalism. Today this position is so unfashionable that Arnheim's calm confidence is unsettling. For many scholars now, all that matters is what divides and differentiates us. But for eighty-plus years Arnheim emphasized ways in which we share a common experience of the world and of art.

In *Art and Illusion* and elsewhere, Gombrich unraveled the artifices of realism, the tricks of the artist's trade that simulated the look and feel of the world. But Arnheim was fascinated by bold stylization. Naturalism, he believed, was a recurrent but superficial approach to visual reality. What endured, what underlay even the most cunning *trompe l'oeil*, were principles of vision we acquired from birth, and these could override academic rules about how things should look. Ingeniously, he argued that the cockeyed crèche in Figure 1.1a conveys a stronger sense of three-dimensionality than the perspectivally correct one presented in Figure 1.1b. The "inverted" perspective encloses baby Jesus's head fully, just as a hollow cradle would.[7]

It's often said that Arnheim favored modernist styles, like Cubism and expressionism, and that his insistence that art surpassed mere copying reflects modern artists' will to distorted form. It is true that his paradigm cases often come from high modernism. His exhaustive study of *Guernica* has become a classic of formal analysis (with, surprisingly, some explanatory

Figure 1.1 a and b
From *Art and Visual Perception: A Psychology of the Creative Eye*, 2nd ed., by Rudolf Arnheim, © 1974 by the Regents of the University of California. Courtesy University of California Press.

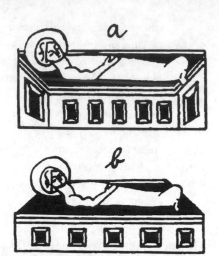

concepts borrowed from Freud).[8] Still, Arnheim saw a deep continuity between classic art and modern art. Both traditions explored the perceptual force of form. Medieval art can look "modern" because both exploit gestalt laws to create satisfying expressive form. Arnheim saw a common form-giving activity at work in "primitive" art, the art of children, and even the art of the mentally ill. It turns out that the universalism of gestalt theory underwrites diversity no less vigorously than the most ardent post-modernism.

At a period when many readers complain that academic film studies have little relevance to filmmaking, it's worth recalling that the two giants of twentieth-century art theory kept in touch with actual practice. Gombrich the historian had a firm sense of how artists did their jobs, always seeking out the technical secrets behind visual effects like sparkling eyes or mirror reflections. Likewise, Arnheim's chapter titles in *Art and Visual Perception* might suggest a how-to manual: "Balance," "Shape," "Form," "Growth," "Space," "Light," "Color," "Movement," "Dynamics," and "Expression." But the book is subtitled *A Psychology of the Creative Eye*, and the section titles give the game away: "The hidden structure of a square" . . . "Vision as active exploration" . . . "Perceptual concepts" . . . "What good does overlapping do?" . . . "Why do children draw that way?" . . . "Gradients create depth" . . . "Visible motor forces" . . . "The priority of expression." No doubt about it: this is a book offering explanations. In these pages the artist's creativity is the result of broader psychological tendencies.

Arnheim delighted in the fact when, visiting a painter's studio, he would find a spattered copy of his book on the workbench.

> All in all, I can only hope that the blue book with Arp's black eye on the cover will continue to lie dog-eared, annotated, and stained with pigment and plaster on the tables and

desk of those actively concerned with the theory and
practice of the arts, and that even in its tidier garb it will
continue to be admitted to the kind of shoptalk the visual
arts need in order to do their silent work.[9]

What academic theorist today would so boldly announce a respect for the
workaday skill of creating images?

The contrasts between Arnheim and Gombrich were felt in their
lifetimes. Arnheim wrote a deeply critical review of *Art and Illusion*. He saw
Gombrich's appeal to prior experience as a residue of empiricism, and at one
point he claimed that Gombrich's argument reflects "the pathological
disturbance in the relationship between man and perceptual reality that has
recently beclouded Western civilization"![10] Yet in reviewing a later Gombrich
collection, after registering disagreements, Arnheim observes that the
book exuded "that effortless charm which Baldassare Castiglione recom-
mended to his courtiers as *grazia*, the most indispensable virtue, he thought,
of a civilized person."[11] The same encomium could apply to Arnheim's
achievement.

flexible striving

Gestalt theorists believed in the primacy of form, which was conceived
chiefly in geometrical terms. Pioneers like Wertheimer and Köhler saw the
relevance of such ideas to the arts, particularly music, but their research
remained focused on perceptual experience. As a young man Arnheim
became the more or less official art theorist of the gestalt movement, but he
took things in a surprising direction.

He inherited the great Viennese territorial division among artistic
activities: representation, expression, and decoration. Gombrich, despite
forays into expression and decoration (in *The Sense of Order*[12]), remained
content to explore representation—how artists, as was commonly said,
learned to capture the look of the phenomenal world. Arnheim went in
another direction. For him the conquest of physical appearances was
secondary. He sought to ground both representation and decoration in the
fundamentals of expression. Like Eisenstein in film theory, he saw the
human apprehension of the world as shot through with feeling.

According to Arnheim, the patterns that the gestaltists disclosed were
inherently expressive. A triangle resting on its base wasn't just balanced; it
was weighty. We see the weeping willow as not merely curved but sad; a
skyscraper isn't just tall, it's aggressively hurling itself upward. Every shape
or movement we grasp has a distinctive flavor and feeling. Indeed, he writes
audaciously, "expression can be described as the *primary content* of vision."

We have been trained to think of perception as the recording of shapes, distances, hues, motions. The awareness of

these measurable characteristics is really a fairly late accomplishment of the human mind. Even in the Western man of the twentieth century it presupposes special conditions. It is the attitude of the scientist and the engineer or of the salesman who estimates the size of a customer's waist, the shade of a lipstick, the weight of a suitcase. But if I sit in front of a fireplace and watch the flames, I do not normally register certain shades of red, various degrees of brightness, geometrically defined shapes moving at such and such a speed. I see the graceful play of aggressive tongues, flexible striving, lively color. The face of a person is more readily perceived and remembered as being alert, tense, concentrated rather than being triangularly shaped, having slanted eyebrows, straight lips, and so on.[13]

A dominant Western tradition conceives the world as an objective array of spaces and surfaces and stretches of time, to which the human mind adds meanings and emotions (thanks either to innate propensities or to acquired cultural conventions). Arnheim found the world bristling with qualities, given directly to our senses but structured, as Kant might put it, through "forms of sensibility." Rendering these qualities with impact was the artist's task. The artist registers not what a fire objectively is, but what it feels like. Paradoxically, that can best be done by "visual concepts" derived from an apprehension of formal properties.

The artist's task is to embody some of the expressive energy of the world in a medium. That energy is as easily depicted in practical tools as in artworks.

In a functional-looking object, we may see the dynamics of pouring, soaring, containing, receiving, etc. We also see such "character traits" as flexibility, sturdiness, gracefulness, strength, etc., which, just as in a representational work of fine art, are intimately and totally related to the theme: the gracefulness of the spout consists in the graceful pouring it displays visually; the sturdiness of the Doric column consists in its supporting the roof sturdily. Expressive properties are adverbial, not adjectival. They apply to the behavior of things, not the things themselves.[14]

For Arnheim, the world was pulsating with movement; hence, perhaps, his early interest in cinema.

moving pictures

In his maturity Arnheim wrote about many art forms: painting, sculpture, architecture, even radio. But as a young man what seized him was the movies. While doing quantitative research on physiognomic perception, he was also reviewing movies for a left-wing newspaper. His reviews were tough-minded, and they often pushed toward speculations on the nature of the medium. His book on cinema, *Film als Kunst* (1932), was published before he was thirty and was quickly translated into English. Always in search of greater clarity, Arnheim rewrote it in 1957. Unsurprisingly, he didn't update its reference points: you'll search in vain for film examples from the 1930s, 1940s, or 1950s. The touchstones remain Chaplin, Keaton, von Sternberg, and the Soviets.

Early and late, Arnheim held that cinema was essentially a pictorial art. Synchronized sound added very little; in fact, it threatened visual experimentation. It was so easy to convey a story point with dialogue that lazy filmmakers would be tempted to create photographed stage plays. Instead, like many cinephiles of the silent era, Arnheim emphasized how film technique reshapes what is filmed. Close-ups, shot design, camera angles, and cutting make cinema no simple medium of reproduction. Film form transforms the world that is photographed. Put more daringly, it is in the very deficiencies of cinema as a realistic record of the world that its artistic resources lie. Black-and-white film automatically stylizes reality; so does the two-dimensional picture plane. The creative film artist uses the limitations of the medium to capture expressive qualities. This position, commonplace today, was a real advance in the silent era and aimed to give cinema cultural respectability, a subject that Arnheim reflected on amusingly in *Film als Kunst*. "Older people will, I hope, see from this book that . . . Charlie Chaplin, Greta Garbo, constructive cutting, or the preventions of oscillation may be discussed just as seriously as Titian, Cézanne, baroque, or sunbathing."[15]

For such reasons, Arnheim's thought is usually taken to be the summation of a certain strain of 1920s film theory. Again, however, he did more than synthesize current ideas. Theorists' hunches that film stylized reality could now be grounded in gestalt ideas about medium and form. In effect, the 1957 *Film as Art* was *Film als Kunst* rewritten in the light of *Art and Visual Perception*. Here is the most famous passage:

> Not until film began to become an art was the interest moved from mere subject matter to aspects of form. What had hitherto been merely the urge to record certain actual events, now became the aim to represent objects by special means exclusive to film. These means obtrude themselves, show themselves able to do more than simply reproduce the required object; they sharpen it, impose a style upon it, point out special features, make it vivid and decorative. Art begins where mechanical reproduction leaves off, where the conditions of reproduction serve in some way to mold the object.[16]

This, you might say, is Arnheim's reply to Walter Benjamin's theory of cinema as mechanical reproduction. Film is not a medium signaling a break with the canonized arts, by virtue of its abandonment of "auratic value." For Arnheim, filmmakers continue the mission of the traditional arts. Like painters, film directors use their medium to create meanings, emotions, and engaging perceptual effects. Chaplin, Keaton, and their peers made cinema a bearer of significant form.

Nevertheless, Arnheim held that film, like photography, has more limits than other arts. Tied to recording the surface of things, film and photography can never achieve the range of expressive form we find in painting. Arnheim clung to this opinion, I suspect, because of his deep love for that creative freedom he found in the traditional visual arts. And I sometimes think that for him, a painting or statue harbored all the nascent thrusts, pulls, and torques you could want. Movies flaunted what was tactfully implied in still images.

envoi

My wife Kristin Thompson and I first saw Arnheim when we were graduate students at the University of Iowa, in March 1972. He gave a lecture that stuck to his principles of 1933.

> Every art medium has a ceiling, beyond which it cannot effectively pass. The ceiling is somewhat low for the reproductive arts. Photography is more limited in what it can do than painting, and so is film.

> Films should be in black and white, the better to stylize reality. Q: *Are there no worthwhile color films?* Pause. A: *Red Desert*, perhaps.

> Q: *Do you see many contemporary films?* A: No.

Some years afterward, I lined up Arnheim for a visiting lecture at my home base, the University of Wisconsin—Madison. But he had to cancel; he had slipped on ice and broken his hip. He was then about seventy-five.

Later in the 1980s I visited Ann Arbor and had lunch with him. It was wonderful. Spotting that I leaned in a Gombrichian direction, he gave a shrewd analysis of the dividing lines: gestalt psychology vs. new look cognitivism, expressive percepts vs. illusions, brain fields vs. schemas. He asked me to send him copies of my publications, which I did on and off during the decade. I never dared to ask what he thought about my fancy sentence in *Narration in the Fiction Film*. In order to contrast J. J. Gibson's theory of optical realism with Arnheim's idea of expressiveness, I wrote: "Gibson likes likeness, Arnheim loves liveliness."[17]

I thought of Arnheim often as I read more perceptual psychology. Gestalt work had once seemed to me a dead-end, but Bela Julesz's researches into

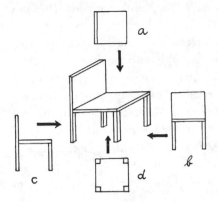

Figure 1.2
From *Art and Visual Perception:
A Psychology of the Creative Eye,*
2nd ed., by Rudolf Arnheim,
© 1974 by the Regents of the
University of California. Courtesy
University of California Press.

"cyclopean vision" showed that the mind can impose vivid form on randomly generated fields of dots; no need for any "prior experience" of three-dimensional objects and layouts to intuit depth.[18] Somewhat later, David Marr's theory of visual perception brought gestalt ideas into computational perceptual psychology. The "3-D model representation" that Marr claimed operated in visual processing uncannily echoes Arnheim's discussion of perception's reliance on "characteristic aspects."[19] (Arnheim illustrates the idea with the various views of the chair, shown in Figure 1.2 above. Which one is instantly recognizable as a chair?) And with contemporary interest in the relation between emotion and cognition, as seen in empathy and motor mimicry, Arnheim's theory of the expressive side of perception is creeping back too.

When Kristin and I oversaw a book series at the University of Wisconsin Press, we were eager to bring out an anthology of Arnheim's film criticism, a collection originally published in German in 1977. Brenda Benthien, a close friend of Arnheim and his wife Mary, composed a sparkling translation and Arnheim supplied a touching introduction. He summed up the crisis of the Weimar republic in a novelistic glimpse:

> Even now I keep as a sort of talisman a bullet which in the
> days of the 1918 revolution, when I was fourteen, flew over
> the neighboring houses, bored a little hole through the
> windowpane, and fell inert on the carpet before my bed.
> Thus it began.[20]

In the same introduction, Arnheim deplores the current state of cinema ("my basic objection to the talking film as a mongrel seems to me just as valid today as then") and he warns against the cheapening of our vision: "Without the flourishing of visual expression no culture can function productively."[21] These tenets are predictably Arnheimian, but more surprising are his comments on Keaton, Eisenstein, Gance, Pudovkin, Chaplin, von Sternberg, and other greats, as well as the essays "Style and

Monotony in Film," "Epic and Dramatic Film," and especially "The Film Critic of Tomorrow."

Scarcely a month goes by when I don't have some idea that can be traced to my reading of Arnheim. In writing a web entry on comic framing, I started with his discussion of Chaplin's *The Immigrant*.[22] His theory of expression goes a long way toward explaining how composition can trigger laughter. I doubt that I'd be so alert to the possibilities of two-dimensional design in film shots if I hadn't been tutored by *Film as Art*, *Art and Visual Perception*, and *The Power of the Center*.[23] My pleas over the last couple of decades that film researchers should reflect upon filmmakers' craft practices are merely clumsy restatements of this, which I discover marked in my copy of *Art and Visual Perception*:

> Good art theory must smell of the studio, although its language should differ from the household talk of painters and sculptors.[24]

In 2004, several of us from Madison visited Ann Arbor, where Arnheim resided in an assisted-living facility. His sunny room was packed with books, a microfilm reader, remarkable drawings and paintings (Feininger, Köllwitz), and a worktable with a gigantic magnifying lens on an articulated arm. A manuscript in progress lay on the desk. Conversation was difficult for him, but he seemed to understand everything we were saying. His smile was quick and his eyes shone. When I showed him the first German edition of *Film als Kunst* I'd brought along, he turned it over in his hands as if he hadn't seen one in years. He signed it, then shook his head apologetically at the uneven penmanship. He had just turned one hundred.

Now that Benjamin and Kracauer have become the prototypical Weimar intellectuals, it's a pity that so many media students and professors are unaware of Arnheim's work. His Leonardo-like interest in merging art and science is discouraged in a climate that posits the cultural construction of everything. Unencumbered by today's puns, slashes, dashes, and parentheses, his writing is clear, his arguments cogently laid out. No one studying visual achievement in any medium can ignore his ideas on composition, lighting, color, and expression. He exemplifies the passion, rigor, and dignity that interwar German intellectuals brought to the study of the arts. One-sided his oeuvre may be, but a great deal of what Arnheim believed remains original, provocative, and true.

notes

1. This is an expanded version of the essay "Simplicity, Clarity, Balance: A Tribute to Rudolf Arnheim" originally posted on David Bordwell's website *Observations on Film Art*, 15 June, 2007. Available online at: <http://www.davidbordwell.net/blog/?p=956>

2. Rudolf Arnheim, "Art History and the Partial God," in *Toward a Psychology of Art*, Berkeley: University of California Press, 1966, p. 161.
3. E. H. Gombrich, *Art and Illusion: A Study in the Psychology of Pictorial Representation*, Princeton: Princeton University Press, 2000, pp. 1–9.
4. See Michael Podro, *The Manifold in Perception: Theories of Art from Kant to Hildebrand*, London: Oxford University Press, 1972, and *The Critical Historians of Art*, New Haven: Yale University Press, 1982.
5. Arnheim, *Film as Art*, Berkeley: University of California Press, 1957, p. 3.
6. For a discussion of Arnheim's early research and training, see Mitchell G. Ash, *Gestalt Psychology in German Culture 1890–1967: Holism and the Quest for Objectivity*, Cambridge: Cambridge University Press, 1995, pp. 299–301. Ash's book is a valuable history of gestalt ideas.
7. Arnheim, *Art and Visual Perception: A Psychology of the Creative Eye*, The New Version, Berkeley: University of California Press, 1974, pp. 265–266.
8. Arnheim, *Picasso's Guernica: The Genesis of a Painting*, Berkeley: University of California Press, 1962.
9. Arnheim, *Art and Visual Perception*, The New Version, p. x.
10. Arnheim, "Art History and the Partial God," pp. 159–160.
11. Arnheim, "Perceiving and Portraying," *The Times Literary Supplement*, 29 October 1982, p. 1180.
12. Gombrich, *The Sense of Order: A Study in the Psychology of Decorative Art*, Ithaca: Cornell University Press, 1979.
13. Arnheim, *Art and Visual Perception*, Berkeley: University of California Press, 1954, p. 430.
14. Arnheim, "From Function to Expression," in *Toward a Psychology of Art*, p. 208.
15. Arnheim, *Film*, trans. L. M. Sieveking and Ian F. D. Morrow, London: Faber and Faber, 1933, p. 7.
16. Arnheim, *Film as Art*, p. 57.
17. David Bordwell, *Narration in the Fiction Film*, Madison: University of Wisconsin Press, 1985, p. 100.
18. See Bela Julesz, *Foundations of Cyclopean Perception*, Chicago: University of Chicago Press, 1971, and *Dialogues on Perception*, Cambridge: MIT Press, 1995. For an enjoyable introduction to random-dot stereograms, see *Stereogram*, San Francisco: Cadence Books, 1994.
19. David Marr, *Vision: A Computational Investigation into the Human Representation and Processing of Visual Information*, New York: Freeman, 1982, pp. 302–328.
20. Arnheim, *Film Essays and Criticism*, Madison: University of Wisconsin Press, 1997, p. 3.
21. Ibid, p. 5.
22. "Funny framings," 2007, available online at <http://www.davidbordwell.net/blog/?p=761>
23. Arnheim, *The Power of the Center: A Study of Composition in the Visual Arts*, 2nd ed., Berkeley: University of California Press, 1988.
24. Arnheim, *Art and Visual Perception*, The New Version, p. 4.

arnheim and modernism

two

malcolm turvey

Rudolf Arnheim's theory of film is normally classified by film scholars as an example of what is variously called the formative or creationist tradition, which dominated silent film theory. This tradition aimed to prove that film can be art by combating the claim that photography, and by extension film, mechanically reproduce what is in front of the camera. Mechanical reproduction, it was widely thought in the nineteenth and early twentieth centuries, cannot be art, and many film theorists in the cinema's first decades attempted to demonstrate, in their different ways, how film diverges from mechanical reproduction, and how these divergences can be used artistically by filmmakers to transform pro-filmic reality rather than reproduce it. In his seminal *The Major Film Theories*, Dudley Andrew groups Arnheim with Hugo Munsterburg, Sergei Eisenstein, and Béla Balázs, arguing that they all adhered to the "formative dictum to transform daily life."[1] And Noël Carroll, in *Philosophical Problems of Classical Film Theory*, selects Arnheim's *Film as Art* to represent the "creationist ethos," according to which "the processes of cinematic articulation . . . are more productive than reproductive—a means for creating rather than merely copying; a means of manipulating reality rather than reproducing it."[2]

Some have gone further, however, arguing that Arnheim's film theory is not just formative or creationist but *modernist*. Gertrud Koch has suggested that the gestalt psychological theory of perception, which Arnheim studied as a student in Berlin in the 1920s and which informed his film theory, is "compatible with aesthetic modernism in its inherent constructivism. Analogous relations between the world of real objects and the world of perception are not established by means of images and imitation, but by similar structural principles."[3] Ara Merjian locates Arnheim's modernism in his doctrine of medium specificity, which in Merjian's view makes him "part of the trajectory of Greenbergian, modernist purity" ascendant in post-World War II American art criticism.[4] And in my own *Doubting Vision*, I argue that Arnheim's film theory betrays the influence of modernism due to its anti-mimetic conception of art, according to which genuine art should not imitate or copy the way that reality standardly appears to human vision. Rather, it should be free from the normal exercise of the visual faculty. The artist should transform or abandon the way that reality usually appears to everyday sight; he or she should not slavishly imitate it.[5]

Certainly, a cursory reading of the most widely available version of Arnheim's film theory—the 1957 reissue of *Film as Art*, which is a condensed and rewritten version of the 1933 English translation of the 1932 German original—would seem to confirm some of these views of Arnheim as a modernist. Arnheim begins this book by stating

> It is worth while to refute thoroughly and systematically the charge that photography and film are only mechanical reproductions and that they therefore have no connection with art—for this is an excellent method of getting to understand the nature of film art.[6]

And he goes on to explore various ways in which film putatively fails at mechanical reproduction and therefore can be art. As Carroll has pointed out, Arnheim's conception of mechanical reproduction is slippery.[7] Usually, however, what he means when he claims that film diverges from mechanical reproduction is that it differs from the way humans normally see reality. Ordinary visual perception, in other words, is for the most part used by Arnheim as the criterion for mechanical reproduction. For example, Arnheim argues that the frame of a shot imposes a limitation on what can be seen by the film viewer that "in the actual range of human vision . . . simply does not exist." This is because our eyes, heads, and bodies are "mobile." Hence, "the field of vision is in practice unlimited and infinite." We can move our eyes, heads, and bodies to see what is at any one moment out of sight, beyond the periphery of our vision. But "It is otherwise with the film or photograph," for the frame of a still shot prevents us from seeing what lies beyond the edge of the frame.[8] Hence, film diverges from mechanical reproduction because the frame of a shot restricts what we can see, and no such restriction obtains in normal perceptual experience. Arnheim makes similar arguments about editing and the absence of depth, color, and sound in silent film. All, for Arnheim, mean that film can be art because it diverges from mechanical reproduction in the sense that they entail that our visual experience of what the film represents is very different from how we would perceive what it represents in reality. This would seem to corroborate my claim in *Doubting Vision* that Arnheim is a modernist because he believes that art should not imitate or copy the appearance of reality to ordinary human vision. In addition, the various ways in which film diverges from mechanical reproduction are all, for Arnheim, specific properties of the film medium. "In order that the film artist may create a work of art it is important that he consciously stress the peculiarities of his medium," he states, and he spends Part 2 of *Film as Art* attempting to "show how the various peculiarities of film material can be, and have been, used to achieve artistic effects."[9] Such statements might appear to support Merjian's contention that Arnheim is a medium-specific modernist of the Greenbergian variety.

Yet, a more careful reading of Arnheim's film theory as well as some understanding of his perceptual psychology, theory of visual art, and art criticism complicate this assessment, as I will show in what follows. I now think I was wrong to classify Arnheim as a modernist *simpliciter*, and Andrew's and Carroll's more cautious labels "formative" and "creationist" seem more accurate to me. Of course, part of the difficulty of categorizing anyone as a modernist is with the term "modernism" itself, which has a number of different meanings. Here, I will untangle some of these, and in the process of showing how Arnheim's work resists the modernist label in some of its senses, I hope to demonstrate just what an original thinker Arnheim was. His originality, however, did not mean that he was able to avoid one of the fundamental problems in film theory, which I will point to in the closing paragraphs.

I

In *Doubting Vision*, I contend that the anti-mimetic conception of art to which Arnheim appears to subscribe—the view that art should not imitate or copy the way that reality standardly appears to human vision—is motivated by a skepticism about human vision, the belief, found everywhere in modernism, that our sense of sight is flawed. I further claim that many film theorists have been influenced by this skepticism. Arnheim's contemporary Dziga Vertov, for example, declared that "The weakness of the human eye is manifest" and rejected all film practices that "copy the work of our eye." Only a technology much more powerful than the eye can reveal reality, Vertov argued, and he viewed film as being this instrument because it "perceives more and better."[10]

Yet, if we turn to Arnheim's work on perceptual psychology and visual art—which he began publishing after emigrating to the United States in the 1940s and where he develops his theories of seeing and art in much greater detail than in his writings on film—instead of arguing that art must diverge from ordinary human vision as he did in his film theory, he now sees a much closer relation between the two. In the introduction to *Art and Visual Perception*, for example, he states that "we recognize the exalted kind of seeing that leads to the creation of great art as an outgrowth of the humbler and more common activity of the eyes in everyday life."[11] And in Chapter 2, on shape, he asserts that "Every man's eyesight anticipates in a modest way the justly admired capacity of the artist to produce patterns that validly interpret experience by means of organized form."[12] This analogy between visual art and sight was to inform Arnheim's work for the rest of his life, and in order to understand it, both his theories of visual perception and art must be clarified.

According to Arnheim's perceptual psychology, vision is not a mechanical recording device. "The world of images does not simply imprint itself upon a faithfully sensitive organ." Instead, seeing "is an eminently active occupation" in at least two ways.[13] First, drawing on the experiments of gestalt psychologists, Arnheim argues that "the most elementary processes of vision ... organize the sensory raw material creatively according to principles of simplicity, regularity, and balance, which govern the receptor mechanism."[14] For Arnheim, there is an "active striving for unity and order manifest in the simple act of looking at a simple pattern of lines," and he spends much of his perceptual psychology detailing the experiments that reveal organization at work in vision.[15] The second is generalization. It used to be thought by perceptual psychologists, Arnheim states, that "perception starts with the recording of individual cases, whose common properties could be realized only by creatures capable of forming concepts intellectually," that we proceed from the particular to the general by way of an intellectual inference about the general from the perceptible particular. Gestalt psychology has shown, however, that we see the general in the particular, that "over-all structural features are the primary data of perception."[16] When we see a dog, we do not see a number of its particular features, such as its shape, color, texture, and so on, and then infer that what we are seeing is a dog. Rather we directly see the dog's doggishness, what it has in common with other dogs, in its particular features. As Arnheim puts it, "Vision deals with the raw material of experience by creating a corresponding pattern of general forms, which are applicable not only to the individual case at hand but to an infinite number of other, similar cases as well." He refers to the general forms created by vision as "perceptual concepts," and concludes that seeing is not something that occurs prior to understanding, but that understanding takes place during seeing, that vision is visual thinking, that "eyesight is insight."[17] Eyesight is insight because we can directly see what something has in common with other things; we do not have to infer its general properties.

While there is little trace of this theory of visual generalization in his film theory, Arnheim's theory of art is already in place. In *Film as Art*, he argues that film's various failures to reproduce reality mechanically do not automatically entail that it is art. Instead, they are artistic only if used for the purpose of "interpreting" what is represented in the film. As he puts it, exploiting film's various divergences from the mechanical reproduction of reality should be used "in such a manner that the character of the objects represented should not therefore be destroyed but rather strengthened, concentrated, and interpreted."[18] In Part 2 of *Film as Art*, titled "The Making of a Film," he shows how these various divergences can be used to interpret what is being represented in a film for the film viewer. The limitation imposed by the frame, for example, "allows of some particular detail being brought out and given special significance; and, conversely, of unimportant things being omitted, surprises being suddenly introduced into the shot, reflections of things that are happening 'off[-screen]' being brought in."[19]

It is because of the role of interpretation in art that Arnheim believes it is like sight. Just as the artist must go beyond merely reproducing reality by interpreting it in some way, so human vision goes beyond merely recording reality by organizing it according to principles of simplicity, regularity, and balance; and understanding it through the general forms or perceptual concepts it creates and sees in the particulars around it.

> There was a wholesome lesson in the discovery that vision
> is not a mechanical recording of elements but rather the
> apprehension of significant structural patterns. If this was
> true for the simple act of perceiving an object, it was all the
> more likely to hold also for the artistic approach to reality.
> Obviously the artist was no more a mechanical recording
> device than his instrument of sight.[20]

In fact, for Arnheim, the connection between the two is even closer. Art, he claims, should not simply interpret what it represents, but should do so with the goal of promoting visual understanding, of helping the eyes in their active effort to understand reality. "When I think of art," he states in "The Form We Seek," an essay first published in 1961, "I think of what makes the nature of things visible . . . All that matters is whether or not the shape makes my eyes understand what they see. If it does, I call it art."[21] The artist aids visual understanding by translating into his medium his "percept," his creative perception of reality with its organizing and generalizing tendencies: "perceiving consists in the creation of patterns of perceptual categories" and "the artist's task includes the representation of such patterns." This does not mean art is a mechanical copy of what the artist has seen, for only some of the "qualities" of a percept "can be reproduced" in art, "others cannot."

Thus the artist must creatively find a "pictorial equivalent of his perceptual concept" using the resources of his medium, "a translation into the pictorial medium rather than a reproduction . . . Representation consists in 'seeing into' the stimulus configuration a pattern that fits its structure . . . and then inventing a pictorial counterpoint for this pattern."[22] Thus, for Arnheim, visual art and human sight are alike because both seek to understand reality through organization and generalization. Using the specific properties of his medium, the artist interprets reality by depicting it using the same principles of simplicity, regularity, and balance that the eyes use; and by representing the general forms or perceptual concepts—what something has in common with other things—that vision creates and sees in the particulars around it.

How, then, to explain the change that appears to take place in Arnheim's thinking between his film theory, where he argues that film can be art only if it fails to mechanically reproduce ordinary vision, and his later work on the psychology of the perception of art, in which he claims that visual art should be fundamentally like everyday sight? Carroll has suggested that in both Arnheim is in fact operating with two conceptions of visual perception.[23] The first he associates with mechanical reproduction and is an impoverished form of seeing. It consists simply of "recording" geometric-technical properties such as "shapes, distances, hues, motions" for pragmatic purposes such as the identification of objects.[24] "For the purposes of everyday life, seeing is essentially a means of practical orientation, of determining with one's eyes that a certain thing is present at a certain place and that it is doing a certain thing. This is identification at its bare minimum."[25] The second is the creative type of vision surveyed above. Although Arnheim thinks the latter is the more natural way of seeing, the former, he believes, has increasingly come to dominate in the technological and scientific culture of modernity.

> The awareness of these measurable characteristics is actually a fairly late accomplishment of the human mind . . . It is the attitude of the scientist and the engineer, or of the salesman who estimates the size of a customer's waist, the shade of lipstick, the weight of a suitcase.[26]

Thus, in his film theory, Arnheim argues that film can only be art if it fails to reproduce ordinary vision because he is conceiving of sight in the first, mechanical sense, whereas in his psychology of visual art, he claims that art must imitate sight because he is conceiving of vision in the second, creative sense.

Things are not so clear-cut, however, if one returns to *Film*, the original 1933 English translation of *Film as Art* on which the 1957 version is based. Certainly, in much of this book, Arnheim operates with the impoverished, mechanical conception of vision as mere identification for practical purposes, which would explain why he believes film art should diverge from sight. "For the ordinary person in everyday life," he writes in a passage that is retained in the 1957 reissue, "sight is simply a means of finding his bearings in the natural world. Roughly speaking, he sees only so much of the objects surrounding him as is necessary for his purpose."[27] However, in the introduction, which he excised from the later version, he points to the similarity between art and vision, much as he will do in his later work on perceptual psychology and visual art:

> It is one of the author's fundamental principles that art is just as much and just as little a part of material life as anything else in this world; and that the only way to understand art is to start from the simplest forms of sensory-psychological impressions and to regard visual and auditory art as sublimated forms of seeing and hearing. A man who considers the ordinary sensory processes as uncomplicated and unspiritual functions and art as a supernormal portent does justice to neither, and moreover denies himself the illuminating realization of the close connection between the two [28]

In a passage on "Fundamental Aesthetic Concepts," also removed from the 1957 reissue, he explains this close connection by way of the theory of visual organization that forms part of his conception of vision as creative and active. "The desire for balance and symmetry manifests itself at every opportunity and very often quite unconsciously," he avers, citing the example of a housemaid who, when tidying, "without being told arranges objects in accordance with the principal of balance and symmetry."[29] And he defines art as an expression of this desire, using a Van Gogh sketch as an example:

> The lines ... make a pleasing design in form and arrangement—the distribution of dark and light in the rectangular space occupied by the drawing is well balanced, the lines are grouped in beautiful patterns, radiate in various directions or are ordered in rows, their shapes harmonise with one another.[30]

This conception of art as organizing reality into balanced patterns is evident even in sections of the original book that are retained in the 1957 version: "In a good film image, all lines and other directions stand in well-balanced relation to one another and the margins."[31]

Why, then, would Arnheim argue that film, in order to be art, must diverge from ordinary vision, if at least some of the time in the original version of his film theory he conceives of sight and visual art as fundamentally alike in their striving for order and balance? I suspect that, in *Film as Art*, Arnheim is trying to reconcile, not always successfully, two

37

competing conceptions of human sight: the modernist one shared by his film theoretical contemporaries such as Vertov, in which vision is denigrated and (film) art is celebrated for its capacity to diverge from ordinary perceptual experience; and the gestaltist conception which views vision in a much more favorable light because of its active and creative powers. Indeed, I am not sure Arnheim ever fully resolves the tension between the two. Although in his later perceptual psychology, especially in *Visual Thinking* (1969), he explicitly rejects the "mistrust" of human vision that he sees as central to the Western tradition from the Greeks onward and praises the eyes for their intelligence, he still at least sometimes continues to conceive of sight as mere mechanical recording, from which art must diverge. But whatever the reason, the fact that there is such a tension shows that I was wrong in *Doubting Vision* to label Arnheim a modernist because of his denigration of sight and his view that art should not imitate the way reality appears to it. While this denigration is present in his theorizing in the form of the conception of vision as mere mechanical reproduction for the pragmatic purpose of identification, it competes with a much more exalted view of sight as "imaginative, inventive, shrewd, and beautiful," something art should imitate and intensify, not abandon.[32]

II

Now to Arnheim's espousal of medium specificity, which Merjian believes anticipates Clement Greenberg's art theory and thereby makes him a modernist. Greenberg proposed a highly influential definition of modernism "as a self-critical tendency" in modernity in his 1960 essay "Modernist Painting," using the philosophy of Kant as an example:

> The essence of Modernism lies, as I see it, in the use of characteristic methods of a discipline to criticize the discipline itself, not in order to subvert it but in order to entrench it more firmly in its area of competence. Kant used logic to establish the limits of logic, and while he withdrew much from its old jurisdiction, logic was left all the more secure in what there remained to it.[33]

Greenberg argued that this self-critical tendency was also evident in modern art, which, in order to prevent itself from being "assimilated to entertainment," had to demonstrate not only "what was unique and irreducible in art in general, but also that which was unique and irreducible in each particular art." The latter was achieved, claimed Greenberg, through an investigation by each art of "all that was unique in the nature of its medium" and an elimination of "every effect that might conceivably be borrowed from or by the medium of any other art." This process of medium purification occurred in painting when artists drew attention to "the limitations that constitute the medium of painting—the flat surface, the shape of the support, the properties of the pigment," which in "realist, naturalistic art" had been "dissembled" and "concealed," and Greenberg saw Manet as the first modernist painter by virtue of the "frankness with which [his pictures] declared the flat surfaces on which they were painted."[34]

Greenberg's definition of artistic modernism as a process of medium purification is a widely accepted one. For example, in his essay "Modernism," Charles Harrison argues that "to label a modern form of art as modernist is to stress both its intentional and self-critical preoccupation with the demands of a specific medium, and its originality with regard to the precedents that medium avails."[35] Certainly, the claim that each visual art, including film, should both exploit and draw attention to the specific properties of its medium is central to Arnheim's theorizing. In the section of *Film* on fundamental aesthetic concepts, Arnheim states that "An essential condition of a good work of art is indeed that the special attributes of the medium employed should be clearly and cleanly laid bare,"[36] and in the introduction to the 1957 reissue, he noted that his "guiding concern" when he had originally written *Film as Art* in the early 1930s was what he called *Materialtheorie*, which was "meant to show that artistic and scientific descriptions of reality are cast in molds that derive not so much from the subject matter itself as from the properties of the medium—or *Material*—employed."[37] Throughout his later work on the perceptual psychology of visual art he claims that "image-making, artistic or otherwise . . . is an equivalent, rendered with the properties of a particular medium, of what is observed in the object."[38] It is statements such as these that lead Merjian to conclude that "the willful stripping of the medium in order to safeguard its integrity, is clearly one of the seminal aspects of Arnheim's writing on film and must be considered part of the trajectory of Greenbergian, modernist purity."[39] In fact, Arnheim's avowal of medium specificity is very different from Greenberg's.

Arnheim never argues, as does Greenberg, that an artist should investigate and foreground the properties specific to his medium *for the sake of purifying it*. Instead, the artist should do this, Arnheim claims, in order to interpret what the artwork represents, i.e., organize it into balanced patterns and general forms, and thereby aid visual understanding. The latter is the goal of art, according to Arnheim, not medium purification.

> In order that the film artist may create a work of art it is important that he consciously stress the peculiarities of his medium. This, however, should be done in such a manner that the character of the objects represented should not thereby be destroyed but rather strengthened, concentrated, and interpreted.[40]

The artist must draw attention to and exploit the particular properties of his medium because this is the way to make the artwork an interpretation,

as opposed to a reproduction, of what it represents. For it is only by emphasizing the medium's attributes that the interpretive dimension of the
artwork becomes visible to its viewer.

> Artistic pleasure is delight in the success of an attempt of a
> particular kind. This pleasure is not possible when the
> means are obliterated and only the object itself is visible . . .
> A deceptively naturalistic battle-panorama may be pleasing
> in itself. There are people who enjoy the sight of a battle . . .
> But for anything to be a work of art the medium employed
> must be obvious in the work itself. It is not enough to know
> that one is looking at a reproduction. The interplay of
> object and depictive medium must be patent in the finished
> work.[41]

Hence, Arnheim tends to reject as unartistic any use of a medium that does
not aid interpretation and visual understanding. In his discussion of camera
angles in *Film as Art*, for instance, he cites a scene from Pabst's *Diary of a Lost
Girl* in which a couple is kissing by the glass door of a shop.

> The scene is first taken from the interior. The camera is
> standing in the shop . . . Then the scene is suddenly shown
> from another angle—the couple remain in exactly the
> same position, but the camera is now outside the door and
> they are seen through the glass. There seems to be no point
> in this change of the camera's position. It signifies nothing.
> And things which have no significance have no place in a
> work of art.[42]

If Arnheim was a Greenbergian modernist devoted to medium purification
for its own sake, he would surely celebrate this change of camera angle for
investigating and drawing attention to variable framing, arguably a specific
property of the medium of film when these sentences were first written. But
he rejects it as inartistic because it does nothing to further the goal of artistic
interpretation and visual understanding. This is also why Arnheim rejects
the use of medium-specific properties in art if they do not further this goal,
most obviously the photographic property of mechanical reproduction. If
he was a modernist in the Greenbergian sense, he would doubtless advocate
a film art that investigates *all* the putatively specific properties of film relative
to the other arts. But as we have seen, he vehemently rejects one of its major
attributes, mechanical reproduction, because it prevents artistic interpretation and visual understanding. Finally, Arnheim is quite happy to
condemn as inartistic the work of visual artists who do not, he believes,
seek to further visual understanding, including Jackson Pollock, one of
Greenberg's major examples of a modernist painter. In his brilliant essay
"Accident and the Necessity of Art" (1957), Arnheim examines the role of

chance in art, arguing that while it has always been a valid subject for art, it has recently become a "compositional principle." In other words, artists have begun "portraying chance" by "producing a chance assortment of shapes."[43] Pollock, he thinks, is a prime example, and he rejects the trend Pollock exemplifies in the following way:

> What objection is there aesthetically to random patterns? Not that they are not interesting, suggestive, stimulating . . . It cannot be said either that such patterns are unbalanced . . . But stimulation, pleasure, and balance are not enough. A work of art must do more than be itself; it must fulfill a semantic function, and no statement can be understood unless the relations between its elements form an organized whole.[44]

What Arnheim elsewhere calls "the active grasp of meaning that characterizes man's relationship to reality,"[45] which in vision manifests itself as creative organization and generalization, is missing from Pollock's work, and he therefore rejects it as inartistic even though it is, arguably, a paragon of Greenbergian modernism. Clearly, Arnheim and Greenberg view the role of medium specificity in art quite differently.

Of course, these differences do not mean Arnheim is not a modernist, for he firmly believes in a version of medium specificity, a doctrine widely associated with modernism. Once again, therefore, as is the case with skepticism about vision, Arnheim is clearly influenced by a major tenet of modernism. However, Arnheim's differences with Greenberg are instructive about his relation to modernism. Modernist medium specificity is consistently subordinated in Arnheim's work to his more original thesis about the creative eye and the goal of visual understanding through art. When it comes to a choice between the two, the latter clearly wins out in Arnheim's art theory and criticism.

III

Another difference between Greenberg and Arnheim is that the latter does not conceive of modern art as "evolving"[46] beyond art of the past, as does Greenberg, and this brings us to a third sense of modernism. Greenberg found evidence of the attempt to purify the medium of painting long before the advent of modernism, for example in the "resistance to the sculptural" starting in Venice in the sixteenth century, and therefore viewed modernism as continuous with art of the past.[47] However, he thought there was something new about modernist art, namely, the self-consciousness and "deliberateness" with which it went about the process of medium purification.[48] He also saw this process as proceeding in fits and starts, and "as by no means finished" when he published "Modernist Painting" in 1960.

Yet, overall he believed modernist painting was making progress toward the goal of "achieving autonomy": "the fact that it becomes deeper as it proceeds accounts for the radical simplifications that are also to be seen in the very latest abstract painting, as well as for the radical complications that are also seen in it."[49] While not all modernists, of course, share Greenberg's conception of what art is evolving away from or toward, they tend to agree with his definition of modernist art as self-consciously *modernizing*, as intentionally differing from art of the past in one or more respects, as deliberately innovative and advanced, pushing art forward in previously unexplored directions in both form and content. In his historical survey of the term, Matei Calinescu sees this as the major meaning of modernism in English since the early twentieth century, using Laura Riding and Robert Graves's 1927 *Survey of Modernist Poetry* as an example:

> Characteristically, Riding and Graves define "modernist"
> poetry (as distinct from "modern" poetry in the neutral
> chronological sense) by its willful deviation from accepted
> poetic tradition, by the attempt to "free the poem of many
> of the traditional habits which prevented it from achieving
> its full significance."[50]

While Arnheim is certainly aware of and points to differences between modern art and its predecessors, his major categorical distinction is between art and non-art, not different styles or periods of art. All visual art, for Arnheim—whether ancient or modern, representational or abstract—by definition pursues the goal of interpretation and understanding, and it often does so using the same means. To demonstrate this, he employs a diverse range of examples from different times and places, emphasizing the principles of pictorial composition they share, such as "the unifying power of consistent form" used by both Paul Cézanne (1839–1906) and El Greco (1541–1614).[51] These include examples from modern, non-representational art, which Arnheim views as fundamentally continuous with art of the past.

> Traditional representational art leads without a break to
> the nonmimetic, "abstract" art of our century. Anyone who
> has grasped the abstraction in representational art will see
> the continuity, even though art ceases to depict objects of
> nature. In its own way, nonmimetic art does what art has
> always done. Each successful work presents a skeleton
> of forces whose meaning can be read as directly as that
> inherent in Michelangelo's story of the first man.[52]

Hence, while he acknowledges that "individual artists and cultures form the world after their own image,"[53] Arnheim for the most part rejects the notion that one style or period of art is superior to another as well as Greenberg's developmental conception of art history: "We do not know what the art of the future will look like. No one particular style is art's final climax. Every style is but one valid way of looking at the world."[54] This is because, in spite of cultural differences, all art worthy of the name contains "a common core of truth, which would make the art of all times and places potentially relevant to all men."[55] This truth consists of the universal, natural properties of sight, primarily visual organization and generalization, which give rise to principles of pictorial composition common to visual art in many cultures and periods such as the unifying power of consistent form. Thus, if by modernist is meant someone who believes modern art must evolve beyond past art in some way, Arnheim was not a modernist. He insisted modern art should continue doing what art had always done, and he criticized it when it didn't, as in the case of Pollock.

IV

Arguably, the exceptions to Arnheim's relatively static conception of art history are those periods, such as "Hellenistic or Renaissance art," in which, he believes, realism is the dominant artistic style, which brings us to what is perhaps a fourth meaning of modernism, although it can be considered a variant of the third.[56] In this sense, modernism is a welcome reaction against a specific artistic predecessor: realism and/or naturalism. "What Modernism and Postmodernism share in common," argues Malcolm Bradbury, "is a single adversary which is, to put it crudely, realism or naïve mimesis. Both are forms of post-Realism."[57] "Adversary" is a good word for Arnheim's view of realism, which, in its extreme form, he tends to condemn as incompatible with art. Uninterpreted reality, argues Arnheim, is "a phenomenal chaos of accident, from which man seeks refuge in art."[58] In order to understand reality, art, like science (and vision), interprets it by organizing it and producing generalizations about it, and Arnheim viewed the relatively abstract artworks of children and "primitive" peoples as "simple" interpretive generalizations about reality which "limit themselves to portraying the things of nature with just a very few structural features."[59] However, as art develops, it aims for greater realism, employing more and more complex patterns in order to represent the "variety of appearances" found in reality. Rather than generalize, artists increasingly depict the "particular" and "accidental" properties of what they represent to the point sometimes where they simply reproduce the phenomenal chaos of accident in reality rather than attempting to interpret and therefore understand it by way of organization and generalization.

> This can be demonstrated by the increasing number of dismal examples that have accumulated in the Western art of the past centuries when the compositional patterns of realism became so complex that the average painter's and

sculptor's eyes could no longer organize them . . . The desire
for the faithful imitation of nature finally conquered man's
natural and traditional need of visual order and meaning
to such an extent that the occasional great master was
increasingly hard put to impose organization and significance upon the multiplicity of appearances.[60]

Realism in this excessive form, Arnheim felt, was a "melancholy surrender
rather than the recovery of man's grip on reality" and therefore incompatible with a major function of art: "discovering order, law, and necessity
in the seemingly irrational world of our experience."[61] Arnheim also
described certain trends in modern art as a "radical countermovement" to
the realism of art since the Renaissance, "a return to elementary shapes and
the elementary schemata of permanent structural norms. The reaction
became conspicuous in the geometrical simplifications of Seurat and
Cézanne and the primitivism pervading much art of the early twentieth
century."[62] Thus, due to his animosity toward realism, and his conception
of at least some kinds of modern art as a reaction against it, Arnheim could
be viewed as a modernist in the fourth, anti-realist sense.

However, even this assessment must be qualified, for as Patrick Keating
also argues, Arnheim's hostility to realism was by no means total, especially
in his later work.[63] The interpretive intervention of the artist could be found
in many realist artworks, he thought, even though it might be less obvious
and extensive than in other styles. In *Art and Visual Perception*, he uses Ingres's
La Source (1856) as an example of a painting that, while seeming to "offer little
more than pretty triteness displayed in a standard naturalistic manner," in
fact employs "formal devices that represent life so fully" that "we marvel at
the intelligence of the interpretation it conveys"; elsewhere he praises
Degas's *Cotton Market in New Orleans* (1873) and Vittorio De Sica's neorealist film
Umberto D. (1952) for similar reasons.[64] For Arnheim, realism seems to be a
style of art in which the goal of reproducing the phenomenal chaos and
accident of reality is aimed for but rarely achieved because it typically
contains at least some artistic interpretation of reality, even though it might
not be obvious. Furthermore, as we have seen, Arnheim does not hesitate
to criticize non-representational modern painting that "repeats and
continues" the "gradual decrease in visibility, complementary to an
increasing surrender of the formative capacity of the human mind to the
raw material of experience" found in realism.[65] In addition to Pollock,
Arnheim cites Jean Dubuffet as an example of such a modern painter
due to his conception of his "materials" as "objects for their own" rather
than "as means of representation." "What else," he laments, is Dubuffet's
art than "an ever more faithful reproduction of nature, nature at its most
amorphous, remote from the formative impact of man and equally
remote from its own formative powers?"[66] Thus, once more we find that
a modernist tenet—hostility to realism in favor of anti-realist modern art—

is subordinated in Arnheim's art theory and criticism to his notion of the creative eye and visual understanding through art. Realist artworks are praised by Arnheim if they in some way interpret reality and aid visual understanding while modern ones are condemned if they don't.

I have distinguished four meanings of modernism: visual skepticism; medium specificity; modernizing; and anti-realist. While Arnheim is clearly influenced by all four, he embraces none wholeheartedly, his adherence to gestalt perceptual psychology, or at least his version of it, complicating his relationship to modernism in all four senses. In the case of visual skepticism, it competes with it; medium specificity and anti-realism, meanwhile, are subordinated to it; and modernization is rejected due to it. This shows that it is in Arnheim's divergences from modernist orthodoxy, resulting from his training in gestalt perceptual psychology, that much of his originality as an art and film theorist lies. Due to this training, he was able to resist, at least to some extent, the mistrust of human vision, the fetishization of the medium, the inability to see what modern art has in common with its predecessors, and the rejection of realism that bedeviled so much art theory and criticism in the twentieth century long before they came to be widely criticized as the influence of modernism began to wane. His work stands as an enduring example of how a genuine engagement with a non-artistic discipline such as perceptual psychology can enable an art theorist to question and see beyond the doxa of his day.

Yet, in equal measure, it also shows how such an engagement can give rise to its own problems and prejudices. Supposing, for the sake of argument, that Arnheim's perceptual psychology is true, why does it follow that visual artworks *must* further visual understanding by interpreting their subjects through organization and generalization? In other words, why is it the case that they *have to* imitate sight in its "active striving for unity and order"?[67] Arnheim provides no explanation for this fundamental premise of his art theory except the circular one that the goal of visual art is visual under-standing, and it gives rise to an overly restrictive definition of art in his work. For artworks, of course, have many other purposes in addition to visual understanding, such as intellectual understanding, emotional expression, and political critique. While such artworks might employ what Arnheim calls visual organization and generalization in realizing these purposes, they also might not, actively pursuing a derangement of the senses and resisting comprehension, as does, say, René Clair and Francis Picabia's *Entr'acte* (1924).

More fundamentally, the comparisons between visual art and human sight upon which Arnheim's theory of art like much film theory is predicated are often vague and tendentious. Take, for example, his claim, examined earlier, that the frame of a shot imposes a limitation on what can be seen that "in the actual range of human vision . . . simply does not exist" because our eyes, heads, and bodies are "mobile."[68] One could quite easily argue the opposite about the frame, that it is equivalent to the "framed" or bounded nature of human vision, the fact that we can only see a portion of our environment at any one time, as do other film theorists such as Gilles Deleuze.[69] Meanwhile, filmmakers such as Stan Brakhage have attempted to replicate the mobile nature of vision, using the camera to imitate the saccadic movement of the eyes as well as the impact of the motions of the head and body on seeing.[70] Another example is editing. Arnheim argues that "in real life every experience or chain of experiences is enacted for every observer in an uninterrupted spatial and temporal sequence," whereas this is "not so in film" due to the fact that "the period of time that is being photographed may be interrupted at any point" by editing.[71] Yet, other theorists, such as Ernest Lindgren, claim that editing can "exactly reproduce the manner in which we normally see," because it enables the filmmaker to cut from one detail of a scene to another, much like our eyes typically move from one feature in our environment to another.[72]

Why is it that the same technique or property of a visual art such as film can be construed as like human vision by some theorists and unlike it by others? One reason is that different theorists emphasize different features of seeing and visual art. If one focuses on the rapidity of saccadic eye movement, for instance, one might claim that the eyes' saccadic shift from one detail to another in an environment is like the instantaneous cut from one shot of an object to another in editing. But if one instead foregrounds the temporal continuity of visual experience, one could conclude that instantaneous cuts make film dissimilar to sight. Likewise, if the perceptual–mental phenomenon of attention is underscored, cutting from one shot of a detail in a scene to another might seem to be like seeing, whereas if an observer's bodily location in relation to such a detail is the focus, then instantaneous cuts between shots of it taken from different camera positions will seem very different from vision. The point here is not that drawing analogies between seeing and visual art is necessarily mistaken. Rather, it is that both are complex phenomena with multiple features, some of which are alike in some ways, others of which are not. General conclusions about whether human vision and visual art are similar or not of the sort that Arnheim traffics in are therefore going to be empty. Such comparisons can be made only at the level of specific features, as well as particular artistic practices. Nor is Arnheim alone in arriving at such conclusions. Film theorists have often erected their theories upon them, from Vertov in the 1920s to more contemporary theorists such as Deleuze, who claims that "cinema does *not* have natural subjective perception as its model" due to the "mobility of its centres" and the "variability of its framings."[73]

A better way of conceiving of the relation between a visual art such as film and human sight might be in terms of *interaction* rather than similarity. Rather than imitating them, visual artworks, one might hypothesize, are designed to interact with the eyes, guiding their attention, surprising or shocking them, confusing or enlightening them, creating beautiful or ugly experiences for them as well as exciting or subdued ones.[74] Of course, much of the enduring value of Arnheim's work lies in the sensitive, meticulous way he examines precisely this dimension of visual art, focusing on the impact of balance, color, "the power of the center," and much else on our visual experience of artworks. It is what he says about visual composition, I suspect, that has the most to teach us today rather than his more abstract theoretical claims about the similarities between visual art and sight.

notes

1. Dudley Andrew, *The Major Film Theories: An Introduction*, London: Oxford University Press, 1976, pp. 12–13.
2. Noël Carroll, *Philosophical Problems of Classical Film Theory*, Princeton, NJ: Princeton University Press, 1988, p. 27.
3. Gertrud Koch, "Rudolf Arnheim: The Materialist of Aesthetic Illusion – Gestalt Theory and Reviewer's Practice," *New German Critique* 51, Fall 1990, p. 171.
4. Ara H. Merjian, "Middlebrow Modernism: Rudolf Arnheim at the Crossroads of Film Theory and the Psychology of Art," in Angela Dalle Vacche ed., *The Visual Turn: Classical Film Theory and Art*, New Brunswick, NJ: Rutgers University Press, 2003, p. 172.
5. Malcolm Turvey, *Doubting Vision: Film and the Revelationist Tradition*, New York: Oxford University Press, 2008, pp. 9, 101.
6. Rudolf Arnheim, *Film as Art*, Berkeley and Los Angeles: University of California Press, 1957, p. 9.
7. Carroll, *Philosophical Problems*, p. 31.
8. Arnheim, *Film as Art*, p. 17.
9. Ibid., p. 35.
10. Dziga Vertov, "Kinoks: A Revolution" (1923), in Annette Michelson ed., *Kino-Eye: The Writings of Dziga Vertov*, trans. Kevin O'Brien, Berkeley and Los Angeles: University of California Press, 1984, pp. 15–16.
11. Arnheim, *Art and Visual Perception: A Psychology of the Creative Eye*, The New Version, Berkeley and Los Angeles: University of California Press, 1974, p. 5.
12. Ibid., p. 46.
13. Ibid., p. 43.
14. Arnheim, *Film as Art*, p. 3.
15. Arnheim, *Art and Visual Perception*, p. 5.
16. Ibid., p. 45.
17. Ibid., p. 46.
18. Arnheim, *Film as Art*, p. 35.
19. Ibid., pp. 73–74.
20. Arnheim, *Art and Visual Perception*, p. 6.
21. Arnheim, "The Form We Seek," in Arnheim, *Toward a Psychology of Art: Collected Essays*, Berkeley and Los Angeles: University of California Press, 1966, p. 355.
22. Arnheim, "Perceptual Abstraction and Art" (1947), in *Toward a Psychology of Art*, p. 35.
23. Carroll, *Philosophical Problems*, pp. 53–54.

24. Arnheim, *Art and Visual Perception*, p. 454.
25. Ibid., p. 42.
26. Ibid., p. 454.
27. Arnheim, *Film*, trans. L. M. Sieveking and Ian F. D. Morrow, London: Faber and Faber, 1933, pp. 52–53.
28. Ibid., p. 11.
29. Ibid., p. 43.
30. Ibid., pp. 44–45.
31. Arnheim, *Film as Art*, p. 74.
32. Arnheim, *Art and Visual Perception*, p. 5.
33. Clement Greenberg, "Modernist Painting" (1960), in John O'Brian ed., *Clement Greenberg: The Collected Essays and Criticism, Volume 4, Modernism with a Vengeance, 1957–1969*, Chicago: University of Chicago Press, 1993, p. 85.
34. Ibid., p. 86.
35. Charles Harrison, "Modernism," in *Critical Terms for Art History*, Robert S. Nelson and Richard Shiff eds., Chicago: University of Chicago Press, 1996, pp. 145–146.
36. Arnheim, *Film*, p. 44.
37. Ibid., p. 44; Arnheim, *Film as Art*, p. 2. On Arnheim's *Materialtheorie*, see Shawn VanCour's essay in this volume (Chapter 10).
38. Arnheim, *Art and Visual Perception*, p. 139.
39. Merjian, "Middlebrow Modernism," pp. 171–172.
40. Arnheim, *Film as Art*, p. 35.
41. Arnheim, *Film*, p. 45.
42. Arnheim, *Film as Art*, pp. 49–50.
43. Arnheim, "Accident and the Necessity of Art" (1957), in *Toward a Psychology of Art*, p. 169.
44. Ibid., p. 170.
45. Arnheim, "Melancholy Unshaped" (1963), in *Toward a Psychology of Art*, p. 190.
46. Greenberg, "Modernist Painting," p. 92.
47. Ibid., p. 88.
48. Ibid., pp. 89, 92.
49. Ibid., pp. 88, 89.
50. Matei Calinescu, *Five Faces of Modernity*, Durham, NC: Duke University Press, 1987, p. 83.
51. Arnheim, *Art and Visual Perception*, p. 89.
52. Ibid., p. 461.
53. Ibid., p. 6.
54. Ibid., pp. 6, 461.
55. Ibid., p. 6.
56. Arnheim, "Perceptual Abstraction and Art," p. 29.
57. Quoted in Christopher Butler, *Early Modernism: Literature, Music and Painting in Europe 1900–1916*, Oxford: Oxford University Press, 1994, p. 1.
58. Arnheim, "Accident and the Necessity of Art," p. 169.
59. Arnheim, *Art and Visual Perception*, p. 145.
60. Arnheim, "Accident and the Necessity of Art," p. 169.
61. Arnheim, "Melancholy Unshaped," p. 191; Arnheim, "Accident and the Necessity of Art," p. 163.
62. Arnheim, *Art and Visual Perception*, pp. 134–135.
63. See Patrick Keating's excellent essay, "Art, Accident and the Interpretation of the Modern World," in this volume (Chapter 8).

64. Arnheim, *Art and Visual Perception*, pp. 152, 156; Arnheim, "Accident and the Necessity of Art," p. 168; Arnheim, "Melancholy Unshaped," p. 188. Patrick Keating offers a plausible explanation of why Arnheim praised *Umberto D.* in his essay in this volume (Chapter 8).

65. Arnheim, "Melancholy Unshaped," p. 189.

66. Ibid., p. 190.

67. Arnheim, *Art and Visual Perception*, p. 5.

68. Arnheim, *Film as Art*, p. 17.

69. Gilles Deleuze, *Cinema 1: The Movement Image*, trans. Hugh Tomlinson and Barbara Habberjam, 1983; Minneapolis: University of Minnesota Press, 1986, p. 62.

70. See William Wees, *Light Moving in Time: Studies in the Visual Aesthetics of Avant-Garde Film*, Berkeley and Los Angeles, University of California Press, 1992, pp. 86–87.

71. Arnheim, *Film as Art*, pp. 20–21.

72. Quoted in Karel Reisz and Gavin Millar, *The Technique of Film Editing*, 2nd ed., Oxford: Focal Press, 1968, p. 213.

73. Deleuze, *Cinema 1*, p. 64.

74. See, for example, the most recent version of Noël Carroll's theory of cinematic attention management in his *The Philosophy of Motion Pictures*, Malden, MA: Blackwell, 2009, pp. 122–124. I thank Scott Higgins for his helpful comments on an earlier draft of this essay.

rudolf arnheim's

early passage between

three   # social and aesthetic

film criticism

eric rentschler

I

To this day the distinction between Rudolf Arnheim the formalist and Siegfried Kracauer the realist is fundamental to classical film theory. Film cannot become an art, argues Arnheim in his canonical *Film als Kunst* (1932), if it only records reality and, in that way, simply duplicates the world. Precisely the technical limitations that render it an imperfect means of reproduction grant it the formative capacity to become an art.[1] Kracauer, as we know well, begged to differ. For the author of the equally canonical *Theory of Film* (1960), the medium shares with photography the propensity for capturing unaltered reality. This is its chief characteristic; for this reason, realism constitutes for Kracauer the very essence of film, indeed its principal criterion of aesthetic value.[2] The clear-cut opposition between Arnheim's formalism and Kracauer's realism seems hardly controversial and virtually unassailable. University course offerings on classical film theory, relying on the disposition of Dudley Andrew's still widely used monograph, *The Major Film Theories* (1978), employ this dramatic disparity between

Arnheim's constructivism and Kracauer's non-interventionism as an organizing principle.[3] And yet there are curious and intriguing affinities between these two seminal thinkers, which complicate such a construction and, at least to a degree, compel us to reconsider our understanding of Arnheim's work on film.

Since Thomas Levin's translation of Kracauer's collection, *The Mass Ornament*, in 1996, Anglo-American scholars who do not read German have gained access to a representative selection from the author's massive corpus of Weimar writings; in the process, a strikingly different Kracauer (beyond the well known realist of *Theory of Film* and the film-mirrors-reality determinist of *From Caligari to Hitler*) has emerged and catalyzed productive discussions within the film studies community.[4] His portraits of the Weimar everyday and its social surfaces provide a compendium of modern mythologies long before Roland Barthes's famous collection of 1957.[5] The articles focus on the commodified amusements, public diversions, and popular rituals of a nascent mass culture and anticipate, by more than a half century, an emphasis which now has become institutionalized within academia under the rubric of cultural studies. These contributions make it clear how marked the discrepancy is between the Kracauer who wrote criticism on almost a daily basis in Germany during the 1920s and early 1930s and the Kracauer who, living as a refugee in New York, authored the books *From Caligari to Hitler* and *Theory of Film*.

A sampling of Arnheim's Weimar film criticism appeared in Brenda Benthien's translation in 1997.[6] These notices assume an estimable place within lively German-language dialogues about film's formative, discursive, and political potential during a time of constant crisis. They arise within the larger context of Arnheim's activity as a cultural journalist (*Feuilletonist*) and an observer of interwar German society. Curiously, the work of the critic has not had much of an impact on the way in which scholars view the theorist. Arnheim's earliest writings on film, I want to argue, deserve closer attention and more careful reading. They enable us both to nuance and enrich our understanding of his relationship to the cinema and give us reason to refine the accepted wisdom that, in matters of film, he was an essentializing and ahistorical formalist.[7] Here we find an Arnheim who is neither rigid nor apodictic,[8] an Arnheim who is often playful and even irreverent, and an Arnheim who is most certainly a public citizen and a political creature. In crucial regards, the film critic and cultural commentator of the Weimar era represents an unrecognized and, at least in North American quadrants, even an unknown Arnheim.

II

At the age of twenty-one and still a student, Arnheim began writing film criticism for the satirical monthly, *Das Stachelschwein*, and the weekly, *Die*

Weltbühne, an influential journal run by prominent Jewish leftists who, in a non-partisan fashion, defended "republic and democratic ideas in opposition to the strong monarchist tendencies in Germany that sought to reestablish the Kaiser-Reich."[9] From 1928 to 1933 he served as an assistant editor of *Die Weltbühne* and was responsible for its art and film criticism.[10] A collection of his early pieces, *Stimme von der Galerie*, appeared in 1928, the year that Arnheim, now twenty-four, received his doctorate. In the introduction, Hans Reimann, editor of *Das Stachelschwein*, offered an affectionate portrait of the irrepressibly energetic young pundit:

> Arnheim is a bright boy.
>> He knows what's going on.
>> He knows what's up.
>> He's always in the picture.
>> No matter, if he ends up at the Oktoberfest, at a police exhibition, or a boxing match; whether his object of discussion is painting, servant girls, Greta Garbo, a parvenu, or psychoanalysis; he is always unfailingly on target.
>> He is a careful observer. And he has a sense of humor.[11]

Among Arnheim's journalistic entries on the cinema we find general reflections on film criticism as well as discussions of single productions (mainly German, American, French, and Soviet features) and portraits of international stars. Indeed, there is a remarkable sensitivity to the quality and nuance of actors' performances. As we might expect, he remains carefully attuned to films' formal shapes, their artistic accomplishments and aesthetic lapses, as well as—and surprisingly so—their political meanings. He registered the impact of contemporary developments and participated in significant public debates. In the Weimar Republic, he would remark in 1977, there was "no safe place for disinterested bystanders."[12] Looking back at his youthful effusions decades later, Arnheim was struck by how strongly the fledgling critic "was bound to all the manifestations of the manners of the day, the art business, the politics, the personalities, and the anecdotes of the big city."[13]

The Weimar Republic stands out, in Peter Sloterdijk's assessment, as "the most self-aware epoch of history; it was a highly reflective, thoughtful, imaginative, and expressive age."[14] It was an intensely critical period in which many intellectuals, especially on the left, cultivated a cold regard and a cynical reason, ardently seeking to see through illusion and deception. After a lost world war and the confusion in its wake, these sobered spirits swore never to let themselves be deceived again.[15] Characterizing the period's clashing discourses, its competing imperatives of official legitimations, advertising strategies, and propaganda slogans, author Robert Musil speaks of a Babylonian madhouse, "the nervewracking particularism and syncretism of political and ideological groups that screamed at each other in public."[16] Given Weimar's mindboggling gallimaufry of positions and per-suasions, identities (including those of critics) vacillated and meandered between perspectives. From one moment to the next, the ground could shift seismically, which is why one needs to be so attentive to the precise situations from which utterances issued. The constellations of 1924 were worlds apart from those of 1928, much less what transpired in 1931. In such an amphibian reality political frontlines and discursive boundaries are often very difficult to distinguish; the universe, concludes Sloterdijk, "becomes a multiverse and the individual becomes a multividual."[17]

During the Weimar years, the most significant film criticism by and large was not to be found in the prominent daily newspapers, but rather in the leftist cultural periodicals like *Die Weltbühne* and *Das Tagebuch*. In that regard Kracauer's extensive reviews for the *Frankfurter Zeitung* were the exception and Arnheim's feuilletons at *Die Weltbühne* the rule. Common to both daily notices and thought pieces published in cultural weeklies and monthlies was a fundamental skepticism regarding the economic legitimations and industrial biases of the film trade press. One should bear in mind that during the 1920s there were a number of quite prominent and influential trade papers, most notably *Der Kinematograph*, *Bild und Film*, *Lichtbild-Bühne*, and *Film-Kurier*. The status of film as a commercial commodity was clearly recognized, particularly as the German film industry competed fiercely with American studios for larger shares of the domestic box office. Indeed, contemporary notices frequently reflected on the links between the business of film and the production of ideology. In this way, Weimar film criticism often became a vehicle of social commentary and even sociological criticism.

The enlightened resolve that guided German film critics of the 1920s owed much to the eighteenth century. Continuing the legacy of Lessing and Schiller, they sought to further the improvement of artworks as well as militate against bad taste and educate their audiences.[18] Critics protected the best interests of a spectatorship that, more often than not, was considered to be unschooled, immature, and easily misled.[19] The film critic, submitted Arnheim, must be a professional (not a mere enthusiast or an opinionated tastemaker) who knows how the film industry operates, but who does not defer to it; the critic should "evaluate the finished work without prejudice" and function "as an impartial authority."[20] German film critics of the 1920s, to be sure, no longer felt the need to legitimate the cinematic medium as an art. Nonetheless, the precise terms of film's ideal aesthetic shape and ultimate social calling still remained a topic of debate. For all their differences, most German film critics viewed themselves as advocates of a medium that was emancipating itself from the other arts and searching for its true identity; for this reason, they challenged those forces that undermined or diminished cinema's viability and threatened its future. More conservative voices, among them some of the so-called cinema reformers (who had been so active and influential during the previous decade), sought to ensure that German cultural values inform the new medium; in response, progressives like Kracauer aimed to disclose the social interests at work in film fantasies.

Film, Kracauer argued in his seminal essay of 1932, "The Task of the Film Critic," is a commodity in a capitalist society that circulates among other commodities.[21] When one reviews films, one should not simply provide normative judgments about how good or well-constructed they are, which is precisely what Arnheim seemed to have in mind when he espoused "aesthetic criticism" in an essay of 1929.[22] Films, be they low-budget or mainstream productions, are anything but indifferent entities; they have material origins as well as social consequences. The critic must interrogate with care and precision what films convey to mass audiences and how they influence spectators. Even films that appear to have no political implications have commercial determinations and, as such, represent political interests. Producers are part of the dominant economic system and their continuing success depends on the box office and on the preservation of business as usual. The film critic must draw attention to social intentions that manifest themselves, often inconspicuously and therefore all the more perniciously, in cinematic fantasies and make these designs visible. The critic should compare filmic illusions with social realities and elaborate how the former obscures, disguises, and falsifies the latter. "Briefly stated," Kracauer submits,

> the film critic of note is conceivable only as a social critic. His mission is to unveil the social images and ideologies hidden in mainstream films and through this unveiling to undermine the influence of the films themselves wherever possible.[23]

This resolve corresponds to what David Bordwell speaks of as "symptomatic criticism";[24] ever on the look-out for concealed social contents, Kracauer's social critic is a discursive detective who searches for the repressed contents and political agendas of film features; he discovers "film as a social fact" and decodes it as ideology.[25] In the assessment of Theodor W. Adorno, Kracauer set a standard for German film criticism "by reading film as a cipher for social tendencies, thought control, and ideological other-direction." Such an approach, maintains Adorno, constitutes "the self-understood precondition for any reflection about the cinematic medium."[26]

III

The young Arnheim worked and wrote in the same culture as Kracauer. In a number of ways, his perspective was quite different. To a degree, however, Arnheim's early notices shared the impetus of the influential social critic; indeed, there are numerous points of correspondence. In the following I would like to sketch Arnheim's profile as a Weimar film critic and outline the central preoccupations of his early work and its combination of both aesthetic and social incentives.

initiatives and emphases

The young Arnheim took great pride that he shared responsibility for the *Weltbühne*'s reputation as a site of a "joyful style of fencing" ("fröhlicher Florettenstil").[27] His early prose is vital and vibrant, devoid of hackneyed touches or schematic formulations, peppered with biting irony, bitter sarcasm, and an undeniable brashness. He has a decidedly wry wit and a wicked sense of humor. In the words of Karl Prümm, he is "always on the lookout for the lively and original turn of phrase, for the truly new and contemporary."[28] Arnheim is an elegant stylist as well as, at times, an impassioned polemicist and engagé social critic. One finds protracted paratactic sentences that nimbly juggle oppositions as well as acidic one-liners and hilarious punchlines. *Der Kongress tanzt* (*The Congress Dances*, 1931), he notes, "is one of the most expensive German films in years. And one of the poorest."[29] "Fritz Lang's films are parvenus, trashy novels that have come into money."[30] Lang and his collaborator Thea von Harbou, Arnheim says elsewhere, love to "train politics and science for the circus ring, to Wagnerize topical problems." In their film epics "decorative beards and human masses surged endlessly across the screen, and thus sober reality was corrected with the aid of costly cosmetic surgery."[31] Arnheim has a penchant for constellating films, typically playing off a positive example against a negative one, or often reckoning with two or more films at once. He describes, for instance, the bizarre juxtaposition of the jungle movie *Trader Horn* with the Ufa musical, *The Congress Dances*: "The screen had no sooner been cleared of mistreated animals and Negroes," he quips, "than it was populated with many hundreds of extras in Viennese dress, who began dancing waltzes in such detail that one might have thought they were trying to propagate a new art form."[32] The Ufa Palast, where Arnheim took in the double feature, was apparently having "a streak of bad luck. It offered us Africa once, Vienna once, boredom both times."[33]

Quite often, as one might expect, the critic Arnheim writes with the assurance of the future theorist. He has no patience for mannerism and considers "indirect portrayal" to be the hallmark of film art; a subdued performance or a subtle approach will always involve the viewer more keenly. He chides Dreyer for what he considers the overuse of close-ups in *La Passion de Jeanne d'Arc* (*The Passion of Joan of Arc*): "An important structural form was taken to excess in an irritating manner."[34] He likewise complains about René Clair's haphazard compositions and the director's lacking sense of structural design. In *À nous la Liberté*, Clair reminds one of a painter who, when he has reached the image's bottom left, no longer remembers what he painted on the top right."[35] *À nous la Liberté* "is not gushing, untamed raw material, but an untamed game of form, due to its lack of contact with the material, with the subject, with the meaning." Clair's films may be light, but there are various forms of lightness. It is easy to be light "when you are not subject to gravity." For Arnheim, the films of René Clair lack the essential measure of substance which grants to those of Charlie Chaplin a lovely lightness of being.[36] *Morocco*, on the other hand, is hyperartificial, but still manages to be aesthetically convincing: "It hurts Sternberg's films," he comments, "that life always take place in the space of just a few feet around the character. But this small circle turns into a magic circle." Von Sternberg knows what few directors do, namely "that art begins with beauty, not with naturalness."[37]

The multiple screens in Abel Gance's *Napoleon* (1927) remind Arnheim of a three-ring circus. Such "imperialism of space" is inappropriate, for "the restriction to a rigid frame is the first prerequisite for any sort of pictorial effect."[38] He expresses chagrin at an early Tobis Studio sound production, *Das Land ohne Frauen* (*Bride 68*, 1929); its sonic track is downright harrowing. Among the cast that includes Conrad Veidt and a lisping female player, only a camel seems "to have found the right pitch for the Tobis machine." After the camel finished his work on the film, Arnheim adds, it returned to the zoo and mingled with its fellow caged creatures, proclaiming "Boy, what a night I had!" "The critic," he concludes, "escaped with similar feelings."[39] In a review of 1930 Arnheim laments that anachronisms of vaudeville theater one had been glad to be rid of were now making a comeback in sound film. He praises *City Lights,* a film of 1931 that mercifully refuses to get with the sound program—and does so to great artistic effect: "Chaplin's quiet art speaks to us as it always did."[40]

One encounters, nonetheless, a number of moments in which the young Arnheim seems less tightly bound to the formative paradigm. The later mortal enemy of sound, while speaking of *The Phantom of the Opera* (1925), expresses regret that the viewer does not get to hear the phantom's "deep, soft voice."[41] And that same mortal enemy will grant that in *M* "the tools of sound film are occasionally used with skill."[42] (It is ironic that the inveterate Lang-basher reserves praise for the director for a sound film!) He praises E. A. Dupont for the "astonishing courage he has in showing reality" and, in fact, even stresses the ways in which artistic choice and the material immediacy of an object work as an ensemble to startle the viewer. In *Variety*, Emil Jannings wears "an everyday, funny, rumpled" hat when he murders his rival. When he moves away from his victim, "this hat is battered from the struggle, crumpled—something that would be a laughable sight in almost any other circumstances. That here the most trivial absurdity can be turned into utter horror is evidence of more than just a good choice on the director's part."[43]

Pudovkin's *Mother* allows us to partake of things in fresh and unusual ways, so much so that we experience them directly. Instead of conventional film images, "we see the thing itself, laden with all the powerful emotion of reality."[44] In such a formulation, surely more redolent of Kracauer's *Theory of Film* than his own *Film as Art*, reality seems to enjoy a privileged status. And, so too, does one of Kracauer's other privileged categories, namely the adventitious.[45] "Everybody," Arnheim writes in a review of *The End of St. Petersburg*, "needs the kind of inspiration that often strikes by coincidence, and he who always spends time with film people from morning to midnight easily becomes a 'professional,' automatically reeling off his films with the help of a fixed 'archive.' "[46] As a documentary, he writes in 1931, *Tabu* "offers less—primarily less in the way of unstaged reality—than we demand today."[47] The young critic disliked the postsynching in *Tabu*, which he deemed "extraordinarily dangerous. When true images imperceptibly become lies through false sounds, confusion and deception result."[48] "What a work of art most desperately needs," Arnheim claims that same year, "are limitations. He who heads out to catch the whole of life will return home with a pile of chaos in his fishing-net, but he who sticks to a small part of it will, perhaps unexpectedly, catch the whole world." The formalist knows that film has a "pedantic sense of reality—against which one may not sin!"[49] Kracauer also had a pedantic sense of reality. He recognized in *Theory of Film*, Arnheim wrote in 1974,

> that in order to produce the strongest effect, raw material is not repressed, but rather emphasized, because the half-formed, the open and the infinite reveal the world to us in a novel way. The French critic André Bazin has also expressed thoughts along these lines.[50]

Clearly, in these passages at least, Arnheim is seeking to negotiate the formative impulse with a respect for reality's integrity; this balancing act goes a long way toward explaining why Arnheim initially praised *Theory of Film*[51] and continued to do so long after the book's appearance.

termite films and white elephants

There is no doubt that Arnheim preferred productions that set out to further film art and do more than just entertain. Some features, he noted, "achieve their aims in a satisfactory and non-controversial manner, by using tested, safe means"; others experiment and "seek to wrest from the film apparatus new forms of expression."[52] Nonetheless, the *Weltbühne* critic surely was not altogether dismissive of mass culture. He sounds a little like Pauline Kael when he remarks that "a bit of pure, rollicking trash which goes beyond good and evil provides a more pleasant, decent sight than does a cultural asset gaudily made-up to suit the public's taste."[53] Arnheim disparages what he calls "the hopelessly old-fashioned productions by Fritz Lang, Paul Czinner, Henny Porten, etc. in which even excellent partial accomplishments cannot erase the impression that there is nothing of film art here."[54] Repeatedly, he maligns Lang for trying to inflate trivial materials into something grander and more significant. The director's films, carps Arnheim, are certainly busy and very complicated; their fussy obsession with machines, media, and gadgets is, however, both irksome and tedious. Lightning may well flash here, quite often in fact, but it does not strike, so that the viewer only gets "cold fireworks."[55] In *Spione* (*Spies*), Lang stages everything "cleverly and cleanly, but without our imagining for a second that this might be film art. The deluxe edition of dime-store detective novel, nothing more!"[56] In Arnheim's view, Lang's films fail because they are pompous and self-important, akin to what Manny Farber would later call white elephant art; they "blow up every situation and character like an affable inner tube" and seek to imbue each frame "with glinting, darting Style and creative Vivacity."[57] On the other hand, Arnheim applauds the unprofessional cast of *Menschen am Sonntag* (*People on Sunday*) and calls the production an "outsider film," looking ahead to Farber's notion of "termite art" with its resolutely unpretentious and seemingly slapdash "signs of eager, industrious, unkempt activity."[58] Live and spontaneous expressions flit across untrained faces in a welcome departure from the contrived features that rely on acting agencies for their criminals and prostitutes. "A studio," he insists, "should be more impudent, should try its hand at the most refined camera art, and should be bold in its selection of topics and intellectual motifs in areas forbidden to the industry producers."[59]

history and ideology

One of the major discoveries in reading Arnheim's Weimar notices is the critic's marked sense of historical context and strong social engagement. In his various programmatic statements, Arnheim is mindful of the critic's historical responsibility; he often expressly foregrounds the historicity of films as well as imagines the perspectives of future historians. Looking back in 1929, he relates that old Chaplin films

> have their style, which some day in the history of film art
> will be called the early style; for they still basically developed
> with a very primitive idea of the possibilities of film: the
> camera serves as a reproductive organ for a situation which,
> seen purely spatially ... could just as well take place in
> reality or on a stage. The setting of the action remains
> constant throughout entire scenes, the continual long shot
> is scarcely broken up by close-ups, there are no elegant
> shots, no characterizations using boldly isolated details.[60]

These reflections on a cinema of attractions before the codification of continuity editing anticipate by a half-century scholarship on early silent cinema. The evolution of film, in Arnheim's mind (and here, to be sure, his perspective assumes teleological contours), involves the medium's path "from reportage to a world of its own."[61] Silent cinema has provided us the opportunity to watch a new art come into being, a notion that we also find in the work of Béla Balázs.[62] The film critic, in writing about new things, does just the opposite of a paleontologist, who deals with old things. "He must preconstruct film art from occasional fossilizations, from impressions of sometimes not very noble parts; the laws of construction with which the film of the future will perhaps, in happy moments, completely comply must also be applied to contemporary film."[63]

Like his colleague Kracauer, Arnheim frequently took critical stock of German cinema and conducted discursive analyses of current features. Arnheim is taken aback, for instance, at how *Metropolis* fuses the old and new worlds. On one hand, the film puts on display engineer-Americanism, on the other, the whole dust-collecting arts-and-crafts of European emotional life. We partake of "mundane genre scenes with nightmarish medieval portraits, painted in machine oil. There is no trace of the new functionalism, not the least sign of an airing out of the soul via the dispassionate-hygienic technological style."[64] The film's upbeat conclusion, he goes on ("The heart must mediate between head and hands!"), suggests that one can find a resolution to class conflict without being burdened by material considerations. Thea von Harbou, the scriptwriter, has a bit of King Midas insofar as just about everything she touches turns into gold; when she comes upon serious material, however, it invariably turns into kitsch. Clearly, Arnheim suggests, she would be well advised to keep her "manicured fingers off socialism."[65]

In a country where effective political and social critique was in rare supply and public complacency an everyday reality, Arnheim submits, *Die Weber* (*The Weavers*) is a great disappointment. If anything, it reduces Gerhart Hauptmann's historical drama about a Silesian workers' revolt to pretty pictures and fetching performances, which provide a diverting evening in the dark. The film, claims Arnheim (whose ideological reading is much harsher than Kracauer's), seeks to replicate the box office successes of Soviet films like *Battleship Potemkin* and *The Mother* by profiting from the caché of dramatist Gerhart Hauptmann and by promising spectacular scenes of mass violence.[66] No doubt, the feature managed to stimulate "genuine and spontaneous emotion," but that also happens when people watch bike races; in fact, it happens all the time. "Professional athletics are a luxury, art is a luxury, but revolution is not." At once a betrayal of cinematic art and of revolutionary thought, *The Weavers* is nothing less than "a profanity. A revolutionary people deserves a revolutionary art."[67] Arnheim's sensitivity for the political dimensions of films, I would add, also extends to their anti-Semitic insinuations.[68] We also find a sensitivity for primitivist and colonial discourse in his review of *Tabu*: "The film people, the missionaries of the

Maltese cross, show the islanders how it is supposed to look on a romantic South Sea island." In this way, the "ideology of bourgeois film production" finds its way into the film; "the naked wild man must make the westerners' national morality palatable to them."[69]

In his notice, "The Russians are Playing" (1931), Arnheim describes a changed cultural ambience in which one no longer finds on German screens and stages the *Potemkin*-inflected projects of the mid-1920s, the "dilettante theater of current events." Instead of "thundering grenades" and "rough noise from the fields," audiences now partake of "lively parties, frightful marches into winsome dance music."[70] Arnheim's characterization of the incongruous profusion of light touches at a moment of acute political crisis is both ironic and incisive. No wonder, he laments, that serious Soviet films like Dziga Vertov's *Enthusiasm* now seem so out of place. Writing a year later, Arnheim wondered whether one might still be able to make the ambitious films of 1931. All indications suggested not. He deplores "the ever-increasing contamination of the public's taste" as well as the neo-Nazi films with Otto Gebühr. "The intensification of censorship, the National-Socialist cell formation in the circles of cinema-owners, the fear of protest demonstrations in the cinema . . . does not even permit people the modest progress of the past few years." Directors are taking flight and turning out frantic escapist vehicles, fleeing "from the horror of reality into the horror of unreality."[71]

IV

When Arnheim's *Film als Kunst* appeared in 1932, Kracauer was one of its most positive reviewers.[72] He lauded it as an aesthetics of film and acknowledged its relationship to the theoretical work of Balázs, Pudovkin, and Moussinac. With its systematic approach to the laws of the silent cinema, the study, in Kracauer's estimation, is admirably sensitive to formal structures. To be sure, remarked the otherwise respectful colleague, Arnheim does not demonstrate equal sensitivity when it comes to the contents of films: "At the very least his reading of the 'confection film' is not very original, and it seems as if he lacks a knowledge of the relevant sociological categories. Herein lie the book's limits."[73] There is, I think, something decidedly territorial about these harsh words in an otherwise appreciative response, as if the reviewer felt that Arnheim's chapter on film content ("Was gefilmt wird") with its discussion of the psychology of mass productions and a subsequent section on the masses and the film industry were treading on Kracauer's turf, as if the two were somehow in competition not only as film reviewers but as sociological critics.[74]

Histories of German film criticism (like histories of film theory) view Arnheim and Kracauer as diametrically opposed voices, the former insisting that film criticism is foremostly aesthetic criticism, the latter, as stated, that "the film critic of note is conceivable only as a social critic."[75] As we have seen, however, the young Arnheim had both aesthetic and social investments. And even as late as 1935, while still maintaining the primary importance of aesthetic scrutiny, he would argue that the critic's "second great task is the consideration of film as an economic product, and as an expression of political and moral viewpoints."[76] A film is never the independent work of an individual artist and therefore cannot be judged as one would a painting or a novel. "In industrialized production, a film today is characterized far more by the company who makes it than by the director." Indeed, a film "is not so much the expression of individual opinions as it is the expression of general political and moral views." (One is reminded here of the introduction to Kracauer's *From Caligari to Hitler*.)[77] Nations dominated by particular ideologies (the German word Arnheim uses is *Weltanschauung*) exercise a strong influence over the political and moral content of film productions. And it is the task of the film critic, he stresses, "to analyze these contents and to evaluate them, positively or negatively."[78] Film is not the product of individual artists, but rather nations, classes, and political conceptions. Here, too, he comes very close to Kracauer's later notion of film as a collective production.

It is important that we bear in mind the strong difference between *Film als Kunst* of 1932 and its English adaptation, *Film as Art* of 1957. The latter edition, which has almost exclusively dominated our understanding of Arnheim's approach to film in Anglo-American circles, incorporates only a small portion of the original edition and appends four articles that Arnheim wrote later in the 1930s after leaving Germany. As Sabine Hake points out, the American text virtually eliminated any "traces of a political consciousness and deleted numerous contemporaneous references."[79] One of the sections to disappear was a significant reflection on film and ideology, which stresses the importance of social and economic conditions for the production of films and also comments on the ideological functions of specific stereotypes and genres.[80] The elision makes us lose sight of a salient earmark in Arnheim's early film criticism. And in losing sight of the social dimension of his writing, we become unable to appreciate the structured complementarity between Arnheim's formative impulse and his awareness of historical and political reality. As a result, Arnheim comes to us, in part of his own doing, as the ahistorical and unpolitical film theorist. Surely, I would suggest that future studies might quite productively probe a similar complementarity between the regard for form and the sensitivity to social and political determinants in the work of Balázs and Kracauer. Indeed, Karsten Witte once described Arnheim, Balázs, and Kracauer as the "ABKs" of German film theory, a formulation that suggests we might productively consider them as a collective corpus rather than as embodiments of altogether different perspectives.[81] And, if we do so, it would be useful to bear in mind Sloterdijk's insights regarding the amphibian quality of discourse within the Weimar Republic and the compelling ways in which it eludes easy generalization and comfortable cubbyholing. "Mostly," he remarks, "the contemporaries found out only afterward what kind of times they had really lived in—and what was simultaneous with them."[82]

Like the two other great German-language film theorists, claims Gertrud Koch, Arnheim derived his film theory from his work as a film critic. His theoretical texts, she argues, "are shot through with material lifted, unrevised" from his journalistic criticism.[83] The claim certainly is correct, but only if one, like Koch, is working with the original German edition of *Film als Kunst*, which was reissued by the Fischer Verlag without any change in 1979 and reprinted as a Suhrkamp paperback in 2002. In fact, when we look at the 1957 University of California Press edition of *Film as Art*, we find few remnants of the early journalism and certainly none of its historical and ideological inflections. In his Weimar era criticism as well as in much of the original *Film als Kunst*, Arnheim frequently writes in ways that would cause us to think again before we characterize his approach to cinema unrelentingly prescriptive and "rather parochial."[84] As we have seen, he often sounds like Kracauer (especially like the ideological critic and at times like the later realist) and, one might add, at times like Balázs. There are passages that seem decidedly out of keeping with his more normative later pronouncements and surely do not correspond to what scholars have often characterized as his "rigidity in aesthetic matters."[85]

A vexing question remains: how are we to account for the repression of the social critic? Arnheim claims that he made the omissions in *Film as Art* "because some of the chapters tangled with tasks for which respectable techniques are now available, such as my sketchy 'content analysis' of the standard movie ideology."[86] At first blush, this sounds plausible and convincing; Arnheim suggests that the strength of the work, which he intends to be read as "a book of standards," lies in its formal emphasis and that the section on content has in the meanwhile been superseded by the more substantial and informed investigations of others.[87] But the fear that this part of the book might not withstand the test of time certainly did not prevent him from allowing it to appear in subsequent post-war German editions. Is the evanescence of his political voice simply a function of his having matured and moved on? Or might the McCarthy era and its suspicion towards progressive sensibilities, especially those of a Jewish emigrant from Germany with a leftist past, have played a role in Arnheim's decision to make the very considerable cuts? Lacking evidence, of course, one can only speculate, at least in the case of Arnheim. We surely do know, however, that given the difficult tenor of the Cold War epoch, Kracauer made certain that all traces of his former political convictions vanished from his work. History, argues Miriam Hansen, disappeared from the post-war writings of Kracauer, both at the level of history at large as well as his intellectual biography; in a fundamental way, the emigrant distanced himself from the Weimar critic.[88]

A valuable resource for the study of classical German cinema as well as an impassioned defense of silent film art in general, Arnheim's early criticism both enriches and complicates our reading of his subsequent film theory. It demonstrates a public citizen's sophisticated awareness of the contemporary historical context in which he was writing and in which films were being made. It also affords us repeated glimpses of a man of strong political persuasions. Addressing a protest rally against the official ban of *Kuhle Wampe* in April 1932, Arnheim intervened in a fierce debate about government film censorship. "Our task," he insisted, speaking as an activist, "is to enlighten, to show the contradictions between what this state does and what it proclaims in constitutions and constitutional celebrations."[89] "He who wants to improve the film must first improve the social order," claimed Arnheim in 1932 on the last page, indeed, in the startling last lines of *Film als Kunst*. "The future of film depends on the future of economics and politics. To predict this does not come within the scope of the present work. What will happen to film depends upon what happens to ourselves."[90] These final sentences, read retrospectively, anticipate developments that will dramatically alter Arnheim's life and, among other things, will necessitate his own imminent departure from Germany. And, as we know, this invaluable documentation of film culture before Hitler will be banned by the Nazis a year later. That the author himself would decide to expurgate the work a quarter of a century later and, in so doing, to alter his own historical voice is yet a further and poignantly ironic sign, both of separation and of loss.

notes

1. Arnheim's exemplary contribution to film theory appeared as *Film als Kunst*, Berlin: Rowohlt, 1932; a full English translation, which Arnheim considered to be unsatisfactory, appeared a year later as *Film*, trans. L. M. Sieveking and Ian F. D. Morrow, London: Faber and Faber, 1933.
2. Siegfried Kracauer, *Theory of Film: The Redemption of Physical Reality*, Oxford: Oxford University Press, 1960.
3. See Dudley Andrew, *The Major Film Theories: An Introduction*, Oxford: Oxford University Press, 1978.
4. Siegfried Kracauer, *The Mass Ornament: Weimar Essays*, ed. and trans. Thomas Y. Levin, Cambridge: Harvard University Press, 1996.
5. Roland Barthes, *Mythologies*, Paris: Éditions du Seuil, 1957.
6. Rudolf Arnheim, *Film Essays and Criticism*, trans. Brenda Benthien, Madison: University of Wisconsin Press, 1997. Aside from the addition of two articles, the collection follows the West German edition of 1977, *Kritiken und Aufsätze zum Film*, ed. Helmut H. Diederichs, Munich: Hanser, 1977. Arnheim explicitly commends Diederichs for having tracked down these journalistic notices; he [Diederichs] "besieged archives, procured copies, and culled the forgotten and obscure from all over the world, particularly in German, but also in English and some Italian." *Film Essays and Criticism*, p. 7.

7. Sabine Hake's study of Arnheim's Weimar film criticism and theory poses a decided exception and a decidedly more contextually acute perspective. I share her focus on the social dimension of Arnheim's early criticism and appreciate her carefully researched analysis of "his contribution to the cultural and political debates of the late twenties." See Sabine Hake, *The Cinema's Third Machine: Writing on Film in Germany 1907–1933*, Lincoln: University of Nebraska Press, 1993, p. 271. Although I concur that these early writings enact "the tension between aesthetic, psychological, and social categories of evaluation," I do not believe that they fully "resolve" them (Hake, p. 271) in a way that will yield "the unity of a work in which formalist tendencies exist side by side with an acute awareness of the functioning of mass entertainment" (p. 290). Hake's attempt to construct Arnheim's work on film as a "unity" is contradicted by her own thoughtful discussion of how, in later re-editing *Film als Kunst*, Arnheim "eliminated all traces of a political consciousness and deleted numerous contemporaneous references" (p. 290). As I will argue, it might well be more accurate to say that Arnheim *repressed* (rather than *resolved*) the tensions posed by the social and historical incentives of his early writings. Likewise, considerable evidence speaks against Hake's generalization that the young Arnheim lacked interest in "sociological questions" and, for that reason, subordinated "everything . . . to the filmic text" (p. 275). Nor did the exuberant and fun-loving young gadabout altogether disregard pleasure (p. 279).
8. Long before Arnheim became a Professor of Visual and Environmental Studies at Harvard in the 1960s, Lewis Jacobs chided the "ivory tower" approach of *Film as Art* in a review of 1934 that appeared in the journal *Experimental Cinema*. Jacobs is cited in Hake, who elsewhere speaks of Arnheim's "rigidity in aesthetic matters." Hake, *The Cinema's Third Machine*, pp. 282–283.
9. Dirk Grathoff, "Rudolf Arnheim at the *Weltbühne*," in eds. Kent Kleinman and Leslie Van Duzer, *Rudolf Arnheim: Revealing Vision*, Ann Arbor: University of Michigan Press, 1997, p. 21.
10. For profiles of the journal and its contributors, see ed. Stefanie Oswalt, *Die Weltbühne: Zur Tradition und Kontinuität demokratischer Publizistik*, St. Ingbert: Röhrig, 2003.
11. Hans Reinmann, "Vorwort," in Rudolf Arnheim, *Stimme von der Galerie*, Berlin: Benary, 1928, pp. ii–iii.
12. Arnheim, *Film Essays and Criticism*, p. 3.
13. Ibid., p. 5.
14. Peter Sloterdijk, *Critique of Cynical Reason*, trans. Michael Eldred, Minnesota: University of Minnesota Press, 1987, p. 389.
15. Ibid., p. 410.
16. Ibid., p. 501.
17. Ibid., p. 509.
18. Béla Balázs, for instance, articulates this position in *Isskustvo Kino* (1945). See the English translation, Balázs, *Theory of the Film*, trans. Edith Bone, New York: Dover, 1970, p. 17: "Thus the question of educating the public to a better, more critical appreciation of the films is a question of the mental health of the nation." For a survey of film criticism in the Weimar Republic, see Heinz B. Heller, "Massenkultur und ästhetische Urteilskraft. Zur Geschichte und Funktion der deutschen Filmkritik vor 1933," in eds. Norbert Grob and Karl Prümm, *Die Macht der Filmkritik: Positionen und Kontroversen*, Munich: edition text + kritik, 1990, pp. 25–44.

19. Heller, "Massenkultur und ästhetische Urteilskraft", p. 28.
20. Arnheim, *Film Essays and Criticism*, p. 103.
21. Siegfried Kracauer, "Über die Aufgabe des Filmkritikers," in ed. Inka Mülder-Bach, *Werke, Band 6.3, Kleine Schriften zum Film 1932–1961*, Frankfurt am Main: Suhrkamp, 2004, p. 61.
22. Arnheim, *Film Essays and Criticism*, p. 103.
23. Kracauer, "Über die Aufgabe des Filmkritikers," p. 63.
24. David Bordwell, *Making Meaning: Inference and Rhetoric in the Interpretation of Cinema*, Cambridge: Harvard University Press, 1989, pp. 71–104.
25. Theodor W. Adorno, "The Curious Realist: On Siegfried Kracauer," trans. Shierry Weber Nicolsen, *New German Critique* 54, Fall 1991, p. 167.
26. Theodor W. Adorno, "Siegfried Kracauer ist tot," *Frankfurter Allgemeine Zeitung*, 1 December 1966.
27. Rudolf Arnheim, "Vorwort zur deutschen Neuausgabe," in *Film als Kunst*, Frankfurt am Main: Suhrkamp, 1974, p. 2.
28. Karl Prümm, "Epiphanie der Form: Rudolf Arnheims *Film als Kunst* im Kontext der zwanziger Jahre," in Rudolf Arnheim, *Film als Kunst*, 1974, p. 276.
29. Arnheim, *Film Essays and Criticism*, p. 174.
30. Ibid., p. 152.
31. Ibid., p. 165.
32. Ibid., p. 174.
33. Ibid., p. 173.
34. Ibid., p. 180.
35. Ibid., p. 182.
36. Ibid., p. 184.
37. Ibid., p. 172.
38. Ibid., p. 127.
39. Ibid., p. 151.
40. Ibid., p. 158.
41. Ibid., p. 114.
42. Ibid., p. 165. Likewise, in a discussion of *Kuhle Wampe*, Arnheim praises the film's uninhibited use of natural ambient sound, claiming it "could reverse many sound technicians' superstitious prejudices." He goes on to laud the sparse and expressive use of dialogue and the creative implementation of sound in Hanns Eisler's songs and musical score. Ibid., p. 94.
43. Ibid., p. 117.
44. Ibid., p. 122.
45. Kracauer, *Theory of Film*, p. 304:

    The small random moments which concern things common to you and me and the rest of mankind can indeed be said to constitute the dimension of everyday life, this matrix of all other modes of reality. It is a very substantial dimension.

46. Arnheim, *Film Essays and Criticism*, p. 132.
47. Ibid., p. 167.
48. Ibid., p. 168.
49. Ibid., p. 162.
50. Arnheim, "Vorwort zur deutschen Neuausgabe," p. 12.
51. See his review of *Theory of Film*: Arnheim, "Melancholy Unshaped," *Journal of Aesthetics and Art Criticism* 21.3, Spring 1963, pp. 291–297.
52. Arnheim, *Film Essays and Criticism*, p. 139.
53. Ibid., p. 188.

54. Ibid., p. 139.

55. Ibid., p. 135.

56. Ibid., p. 136.

57. Manny Farber, "White Elephant Art vs. Termite Art," in *Negative Space: Manny Farber at the Movies*, New York: Praeger, 1971, pp. 139–140.

58. *Negative Space*, p. 135.

59. Arnheim, *Film Essays and Criticism*, p. 155.

60. Ibid., p. 146.

61. Ibid., p. 147.

62. Balázs, *Theory of the Film*, p. 21: "The fact that the art of the film is not yet fully developed offers an unprecedented opportunity for aestheticists to study the laws governing the evolution of an art in the making." Critics and scholars of silent cinema, Balázs elaborates, "were offered the opportunity of watching a new art being born before their eyes."

63. Arnheim, *Film Essays and Criticism*, p. 184.

64. Ibid., p. 119.

65. Ibid., pp. 118–119.

66. Cf. Kracauer, "Die verfilmten *Weber*" [1927], in *Werke, Band 6.1*, pp. 350–351. Kracauer's review pays careful attention to the film's form, the way in which individual parts serve to suggest something larger, the use of contrast and repetition in the editing, the construction of space, and the creative lessons that the director Friedrich Zelnik has learned from Eisenstein and Pudovkin. It is a good film, claims Kracauer, but it does not compare well to its Soviet prototypes because it is anachronistic. *The Weavers* restages a conflict from a transitional era, which every worker in the audience knows has been "overcome by social policy and unions." For that reason, "it does not serve a revolutionary function, but rather demonstrates how remarkably times have changed." (p. 351).

67. Arnheim, *Film Essays and Criticism*, p. 125.

68. In her screenplay for *Frau im Mond* (*Woman in the Moon*), Thea von Harbou "imagines that big business people or scientists are like Ludendorff imagines the freemasons and the Jews. The 'five richest people in the world' are sitting around a table like the wise men of Zion." Ibid., p. 153.

69. Ibid., p. 167.

70. Ibid., p. 168.

71. Ibid., p. 188.

72. Kracauer's comments on the book appeared both in the literary supplement of the *Frankfurter Zeitung* on 10 January 1932 and in the January 1933 issue of *Neue Rundschau*. The notices are quite similar; references are taken from the first one, "Neue Filmliteratur," reprinted in Kracauer, *Werke, Band 6.3*, pp. 15–19.

73. Kracauer, "Neue Filmliteratur," p. 18.

74. See Arnheim, *Film als Kunst*, 1932, esp. pp. 159–223 and pp. 325–328.

75. See the section on aesthetic and sociological film criticism in Helmut H. Diederichs, *Anfänge deutscher Filmkritik*, Stuttgart: Fischer, 1986, pp. 24–35, 107; Kracauer, "Über die Aufgabe des Filmkritikers," p. 61.

76. Arnheim, *Film Essays and Criticism*, p. 108.

77. Siegfried Kracauer, *From Caligari to Hitler: A Psychological History of the German Film*, Princeton: Princeton University Press, 1947, p. 5: "The films of a nation reflect its mentality in a more direct way than other artistic media . . . Films are never the product of an individual."

78. Arnheim, *Film Essays and Criticism*, pp. 109–110.

67

79. Hake, *The Cinema's Third Machine*, p. 290.
80. For an intriguing reading of Arnheim's approach to cinematic standardization and stereotyping, see Jörg Schweinitz, *Film und Stereotyp: Eine Herausforderung für das Kino und die Filmtheorie*, Berlin: Akademie, 2006, pp. 178–196.
81. Karsten Witte, "Von der Diskurskonkurrenz zum Diskussionskonsens," in *Die Macht der Filmkritik; Positionen und Kontroversen*, eds. Norbert Grob and Karl Prümm, Munich: edition text + kritik, 1990, p. 160.
82. Sloterdijk, *Critique of Cynical Reason*, p. 501.
83. Gertrud Koch, "Rudolf Arnheim: The Materialist of Aesthetic Illusion," *New German Critique* 51, Fall 1990, p. 164.
84. Andrew, *The Major Film Theories*, p. 27.
85. Hake, *The Cinema's Third Machine*, p. 282.
86. Arnheim, *Film as Art* (1957), p. 4.
87. Ibid., p. 7.
88. Miriam Hansen, "Introduction," in Kracauer, *Theory of Film*, p. xiii.
89. Arnheim, *Film Essays and Criticism*, p. 98.
90. Arnheim, *Film als Kunst* (1932), p. 330. Quoted as translated in *Film* (1933), p. 296.

eric rentschler

screening out sound

arnheim and cinema's silence

n o r a   m .   a l t e r

f o u r

> *New means to knowledge do not necessarily imply new knowledge . . .*
>
> (Arnheim, *Radio*, p. 235)

> *Was sound film a totally new art medium with laws of its own? And in addition, were the means of expression of this new medium sufficient to be of some account artistically?*
>
> (Arnheim, *Film*, p. 207)

Media theorist Rudolf Arnheim is perhaps best known for *Film als Kunst* (*Film as Art*), his pioneering text first published in Germany in 1932.[1] This volume had an immediate success and was translated into English and published with a foreword by Paul Rotha by the British company Faber and Faber the following year under the title *Film*. In 1940 Arnheim emigrated to the United States, and in 1957 he reissued a somewhat altered version of this work with University of California Press under the title *Film as Art*.[2] In this book, Arnheim advanced a theory of film that sought to legitimate the relatively new medium by positioning it firmly within the sphere of art. To that extent, he aligned himself with his German-language contemporaries, such as Hans Richter, Walter Ruttmann, and Béla Balázs, who theorized film as a primarily *visual* image-based medium and linked it to the other visual arts such as painting.[3] In contrast to the works of critics such as Siegfried Kracauer or Walter Benjamin, who approached their discussion of the new mass medium from a sociological and/or historical point of view, Arnheim's essay was anchored in an aesthetic formalism.

At the same time that Arnheim was formulating his essentially visual theory, however, important technological advances led to the advent of the *sound* film. In an early film review, "The Sad Future of Film" (1930), Arnheim lamented,

> no sooner did sound film appear than bluff triumphed over quality, and from one day to the next the people's darlings saw their life's work in question. The wide country road of *film art* [emphasis mine], whose lovely goal was becoming ever clearer in the distance, was closed for technical renovations, with a detour erected on a bumpy path over the fields.[4]

Arnheim's initial response to the "talkies" was indeed overwhelmingly negative. Although, over the years, he gradually tempered and rationalized his critique, much of his earlier ambivalence remained even in his final works.

When the 300-page *Film als Kunst* first appeared in German, it marked a major step in the theory and criticism of film. Arnheim's opus was composed of six sections, each divided into subsections. Most relevant for my purposes here is Section V, an 80-page excursus on sound film. It is significant and surprising that, when Arnheim prepared *Film als Kunst* for its American edition in 1957, this entire section was omitted.[5] In its stead, Arnheim substituted an essay from 1938 which he had published while living in Rome: "A New Laocoön: Artistic Composites and the Talking Film."[6] In the 1932 original and the British translation of the following year, Arnheim divided Section V into eleven subsections, each honing in on one aspect of sound in film with the purpose of critically challenging the new medium. He posed two fundamental questions:

> Who could discern whether sound film really contained the seeds of artistic endeavor, and if so, whether they would be so distinctive, so different from the media of all other forms of art, as they had been from silent film.

He concluded pessimistically that the "language problem is not confined to sound films, but is part of the general development of modern life."[7] In between these words Arnheim engaged in a lengthy critique about almost every aspect of sound film as it manifested itself in the early thirties. Six years later and after it was undisputed that sound film was here to stay, Arnheim still retained his ambivalence—however, he was more cautious and careful in his wording. He thus began the substituted "New Laocoön" section by acknowledging that "the following inquiry was suggested by a feeling of uneasiness that every talking film arouses in the author and that is not appeased by increased acquaintance with the new medium." He ended by saying, "There is comfort, however, in the fact that hybrid forms are quite unstable. They tend to change from their own unreality into purer forms, even though this may mean a return to the past."[8] The coupling of sound with the image preoccupied Arnheim for most of his rather long life. In 1999 in one of his last essays, "Composites of Media: The History of an Idea," Arnheim revisited his theory of film (and sound) for the last time. He explained, looking back over the waning twentieth century, "cinema worked very well, as long as the medium was left alone; but it was exposed to an aesthetic *crisis* [my emphasis] when technical inventions and a popular appetite for lifelikeness threatened the purity of the medium. Spoken dialogue in particular wreaked havoc on artistic expression."[9] In this essay, I will examine more closely this "aesthetic crisis" and trace Arnheim's own "bumpy path" over the field of sound to see what obstacles kept him from accepting this innovation as an art form and what theoretical and critical detours he traveled to at least partial acceptance.

> It is obvious that sound film gets under your skin far more
> than silent film . . . the advantages of sound film in the areas
> of instruction and journalism work as disadvantages on an
> artistic level.[10]

Arnheim's first comments on sound film appeared in an article of the same name from 1928. Here we find the beginnings of his antipathy to the medium that will survive more or less unabated for the next seventy years. It is important to note that Arnheim was not against music accompanying and/or structuring silent film; nor was he opposed to the careful use of noise punctuation or markers. Rather, it was sound as a wholly integrated and synchronized component of film that irked him.[11] Compounding his artistic objections to the new medium was his fear that when given the choice between a sound film and a silent one, the public would inevitably choose the former, resulting gradually in the death of silent film. At the time he wrote "Sound Film," Arnheim did not yet clearly distinguish between "Tonfilm" and "Sprechfilm" (sound film and dialogue film), a distinction which later became crucial for him. As his career progressed, it was the "Sprechfilm" that posed the greatest problems for him.

Arnheim opened "Sound Film" in a sardonic tone that was highly critical of the technological innovation: he announced that

> the thrifty among us will be relieved to know that the music
> no longer has to be played anew every evening, and in the

villages the barber's wife will not have to be coerced to
appear Wednesdays and Saturdays at the horse-hair piano
in the ballroom of the Golden Lion, for now the music will
be provided up front by the distributor.[12]

Revealing here is the manner in which Arnheim characterized both the
new medium of sound film and its potential audience. Arnheim singled out
the "thrifty" or parsimonious spectator who sought to receive entertainment at bargain prices and hence did not want to pay for the extra cost of
live entertainment. In addition, in opposition to the cosmopolitan cinemagoer who, it is implied, has sophisticated tastes, Arnheim imagined with
condescension a rural audience in which the barber's wife played on a cheap
piano.[13] His words betray the class, gender, and geographical biases that he
shared with many other modernist thinkers during the twenties.[14] It is in
his writing about sound film in particular that Arnheim revealed his own
prejudices, privileging cinema as a new art form instead of acknowledging it as a mass medium for popular entertainment or education. The
unwelcome entry of sound into his silent world allowed him to explore the
modernist division between high and low culture; he definitely favored the
former.

The high/low, art/mass culture divide was further reinforced by
Arnheim's feminization of popular entertainment. The musical accom-
panist in his derisive fable was a lower-middle-class housewife. In his
discussion of The Jazz Singer, Arnheim characterized the advent of sound in
terms of a "birth" instead of a technological advance. He wrote that the
"midwives had long fought over which forceps were best and who would be
allowed near the mother, and even now they have only brought the baby
into the world to fight for their rights to it in peace."[15] After birthing the
baby, the next step is raising it and introducing it to language. In this area
too Arnheim extended his feminizing metaphor when referring to the labor
involved in the production process. For Arnheim, the demands of the new
sound medium contradicted the aesthetic ideals of poets. In "Sound Film by
Force" (1931) Arnheim declared that "there are cookbooks on how to whip
up inexpensive art works, aesthetic recipes travel from housewife to
housewife, poets are transformed into film-script writers without any
interruptions in their careers."[16] In other words, the words and dialogue that
have been created for this new baby are formulaic and degraded. Cinema is
reduced from an art to a recipe for serial production; the result is a
consumable but, for Arnheim, barely nutritious meal. Sound film is thus
characterized as being born, nurtured, and raised in the female domestic
sphere. This organic system of logic allowed Arnheim to describe "silent film
and radio play are the father and mother of sound film."[17] Or to state it in a
more reductive form: sound cinema is product of a silent father and a talking
mother.

Arnheim's early antagonism toward the sound film was clearly rooted in the modernist antipathy toward mass culture. Sound for Arnheim led to the total commercialization of film.[18] In "Sound Film Confusion," written in 1929, he argued vehemently against works that were shot in more than one language version (e.g., German and English), concluding that such "processes are only possible when the film is a piece of industrial waste for the masses and not art. For a work of art is not a shirt with removable sleeves."[19] The addition of dialogue to images fundamentally threatened film's status as a unique and discrete art object, which, despite its inherent reproducibility, should not be churned out in multiple versions like merchandise on a factory assembly line. Nonetheless, in *Film* Arnheim was adamant in stressing that his ambivalence regarding sound was grounded in aesthetics and was not merely a knee-jerk reaction to the commercial film industry and its push towards sound.

The notion that high art is by definition opposed to commercialization was in the late 1920s and early 1930s primarily maintained by champions of an aesthetic theory that is both gendered and elitist. But, Arnheim evidently (though perhaps somewhat reluctantly) realized that this line of thinking led to a dead end: it was a theory that could not face the test of logic, since film's innate goal (its measure of success) *is* to be a mass medium dependent on public support and driven by a commercial market.[20] In the opening words of "A New Laocoön" (1938), Arnheim explained that "the following inquiry was suggested by a feeling of uneasiness that every talking film arouses in the author"; he acknowledged that even to "bring up this question [the question of whether or not a sound film could be a work of art] was considered by now offensive, defeatist, reactionary."[21] By the late thirties, with the popular success of film, Arnheim concluded that his uncompromising anti-sound-film stance was doomed. In turn, he developed a more complex theory of film's relationship to sound.

sprechfilm

In attempting to theorize this new medium, Arnheim fell back on one of the oldest and classical forms of the arts: namely drama. In seeking to make sense of the new hybrid form, Arnheim posed a fundamental question: "*Can image and word be combined in a manner different from that of the theater?*"[22] Arnheim's comparison of theater and sound film is natural, since written drama, like a film script, constitutes a significant art form, and when it is materialized on the stage (as sound film is on the screen), it brings together two media: text and performance. Arnheim was quick to point out the differences between the two media, but in order to do so he had first to construct an argument that was based on a complex understanding of theater, which relied on deconstructing theater according to different genres.

For Arnheim, melodrama was theater's feminized form par excellence. It transformed high art into easily digestible and consumable mass culture. As he observed, in the rush to embrace sound film, "producers fell back upon the stalest and most hackneyed musical comedy and sobstuff stories."[23] With obvious disappointment, he lamented that "music and song should have opened a new field to film. The mistake began with the takeover of the theater operetta form."[24] And he denounced a manipulative musical accompaniment for turning "sound film into a melodrama, thereby tarnishing its artistic purity unbearably."[25] It is to be noted that the operetta, like the melodrama, was considered to be mere entertainment whose audiences were predominantly female—perhaps if the source had been opera, Arnheim would have felt differently.

In Germany, the highest form of accepted literary expression was the written drama. Unlike in France or Britain, where the competing novel had been developed over hundreds of years and reached its peak in the nineteenth century, in the German language, literary efforts until the twentieth century primarily concentrated on dramatic composition.[26] It is precisely this elite status of written drama, not to be confused with the theatrical performance on the stage, which helps us understand Arnheim's constant ideal reference to theater in his discussions of cinema. Whereas melodrama is a cheapened form of popular entertainment, scripted theater or drama is part of the classical tradition and forms the cornerstone of German *Bildung* (education, development). It is this against which Arnheim pitted the sound film (especially in his "A New Laocoön"). Arnheim had an historical view of film and was very aware of its origins and success during its first decade: first as fairground curiosity and later as a nickelodeon entertainment for the masses. Through careful cultivation he argued that film by the 1920s had shed its past association and had attained the status of art. As he stressed in the opening of the section on sound in *Film*: "A few years have sufficed to turn a peep show into an art that must be taken seriously."[27] The advent of sound threatened this newly achieved cultural status.

From the beginning Arnheim conceded that there might be a role for music and songs in the cinema. However, in their "popular" incarnation, he felt that they ruined the high art of the silent screen, appealing to the lowest common denominator. An exception for Arnheim was the figure of Al Jolson who in *The Jazz Singer* "turns a silly melodrama into a tragedy that begs for tears."[28] This may be due to Jolson's gender since, for the most part, Arnheim praised male performers such as Charlie Chaplin or Buster Keaton over female stars of the silver screen. "[T]hose women who embodied a certain beauty appropriate to the image and movement of a silent film demonstrate an art of song and speech that does not amount to much more than a third-rate provincial theater," he sneered.[29] Better to keep the women beautiful and silent rather than vocal and crass—the subtending of gender with class is again striking. Elsewhere he suggested that sound film's

tendency to nurture low-brow entertainment stemmed from the entre-
preneurial nature of film producers and their pursuit of profit.[30]

Arnheim nuanced his critique of sound in cinema to account for what
he saw as the fundamental differences between sound films and speaking (or
dialogue) films. In *Film als Kunst*, he vehemently stressed—with italics—that
"*Der reine Sprechfilm hat mit Filmkunst nichts zu tun*" (The pure dialogue film has
nothing to do with film art!).[31] With this declaration he split the subject of
his analysis into two parts: setting or ambient sound and speech. It is this
ontological duality that enabled him to go back to Lessing's theory of
medium specificity. The duality also allowed him to posit that the composite
medium of sound film, comprised of a visual and an aural component, leads
to the dilution of not only images but also of sounds. In this reduced state,
sound film cannot be considered an art. Thus, well in advance of Clement
Greenberg, whose "Toward a New Laocoön" would not be published until
1940, Arnheim passionately opposed any fusing or mixing of media. As he
explained, in a critique of both theater and sound film, "great artists . . . work
in perfectly clean media . . . We have seen that the possibility of merging the
peripheries of two arts implies no identity."[32]

But, at least in its performed state theater, like sound film, combines both
the aural and the visual. Moreover, for Arnheim, theatrical performances
were certainly part of high culture thereby posing somewhat of an Achilles'
heel in his argument. He spent a considerable amount of time, both in *Film
als Kunst* and in "A New Laocoön," trying to explain why film should not be
compared to theater. At the same time, he acknowledged that sound film
brings the two previously separate spheres—visual and acoustic—closer
together. In almost defeatist terms he stated that sound leads directly back
to theater, and compared pioneers in that field to Christopher Columbus.
But instead of discovering a new world, they only find a new way back to
their old one: i.e., the stage.[33] In a similar vein, in one of his many attacks
against René Clair's work, he dismissively stated that "what is being made
here is literature."[34] What Arnheim is arguing here is that if sound film is to
come into its own as an art form, it cannot imitate previous art forms that
have language as a base: namely theater and/or literature. Already in "The
Sad Future of Film" (1930), Arnheim cautioned the reader: "We will never
arrive at any sort of understanding if we treat film as a variant of earlier arts.
The majority of all misjudgments on this point arise when theatrical,
painterly, or literary standards are applied to film."[35] However, nearly a
decade later in "A New Laocoön," he revised this position and declared: "One
thing seems certain: if one tries to ignore the properties that film shares with
other media—as has been done *ad majorem gloriam* of the movies—one cannot
hope to evaluate correctly the art of the film."[36]

Theater haunted Arnheim, and its relationship to cinema presented a
conundrum with which he had to contend. He focused on language in order
to demonstrate how theater was different from film. He posited that in

drama the most essential aesthetic component is the word.[37] Words carry the play in theatre; a drama exists first and foremost in its written form as a text that "does not require staging—it merely permits it."[38] The written drama, Arnheim contended, is a "pure wordartwork" (*reines Wortkunstwerk*) that stands alone.[39] Because of this, language and literature seem to hold a special place in his hierarchy of the arts: "the word has the range of all the other media together:" he said in "A New Laocoön,"

> it can describe the things of this world as immobile or as
> constantly changing; with inimitable ease it can leap from
> one place to another; from one moment to the next;
> it presents not only the world of our outer senses but also
> the entire realm of the soul, the imagination, the emotion,
> the will.[40]

When the word appears in film, however, it is diminished. A screenplay, Arnheim believed, was not a piece of literature but only a "recipe." The language employed in film and the manner in which it is delivered was not literary. Here Arnheim was particularly unforgiving as he mocked the pathetic attempts of film actors with no experience in elocution to deliver their lines.[41] But the failure of the speaking film could not be attributed to lack of articulation alone; it also stemmed from a problem of translation, namely from everyday "natural language" to the stage. It was Arnheim's position that in plays language was formal, it did not seek to imitate colloquial practice. As he stated, a good playwright must use words the way a painter paints nature, without attempting verisimilitude.[42] Even when film attempted to represent the classics it was, Arnheim felt, doomed to failure. As he noted in an intriguingly titled article from 1933, "The Philosophy of the Aha," "the grand gestures and the pathos of the voice that go with them do not work before the relentless camera lens, as the filmed Faust and Iphegenie scenes from Goethe films have proven."[43] For Arnheim, the lack of correspondence between the verisimilitude of the visual plane and the hyperbolic artificial speech emanating from the sound track resulted in an irreconcilable confusion.

It is essential to understand that Arnheim's theory of film was based on his belief that film should not copy nature but mold it.[44] That led him to dismiss modern drama and avant-garde theater. Arnheim never mentions nineteenth-century naturalists such as Gerhard Hauptmann (in plays such as *The Weavers*) who attempted to reproduce regional dialects as closely as possible; or visionary playwrights such as Georg Büchner whose *Woyzeck* is only comprehensible when staged. Thus, in order to bolster his theory of film as the new aesthetic medium, Arnheim returned to the classic dramas of Goethe and Schiller—as if the avant-garde had never taken place in theater. He even went so far as to suggest that cinema had had a particularly deleterious effect on contemporary theatrical practice, that "certain stage producers, who, also following the mistaken example of the film, turn the theatre—the home of poetry—into a traveling circus."[45] The reference to circus harkens back to the notion that cinema is but fairground entertainment. Even stronger is Arnheim's reaction to the introduction of film screenings on the theater stage. In one alarming passage, he wrote that a Piscator performance, with its

> screens and loud speakers is or was remarkably like those circus-pantomimes, where the arena was flooded and niggers [sic] and crocodiles battled in the waves, while horses and artillery rattled over pontoon bridges to the accompaniment of thunder and lightning.[46]

Film appeared to Arnheim to be part of an untamed and "savage" nature that threatened the culture of the stage. But more was at stake than the paucity of screen dialogue. Arnheim questioned the fundamental manner in which text and image combined on the screen. He observed, at this point in his writing, that the sound cinema model was one in which the visualization (or image track) accompanied the dialogue rather than completing it. Arnheim advised the author to "take care in detail of the visual production since it would represent 'the other half' of his work itself rather than simply a subsequent 'performance' of it."[47] Thus he proposed a form in which image and text would have equal weight and be developed in an egalitarian fashion. Arnheim pessimistically projected that this fusion would provide an almost insurmountable challenge for the filmmaker, since any combination of two separate media is doomed to failure. The effect is more often than not like two voices trying to speak simultaneously—the result is that both are frustrated and incomplete.[48] Instead of theater as a model, Arnheim, at this stage, proposed looking to opera, where music and text are harmoniously combined. But even in this brief excursus on opera he was quick to sound a warning. He cautioned that the libretto is used primarily to support the music and pure voice.[49] Similarly he concluded that in film the dominant element is the "moving image," and that therefore any dialogue would necessarily play a secondary or supporting role.[50] The only possibility for a successful fusion of sound and images would be to bring the two media together in order to "express something that could not be said by one medium alone . . . A composite work of art is possible only if complete structures, produced by the media, are integrated in the form of parallelism."[51] At the end of "A New Laocoön" Arnheim echoed V. I. Pudovkin who declared that "music . . . in sound film must *never be the accompaniment*. It must retain its own line."[52]

radio

The crux of the problem for Arnheim was in the translation of linguistic text into a combination of the acoustic and the visual. Silent film with intertitles was lauded, and similarly Arnheim championed the medium of radio. According to him radio presented the true new technological art form based on the spoken word. What silent film achieved as a visual art, so, Arnheim felt, radio had achieved as a purely audial medium.[53] Radio exists only in the realm of the acoustic; its reception is not muddled by images. For Arnheim, this singularity of the medium guaranteed success, whereas in sound film the combination of the audio and visual led to a "lawless jumble" and resulted in a "hybrid form."[54] The new medium was so intriguing to Arnheim that four years after the publication of *Film als Kunst*, he devoted a full-length study to it: *Radio* (later reprinted as *Radio: An Art of Sound*)[55]. As he put it:

> an alluring, exciting world has been revealed, containing
> not only the most potent sensuous delights known to
> man—those of musical sounds, rhythm and harmony—
> but capable also of reproducing actuality by transmitting
> real sounds and, what is more, commanding that most
> abstract and comprehensive of all means of expression:
> speech.[56]

In this work, Arnheim revisited the topic of sound film albeit from the perspective of radio. He proposed the thesis that radio and film, though related, function according to opposite principles: radio is unbounded and abstract, whereas film is grounded by its strong visual resemblance (iconic) to that which it represents.[57] In radio the art of making sound is perfected just as in silent film the art of making images reaches its apex. Radio's lack of images is what provides it with strength and aesthetic potential. Radio creates an acoustic organic whole by bridging and linking together myriad sounds.[58] The unifying of different sounds into one acoustic sphere is similar to the process in which disparate images are brought together in the cinematic frame. Yet, whereas images are bounded and confined by a clear frame, wireless transmission breaks "through boundaries of class and country . . . it invades with naïve impetuosity . . . it passes all customs-officers, needs no cable, penetrates all walls."[59] Radio has the ability to bring together time and space in one channel. By transmitting from the outside into the intimate interior spaces of the home it can also dissolve the barrier between public and private. "You . . . listen to events," Arnheim told the reader, "that sound as earthly as if you had them in your own room, and yet as impossible and far-away as if they had never been."[60]

In *Radio* Arnheim proposed that speech as broadcast on the radio, in contrast to that transmitted on the screen, served as a much needed corrective to the degradation of language in society:

> "People who during the day only hear the language of their
> environment, ruined by slang and journalese, and in the
> evening the cheap dialogue of film, should get from the
> loudspeaker an example of natural, simple, individual, but

absolutely pure and logically unequivocal speech, even
when it is only an unpretentious chat."[61]

Like theater, but unlike film, radio offered the possibility of word art. Unlike
cinema, where, in Arnheim's opinion, grand speeches and soliloquies
appeared absurd and detracted from the overall viewing experience, "the
wireless is not, like the sound-film, tied to naturalistic pictures; it can embed
a poetically 'heightened' speech in a sound-world that will not contradict
it."[62] Being free of a contradictory or disjunctive image track allowed for the
combination in a "sensuous unity" of all sorts of voices, noises, and music,
which resulted in pure "acoustic art."[63] Through interesting and unusual
combinations it allowed the listener to hear anew and to "present the world
to the ear."[64] And in so doing, it played a similar role to that proposed
by Schlovsky with regard to literature: it made everyday life "strange." For
Arnheim, it was through this transformative process that life became art.
He observed that "sound is functional as a means of communication, in
everyday speech it is impoverished, blunted, without beauty"; it was for the
wireless to restore language to the status of a "non-functional" art.[65]

But was it? Once again Arnheim's writings on the topic reveal a
contradictory stance. Thus, he writes in the last pages of *Radio*, "wireless,
realm of the ear and not the eye, realm of the word, of poetry, of learning
and of music, was from the outset a field for teachers, educators, and
litterateurs; and as a State institute it was run, not by business men but by
officials."[66] In this passage we hear familiar rumblings that had earlier
surfaced with the advent of sound film against the business of culture or
what Adorno and Horkheimer infamously would refer to as the "Culture
Industry."[67] Arnheim clearly put more trust in the democratic ideals of the
state than in the logic of capital. In this passage he argued that radio, unlike
film, is a combination of purposelessness with purpose, or non-function
with function—in sum, art with the mission of educating the public. Radio,
like theater was linked to a broader cultural program or project:

> Wireless brings an entirely new element into the multi-
> farious attempts at popular education, because for the first
> time it is not directed at the uneducated only, to raise them
> to the level of the educated, but is attempting to draw a
> cultural programme equally appropriate for uneducated
> and educated.[68]

Arnheim's faith in the benevolence of the state and its commitment to *Bildung*
is striking given that he had been forced to leave Germany, and the National
Socialist Party's abuses of the medium of radio were already well known.

But radio's educational mission went further for Arnheim: because
it transmitted "live broadcasts" and "real" events it had, he felt, a strong
indexical quality which affirmed its status as a recorder of "the real." To the

extent that it evoked reality it became a documentary medium and was used to produce news bulletins and broadcasts. Whereas this documentary quality detracted from sound film's artistic potential, in radio this was not the case.

What makes Arnheim's stance against sound film even more inconsistent is his response to the nascent medium of television. Following his writings on sound film, one would have expected Arnheim to be equally dismissive of television, however the opposite was the case. In his remarkable essay of 1935, Arnheim hypothesized that

> through *television* radio becomes a documentary medium. Only when it ministers also to the eye, radio fulfills its task— not its only task and perhaps not its most important—of making us witness immediately what is going on in the wide world around us.[69]

Whereas Arnheim saw this direct access to reality as a positive attribute for radio and television, he felt it was a negative attribute in film and especially sound film. It is precisely Arnheim's conception of film as an *art* and its relationship to reality that lies thus at the crux of his problem with sound film.

reality vs. art

Arnheim's initial essay in 1928 contained an intriguing encounter with an actor whose recorded voice spoke from the screen: "The impression that this is not a copy but a living being is completely compelling. In the split second that this happens, however, film art abdicates its hard-won place back to the good old peepshow."[70] The voice, in Arnheim's opinion, propels film into greater verisimilitude or realism, and it is this realism that moves it out of the sphere of high art and into entertainment for the lower classes. To drive his point home, Arnheim suggested that perhaps only when film entirely abandoned photographic realism and became animation would it really achieve its true artistic potential.[71] Writing in 1999 he observed, "In the case of silent film, a given photographic reality had to be exploited by its *deficiencies*. These *deficiencies* were what I scrutinized jealously when I considered the theory of film art."[72] For Arnheim film became an art—and differentiated itself from photography (and later radio and television)— precisely when it did not seek to proximate reality. He was equally troubled by the successful matching of sound and image into a seamless whole. Once again René Clair became his target: "the things which do not go together are fit together so cleverly that the viewer cannot help combining them psychologically. The result? Not a metaphor, but a fake."[73] The synchronization of sound increases the dreaded effect of verisimilitude, and the closer that film approaches reality, the further it moves away from art. The presence of sound immediately increases film's documentary potential, but, for Arnheim, documentary was not art. According to Arnheim, sound in cinema by its very nature lends itself to naturalistic deception.[74] In contrast to light, which can bring into focus what already exists, sound creates new things that don't exist.[75] But in so doing, it intensifies the reality effect and thereby fundamentally affects the art of cinematic experience. In "Sound Film," Arnheim described what happens when a spectator sees and hears a violin playing in a film:

> When real sounds are emitted by the filmed virtuoso's violin, the visual picture suddenly becomes three-dimensional and tangible. The acoustics perfect the illusion to such an extent that it becomes complete, and thus the edge of the picture is no longer a frame, but the demarcation of a hole, of a theatrical space: the sound turns the film screen into a spatial stage!"[76]

Not only does film come close to theater here, but the integrity of the entire representational frame is also exploded. Sound ruins the "beauty of the picture" since the acoustics interfere with the image by destroying the homogeneity of the visual plane. Note that at this stage, Arnheim seems dismissive of all sound tracks—not just speech.

Arnheim argued that whereas all images on the screen are equivalent when the film is silent, with the addition of sound, certain images speak and can be heard more loudly than others.[77] Sound functions like a spotlight creating priorities that are not dictated by framing, placement, movement, montage, or visual composition but by an aural pointing. With sound, "things which were previously kept on the same footing and which flowed together effortlessly by means of common visual characteristics, despite all discrepancies in content, now stand, disjointed, next to each other."[78] Here, it is almost as if Arnheim were suggesting that by destroying the equality among images, sound reintroduced hierarchy to the putatively democratic medium of film. The addition of sound interferes in the reception of two-dimensional pictures: "the producer cannot pay adequate attention to the beauty of the picture, since it is no longer only the visual, but now also the acoustic that is part of the composition."[79] According to Gertrud Koch, Arnheim's rejection of realism and imitation in film was related to his theoretical training in gestalt theory, which instead of connecting objects to perceptions through images and imitation, seeks to do so through basic structural principles.[80] In addition, the idea of a frame is very important in gestalt theory, and, as I mentioned earlier, Arnheim posited that sound radically breaks apart the frame in film. First of all, sounds come from everywhere; unlike vision it is impossible to direct hearing.[81] Just as sound can highlight images it can also make what is invisible or off-screen present.[82] Sound thus constitutes a potentially subversive element which paradoxically both grounds the image in reality while concomitantly introducing presences that only exist acoustically.

81

But, there is another dimension that sound unforgivingly introduces into the aesthetics of montage: Arnheim cannily detected that montage becomes irreparably destroyed by speech as it is inextricably bound to time.[83] Arnheim pointed to the fundamental difference between the way images and sounds work in film. The image can be stilled, slowed down, or sped up and still remain comprehensible—still retain its basic aesthetic logic as it were. In contrast, sound has to be carefully synchronized and played at an exact tempo in order for it to work. The soundtrack of a film in fast-forward is transmitted as a completely garbled and incomprehensible stream of sounds, whereas the images may still be followed. Thus, sound is controlled and inextricably linked to the speed of projection—it is the medium of time. Further, sound has to be played, it must move forward, as Jean-Luc Godard observed in *Germany Year 90 Nine Zero* it is absurd to play a single note for over an hour whereas projecting a still shot is possible.

Based on his observations regarding the relationship between time and sound, Arnheim concluded that the aesthetics of the film sequence is irreparably damaged by the addition of sound, since "the shot has almost entirely lost its formative function and serves as a mere organ for reporting, as it did at the beginning of the silent film era."[84] Sound film thus tends to return to its status as documentary, coming too close to copying reality and thereby moving farther away from art.

conclusion, or ending on a positive note

Despite his deep misgivings, Arnheim obviously realized over the course of his long career that sound film was here to stay and that he had to come to terms with its possibilities. If early on, he held on to the belief that film could only develop as art in silence and black-and-white,[85] by the late thirties he stated:

> Only experiment can show whether the world of sound is ample enough to provide conjointly with words the material for first-class works of art. For it cannot be said at once that since for silent film there is enough matter in the visible world to create a great art, the same can be true of acoustics.[86]

One such "experiment" presented itself in Walter Ruttmann's 1930 film *Weekend*, a ten-minute sound film without images, which Arnheim discussed in *Film*. *Weekend* is entirely composed as an eleven-minute and ten-second carefully montaged sound track: the location according to Ruttmann is Berlin; the temporal frame is a weekend. The film is composed of more than a hundred different sounds which had been gathered for the project including, cuckoo clocks, whistles, sirens, roosters, dogs barking, sawing, hammering, singing, engines, church bells and voices. Although *Weekend* may bear a strong resemblance to a radio broadcast, it is important to stress that the sounds were recorded onto the sound track of a film and projected in a theater, thus insuring its status as, in Ruttman's words, a "cinema for the ears." In the dense montage of sounds, several stand out and are repeated: a siren, a man's voice that calls out "Hallo Fräulein" at regular intervals, and the ka-ching of a cash register. We also hear a young girl's voice announce the title of one of the main staples of German culture, Goethe's "Der Erl Koenig" (1782). In this instance, for Arnheim, sound film may achieve the status of art precisely because Ruttmann is keenly aware of how a "*montage* of sounds separated in time and space would then provide similar formative potentialities as those which have been described in detail for visible things."[87]

Arnheim was open to the possibilities of the development of a sound montage in relationship with the visual track. In *Film* he acknowledged, referring to *Sous les Toits de Paris* (1930), that there are many more possibilities for layering multiple sound tracks than for superimposing images.[88]

> In the sphere of acoustics, on the other hand, there are innumerable grades of "transparency". For while but few bodies admit the passage of light, almost all let sound through but they modify it. Thus we hear it toned down by thick or thin walls—as, for instance, in "Sous les Toits de Paris", where the refrain of the song which all the characters sing over and over again is given variety by means of such graduated transparency—it is heard coming up through the floor, down through the ceiling, through an open window, through a closed one, from the public house.[89]

Similar to visual composition, sound montage has the potential to bring together spatially and temporally disparate objects. "Acoustic superimposition consists in providing several different sounds, or notes, simultaneously. In this manner a certain formative picture of the world may be achieved similar to that attained by various optical 'angles.' "[90]

Sound—again not dialogue—if properly used, can also function according to the same rhyming and matching principles as images, Arnheim acknowledged in *Film*.[91] Other creative possibilities of sound may be found, for example, in its metaphoric use. Arnheim extolled a scene from Vertov's *Enthusiasm* in which images of marching colonnades of workers are matched to industrial noises of machines. Interestingly, references to Vertov as well as other Soviet directors are omitted in the 1957 American edition, *Film as Art*.

In addition to montage, Arnheim examined sound as a rhythmic measuring force that drives the film. In his 1933 "Sounds in the Left Hand," he transposed a theory of musical composition in which the left hand plays a repetitive, monotonous rhythmic score while the right hand in contrast plays a varied melody. The contrast of the continuity on the one hand and the variation on the other, he found, produces an aesthetic of "unity with diversity."[92] In film, the sound track is the left hand and the image the right. And it is this principle of "unity with diversity" on which Arnheim settled as the only viable possibility of a successful sound film. Again he turned to a musical analogy to refine this theory as he observed in *Film* that in a duet, although neither hand plays the same piece, they must be played together and not separately.[93] What emerges here is a theory of a parallel or double track, each of which has different but complementary functions. But by 1999, as media became ever more mixed and sound tracks further complicated, Arnheim concluded that

> there are and were then all sorts of subdivisions, not just the one of the parallelism I had singled out for my special purpose. A variety of media could be involved, as is the case of an orchestra where every instrument plays its part in the whole performance. Each instrument contributes according to its character, the viola different from the bassoon, and all together at the service of what Schoenberg has called the Gedanke [thought, idea] of music.[94]

He had thus reconciled the aesthetic crisis that so concerned him in his earlier writings and come to accept the transformations that came with the technological development of film. But only partially.

notes

1. Rudolf Arnheim, *Film als Kunst*, Baden-Baden: Suhrkamp, Carl Hanser Verlag, 1932, reprinted 2002. The book was withdrawn from circulation in 1933 due to the Nazi laws forbidding publications by Jews.
2. Arnheim, *Film*, trans. L. M. Sieveking and Ian F. D. Morrow, London: Faber and Faber, 1933. Rudolf Arnheim, *Film as Art*, Berkeley: University of California Press, 1957. Note that for the 1957 version no translator is credited. Throughout this essay I will be citing from all three texts: when I refer to the original German it will be noted as *Film als Kunst*; the 1933 English translation will be *Film*; and the 1957 edition *Film as Art*.
3. For a useful comparative overview of the film theories of Arnheim, Balázs, Munsterberg, and later Kracauer, see Dudley Andrew, *The Major Film Theories*, London: Oxford University Press, 1976.
4. Arnheim, "The Sad Future of Film" [1930] in Arnheim, *Film Essays and Criticism*, Madison: University of Wisconsin Press, 1997, p. 11.
5. Arnheim, *Film as Art*. Interestingly, when this book first appeared in a British translation published by Faber and Faber in 1933 the part on sound remained intact.
6. After the Nazis came to power in 1933, Arnheim emigrated to Rome where he worked for the film division of the League of Nations. After Italy withdrew from the League in 1938, Arnheim moved to London and then to the United States.

7. Arnheim, *Film*, pp. 202 and 280.

8. Arnheim, "A New Laocoön," in *Film as Art*, pp. 199 and 230.

9. Arnheim, "Composites of Media: The History of an Idea," *Michigan Quarterly Review*, Vol. 38, No. 4, Fall 1999, pp. 558–561.

10. Arnheim, "Sound Film" [1928] in Arnheim, *Film Essays and Criticism*, p. 30.

11. Thus, he notes, "Music transmits such ideas more directly, more purely and forcefully . . . This is why music completes the dance and the silent film so perfectly: it vigorously transmits the feelings and moods and also the inherent rhythm of movements . . ." Arnheim, "A New Laocoön," p. 216.

12. Arnheim, "Sound Film," p. 29.

13. Arnheim's father owned a piano factory in Berlin, and presumably Arnheim had first-hand knowledge about the varying quality of pianos.

14. On this topic see Andreas Huyssen, Patrice Petro, Anke Gleber, and Bernd Wittig among others.

15. Arnheim, "The Singing Fool" [1929] in *Film Essays and Criticism*, p. 36.

16. Arnheim, "Sound Film by Force" [1931] in *Film Essays and Criticism*, p. 39.

17. Arnheim, *Film*, p. 215.

18. "Silent film was not ripe for replacement. It had not lost its fruitfulness, but only its profitability." Arnheim, "The Sad Future of Film," p. 12.

19. Arnheim, "Sound Film Confusion" [1929] in Arnheim, *Film Essays and Criticism*, p. 31.

20. Arnheim, *Film als Kunst*, p. 190.

21. Arnheim, "A New Laocoön," pp. 199–200.

22. Ibid., p. 212. Italics in original.

23. Arnheim, *Film*, p. 203.

24. Arnheim, "Sound Film Gone Astray" [1932] in *Film Essays and Criticism*, p. 43.

25. Arnheim, "The Singing Fool," p. 37.

26. In the latter part of the nineteenth century, authors such as Theodor Fontane or Theodor Storm tried to develop a serious German novel but the genre within the German language was not fully developed until the first quarter of the twentieth century by authors such as Thomas Mann and Alfred Doeblin.

27. Arnheim, *Film*, p. 201.

28. Arnheim, "The Singing Fool," p. 38.

29. Arnheim, "Sound Film Gone Astray," p. 43. In praise of Keaton and Chaplin and their appellation as "grossen Künstlers," see *Film als Kunst*, pp. 192–193. Later in the book, Arnheim maintains that sound film will bring about the death of the art of pantomime and the visual gag that has been perfected by Charlie Chaplin and the like: p. 232.

30. In his comparison of radio to film Arnheim champions the state-administrated quality of the former over the entrepreneurially produced nature of the latter: "Film production, directed by capable entrepreneurs of the lowest level of taste and culture, has even to its best productions never lost a flavour of the demi-monde, of drawing-room passion and public house philosophy." Arnheim, *Radio* [1936], New York: Arno Press, 1971, p. 285.

31. Arnheim, *Film als Kunst*, p. 218. I have offered my own translation since the British one does not quite capture the tone of Arnheim's prose: "The truth is that talkie is no part of film art." Arnheim, *Film*, p. 232. Italics in original.

32. Arnheim, *Film*, p. 209.

33. Ibid., p. 208.

34. Arnheim, "Sound Film By Force," p. 41.
35. Arnheim, "The Sad Future of Film," p. 14.
36. Arnheim, "A New Laocoön," p. 213.
37. Arnheim, *Film als Kunst*, p. 197.
38. Arnheim, "A New Laocoön," p. 217.
39. Arnheim, *Film als Kunst*, p. 199.
40. Arnheim, "A New Laocoön," p. 217.
41. Arnheim, *Film als Kunst*, p. 193.
42. Ibid., p. 199.
43. Arnheim, "The Philosophy of the Aha" [1933] in Arnheim, *Film Essays and Criticism*, p. 45.
44. Arnheim, *Film*, p. 201.
45. Arnheim, *Radio*, p. 210.
46. Arnheim, *Film*, p. 210. The term "nigger" here is an unfortunate mistranslation by the British translators of the original "Neger" which more appropriately would be translated as "Negro."
47. Arnheim, "A New Laocoön," p. 221.
48. "Since the two media are striving to express the same matter in a twofold way, a disconcerting coincidence of two voices results, each of which is prevented by the other from telling more than half of what it would like to tell." Ibid., p. 199.
49. Ibid., p. 221.
50. Ibid., p. 224.
51. Ibid., p. 215.
52. V. I. Pudovkin, "Asynchronism as a Principle of Sound Film," in Elisabeth Weis and John Belton eds. *Film Sound: Theory and Practice*, New York: Columbia University Press, 1985, p. 89. Italics in original.
53. Arnheim, *Film als Kunst*, p. 203.
54. Arnheim, *Film*, p. 211.
55. Arnheim, *Radio: An Art of Sound* [1936] New York: Arno Press, 1971.
56. Arnheim, *Radio*, p. 15.
57. Arnheim, "Film and Radio" [1933] in *Film Essays and Criticism*, pp. 16–17.
58. Arnheim, *Radio*, p. 195.
59. Ibid., pp. 226–227, 233.
60. Ibid., p. 20.
61. Ibid., p. 219.
62. Ibid., p. 42.
63. Ibid., p. 28.
64. Ibid., p. 32.
65. Ibid., p. 69.
66. Ibid., p. 286.
67. Theodor Adorno and Max Horkheimer, *The Dialectic of Enlightenment* [1944], trans. John Cumming, New York: Continuum, 1972.
68. Arnheim, *Radio*, p. 248.
69. Arnheim, "A Forecast of Television," in *Film as Art*, p. 193. Arnheim underscored this point in *Radio* when he stressed "finally wireless and television enable any number of people to hear and see simultaneously what is happening everywhere in the world" and "With television the documentary potential of wireless will increase enormously." *Radio*, pp. 230, 278. For a detailed discussion of this argument, see Doron Galili's essay in this volume (Chapter 11).

70. Arnheim, "Sound Film," p. 30.
71. "I would venture to predict that the film will be able to reach the heights of the other arts only when it frees itself from the bonds of photographic reproduction and becomes a pure work of man, namely as animated cartoon or painting." Arnheim, "A New Laocoön," p. 213.
72. Arnheim, "Composites of Media: History of an Idea," *Michigan Quarterly Review*, October 1999.
73. Arnheim, "Sound Film by Force," p. 41.
74. "It is obvious that sound film gets under your skin far more than silent film." Arnheim, "Sound Film," p. 30.
75. Arnheim, *Film als Kunst*, p. 204.
76. Arnheim, "Sound Film," p. 30.
77. Ibid.
78. Arnheim, "Asynchronism" [1934] in *Film Essays and Criticism*, p. 31.
79. Ibid.
80. Gertrud Koch, "Rudolf Arnheim: The Materialist of Aesthetic Illusion," *New German Critique* Vol. 51, Fall 1990, p. 171.
81. Arnheim, *Film*, p. 220.
82. Arnheim, *Film als Kunst*, p. 226.
83. Arnheim, "Sound Film Confusion," p. 35.
84. Arnheim, "Sound Film Gone Astray," p. 43.
85. Earlier on, Arnheim hypothesized "a healthy development might occur as follows: the acoustical film attains perfection as the three-dimensional film, with natural colors and true to life sound reproduction. It will become a replacement for theater . . . Independent of this, silent ('illustrated'), black-and-white, two dimensional film develops according to its own, totally unique rules as a separate art form": Arnheim, "Sound Film Confusion," p. 36.
86. Arnheim, *Film as Art*, p. 216.
87. Ibid., p. 222. Italics in original.
88. Ibid., p. 221.
89. Ibid.
90. Ibid., p. 219.
91. "As optically the round belly of the student dissolved into a hillock (cf. p.94), so the buzzing of a fly and the roaring of the propeller of an aeroplane may be made perfectly congruent by adjustment of intensity": Ibid., p. 226.
92.

> Thus, according to the principle of contrast—one of the most basic and effective aesthetic means there is—the intense turbulence of the "plot" is accentuated by its most radical opposing part, the extreme stasis of monotony; at the same time a continuous basic motif emphasizes the "unity within diversity" that is always required.

"Sounds in the Left Hand" [1933] in Arnheim, *Film Essays and Criticism*, p. 48.
93. "Piano and violin are not doing the same thing simultaneously—they would only distract one another or make the other superfluous. They mutually fulfill one another in their several functions": *Film*, p. 278.
94. Arnheim, "Composites of Media," p. 561.

a gestalt approach

to film analysis

five

m e r a j   d h i r

fundamentals of arnheim's art theory

The categorization of Rudolf Arnheim's *Film as Art* (1957) as a canonical work of "classical film theory," while pedagogically useful, has led to a kind of conceptual filtering of the author's rich and varied contributions to the study of film and the visual arts. To be sure, Arnheim's thesis, couched within a conception of how the formal properties of the new medium deviate from the simple mechanical transcription of reality, constitutes the core argument of his book. His concern with the artistic stature of film and the medium's expressive qualities ally him with what Dudley Andrew terms the "formative tradition" of film theory. So too, Arnheim's commitment to medium specificity, and exaltation of silent era cinema as paradigmatic of film art open him to charges of essentialism and historical presentism.

Yet, while labels such as "formative" (or "formalist") and "classical" film theorist serve useful didactic and historical imperatives, they have perhaps prevented film scholars from recognizing the present-day viability and application of Arnheim's ideas, as well as blinkering our understanding of the multiple insights and finer grained complexities his work affords. More importantly, too narrow a focus on Arnheim's "film theory" has had the effect of severing Arnheim's ideas on film from his larger examination of the visual arts. Thus Arnheim's work on "visual thinking," perception, style, composition, emotion, and meaning making has gone largely ignored by the majority of film scholars.

The aim of this paper is twofold: first I underline the key assumptions informing both Arnheim's writing on film in *Film as Art* and his broader project of analyzing composition and design principles in the visual arts. Second, I argue that the conceptual tools Arnheim enlists to analyze artworks as diverse as painting, dance, or sculpture can help us enrich our understanding of film form and interpretation. Though some of the implications of his general theory of cinema, such as his conviction in the purity of artistic media or his denigration of sound cinema may strike us as flawed or unconvincing, I argue that the lasting value of Arnheim's thought is more usefully recast as an open-ended methodology and approach to film analysis. As a case study to illustrate the utility of Arnheim's thought, I examine Hal Ashby's *Harold and Maude* (1971), a film that evinces a particularly systematic and dense approach to visual composition at both the global and local levels of its stylistic structure.

Three fundamental assumptions inform Arnheim's understanding of artistic media. The first is that vision is active; the mind organizes relations amongst visual stimuli. Artworks are extensions of the structuring capacities of perception and thus function as organized wholes. The second assumption holds that artistic composition constitutes an interpretation of human experience; the meaning of an artwork is coincident with its composition. Finally, for Arnheim artistic form is intrinsically expressive.

a gestalt approach

As its name suggests, "gestalt" ("shape" or "form" in German) theory explained the mind's innate capacity of imposing organization on our visual array. Principles such as "good continuation" (our propensity to "fill in the gaps" of particular patterns), figure–ground differentiation, and the mind's ability to infer three-dimensional relations from two-dimensional depth cues were path-breaking discoveries explained by the gestaltists. Central to this view was the recognition of the active, form-giving tendency of the human mind to process and organize visual stimuli. Arnheim's contribution to art theory was to recast gestalt principles into a broader methodology for understanding artistic phenomena. In an artistic drawing, we do not only see an array of lines, but an underlying skeleton of visual forces, points of attack and intensity. These directional vectors and patterns of form add up to the work's meaningful expression. For the analyst, the primary value of gestalt psychology is a heuristic one: we approach an artwork with the provisional assumption that there exists a dynamic interrelationship amongst its parts. Seeing is always seeing relations. This does not mean that every component of an artwork plays an equal value in the work's effect or that every minute detail must be exhaustively scrutinized to apprehend its meaning. Rather, which parts of an artwork achieve salience depends on the range and scope of our study, the level of magnification or granularity at which we pitch our inquiry, or the specific problem we wish to solve:

> A successful work of art, for example, has its own completeness but changes its character when it is seen in the broader context of the artist's total lifework, the historical setting in which it came about, or the cognitive and motivational traits of the person who made it. [. . .] As a practical consequence, the range of a problem singled out for investigation cannot be arbitrarily staked out but depends strictly on what is relevant for the process under scrutiny. To discover the proper range of a problem is nearly tantamount to finding its solution.[1]

A gestalt approach does not prescribe what kinds of questions can be asked about an artwork, but it does recommend that the phenomenal and formal properties of the work be given a methodological priority in any explanation. Since a gestalt view of art has its roots in the scientific method, it shares many of the epistemological assumptions of scientific inquiry. This is different from claiming that the study of art is cognate with the work of scientists, even though certain questions (the phi phenomenon, the physiology of perception, etc.) may fall under the purview of science. Like scientists, art historians advance hypotheses. With artworks as evidential data, art historians use processes of inductive and/or deductive reasoning to test hypotheses. Arnheim advocates that the analyst of art engage in "careful observation and description," even while he acknowledges that this view of art "presupposes some trust of the analyst in his own ability to view certain psychological appearances objectively and relevantly."[2] Two strategies help the analyst safeguard against subjective error. First, observational data "should be subjected to the judgment of other viewers, professional and otherwise."[3] This provision not only serves as a kind of fact-checking capacity, but also encourages scholars to submit their theories to scrutiny and counterargument. Whether intentionally or not, Arnheim echoes two Mertonian norms of scientific practice such as "organized skepticism" and "disinterestedness," at least insofar as the advancement of functional claims and denotative description are concerned.[4]

Second, Arnheim advises that formal analysis must be carried out "in the context of the work's total structure at a level of abstraction appropriate to the particular objective of the study."[5] The "total structure" may denote an individual work but can also extend beyond to such categories as an artistic corpus, "genre," or "historical period"; finding the "proper" range for the analysis is paramount. For example, an art historian studying the iconographic oddities found in the paintings of Hieronymus Bosch might form exaggerated or false conjectures if she were to ignore the proximate tradition of manuscript illumination in which bizarre and grotesque marginal imagery was prevalent. Similarly, for a film historian to substantiate adequately the claim that Godard's employment of long-tracking shots is distinctive, she must not only explain how such tracking shots function within the "total structure" of Godard's films, but also how Godard's usage of the device deviates from the filmmaking tradition in which he worked.

art and composition

Arnheim explains how two underlying spatial systems, "centricity" and "eccentricity," form the "master key" to all artistic composition, including painting, sculpture, architecture and even film. Arnheim defines art as:

> The ability of perceptual objects or action, either natural or man-made, to represent, through their appearance, constellations of forces that reflect relevant aspects of the dynamics of human experience. More specifically, a "work of art" is a human artifact intended to represent such dynamic aspects by means of ordered, balanced concentrated form.[6]

This definition commits Arnheim to several views about art: artworks are intentional, man-made objects that in some way "reflect relevant aspects of the dynamics of human experience." That Arnheim ties the representational function of artworks to their "appearance" suggests that artworks declare themselves primarily through their phenomenal or formal properties. According to this view art must reflect some aspect of human experience, even if only abstractly, thus Arnheim's unfashionable tendency to anthropomorphize visual relations found in non-figurative artworks. A further criterion is that artworks display a sense of "ordered, balanced, concentrated form." For Arnheim, terms such as "order" and "balance" do not mean something like symmetry or a completely regularized arrangement. Asymmetrical formal relations may also display balance and order as long as the "forces" within the work ultimately compensate for one another. Arnheim admits that the terms "balance" and "order" introduce a set of associations to the formal description of art, such as strivings for social balance or psychological equilibrium, and may also signal a bias towards historically contingent styles.[7] He specifies that by "balance" we are to understand that all the parts demonstrate a compositional necessity. If the artwork is unbalanced or displays an "amorphous" form, it is thus incomprehensible—it is not art.

In Arnheim's usage, balance and order mean something more akin to "coherence," or "unity," in the sense that the work's formal properties serve an identifiable purpose and function in concert to express a specifiable theme or meaning. This explains Arnheim's aversion to thematic and formal ambiguity and his distaste for certain types of European art cinema (Antonioni, for example) and avant-garde styles that utilize dissonance or other formal strategies to thwart the interpretative activity of the viewer. He does not imply that the meaning of an artwork must be readily transparent or easily understood. Rather, Arnheim places a high currency on the different types of cognitive difficulty an artwork may elicit, and good works of art require the viewer to actively marshal their hermeneutic resources in order to comprehend the work's sophisticated and subtle shades of meaning. These meanings are only accessible through understanding the compositional dynamics at play in a work of art.

For Arnheim, composition and visual form designate the totality of the artwork, and he acknowledges no distinction between a work's formal composition and its content, subject matter or theme: meaning and form are coincident. In "Form and the Consumer" (1959), Arnheim explicitly criticizes the reified formalism practiced by members of the Bloomsbury group such as Roger Fry and Clive Bell who give analytical priority to the shape and design of an artwork, ignoring its representational content. Re-examining the same painting by Poussin in which Fry had singled out only the dynamics of volumes and shapes, Arnheim guides the reader through a set of questions:

> We would ask what the arrangement of the figures and the pattern of their gestures bring to the interpretation of the story, and we would try to discover meaning in the distribution of space and light. Perhaps we would find that all aspects of the picture, large and small, combine in presenting the story as a pattern of visual forces, which draws from the legendary episode the deeper theme of revealed masculinity, of power in the guise of grace. And, faced with a complete coincidence of eloquent shape and profound meaning, we might feel willing to say that we are in the presence of art.[8]

The provisional nature of this passage emphasizes the open-ended process of analysis and interpretation engaged in by the attuned viewer. Arnheim stresses the holistic interrelatedness of artistic composition by stating that every aspect of the work participates in unison to facilitate a deeper apprehension of the painting's theme. In Arnheim's view an *artistic* composition acts as a catalyst for soliciting interpretation; the artist interprets a theme and in turn invites the viewer to measure how that interpretation measures up to experience.[9]

The subject of expression constitutes a fundamental component of Arnheim's art theory. As he explains, the expressive property of an artwork constitutes an intensified or concentrated form of the expressive properties inherent in all perceptual phenomena. Arnheim argues that the affective, expressive dimension of perceptual phenomena is anterior to abstract considerations of geometric shape, size, or weight:

> when I sit in front of a fireplace and watch the flames, I do not normally register certain shades of red, various degrees of brightness, geometrically defined shapes moving at such and such a speed. I see the graceful play of aggressive tongues, flexible striving, lively color. The face of a person is more readily perceived and remembered as being alert, tense, concentrated rather than being triangularly shaped, having slanted eyebrows, straight lips, and so on.[10]

In "The Gestalt Theory of Expression" (1949), Arnheim advances the hypothesis that the expressive properties of percepts inhere in their "structural kinship" to certain corresponding mental states.[11] His aim is to determine the connection between perceptual stimuli and the type of mental processes involved in the experience of expression. He begins by outlining the traditional approaches to explaining the problem of expression. To say that something is "expressive" is to indicate that it outwardly manifests an emotive property. Our usual understanding is that emotive properties are the products of particular mental states, as when we detect sadness in another at the sight of certain perceptual features such as their frown, slumped shoulders and teary eyes. Traditional "associationist" and "empathy" theories of expression rely on mechanisms of experience, social enculturation and stereotype to explain how we ascribe expressive properties to perceptual phenomena. According to these views the existential relationship between expression properties and the structure of a work of art is unmotivated.

Arnheim supplants the traditional view by introducing the principle of *isomorphism*, contending that expression operates through "psychophysical parallelism" and an inner structural kinship between observed perception and mental state.[12] As with his numerous discussions of artistic composition, Arnheim emphasizes that all percepts are dynamic, relational and possess directed tensions. When we observe or experience a perceptual configuration, such as the look on a person's face, listen to piece of music, or view a natural landscape, we do not register these phenomena as made up of individual, static components, but experience them holistically, as a structural totality, a gestalt. Arnheim also indicates that we are able to register basic emotion states in others fairly rapidly and automatically, without the need for introspection or inference.

According to the gestalt view, perceptual configurations are carriers of expressive properties. When we say that the weeping willow tree looks sad, we are not applying an arbitrary or socially conditioned metaphor. The tree actually looks sad to us, because its perceptual configuration resembles the perceptible features of sad people. It is this structural kinship that leads to the secondary process of applying metaphors appropriate to our experience of mental states. Artworks of all kinds enlist and modulate the expressive properties of everyday percepts to produce particular effects. Arnheim notes, for example, how the gestalt theory of expression underscores the connection between artistic and "practical" behavior: "The dancer, for instance, does not have to endow movements with a symbolic meaning for artistic purposes, but uses, in an artistically organized way, the unity of psychical reaction that is characteristic for human functioning in general."[13] While Arnheim's theory of expression is pitched as a broad hypothesis, much recent experimental research supports his claims.[14]

An analysis of Claude Monet's painting, *Bazille and Camille* (1865, a completed study for the artist's larger *Déjeuner sur l'herbe*), demonstrates a gestalt approach.[15] In Monet's painting, the length of the rectangular frame stresses the vertical orientation and he stages his two figures, almost precisely, on either side of the format's geometric center, creating a bipolar composition. As we scan the image, we may puzzle at the nature of the relationship between the man and women: what is depicted? And how does composition guide our attention to the scene's salient features and shape its expressive qualities? It may strike us as unusual that Monet would have chosen to position the two figures obliquely to the picture plane. The woman's face is lost in profile, and her body is turned away from our view. Monet thwarts our ability to see her facial expression or identify her features. Arnheim's comments about an artist's choice of view are especially illuminating in light of Monet's *mise en scène*:

> the draftsman may deliberately choose a view that misleads and hides rather than informs. Early stages of pictorial representation avoid any such concealment. They aim for the clearest and most direct sight, and so do all illustrations aimed at straight instruction. At levels of higher sophistication, back views, tilted heads, and the like are admitted for the enrichment they bring to the spatial conception.[16]

The picture provides minimal information about the relationship between the two figures. To understand the meaning of the picture, we must attend to its perceptual organization. What is revealed in perception is not simply the constituents of form (shape, line, color, etc.) but the expressive dynamics they carry. Directed forces of energy, or vectors, may be explicitly marked through line or shape, or "induced" by such cues as the glance of a human face, or gesture. Artists enlist the directing power of vectors to draw the viewer's attention from and towards points of compositional interest. Arnheim points out that "compositional weight" is also affected by "intrinsic interest" and in any representational work, the human form, especially the face and hands constitute such privileged "expressive nodes."[17] Representational artists may capitalize on such natural human propensities or thwart them in favor of particular effects. In Monet's picture, the female figure is not simply turned away from the viewer, but her partner as well. We can witness the expressive power of vectors in the way Monet cannily directs the eye to the central "event" of the picture. He places a daub of bright paint close to the geometric center of the composition, drawing our attention to the place where the two bodies meet. The woman's left elbow and torso overlap and occlude the man's left hand and forearm. With his slightly off-center, leaning posture, directed gaze, and the diagonal vector of his stick, he seems to be reaching out to her, both literally and psychologically, and whether his gesture is tender or subtly aggressive we cannot discern.

By denying access to the woman's face, the viewer must search for the more subtly expressive cues found in her posture, such as the downward crook of her head and the contraction of her upper arms "inwards" towards her torso, in order to apprehend her mental state. By using form carefully to orchestrate our attention towards the female figure, only to suppress any clearly expressive facial characteristics, Monet uses concealment as an expressive device. This is especially true in relation to contemporary expectations that such genre scenes required clearly legible relationships and narrative contexts, supporting art historian John House's claim that in their overall effect, the artist's figure compositions of this period evince a "rejection of stereotyped images of courtship and parenthood, in favor of more open-ended, ambiguous images of human relationships."[18]

film art and "expressive implication"

Having sketched the fundamental assumptions informing Arnheim's gestalt approach to art, we are now in a better position to understand how they shape his thinking about film. Two fundamental principles guide Arnheim's film theory: 1) the "reality" of the filmic image is always "partial"; and 2) film artistry consists in the "transposition," of making non-visible phenomena visible.[19] While Arnheim refers to "transposition" only with reference to visualizing sound effects and dialogue in the context of silent film practice, I would argue that the formal processes suggested by "transposition" guide Arnheim's comments about film technique more broadly.[20] The two principles bear a causal relation: it is because the film medium limits the presentation of reality to a partial illusion that the filmmaker must use techniques of transposition to expressively complete that illusion.

The principle of "partial illusion" is a direct offshoot of the gestalt model of perception. In everyday experience, visual perception arises from the interaction of the mind's active, organizing capacities, and the stimuli found in the sensory environment. Recall the gestalt principle of "good continuation," which allows us to see a line when given only a minimal number of graphic elements grouped together, or a square, even though the corners are missing. "Good continuation" suggests that given particular stimuli, perception "fills in" the gaps. Like other artists, filmmakers use this natural human propensity in the service of creative effects. In figurative painting, interposition of planes, perspective, and variations in size allow us to perceive depth where no depth exists. In Arnheim's gestalt approach to art, something like "good continuation" is also intended to characterize the activity of the spectator's relationship to the artwork, beyond the literal sense it is used in gestalt perceptual psychology. When Monet portrays the female figure in *Bazille and Camille* from behind, he creates a kind of gap in our knowledge, encouraging us to exert our perceptual and cognitive resources, to scan the rest of the image relationally, so as to "fill in" what is not shown and apprehend the meaning of the work.

In film, the condition of "partial illusion" encourages the filmmaker to develop an array of expressive devices to complete the illusion. In a sense, Arnheim organizes his theory of film through a homology between the mind's structuring capacities in relation to reality—processes that occur largely automatically—to the relation that exists between the spectator and the artistic use of film form. Through the concept of "partial illusion" Arnheim develops an especially sophisticated understanding of the various levels of motivation operative in cinematic construction:

> within any particular scene value is laid on naturalism. The characters must talk as people do in real life, a servant like a servant, a duke like a duke. (But even here we have this restriction: the servant and the duke are to talk clearly and sufficiently loudly, that is really, too clearly and loudly.)[21]

In addition to producing arresting imagery, narrative filmmakers adhere to certain conventions of verisimilitude and naturalism, while simultaneously using the medium to direct the audience's attention to salient story information.[22] These varying motivations are densely interwoven into the stylistic texture of the film and serve as a criterion of value: "In a good film every shot must be contributory to the action."[23] Arnheim derides Dreyer's narratively unmotivated camera angles in *The Passion of Joan of Arc* (1928), allying it with an empty formalist tradition: "Form for form's sake—this is the rock on which many film artists, especially the French, are shipwrecked."[24] Of a seemingly arbitrary shift in camera position in G. W. Pabst's *The Diary of a Lost Girl* (1929) he comments: "It signifies nothing. And things which have no significance have no place in a work of art. The reason for the sequence is wholly superficial and decorative. [. . .] Here the device is insufficiently motivated and therefore artistically weak."[25] Arnheim conceives the optimal use of style as unobtrusive and subservient to the demands of plot. And while he encourages filmmakers to heighten the expressive appeal of their images, his comments forestall the artistic possibilities of modernist, serial, or what film scholar David Bordwell has termed "parametric" modes of narration.[26] Again, we might explain Arnheim's dismissal of such modes by the gestalt insistence that percepts always function relationally. Those elements of an artwork that call attention to themselves for purely decorative purposes threaten to sever the dense interrelationship of form.

Arnheim seems to have tacitly formulated something like an aesthetics of "expressive implication," which functions as a through-line, connecting his writing on static media such as painting, sculpture, and photography, and his writing on film. It is telling that most of Arnheim's examples of film artistry reveal a tendency to favor more indirect, subtle and oblique modes of visual narration. To explain "transposition," Arnheim praises the way a film uses a flock of rising birds to relay indirectly the "sound" of a shooting gun: "the spectator does not simply *infer* that a shot has been fired, but he actually *sees* something of the quality of the noise."[27] He goes on to suggest, with an example from Dante's poetry, that "indirect representation" is "a favorite method in all art."[28] In sound film, Arnheim argues, directors are encouraged towards a less "artistic," more direct presentation of events and character psychology: "*The dialogue paralyzes visual action.*"[29] To tell a dramatic story filmmakers must obviously develop methods to compensate for the lack of sound; but Arnheim's preference for indirection extends to principles of shot design and cinematography, in which the absence of sound is not a determining factor.

In *Film as Art*, Arnheim's filmic citations repeatedly underscore the value of oblique staging methods and visual opacity in favor of maximally informative views. He cites the way Chaplin's *The Immigrant* (1917) produces the cinematic equivalent of a gestalt switch through visual suppression and revelation:

> Then comes the first shot of Charlie Chaplin: he is seen hanging over the side [of the boat] with his back to the audience, his head well down, his legs kicking wildly—everyone thinks the poor devil is paying his toll to the sea. Suddenly Charlie pulls himself up, turns round and shows that he has hooked a large fish with his walking stick.[30]

Arnheim relays that in order to produce this comedic effect, Chaplin's framing works "contrary to the principle of 'the most characteristic view.'"

While film scholars often single out Bazin for his analysis of the long-take, deep-staged image, Arnheim is no less illuminating about the poetics of cinematic staging. In *Film as Art*, though he carefully enumerates various editing strategies and methods of joining shots based on conceptual, associative, and poetic relations, he is critical of Pudovkin's view that editing constitutes the essence of film art. Over and again, Arnheim demonstrates how the act of carefully composing and staging action for the bounded film screen is sufficient in itself to fundamentally differentiate cinema from the stage, allaying any fears that the medium offers only a debased form of "canned theater."[31] Arnheim's perspicuous observations about staging and composition, unfettered by Bazin's murky ontology of cinematic realism, are enhanced by his sophisticated attunement to form, character psychology, and narration. He notes how the narrative context of a strong foreground–background opposition in a shot from Pudovkin's *The End of St. Petersburg* (1927) encourages a symbolic association. Discussing variations for filming two actors in conversation, Arnheim notes the expressive effect of withholding the alternating phase of the conventional shot–reverse–shot schema in Clarence Brown's *A Woman of Affairs* (1928): "The father is seen in dark silhouette in the foreground with his back to the camera, very large, very near. [. . .] Hence the father's face is not visible. But what he is saying can be conjectured from his attitude and gestures and, above all, from the play of expression on the son's face."[32] He praises the "expressive" occlusion of a character's face by the darkly silhouetted head of another in Jacques Feyder's *Le nouveaux messieurs* (1929), remarking that "The bisection is most expressive. One seems to see more by seeing less."[33] And of German actor, Emil Jannings, Arnheim writes that a view of his "back is as expressive as his face."[34]

In his consideration of film acting, Arnheim favors bodily communication over the resources offered by spoken dialogue:

> For if a man is heard speaking, his gestures and facial expression only appear as an accompaniment to underline the sense of what is said. But if one does not hear what is said, the meaning becomes *indirectly* clear and is artistically interpreted by the muscles of the face, of the limbs, of the body. The emotional quality of the conversation is made obvious with a clarity and definiteness which are hardly possible in the medium of actual speech.
>
> (italics mine)[35]

Arnheim argues that facial and bodily performance can be *more* effective than actual speech in relaying psychological and behavioral characteristics. Arnheim's deep background in psychology and studies of visual perception attuned him to the expressive potentials of the human body. In "The Face and the Mind Behind it" (1993) he relates: "An interest in the eloquent expression of the human body has accompanied and almost haunted me since my student days."[36] Our analysis of Monet's painting helped illustrate

Arnheim's contention that the human body presents a "prime quality of all perception of shape."[37] Bodily expression acts "as a vehicle of the mind. [. . .] Perception refers mainly to the forces made visible in the outer appearance of the body."[38]

Arnheim argues that the prime content of the film medium is not storytelling per se, but "mental processes" rendered through the expression of the actors' bodies.[39] One implication of Arnheim's emphasis on the cinema's ability to foreground naturalistic human behavior is that it highlights the medium as a way of understanding social cognition. At the same time, Arnheim's film aesthetics is shaped by his conviction that film is primarily a *pictorial* art and informs his commitment to the plasticity of the film image, and the use of stylistic techniques that "serve in some way to mold the object."[40] In *Film as Art*, his discussion of the historical development of film form precisely echoes his comments about "characteristic views" and the historical emergence of pictorial art in *Art and Visual Perception* cited above. He writes that in the early days of cinema: "Whatever was to be shown was taken from the angle which most clearly presented it and its movement. The task of the camera was in fact considered to be merely that of catching and registering life," and only gradually did filmmakers begin to frame and stage pro-filmic material with an eye towards producing expressively nuanced effects.[41]

composition in motion

How does Arnheim's theory of composition in static media translate to film? Arnheim notes that in film composition does not function as "a succession of statically composed highpoints connected by transitions."[42] Rather film composition operates as "a flow of transformations, during which its center moves from place to place."[43] Also, for composition to function as an artistic device, it must serve as a vehicle for the expressive interpretation of experience. Hence, not all uses of film form will satisfy Arnheim's conditions for film artistry. For example, a film that uses dialogue for straightforward exposition, or shot compositions that are clear and informative, albeit expressively dull, lack artistry because they convey plot and character information too directly, without using visual composition to communicate implicit, thematic, and expressive meanings.

An analysis of shot design in *Harold and Maude*, directed by Hal Ashby, helps illustrate how Arnheim's approach to analyzing pictorial composition deepens our understanding of the film's formal system and its effects. The film presents the story of an improbable romantic relationship that develops between Harold, a repressed twenty-year-old man, and Maude, an eccentric concentration camp survivor. On a thematic level, the film schematizes the opposition between two incompatible forces, each vying to shape Harold's identity. On the one hand are the rigid, conservative values of his mother who attempts to mold him along the lines of a prescribed identity broadly dictated by his social class and the rigid authoritarian values that subtend it. Alternatively, Maude exerts a kind of rebellious influence and awakens Harold's aesthetic appetites. She introduces him to various tactile and sensual pleasures, including music, exotic foods, and sex. As the displaced survivor of a concentration camp, Maude is herself the victim of fascist, authoritarian forces, and she alludes to a youth engaged in political activism, fighting for "liberty, rights, justice," which she now continues, in her "own small, individual way." In her attitude and actions, Maude is thus broadly representative of the non-conformist spirit and a commitment to anti-establishmentarianism. While the film's plot refers to a clash between these two ideological poles, the visual composition dramatizes this conflict pictorially. Recall the three fundamental precepts of Arnheim's gestalt approach to art: 1) perceptual configurations can only be apprehended and understood through their interrelatedness within a total structure, 2) the composition of a work is coincident with its meaning, and 3) form is intrinsically expressive. In the context of film we can understand "total structure" as operating on several levels, from the basic unit of the shot, to the organization of scenes, and finally, to the global structure of the overall film. The value of our analysis hinges on whether Arnheim's gestalt approach can help us better understand the construction and effects of Ashby's film.

The film uses three interdependent techniques to heighten expressively the graphic properties of individual shots. First, long-scale shots subordinate the human figure to the total composition. As a result, the longer shot-scales also function to foreground the film's densely textured *mise en scène*. Finally, by progressively drawing the viewer's attention to overall features of shot design, the careful patterning of similarly composed images rhyme and echo across the film, encouraging the viewer to form both visual and semantic parallels.

At the level of the individual shot, the film displays a strikingly fluid approach to moving the human figure, especially its protagonist, around the frame. At times, Harold is wedged into a particular segment of the shot submitting him to the larger architectonics of the *mise en scène*. In a medium-long shot-scale at his uncle's office, Harold is slotted neatly into the geometricized space articulated by the intersecting vectors of the furniture and blinds. The oblique angle of the foreground table juts out threateningly, producing a vector that pins Harold to his seat. Angular, centric vectors create a closed system, and together with his rigid posture, accentuate the pictorial sense of containment and oppression. This contrasts with the open compositional system of the next shot in which Harold practices his banjo. After Maude presents him with the musical instrument, we see him decentered into the lower left foreground, in a relatively long-scale framing. The shallow, vine-covered background creates an expansive pattern of arabesques, reminiscent of the flat, all-over compositions produced by Matisse, in which the human figure is integrated within a larger decorative arrangement. The comparison demonstrates how Arnheim's principles help us to analyze the expressive effects of individual shots, as well as how they may work relationally, intensifying their effects across the total structure of a film.

For Arnheim, artistic composition is always the result of form "structured in such a way that the configuration of forces reflects the meaning of the artistic statement."[44] Let us examine how Ashby uses long shot-scales, coupled with the decoratively flattening effects of the telephoto lens, to render a potent visual association across two discrete scenes. An extreme long-scale establishing shot presents the film's titular characters as tiny specks, barely locatable in the upper left register amongst a field of daisies. As the scene progresses through closer views, Maude remarks on the uniqueness of an individual daisy when observed distinctly. Articulating a metaphor about the human condition, she says, "I feel that much of the world's sorrows comes from people who are *this*, yet allow themselves to be treated as *that*," as she gestures towards the larger expanse of daisies seen as a group. The following shot displays the two in the upper right corner of a veteran's cemetery. The isotropic arrangement of deindividuated, uniformly shaped headstones recalls the previous long-scale framing of the daisies, extending Maude's metaphor to include the dehumanizing effects of war. The example illustrates Arnheim's principle that an artistic use of form is intrinsically expressive. Here, Ashby translates visually an abstract idea, something like "mass conformity," "anomie," or "alienation," by capturing the expressive attributes of the subject: uniformity, dedifferentiation, anonymity, and the absence of any stable center or hierarchical gradient.

When applied to film, Arnheim's theory of compositional vectors helps explain how the viewer's attention is guided across the duration of a shot. For example, in film vectors may shift and change producing new or competing centers of attention over the span of an individual shot. Take the film's use of deep staging to produce humorous foreground–background juxtaposition and vary hierarchies of knowledge in the scene where Harold's mother interviews one of his prospective dates. The two figures are separated by the grid-like structure of a large window that looks out onto the exterior garden. As they engage in light banter, we see Harold walk into the background and climb onto a bench; he appears perfectly framed by a section of the windowpane. The rectangular aperture functions as an internal framing device, guiding our view. The angle of the young woman's head induces a diagonal vector that connects through the top of a silver teapot (itself conspicuously occupying the geometric center of the frame), out through to Harold who is staged in deep space. The shot contains dual centers of attention that change and shift through time. When Harold enters the background, our attention turns to him, but we also continue to observe the back of the girl's head and posture to see if her movements betray any sense that she has caught sight of what is happening.

Arnheim's emphasis that gestalt forms are perceived relationally characterizes the viewer's experience of rhyming and contrasting compositions across the film. Throughout, protracted shots of Harold with his mother, and at home, are composed according to an emphatically bilateral symmetry. In contrast, the spaces associated with Maude, including exteriors, are treated as an aggregation of dissonant, eccentric forms. Long-scale shots of Maude's interiors are congested with diaphanous screens, ornamental latticework, and are populated with all sorts of junk and *objets d'art* layered with the textural density of a Dadaist collage. While the enveloping décor of Harold's home and the institutions which are in some sense an extension of its values are aggressively symmetrical, the entangled, clashing vectors of Maude's spaces derange and overburden our sense of vision, perceptually resisting the mind's ordering capacities. The pictorial disorganization of Maude's environment in relation to the highly ordered, symmetrical compositions of Harold's home strengthens the sense that her influence threatens to derail the repressive forces that attempt to mold and constrain him. Arnheim describes the viewer's experience of composition through time as a process of constant "anticipation," and a "gradual accretion" of compositional forces.[45] In *Harold and Maude*, the film's distribution of rhyming and contrasting compositions across the film invite the viewer, through precisely such a process of "gradual accretion," to take note of large-scale pictorial relations. Arnheim's analysis of composition emphasizes that we cannot be satisfied to rest at only a descriptive level of stylistic analysis. Rather, forms themselves are intrinsically expressive extending even to symbolic forces within the social field.[46] The interaction of symmetry and asymmetry, equilibrium and entropy, enacts a counterpoint between two semantically antithetical forms. Whereas paratactic arrangements disperse pictorial elements and encourage the viewer to scan and search the image for referential and interpretive connections, symmetry subordinates pictorial units to a predetermined and rigid hierarchy. Arnheim's provision that pictorial form can only be adequately understood relationally provides an important check against the interpretive abuses of "top-down" theorizing or the attribution of implicit or symbolic meanings to selective aspects of form, without first accounting for how form functions within the overall structure of the artwork.[47] In *Harold and Maude*, the use of alternating compositions serves to strengthen and visually "interpret" the film's implicit themes across the film. A gestalt approach to understanding pictorial composition in film both provides us with an array of tools for explaining and analyzing the compositional strategies and effects of individual shots, and also helps us explain how composition functions relationally within a film's overall formal system. Interestingly, we find confirmation of our analysis from the film's cinematographer, John Alonzo, who recounts that

103

Ashby's only instruction during preproduction had been that "all the sequences with Harold in his home should have a certain sort of sterility; sort of clear, clean, pure, no diffusion. The angles were to be more symmetrical; sort of meat and potatoes. And every time we ended up with Maude, it would have a slight craziness to it, just a little kookiness . . ."[48] Such anecdotal support of our analysis illustrates that film theory and analysis can be empirically tractable and supports Arnheim's claim that: "Good art theory must smell of the studio, although its language should differ from the household talk of painters and sculptors."[49]

This paper has been motivated by the desire to show how Arnheim's theories of pictorial composition, the relational and expressive qualities of form, and his study of different media provide a wellspring of analytical tools that have gone relatively unused by most film scholars. But I have also been motivated by another goal, informed by one of the core debates within our field and which concerns the question of meaning and interpretation. Such debates have clustered around the legitimacy of theories, rhetorical strategies and methods to interpret the meanings of films. For Arnheim, the question of meaning and form are inextricable. In his insistence that the composition of an artwork is coincident with its meaning and that form can only ever be adequately understood as it operates within an overall "comprehensive structure" that includes the work's "temporal" context or history, I believe, and hope to have demonstrated, he offers us the most coherent approach to explaining the expressive and interpretive appeals of art.

notes

1. Rudolf Arnheim, "What is Gestalt Psychology?," in *To the Rescue of Art: Twenty-Six Essays*, Berkeley: University of California Press, 1992, p. 203.
2. Arnheim, "But is it Science?," in *To the Rescue of Art*, p. 181.
3. Ibid., p. 181.
4. For Merton's norms see Peter Godfrey-Smith, *Theory and Reality*, Chicago, IL: University of Chicago Press, 2003, pp. 122–125. See also Paisley Livingston, *Literary Knowledge: Humanistic Inquiry and the Philosophy of Science*, Ithaca, NY: Cornell University Press, 1988.
5. Arnheim, "But is it Science?," p. 185.
6. Arnheim, *The Power of the Center: A Study of Composition in the Visual Arts*, Berkeley, CA: University of California Press, 1988, p. 225.
7. Arnheim, *Art and Visual Perception: A Psychology of the Creative Eye*, The New Version, Berkeley: University of California Press, 1974, p. 19.
8. Arnheim, "Form and the Consumer" (1959), in *Toward a Psychology of Art: Collected Essays*, Berkeley: University of California Press, 1972, p. 15.
9. Arnheim seems to use the term "interpretation" in several senses. At the most basic level an artist's "interpretation" can mean the expressive qualities the artist uses to render their motif. A painter "interprets" a woman's hair by using a particularly fiery shade of red or gestural brushstroke to produce a particular effect, thereby strengthening or "interpreting" reality. But it is

clear Arnheim also uses the term to denote the activity of ascribing implicit, symbolic, and symptomatic meanings to compositional form, as he does in many of his own interpretations of individual artworks. For example, see Arnheim, "Seven Exercises in Art Appreciation," in *To the Rescue of Art*, pp. 61–73. Within the gestalt approach Arnheim prescribes, two important conditions guide the ascription of interpretive meanings. First, interpretation arises out of a thorough consideration of the overall formal properties and relations operating in the work; in the language of cognitive psychology, interpretation arises from "bottom-up" processes. Second, a work of art always appears within particular contexts, including a "temporal context," and such factors as the viewer's past knowledge or knowledge of history condition the types of interpretation viewers ascribe to works. For the importance of "temporal context" see Arnheim, "The Gestalt Theory of Expression" (1949), in *Toward a Psychology of Art*, p. 65. For a consideration of "top-down" and "bottom-up" processes with respect to film interpretation see David Bordwell, *Making Meaning: Inference and Rhetoric in the Interpretation of Cinema*, Cambridge, MA: Harvard University Press, 1991.

10. Arnheim, *Art and Visual Perception*, pp. 454–455.

11. Arnheim, "The Gestalt Theory of Expression," pp. 51–73.

12. Arnheim, *Art and Visual Perception*, p. 58.

13. Ibid., p. 70.

14. Margaret S. Livingstone, *Vision and Art: The Biology of Seeing*, New York, NY: Henry N. Abrams, 2002.

15. For an online reproduction see the National Gallery collection at http://www.nga.gov/fcgi-bin/timage_f?object=52185&image=12029&c=gg86 (accessed 24 May, 2009).

16. Arnheim, *Art and Visual Perception*, p. 109.

17. For "compositional weight" and "intrinsic interest" see Arnheim, *Art and Visual Perception*, pp. 24–25.

18. John House, *Monet: Nature into Art*, New Haven, CT: Yale University Press, 1986, p. 34.

19. Arnheim, *Film as Art*, Berkeley: University of California Press, 1957, p. 24.

20. Ibid., p. 109.

21. Ibid., p. 24.

22. Arnheim's argument that artistic form relies on different types of motivations and the parts of an artwork are relationally interdependent loosely parallels Kristin Thompson's "neoformalist" approach to film analysis. See Kristin Thompson, *Breaking the Glass Armor*, Princeton, NJ: Princeton University Press, 1988.

23. Arnheim, *Film as Art*, p. 40.

24. Ibid., p. 41.

25. Ibid., p. 50.

26. See David Bordwell, *Narration in the Fiction Film*, Madison, WI: University of Wisconsin Press, 1985, pp. 274–310.

27. Arnheim, *Film as Art*, p. 107.

28. Ibid., p. 107.

29. Ibid., p. 228. Italics in original.

30. Ibid., p. 36.

31. Ibid., p. 17.

32. Ibid., p. 55.

33. Ibid., p. 56.

34. Ibid., p. 57.

35. Ibid., p. 58.
36. Arnheim, "The Face and the Mind Behind It" (1993), in *The Split and the Structure: Twenty-Eight Essays*, Berkeley: University of California Press, 1996, p. 139.
37. Ibid., p. 139.
38. Ibid., p. 140, p. 141.
39. Ibid., p. 134.
40. Ibid., p. 57.
41. Ibid., pp. 41–42.
42. Arnheim, *The Power of the Center*, pp. 213.
43. Ibid., p. 214.
44. Ibid., p. 226.
45. Ibid., p. 213.
46. Ibid., p. ix.
47. For a criticism of top-down theorizing see David Bordwell, "Contemporary Film Studies and the Vicissitudes of Grand Theory," in *Post-Theory: Reconstructing Film Studies*, edited by David Bordwell and Noël Carroll, Madison: University of Wisconsin Press, 1996, pp. 3–36.
48. From Dennis Schaefer and Larry Salvato, *Masters of Light: Conversations with Contemporary Cinematographers*, Berkeley: University of California Press, 1984, p. 25.
49. Arnheim, *Art and Visual Perception*, p. 4.

deft trajectories

for the eye

bringing arnheim to vincente

minnelli's color design

scott higgins

Within the field of film studies, Rudolf Arnheim has a reputation as a narrow and stalwart adherent to black-and-white aesthetics, a "chromophobe" to use David Batchelor's influential term.[1] In *Film as Art*, Arnheim's theory famously consigned color and sound to the realm of "wax museum ideals" and intractably referred to film art as an experiment that took place in the first three decades of the twentieth century.[2]

Arnheim revisited the question of color cinema in a brief essay in 1935, after the premiere of the first three-color Technicolor feature, and he was cautiously optimistic about the theoretical possibilities of color film, though for him cinema as practiced remained artless. And yet, from the 1950s through the late 1990s Arnheim returned to the problem of color in art, seeking to explain and describe its power with remarkable exactitude. Taken as a whole, this work offers a unique conception of color's compositional power, and a compelling analytical model. I argue that Arnheim's model is particularly suited to colorist filmmakers like Vincente Minnelli, who challenge design norms and exercise perception by playing on color's compositional power. Arnheim's way of thinking provides valuable tools for grasping and explaining Minnelli's elegant chromatic control.

Writing on the heels of the first three-color Technicolor feature and its attendant publicity in 1935, Arnheim returned to the question of color cinema. In "Remarks on Color Film," he nuances his rejection of color in *Film as Art* by delineating the specific ways that it might structure composition. Color, for Arnheim, is first and foremost a tool for guiding the eye within the frame, or rather, organizing the frame as a whole as it meets the eye, and in this short essay on film we find him working through ideas that he would develop in *Art and Visual Perception*. Remarkably, the champion of black-and-white suggests that color may have greater flexibility and subtlety in organizing the image. In monochrome, light and dark contrast can serve to direct attention, but in color differences of hue and saturation contribute another range of visual distinctions:

> the clear standing out of an object—a principle factor in optic dramaturgy—thereby loses much of its violence: the severity of the contrast is removed when it can be divided into more than two fundamental types and, as it were, stretch out into several dimensions.[3]

Instead of light against dark, film artists could now manipulate hue against hue at various levels of brightness. Moreover, the interaction of hues adds an unprecedented layer of complexity. Contrasts among primaries, for Arnheim, are rather stable, but adding mixed colors creates new tensions that have no analogue in black and white: "such a relation can now contain both equality and contrast at the same time, e.g., orange (red plus yellow) and violet (red plus blue)."[4] This is one of Arnheim's earliest articulations of his theory of tertiary colors, the idea that mixtures of primaries could act as compositional switches, both attracting and repelling one another. An orange, for instance, can throw its weight toward a red or yellow area of the image, binding or separating from other figures.[5]

However, at the end of the essay Arnheim shifts to an unfavorable comparison between color film and painting. Where great artists might exercise confident control of myriad color contrasts, filmmakers lack the necessary discipline; as he puts it, "the art of directing the mechanical process has not yet been discovered."[6]

Arnheim traces the flaw in color filmmaking to a confusion of practical and aesthetic vision, and in this he directly confronts Hollywood practice. Natalie Kalmus, the head of Technicolor's color advisory service, had appealed to nature as a guide for successful color design in her famous essay "Color Consciousness," also published in 1935 (and cited by Arnheim in his essay). It was Kalmus's charge to ensure that all Technicolor productions met particular design specifications revolving around taste, harmony, and dramatic appropriateness. Her department would help set the colors for each film from the script forward, and work to enforce the Technicolor look. Kalmus contends, "if color schemes of natural objects were used as guides, less flagrant mistakes in color would appear . . . natural colors and lights do not tax the eye nearly as much as man-made colors and artificial lights."[7] For Arnheim, however, our view of the natural world is distinct from the vision we bring to an artwork. Natural palettes appear agreeable, in part, because viewers direct their attention to the single objects, rather than unified wholes, as they navigate the world. Thus when confronting nature "we see neither harmony nor discord."[8] The "aesthetic way of seeing," on the other hand, grasps structure, organization, and meaning at once. Paintings can deliver "unambiguous representations" and be "taken in at a glance" because "every color has its place in a system of colors and shapes, which system forms a correct balance of intensities, because intensities and sizes of surfaces stand in a correct relationship to each other; and because there are no colorless characterless tones."[9] Appealing to natural rules for color design fails to please the aesthetically oriented eye. Arnheim suggests:

> we have become used to seeing a painting as a structure full of meaning; hence our helplessness, our intense shock on seeing the majority of color photographs. We do not find any form in them; neither can we decide to see them as nature.[10]

Inasmuch as Technicolor designers sought to emulate natural colors rather than highly structured composition, color films would fail. This, of course, returns us to his argument in *Film as Art*, which pits cinema's mimetic aims against its artistic potential. Where Arnheim originally viewed color, like sound and widescreen, as infringing on the medium's transformative properties and so narrowing the artist's ambit, in "Remarks on Color Film" he has reformulated color film as a potential artistic tool if, and only if, it is approached from an aesthetic standpoint. As we will see, Arnheim's approach is most valuable for those filmmakers who challenge Technicolor's conventions of verisimilitude with complex color patterning.

After his 1935 essay, Arnheim rarely took up the problem of color in cinema. Rather, he developed his ideas with reference to art history in his major works from the 1950s forward. The color theory that emerges from this work is rooted in two sets of assumptions. The first is a model dating back to Delacroix's color triangle of 1832 and Chevrul's *Principles of Harmony and Contrast of Colors*, first published in 1839, which isolates red, yellow, and blue as primaries, or fundamental colors, from which a painter could mix any hue. This tradition relies on the hypothesis that viewers crave chromatic completion. A balance of the three fundamentals satisfies the eye, while an absence creates tension or discord. Even as contemporary research argued for green as a fundamental color to our visual system, Arnheim defended the red–yellow–blue triad.[11] Ultimately, he appealed to authority to make his case, asserting that

It so happens that the assertion (of green as a primary) is opposed by the majority of painters who can be expected to know something about how colors look and who . . . have based their color systems on red, blue, and yellow as pure primaries.[12]

Unlike most other writers in this tradition, however, Arnheim did not direct his attention to the question of harmony, but to color's role in structuring composition and guiding the eye.

The source of Arnheim's innovation was his employment of a second set of assumptions deriving from gestalt psychology and his broader theory of art. Color was not decoration or elaboration, but tectonic. From Arnheim's gestalt perspective, the organizing mind reaches out to artwork searching for clear-cut patterns and governed by sharpening and leveling. While color could be broadly expressive, which Arnheim associates with a sensual immediacy and a passive viewer, it could also tend toward active control. For Arnheim: "a picture can be painted or understood only by actively organizing the totality of color values."[13] With red, yellow, and blue as his anchors, he traced how artists guide perception by exploiting the viewer's desire for balance. A successful composition, for Arnheim, was one in which "hue, place, and size of every color area as well as its brightness and saturation are established in such a way that all the colors together stabilize one another in a balanced whole."[14] As Arnheim noted, precompositional models of color harmony inevitably fail because colors shift in relation to one another; theorizing combinations in the abstract was a fruitless enterprise. Thus he dwelt on the relations of colors within a given composition, parsing their contribution to the whole.

From traditional art theory Arnheim inherited the blue–yellow–red triad and the completion hypothesis, and from gestalt psychology the notion that the eye contributes form by seeking patterns of these basic fundamentals. He explains this in his book *Visual Thinking*:

> Just as perceived shapes are more or less complex elaborations of simple shapes, so color patterns are seen as elaborations of the elementary pure qualities of yellow, red, blue. Here and there, these qualities are encountered in their purity, but most of the time there are mixtures which are understood perceptually as combinations of underlying primaries.[15]

Indeed, Arnheim was attracted to Delacroix's color triangle because it evinced the very rules of simplicity and order that gestalt psychology celebrated. Here was a system of logical relations with which to create ordered patterns. As he put it:

> this simple order recommends itself to the painter as a musical scale recommends itself to the musician because

there springs from it a network of kinship relations by which colors exclude or contain each other. There are also contrast and mutual attraction, clashes and bridges.[16]

The assumptions of both traditional color theory and of gestalt psychology are open to question. Whether we do, in fact, seek completion of primaries, or whether green, for instance, is perceived as a mixture of blue and yellow fundamentals or as its own unique property, are subjects of ongoing research and speculation.[17] My aim in this chapter, though, is to dwell within Arnheim's theory to uncover what I think are particularly sophisticated analytical concepts. According to this theory, color composition engages the viewer in what Arnheim called "the dynamic interplay of perceptual forces."[18] The three primaries tend to be static, presenting the eye with a climax, a place of rest, or a keynote for the composition. Mixed colors form bridges between the primaries, creating a web of connections and segregations. Secondary colors (orange, purple, and green) possess what Arnheim called a "vibrating duality"; they strain between their two parent hues. Finally, tertiary colors (uneven mixtures of primaries like reddish yellow and bluish green) are particularly dynamic as they could tip the balance toward one pure hue or another.[19] Arnheim speculates that tertiary colors that share a dominant hue (yellowish red and bluish red, for instance) will resist one another, as red is pushed in two directions. Tertiary hues made up of color mixtures in which the dominant and subordinate colors mirror one another (reddish blue and bluish red, for instance) should strongly harmonize and attract since they symmetrically balance one another. These clashes and bridges are powerful for Arnheim. They can "help detach the foreground from the background or the leaves of a tree from its trunk and branches, or keep the eye from traveling a compositionally undesirable path."[20]

The frame for Arnheim is a field of attractions and repulsions that form "the basis for all color organization."[21] Because the eye strives for contrast or assimilation of colors, colors tend to call out to one another or oppose one another across a canvas. Arnheim explains color interactions with reference to perceptual routines of sharpening and leveling: "Since perceptual patterns tend toward the most clear-cut organization available, a configuration of colors will strive either toward contrast or toward assimilation, depending on which is closer to the given stimulus information."[22] Complementary colors attract and connect distant portions of an image, while unbalanced tertiary mixtures push apart. Shape, contour and line tend to take precedence in defining space, but the pushes and pulls of color can torque a composition. As Arnheim observed, "perhaps no two shapes, not even a circle and a triangle, can ever be so completely different from each other than can be a pure red from a pure blue from a pure yellow."[23]

Arnheim's examples reveal the power of his model to countenance color's contribution to composition. Most basically, perception of similarity links areas of a composition, as when Titian used strong spots of red to tie together Actaeon and Diana when he discovers her in her bath, in Arnheim's words "setting them off against the complex accessories of landscape and attendants and connecting them across a large interval of space."[24] Color can also interact with other compositional cues, as in El Greco's *Agony in the Garden* when Christ's red garment and blue coat are completed by the yellow in the Angel's robe, uniting the two figures through primary completion, while Christ is also held back from the compositional center by the weight of the rock that surrounds him. Here, color and "the power of the center" (Arnheim's term for graphic arrangements organized around a central point) create the composition's tension and dynamism. Christ is pulled upward toward the angel and yet grounded, just off-center, by the earth, creating what Arnheim would call a cognitive statement about the nature of deity.[25]

One of Arnheim's masterpieces of color analysis is his discussion of El Greco's *The Virgin with Saint Ines and Saint Tecla*, published in *Art and Visual Perception*.[26] El Greco places Mary holding baby Jesus in the center of his frame, where she is borne aloft by angels and clouds. Below her are Saint Tecla with her lion on the left and Saint Ines with her lamb on the right. Arnheim notes that composition is strongly symmetrical, but this is complicated by a slanted axis that leads from the Virgin to Saint Tecla at the left, emphasized by the figures' glances toward one another and the woman's outgoing gesture. Color bolsters these compositional features. The Virgin is self-contained, and her cloak creates a central symmetry around the Christ child. His yellow hair completes the triad of primaries in her reddish blue and bluish red cloak, creating the composition's keystone. This yellow also relates to the hair, cloak, palm branch, and lion of Saint Tecla, while the blue of the Virgin's coat is picked up by the saint's blue sleeve. For Arnheim this creates an easy union between the Virgin and the leftmost figure, while Saint Ines, cloaked in orange on the right, clashes. Purple and orange segregate because, as he puts it, "the red, dominant in both areas, is torn into the conflicting scales of red-blue and red-yellow."[27] This color scheme discourages the eye from gliding from Saint Ines on the right up to the Virgin, and encourages an itinerary that unites the two saints and then travels from the right figure of contemplation and meditation to the left figure of inspiration and reception, upward to the Virgin.[28] Though Arnheim uses the language of linear eye movement from area to area, his gestalt assumption is that this happens instantaneously; the image is grasped as a whole. Color arrangements, webs of connection and repulsion, can make intricate perceptual demands on the viewer's eye. Arnheim presents us with a system for capturing color's role in organizing space, cuing attention, and unifying compositions.

One challenge in bringing Arnheim's model for analyzing paintings to film analysis lies in squaring his ideas about how composition can function in the two media. As noted earlier, in 1935 he cast the problem largely in terms of viewing strategies. Aesthetic observers processed compositional wholes and could contemplate the structural webs that shaped the artwork. Practical observers, however, tend to focus on particular things in the world as they navigate through it. Writing in 1982, the distinction between the media seems to have hardened for Arnheim. He emphasizes what he sees as a fundamental difference between the modes of contemplation encouraged by painting and cinema. While a painting's composition can exert structured control over perception, Arnheim views the cinemagoer as "caught up in the course of events which he perceives from the constantly changing vantage point of the present moment."[29]

To a certain extent we must admit that Arnheim is correct. Cinema trades in a kind of sensual immediacy and visceral reaction that does not square with the rapt contemplation of a frozen image. However, the gap between media and modes of viewing may be bridgeable. Classical continuity privileges attentional patterns used to follow individuals through space; that is, we tend to watch characters rather than compositions.[30] Yet, some filmmakers overtly compose their frame and drive attention around it in a way more in tune with Arnheim's aesthetic observation. Moreover, where directors do not offer an invitation to contemplate a long take, they can build patterns from shot to shot, or from camera movement to camera movement, in a manner functionally equivalent to a grand compositional scheme.[31] Some filmmakers, whom I refer to as colorists, are adept at engaging this sort of aesthetic observation within the moving image using the color properties that Arnheim describes. Notably, and especially in Vincente Minnelli's case, these techniques blend rather than conflict with more traditional attentional patterns. At its most successful, Minnelli's work rewards both practically and compositionally oriented viewing, both contemplation and sensual engagement; indeed, they seem inseparable.

Classical Hollywood filmmakers of the Technicolor era attended to color with a care and precision that Arnheim might appreciate, but in normative schemes color generally served a supporting role to other compositional cues like centering, contour, and lighting. As I have argued elsewhere, much of the beauty of Technicolor design came from the elegant integration of color into the established regime. Near-complementary contrast between a blue costume and a yellow-gold set, for instance, could center and reinforce Claude Rains' presence in *Adventures of Robin Hood* (see Figure 6.1).[32] But Arnheim's conception of the frame as a dynamic web helps us capture the work of filmmakers who consciously depart from this classical norm and grant color a higher place on the compositional hierarchy to generate perceptual challenges.

Some obvious and important examples come from the European Art Cinema of the 1960s where filmmakers deliberately rethink and challenge Hollywood norms. One technique involved emphatic accenting to channel

Figure 6.1 Near-complementary contrast between cape and background in *Adventures of Robin Hood*. Frame enlargement

attention in non-traditional directions. Color accents within a controlled frame call to one another, multiplying points of attention within the frame. In the opening of *Playtime* (1967), for instance, Jacques Tati flattens out competing cues like centrality of action or lighting contrast so that spots of red in his airport interior create a game of perceptual pinball (see Figure 6.2). We can scan from accent to accent, searching for a pattern that never emerges. Other filmmakers stressed relationships between contrasting and converging colors. For example, Arnheim's observations offer tools to open up Jacques Demy's fantastically complex *Umbrellas of Cherbourg* (1964). The opening scene offers a near-constant revelation of connections and completions as Guy, clad in dark blue overalls with a bright baby-blue shirt collar poking out, finishes his workday at the service station. When he closes the hood of a car in the foreground, Guy (Nino Castelnuovo) reveals a connecting baby-blue accent of an air compressor on the back wall, and as he walks forward a track backward introduces completing triadic colors. As the camera moves to follow Guy, reds and yellows emerge and recede to create a composition that is continually rebalancing itself. We can attend primarily to the character, but in the meantime the color scheme around him is alive and pulsing. Elsewhere, Demy uses color harmonies to segregate the composition. As tension simmers between Genevieve (Catherine Deneuve) and her mother (Anne Vernon), Demy offers a shot split down the middle (see Figure 6.3). The right half of the frame, which shows Genevieve's bedroom, employs triadic completion of pink and blue floral

Figure 6.2 Red accents include the soldier's gift, the flowers, the sign above the bar, and the no-entry symbols, against uniformly gray *mise en scène*. *Playtime*, frame enlargement

Figure 6.3 Mother and daughter are separated by color harmonies and architecture in *Umbrellas of Cherbourg*. Frame enlargement

wallpaper and dress to offset her yellow hair. The left half, dominated by an open doorway into the dining room where her mother stands in a green coat before pink and green striped wallpaper and red and green curtains, is a self-contained set of red and green complementaries. Scenic architecture of the doorway separates off the mother and daughter, but color imparts a mutual exclusion between the spaces.

Within Hollywood filmmaking we find colorists like Vincente Minnelli, who did less to break the rules than to work remarkably and innovatively within them. Minnelli develops color structures across extended sequences, rather than in isolated moments. When staging a scene of elaborate action he could array strong saturated accents across the frame and keep them in continual motion. His musical numbers present constantly evolving sets of color relationships that draw the eye through space and are not reducible to Technicolor norms of accent against neutral. Remarkably, Minnelli's mosaic designs often help reinforce the central narrative action, but they do so in a perceptually demanding way.

The 42nd Street arcade set in *The Band Wagon* where Fred Astaire and Leroy Daniels perform "A Shine on Your Shoes" offers a vivid example. The set initially disperses attention across its expanse through the multiplication of blue–yellow–red triadic accents, interspersed with secondary highlights. But as Astaire begins moving through the crowded space, key contrasts begin to harness our attention, as when Leroy Daniel's red and green Hawaiian shirt appears in the background (see Figure 6.4). Once the dance is under way Daniel's shirt is Minnelli and choreographer Michael Kidd's secret weapon, offering a chromatically complete complementary set that holds its own against the shifting field. At the same time, the passersby present an unending stream of blue, yellow, pink, green, lavender, and red accents that might briefly draw our attention. At each turn, though, our visual itinerary is rerouted to Astaire and Daniels, partly because of centering and action, but also because Astaire's contrast with his surroundings is constant (gray suit in a field of assertive color) while his socks generate strong connections with other stable blue accents (like the neon sign) and fluidly join passing

Figure 6.4 Leroy Daniel's red and green Hawaiian shirt attracts attention in the background of the 42nd Street arcade in *The Band Wagon*. Frame enlargement

reds and yellows for triadic completion (see Figure 6.5). Minnelli exercises our perceptual dispositions in a particularly captivating and rewarding contest of contrast and convergence.

But if Arnheim's approach bequeaths anything to film studies it is a set of tools with which to conduct very close, moment-by-moment analysis of detail and the way it might engage perception. Few scenes better exemplify Minnelli's command of color accenting and framing than the "Skip to My Lou" dance number in his first color film *Meet Me In St. Louis*. The scene is a highpoint of 1940s Technicolor design crafted out of seven shots that deftly integrate staging, color, and camera movement. The complexity of the dance comes not from choreographed performance, but from the interactions of composition and *mise en scène*. Minnelli likely collaborated with a dance director to stage the scene (no choreographer is credited) but we sense that his experience in composing images as department store window designer and director at Radio City Music Hall certainly served him well. The dance itself, rooted in colloquial and folk traditions, is designed as a display of community and courtship in the Smith home as three siblings lead the party in a version of a familiar song. The dance is clearly centered on Esther (Judy Garland) and her flirtation with John Truitt (Tom Drake), the boy next door, but Esther's older brother Lon (Henry H. Daniels Jr.) and sister Rose (Lucille Bremmer) weave in and out of the song.

It is worth noting how unusual Minnelli's style is in the context of the 1940s musical. The scene's color design is extraordinarily intricate. From the standpoint of Technicolor's color advisory service, Minnelli's dispersion of

Figure 6.5 Astaire's blue socks connect with the blue neon sign in *The Band Wagon*. Frame enlargement

accents courts disaster because they regarded color highlights as notoriously unruly, threatening to divert attention from the action at hand.[33] Minnelli peoples his numbers with dancers in varied costumes that generate fluid patterns of connection and divergence with the lead players. Arnheim's model is useful in exploring this artful combination of varied highlights, and it can help explain how Minnelli works with a constantly shifting field of accents to guide attention and build compelling trajectories for the aesthetic eye.

The sequence opens with a dolly shot that brings the viewer from the Smiths' moonlit front porch, through a window and into their warmly illuminated living room. This is both an establishing shot and an invitation into a perceptually rich and elaborately ordered space. The camera movement begins by following a partygoer as she passes through the dappled blue light on the porch and crosses the threshold into the living room. But after she exits the frame, the camera independently continues its forward trajectory through the window. Without a character to follow, the movement becomes more purely revelatory, leaving the viewer to contemplate the *mise en scène* rather than chase a figure through space. The shift in color temperature from exterior to interior, and the masking of the window frame emphasize color saturation, a Technicolor technique that pulses and renews color through its suppression and revelation. It also calls attention to the frame *as* a composition, recalling Arnheim's observations on the distinction between color in art and nature: the viewer briefly ceases to navigate among independent objects and is confronted with a total composition "taken in at a glance."

This composition channels our attention among colors in a classic Minnelli strategy (see Figure 6.6). The central figure is ringed by observers who help direct the viewer inward while also providing a circuit of cues around the frame. Cornet player Ida Boothby (Mary Jo Ellis) commands the center of the frame with a light lavender-blue blouse, light blue hair bow, and blue skirt with pink, blue, and magenta stripes. She is the camera's new target and composition's visual anchor, providing a sonic and graphic rationale for the journey forward (her cornet blasts dominate the sound track). As the camera passes through the window frame it progressively reveals space around Ida, rewarding the eye with a spatial context that reinforces the center while guiding our attention around and into the depth of the image. Red accents stretch from the right foreground plaid dress of a seated guest, to a magenta hair bow just left of center foreground, to a red lamp on a background table. All of these reds receive brief emphasis from their complementary contrast with the green ivy framing the window that obtrudes into the foreground as the camera travels through it. Arnheim might say that the green generates a connection with the reds across the space of the frame. So primed, these red accents provide a course around Ida Boothby from fore right (dress) to left-of-center rear (lamp).

Figure 6.6 *Meet Me in St. Louis* frame enlargement

The circle around Ida supplements the diagonal of blue accents into the depth of the shot, with our central figure as the first and foremost station. Moreover, the extreme background plane is highlighted by an extra standing midway up the staircase in a blue-green dress with a vibrant red belt. She does several things for the composition's order. The split complementarity of belt and dress give the background a graphic spike that highlights the depth of the frame. This, in turn, helps mark out the area where John Truitt, Rose, and Lon stand, just before the staircase. Since they are the only major characters in the frame, the composition gives them prominence but Minnelli avoids conferring overpowering centrality. The technique supports the theme of community in the dance, where family and romance appear to emerge out of a larger social network. Color, in this case, is a redundant cue, for Minnelli has also cleared a path through the crowd and has centered and top-lit our trio of familiar characters in the background. Color, though, is important. If the woman on the stairs presents another station-point in the ring of red accents around the central figure, or the diagonal of blue, she also helps nudge our vision forward to the narratively important characters. Finally, her blue-green and red combination has a very strong affinity to the blue-green and magenta stripes on Ida Boothby's skirt, an echo that unifies mid- and background and reinforces the composition's structure. We can find this sort of complex compositional balance of accents elsewhere in Minnelli's work, notably in *The Band Wagon*, and it is one of the director's distinctive strengths. Color forms a network in the frame that can both be "seen at a glance" and that rewards contemplation. The semantic force of

119

the image, its expression of community and family, lends it the kind of formal significance that Arnheim praised in the silent cinema he regarded in *Film as Art*.

Having led the eye through this space, Minnelli rearranges composition through staging, camera movement, and cutting. Without pause, as the camera lands on this tableau, Minnelli begins moving the figures around. Lon comes forward, takes Ida's cornet and exchanges it for a mandolin as guests rise and move to the background. Character movement changes everything. Lon, Ida, and several other guests move up to the foreground, stretching across the frame and facing the camera, as he delivers the song's refrain (see Figure 6.7). This simplified, performative composition is fleeting however, as guests move the furniture that Lon had been leaning on to clear room for the dance. The fluid dynamics of the community dance overtake the brief moment of stability focused on a select group. Lon, Ida, and their friends turn and recede into the mid-ground, helping to motivate an axial cut forward to the threshold between the living room and staircase.

A match on action brings Lon and his mandolin into the foreground, binding this frame to the last. But other compositional cues might draw attention beyond Lon's action (see Figure 6.8). The guest with the red hair bow who had occupied the foreground of the first shot has now moved to a chair on the left foreground of this shot, and the lamp that served as a station-point in the ring of red accents in the first shot now appears on the far left. Where matches-on-action tend to highlight the movements of single figures (Arnheim's event over composition) Minnelli's repetition and

120

Figure 6.7 *Meet Me in St. Louis* frame enlargement

Figure 6.8 *Meet Me in St. Louis* frame enlargement

rearrangement of accents encourages us to view the frame as a whole, and by extension the series of shots as part of a larger, unfolding composition. This rearrangement and repetition of elements lend to the sense of determination, of everything in its right place that so often characterizes Minnelli's designs.

But these accents also prime the viewer for Esther's arrival from the background, carrying the tune. The red accents on the left and Lon, turned away from the camera in his dark blue jacket on the right, effectively frame Esther's emergence. An architectural detail, the off-white pillar that helps separate the living room from the hall and stairs runs down the center of the frame and quite literally frames Esther's arrival. Once she steps on the scene, in her light blue dress and mustard greenish-yellow scarf, Esther commands the scene. Esther's colors, red hair, yellow scarf, blue dress, form a sort of primary triad that Arnheim described as static and complete. Not only is she the only character to bring all three colors together in one figure, Esther also constitutes a unified, self-sufficient palette. Like El Greco's Virgin, Esther is the compositional keystone. Other figures seem ordered around her. A character in an orange blouse standing near the foot of the staircase, for example, is locked into a complementary relationship with Esther's blue, and the red accents planted in the scene participate in Esther's red–yellow–blue triad. As Minnelli begins the longest take of the sequence (one minute twenty-seven seconds) he draws on the resources of color and centering to anchor attention to his star and to unify the composition around her. And yet, describing Esther's colors as a stable triad isn't quite

121

accurate, and Arnheim can help us see why. Neither the yellow of her scarf (which is decidedly greenish) nor the red of her hair (much closer to dark orange) are pure colors, and this puts them into a more dynamic relationship with their chromatic environment. Esther's hair color falls somewhere between the red lamp and the background dress, lending contrast, while the scarf yields a point of coordination with a green/yellow plaid dress at the rear; she is both individuated from and coordinated with the community around her. The example illustrates Minnelli's penchant to complicate and unify composition even when the viewer's attention is firmly and easily fixed on his star's performance. Indeed, Minnelli is elaborating Technicolor's convention of keying *mise en scène* to the female star's coloration. Rather than resting with easy harmonies, "Skip to My Lou" deploys echoes, completions, and variations of Esther's keynote colors to unfold and develop its grand, dynamic composition.

Throughout the long take Minnelli faces the problem of tracking the main characters as they carry the song while also embedding them in the community's spontaneous dance. His job is fairly simple when Esther is singing, as the camera can center and track her movements with the red—yellow—blue triad ensuring that the visuals will match her vocal dominance on the soundtrack. The shot's highpoint of color patterning, however, is remarkably complex. Party guests arrange themselves into a square-dance aisle with boys on the left and girls on the right. Esther dances down the aisle to the far end where she breaks off from her partner and begins weaving her way up the line of boys on the left. Minnelli and his cinematographer Charles Rosher dolly backward, keeping Esther centered in long shot as she swings from partner to partner, passing behind and around each boy. The movement, timed with the lyric "if I do it's up to you to let me dance with Harry, Johnny, Charley," reinforces the theme of balancing individual romance within a larger community. As she dances her way up the line, Esther briefly locks hands with John Truitt, quickly recognized because of his uniquely blue sport jacket, and exchanges a meaningful glance, but the dance must continue (see Figure 6.9).

The moment of flirtation takes place at the peak of kinetic momentum. As she swings from partner to partner, Esther is briefly occluded and then revealed, vanishing and reappearing along a chain of black, blue, and gray sport coats (see Figures 6.10 and 6.11). Other women begin weaving in behind her, extending and complicating the pattern of occlusion and revelation. First the guest in the red plaid dress (who held the foreground in the first shot), then Ida Boothby, and finally a dancer in a nearly neutral off-white dress joins the chain. When Esther reappears in the foreground, primary triad locked firmly together, she is mirrored in the background first by red accents, then by Ida's blue, lavender, fuchsia, and pink details, followed by the chromatically less prepossessing girl in beige. Like a comet, Esther gathers a tail of color streaking through the depth of the frame.

Figure 6.9 *Meet Me in St. Louis* frame enlargement

123

Figure 6.10 *Meet Me in St. Louis* frame enlargement

In a proper 35mm print which display's Technicolor's remarkable registration of texture and detail, this movement is a climactic perceptual event, and Arnheim's ideas can help show us why. Sharpening and leveling heighten the binary of color and neutral while the line of dresses deal a pattern of connection and segregation. Different components of Esther's

Figure 6.11 *Meet Me in St. Louis* frame enlargement

modified triad are pushed and pulled by her companions. The dancer in the red dress reinforces the hue of Esther's hair (indeed the most muted of her triadic colors), while her blue bow joins to Esther's dress. A step further down the chain, Ida's blue skirt binds to Esther's blues and her red stripes converge with the dancer between them. The dancer in soft tones ties off this play of connection and contrast, a sort of stable endpoint to the visual game. The unfolding composition engages the eye in an arresting double pattern of color and neutral, and hue on hue.

This is a moment where the sensual immediacy of Minnelli's dance encourages and rewards a kind of contemplation, a more or less instantaneous appreciation of unified form. Moreover, the phrase is semantically significant in that Esther and John snatch a moment of flirtation amid the whirlwind of the group dance. The couple is kept apart at the same time that the community is most united, the sort of meaningful form that Arnheim praised in *Film as Art* and *Art and Visual Perception*.

As Arnheim wrote in *Art and Visual Perception*, it is "our task to search the perceived object for the formal factors that determine what the eyes see."[34] In reaching beyond the norms of easy harmony and legibility, filmmakers like Minnelli test and control perception through the deployment of color, and Arnheim's model provides insight. Certainly, in Minnelli we find an artist who exploits color's structural ability in a deep way; his is not a work of shape and line in which color serves as mere embellishment, but a structured web of chromatic kinships that direct the eye and lend formal significance. Viewing a color composition as a system of pushes and pulls, attractions and repulsions, brings us closer to a formal understanding of why certain films engage us.

notes

1. David Batchelor, *Chromophobia*, London: Reaktion Books, 2000. Batchelor uses the term to describe a devaluation of color in art and culture, stretching back to Aristotle's *Poetics* and represented in the tradition of *disegno* versus *colore*.
2. Rudolf Arnheim, *Film as Art*, Berkeley: University of California Press, 1957, pp. 1, 154.
3. Rudolf Arnheim, "Remarks on Color Film," trans. F. G. Renier, in *Film Essays and Criticism*, Madison: University of Wisconsin Press, 1935 (1997), pp. 19–20.
4. Ibid., p. 20.
5. This theory has been elaborated into a full account of color behavior by artist and designer Augusto Garau. See Garau, *Color Harmonies*, trans. Nicola Bruno, Chicago: University of Chicago Press, 1993.
6. Arnheim, "Remarks on Color Film," p. 22.
7. Natalie Kalmus, "Color Consciousness," in eds. Angela Dalle Vacche and Brian Price *Color, The Film Reader*, New York: Routledge, 1935 (2006), p. 25.
8. Arnheim, "Remarks on Color Film," p. 22.
9. Ibid., pp. 21–22.
10. Ibid., p. 21.
11. John Gage traces this primary triad to Aristotle and the fifth-century BC poet Xenophanes. He notes that the triad "had established itself as fundamental among artists all over Europe by the early seventeenth century." Gage, *Color in Art*, London: Thames & Hudson, 2006, pp. 24–25.
12. Rudolf Arnheim, "Foreword," in Garau, *Color Harmonies*, p. x.
13. Rudolf Arnheim, *Art and Visual Perception*, The New Version, Berkeley: University of California Press, 1974, p. 336.
14. Ibid., p. 345.
15. Rudolf Arnheim, *Visual Thinking*, London: Faber and Faber, 1969, p. 30.
16. Rudolf Arnheim, "Colors Irrational and Rational," *The Journal of Aesthetics and Art Criticism*, 1974, Vol. 33, No. 2, p. 153.
17. Recent research by Stephen Palmer's visual perception lab at University of California, Berkeley suggests that we view similar rather than complementary colors as harmonious. Stephen Palmer, "Aesthetic Science: Understanding Preferences for Color and Spatial Composition," http://videolectures.net/google_palmer_colors/ (accessed 4 June 2009). Research on color processing in the human visual system is ongoing and the subject of debate. As yet, there doesn't seem to be consensus that the painter's primaries are favored. For an excellent overview of the research, see Bevil R. Conway, "Color Vision, Cones, and Color Coding in the Cortex," *The Neuroscientist*, 2009, Vol. 15, No. 3, pp. 277, 279–282.
18. Arnheim, "Colors Irrational and Rational," p. 153.
19. Arnheim, *Art and Visual Perception*, pp. 351–357.
20. Ibid., p. 355.
21. Ibid., p. 357.
22. Ibid., p. 363.
23. Arnheim, "Colors Irrational and Rational," p. 152.

24. Ibid., p. 151. A reproduction of Titian's *Diana and Actaeon* (1556–1559) is available at <http://www.nationalgallery.org.uk/paintings/titian-diana-and-actaeon>

25. Rudolf Arnheim, *The Power of the Center*, Berkeley: University of California Press, 1982, pp. 78–81. A reproduction of El Greco's *The Agony in the Garden* (1590–1595) is available at <http://www.toledomuseum.org/Collection/El_Greco.htm>

26. A reproduction of El Greco's *The Virgin with Saint Ines and Saint Tecla* (1597–1599) is available at <http://www.cts.edu/ImageLibrary/Images/July%2012/grcovrgn.jpg>

27. Arnheim, *Art and Visual Perception*, p. 367.

28. Ibid., pp. 366–368.

29. Arnheim, *The Power of the Center*, p. 234.

30. This line of research is currently undertaken from a cognitive perspective by Tim Smith at Edinburgh University. In relation to color, see his analysis of the "Famous Color Changing Card Trick" on his website: <http://continuityboy.blogspot.com/2007/11/famous-colour-changing-card-trick.html>

31. This notion derives, in part, from Sergei Eisenstein's late conception of the "montage unit" which considers the shot as part of a grand, unfolding composition. For a discussion of this concept see David Bordwell, *The Cinema of Eisenstein*, Cambridge, Massachusetts: Harvard University Press, 1993, pp. 146–155.

32. Full color versions of the frame enlargements for this essay are available at the author's website: <http://shiggins.web.wesleyan.edu/My%20Home/>

33. For a discussion of the color advisory service, see Scott Higgins, *Harnessing the Technicolor Rainbow*, Austin, Texas: University of Texas Press, 2007, pp. 39–47.

34. Arnheim, *Art and Visual Perception*, p. 371.

perfecting the

complete cinema

seven

rudolf arnheim and the digital

intermediate[1]

j i n h e e   c h o i

Classical film theorists have considered cinema's reproductive capacity to be the principal characteristic of the medium, even as they have disagreed on the artistic potential arising from it. Unlike André Bazin, who claims that the invention of cinema arose from the impetus toward realism, or the creation of a reality, Arnheim attributes the artistic effects of film form to the limitations of the medium, that is, to the fact that cinema's reproductive capacity falls short of being a complete replica of reality. Film art is located somewhere between nature and a complete replica of nature (the complete cinema) and technological development within the film industry would curb the range of the medium's artistic possibilities, as the phenomenal gap between a filmic reproduction and the reality would become decreased.

For film scholars, classical film theorists such as Rudolf Arnheim's medium-specific approach may be viewed as outdated or irrelevant to the discussion of contemporary film aesthetics, as media convergence has become the norm within the global film industry. Nonetheless, Arnheim's reservations on "the complete film" are worthy of re-examination, especially when industry discourse on technological development heavily emphasizes the novelty and limitlessness of the moving image, be it photographic or digital.[2] This chapter will carefully reassess Arnheim's criticism of the complete film by turning attention to the tension that often exists between a new medium and a burgeoning aesthetic mode. Although new media scholars often attempt to establish aesthetics by isolating the specificity of the medium or material, as this chapter hopes to show, new media aesthetics are often assimilated to the aesthetic norms and conventions of the media that preceded them or those developed across media. This chapter further attempts to show how a contemporary debate about digital technology, digital intermediates (DI) in particular, embodies such a tension.

the notion of the complete cinema

Arnheim aims to advance a material film theory with two distinct but related objectives: to establish film as a genuine art form and to underscore the compatibility between the film medium's reproductive capacity and artistic expressivity. The artistic function of the medium should not be found in its emulating of other art forms, but in the exploring of its own medium—its very material, technical constraints. Arnheim demonstrates how film is far from a perfect copy of reality and that the imperfections of the "mechanical" reproduction process should serve as the basis for the artistic use of the medium: from the reduction of depth, to lighting, to the delimitation of the screen, to the absence of the space–time continuum, and to the absence of color and of non-visual sensory coordination, each "defect" or "drawback" can render artistic effects.

As Jon Elster reminds us, creativity comprises both a "choice of constraints" and "choice within constraints" and the filmmaker's initial choice of the medium would impose certain intrinsic, technical constraints, within which he or she can pursue the medium's artistic potentials.[3] Consider, for example, depth of field in the cinema, which can underscore the psychological state of a character. Arnheim takes an example from King Vidor's *The Crowd* (1928), which showcases an aesthetic inclination of the medium. A boy hurries home, as he sees a crowd gathering around his house at the sound of an ambulance. The camera is located on the second floor, looking down at the door, as the boy enters. As the boy nears the end of the stairs, he appears disproportionately large—an effect of the camera lens—which nevertheless artfully expresses his fear of hearing the dreadful news that his father is dead.[4]

Given the artistic potentials of the medium, filmmakers aim not to "re-present" reality, unfolding in front of the camera, but to transform its material constraints into cinematic expression. However, as film technology advances, Arnheim claims, it not only jeopardizes the film's status as an independent art form—the boundary between theater and film becomes blurred—but also brings about aesthetic consequences. Newly developed technologies such as sound, color, and widescreen would enhance the reproductive capacity of the film medium, which would then limit the range of artistic choices that filmmakers make.

The pursuit of the complete cinema, according to Arnheim, is a natural outcome of "the fulfillment of the age-old striving for the complete illusion."[5] Arnheim acknowledges that the history of visual art has been driven by the desire to create a replica of reality—what Bazin later calls the "mummy" complex, an impulse to immortalize an appearance against the passage of time.[6] At the same time, he claims, there has been a counter tendency "to originate, to interpret, to mold."[7] Arnheim is not concerned with providing a psychological explanation of whether the mimetic impulse or the expressive tendency propelled the evolution of the visual art. Rather his point is that in the case of film, the two are often in conflict, with the mimetic desire deterring filmmakers from exploring the expressive qualities of the medium. This duality of mimetic and expressive functions manifest in the aesthetic pursuits of the film medium continues to provide a theoretical framework for the aesthetic debate for the digital medium.

Arnheim's resistance to the complete cinema—or at least a move toward it—resides in his deep-seated conviction that film is a visual medium. In his article entitled "A New Laocoön," Arnheim considers the artistic possibility of the hybrid arts, through which he attempts to demonstrate that sound film curtails, rather than strengthens, the aesthetic merits of the medium. One of the major differences between theater and film, according to Arnheim, is found in their principal medium: the former is a verbal medium, while the latter is visual. Even within the so called hybrid arts, they can be distinguished from one another by virtue of the "dominant medium" that is in place.[8] Opera, for instance, incorporates dialogue but musical performance still is its dominant medium. In theater, it is the dialogue, and in film, visual action. But if both theater and film employ dialogue and visual action, the difference between the two will be a matter of degree, rather than of kind.

One may level various criticisms against Arnheim's controversial claim that visual action is the principal medium for film art. It can be granted that the introduction of technologies like sound, color, and widescreen removed some of the constraints of representing the reality embedded in the medium. Yet Arnheim does not view the technological imperfections manifest in the film medium as, in and of themselves, aesthetic merits: instead they *can* be employed to produce artistic effects. Any technological novelty has its own material constraints—sound, color, or any other technology—and filmmakers can explore aesthetic possibilities of new technology under Arnheim's aesthetic provisions, by tuning into its formative, instead of mimetic, capacity.

One can further interrogate Arnheim's uncontested assumption that each art form has only *one* dominant medium. Film art can be viewed as a composite art, yet the medium-specificity thesis can still be defended through a relational approach: the way image and sound are coordinated differs from that of theater or opera. Or one can take an alternate route: despite the fact that certain art forms *may* share the principal medium, the materiality or physicality of each medium would provide sufficient ground to be distinguished from each other.[9] Arnheim entertains a scenario in which theater uses a projected image as a backdrop or a rotating set that can emulate the camera movement, effacing the difference between theater and film. But one can still disprove Arnheim's claim by pointing out how three-dimensionality of performance space in theater (not the backdrop) departs itself from two-dimensional projected space in film.

These criticisms are valid as well as valuable in and of themselves, and Arnheim's medium-specificity thesis may be untenable. But for the purpose of this chapter, it is too hasty to dismiss entirely Arnheim's concern for the aesthetic implications and consequences that result from the industry's gradual move toward the creation of the complete cinema. Instead of providing counterexamples to Arnheim's thesis, what would be of greater value when discussing contemporary digital technology is uncovering the *overarching aesthetic principles* that he views as breached by new technology and whether these are indeed rooted in the postulated ontology of the new medium. By dissociating Arnheim's aesthetic principles—naturalism and homogeneity, as will be shown—from his ontological argument, one can see how his aesthetic categories are still pertinent to the current discussion of digital technology, regardless of whether one may or may not adopt his ontological presuppositions on the photographic medium.

principles of naturalism and homogeneity

Arnheim demands that film art should abide by two aesthetic principles: naturalism and homogeneity. However, these do not constitute a medium-specific aesthetic mode. Arnheim's film theory is often classified as "formative" or "creationist," yet throughout his discussion of film art, his aesthetic is heavily circumscribed by the notion of the "natural." Film art is not an imitation but a transformation of nature: it "strengthens," "concentrates," and "interprets," but not to the extent that it completely "restructures" nature or imposes a new reality.[10] With his emphasis on "nature" Arnheim does not align himself with any artistic movement of the eighteenth or the nineteenth century, but rather uses it as an umbrella term, encompassing both his ontological assumptions about the medium and general aesthetic principle. Film art should explore and foreground the formal, as well as phenomenal, gap between nature and film, but not to the extent that its relationship to reality is compromised.

The concept of "natural" in Arnheim's aesthetics is construed as a relative concept, the scope and phenomenal experience of which being varied in accordance with the category and conventions to which film belongs. One of the principal reasons for Arnheim to reject sound films has to do with the film's auditory proximity to reality, but it also has to do with the changing conception of "natural." Arnheim's observations on the film industry and its relationship to aesthetic norms are worthy of note here. Arnheim argues that so long as silent film, sound film, and complete film can coexist, there is nothing *inherently* deplorable about the invention of the complete cinema. The complete film can serve a function different from that of the silent cinema—such as the filming of a stage play. Nevertheless, Arnheim states, "since on economic grounds film is much more dependent on the general public than any other form of art, the 'artistic' preferences of the public sweep everything before them."[11] With the incorporation of new technology, a new set of conventions would become the industry norm with no room left for the silent cinema to coexist alongside the sound film. The viewer's conception of the naturalistic film would change and sound film would make silent film feel artificial, as color film would make black-and-white film look unnatural.[12]

The notion of "natural" also carries other assumptions in Arnheim's theory, one of which concerns narrative.[13] Arnheim at times equates narrative film with "naturalistic" films, and an unmotivated use of film device or style would result in a disruption of the diegesis. He claims that the close-ups and camera angles used in the court scene of Carl Theodor Dreyer's *The Passion of Joan of Arc* (1928) are unnatural and disruptive, since such devices are narratively unmotivated: "Form for form's sake— this is the rock on which many film artists, especially the French, are shipwrecked."[14] While commenting on the intellectual montage, Arnheim also notes,

> Putting actual pictures in juxtaposition, especially in an otherwise realistic film, often appears forced. The unity of the scene, the story of the prisoner who is rejoicing, is suddenly interrupted by something totally different. Comparisons and associations like the brook and the sunbeams are not lightly touched upon in the abstract but are introduced as concrete pieces of nature—and hence are distracting.[15]

Unlike literature, in which a writer can freely draw on discrete ideas and imageries to forge a symbolic link between them, cinema, due to the concreteness of photographic image, prevents the filmmaker from connecting various shots of objects that fall outside the immediate unity of narrative space.

In addition to the hampering of the naturalistic aesthetics, new technology—both sound and color—significantly impedes the homogeneity of the film medium. Arnheim asserts that unlike human expression, which is anchored on the biological unity of a person, sound films lack such a center. The juxtaposition of two sensory modes in a sound film—visual action and dialogue—does not automatically guarantee the expressivity of a work. Expressivity, according to Arnheim, is achieved at the higher level, only when there can be found the "kinship of expression" between different sensory modes. The fusion of two distinct media can be obtained by virtue of the expressive structure shared between such modes.[16] For instance, sadness can be expressed and enhanced through the "kinship of expression" between the patterns of bodily movement and the patterns of the melody. However, Arnheim is concerned that the combination of image and sound in film would divert the viewer's attention from the visual component to the source of the sound. Dialogue would center the action on the human figure, and the "homogeneous" relationship held between human figure and inanimate objects in the silent cinema would disappear with the coming of sound.[17]

Arnheim denies the artistic potential of color films on a similar ground. Color films not only approximate reality more than black-and-white film, but also lack the homogeneity and harmony of the latter.[18] Chromatic films present a wider range of contrasts and relations among colors than achromatic black-and-white films at the level of hue, value, and saturation, creating "the possibility of discord."[19] The three primary colors would render different pairs of contrasts (blue–yellow, yellow–red, red–blue) and other variables such as value and saturation would further complicate color harmony in contrast to the single optic scale of black-and-white film. The homogeneity of black-and-white film can be easily disrupted in color film, unless an image contains objects with colors that fall within a single range of hue or value.

Arnheim often uses metaphorical expressions such as "truth to nature," "violence to nature," or "unfaithfulness to nature," as if his "naturalistic" aesthetics are an aesthetic corollary of the film medium's ontological commitment to the reality.[20] Naturalism, however, is not a veridical concept whose truth or falsity can be judged by the resemblance or faithfulness to the external world. Naturalism construed as such—or "naturalness"—would indeed count as an aesthetic defect for Arnheim rather than a merit, since for him nature is indeterminate, formless, and only accidentally harmonious. As much as our conception of the natural and naturalistic is in part shaped by the experience of the real (and perhaps an extension of it), it is also influenced and governed by both aesthetic conventions and norms, facilitated by the artistic motivations within a particular work.

Homogeneity, which I take to be one of the conditions that can contribute to artistic expressivity and enhance unity and/or harmony in film art, is not medium-specific. By homogeneity Arnheim refers to the equivalence of *functions* and *values*, which are "exchangeable" as well as "fusable."[21]

In the universal silence of the image, the fragments of a broken vase could "talk" exactly the way a character talked to his neighbor, and a person approaching on a road and visible on the horizon as a mere dot "talked" as someone acting in close-up. This homogeneity, which is completely foreign to the theater but familiar to *painting*, is destroyed by the talking film: it endows the actor with speech, and since only he can have it, all other things are pushed into the background.[22]

(My italics)

In a silent film, lack of dialogue frees an image from a usual hierarchy within a frame with priority given to human presence or performance. Instead, it allows any element in an image to bear as much significance/value as the human figure. However, homogeneity in this sense is present in any visual medium unaccompanied by an additional sensory mode, since the viewer's attention would not be directed to any specific aspect within the frame with the added mode. In a black-and-white film, in a similar vein, each tone has an equal value, for no particular hue visually dominates over others.[23] Nonetheless, as Arnheim himself notes, homogeneity of this kind can also be obtained in a color film, if it is shot with a single tint or if it is based solely on equal values of primary colors.[24] In each case, Arnheim's aesthetic principles might be fulfilled by a variety of technological configurations, despite his preference for a particular kind of medium specificity.

Film as art, according to Arnheim, should strive for a subtle balance in its transformation of and adherence to nature, yet the aesthetic principles that he provides to guide the artistic practices of the medium do not result from the unique qualities and/or materiality of the medium. Arnheim often conflates these two, and his reservations about new technology have more to do with technical feasibility than an ontological predisposition of the medium. It is here that the recent development of digital technology poses a challenge, as well as provides a solution, to Arnheim's film aesthetics. Digital technology may perfect the complete cinema in enhancing photographic realism, but it also facilitates and extends the existing expressive possibilities of film as a photographic medium. As Stephen Prince points out, the use of digital technology is not monolithic, as it often conforms to, and reinforces, the naturalistic aesthetics of the photographic medium instead of forging a new distinctive mode of aesthetics.[25] My discussion that follows will focus on the debate about the visual effects of digital technology, and especially DI, particularly how it can be viewed as both continuing as well as redirecting the debate about a new medium and its aesthetic strategy.

arnheim and digital intermediates

Arnheim advances criticisms against both sound and color on a common ground: art perception requires a different or additional set of conditions than those required for natural perception. Even if you transfer beautiful scenery into a film, its beauty would not automatically be rendered: "as soon as a piece of nature becomes an image, we consider it with different eyes."[26] If the unity in nature is either given—as in the organic unity of a human being—or accidental—as in natural beauty—artistic unity can only be achieved via a precise patterning and formal relationship.[27]

> The color confusion in color film, the disturbing promi-
> nence of single tones, the difficulty of seeing the images at
> a glance, and the diversion from the object because of color
> have at most secondary technical reasons. The main reason
> is the "naturalness," *the lack of form*.[28]
>
> (My italics)

However, it is not just the lack of form that makes a color film look "atrocious."[29] In his discussion of color films, Arnheim constantly foregrounds the difference between filmmakers and painters by contrasting how the former lacks the selective color control that the latter enjoys. Given the traditional methods of photochemical color processing, which tend to affect the entire image, a filmmaker's control of *individual* colors relies on the configuration of elements of *mise en scène*. Such a process, to the eyes of Arnheim, would amount merely to a mechanical shift—a "transposition," not a "transformation," of a physical reality.

> All kinds of fine procedures are conceivable, especially in the
> montage of colored pictures, but it must not be overlooked
> that in this way the subjective formative virtues of the
> camera, which are so distinctive a characteristic of film, will
> be more and more restricted, and the artistic part of the
> work will be more and more focused upon what is set up
> and enacted *before* the camera.[30]

One may be surprised by Arnheim's assertion above, even if one puts aside the implicit hierarchy within the functions of "cinematic" devices—that is, cinematographic qualities are more essential to the medium than non-cinematographic ones such as *mise en scène*. *Pace* Arnheim, the image created on film is not a direct transposition of the image variables in *mise en scène*. As Prince points out, an image created *in* camera is "latent" form, further subject to transformation and manipulation during development and printing.[31] I would even speculate that the physical limitations of color films could indeed serve an aesthetic purpose given Arnheim's aesthetics of constraints. Technicolor film, for instance, may create problems for lighting and creating depth, but such constraints can be turned into aesthetic merits.[32]

In fact, Arnheim's disapproval of color films is based less on the ontological assumptions about the medium than on the violation of general aesthetic principles: the lack of artistic control, which would deter the filmmaker from achieving the unity and harmony needed to engage the viewer's artistic perception. But the development of DI, many argue, provides a wider range of controls to filmmakers comparable to painters. DI is a process that digitizes filmed images so that they can be manipulated and then recorded back out onto film or stored on a digital medium.[33] It provides a tool to filmmakers not only to alter the tone and temperature of an image as a whole but also to work at the micro level of color correction, which is unavailable in photochemical lab-based color processing. Reliance on DI for color correction makes the industry increasingly depend on post-production to create the look desired. The director of photography, as well as the director, needs to communicate closely during both pre- and post-production stages with DI colorists in order to plan what should be carried out or materialized during or after production.

It is quite intriguing to observe how the scholarly discussion of the impacts of DI echoes Arnheim's aesthetic concerns: naturalism and homogeneity. John Belton claims that films such as *Pleasantville* offer a new mode of digital aesthetics, successfully showcasing the expressive potentials of the digital medium. *Pleasantville* was made shortly after the heated debate about the role of digital colorization—the public disapproved of Ted Turner's attempt to color classical Hollywood black-and-white films—and self-reflexively thematized the issue of colorization. *Pleasantville* is neither the first nor the only film that blends black-and-white and color in a single image. Films such as *Schindler's List* (1993) and *Sin City* (2005) contain colored elements within the overall achromatic tone. But for Belton, what distinguishes *Pleasantville* from the films that had preceded and would follow is that it narrativizes the juxtaposition of color and black-and-white.

> Within the narrative, the transformation of black-and-white images into color images functions as an *expressive device* that documents the progressive movement of characters on the paths of self-discovery/self-actualization.[34]

(My italics)

When David and Jennifer, the protagonists in the film, are transposed into the black-and-white television show *Pleasantville*, their transformation, as well as the transformation of the townspeople, is expressed through the shift from black-and-white to color. Contrary to the inverse relation posited by Arnheim between the emergence of a new technology and the delimitation of the artistic scope of the medium, the perfecting of the complete cinema through digital technology can increase the expressive function of the moving image.

Pleasantville may be viewed as "naturalistic" by Arnheim's standard, since the presence and absence of color are narratively motivated, but they do make "DI visible—even if that visibility is narratively recuperated," as Belton admits.[35] Arnheim's endorsement of naturalism is complex, encompassing not only narrativization of film devices but also a subtle use of film techniques. The film may successfully thematize the diverging capacity of the photographic and of the digital medium but their juxtaposition is still perceptually palpable. But according to Belton, such a visibility carries an additional function—self-reflexivity: it enables the viewers to revisit their understanding of the photographic and digital image—the wholeness of the photographic image vs. an array of discrete picture elements in the digital image.[36]

Belton's digital aesthetics shares theoretical assumptions with Arnheim's in that he devises "new" aesthetics in accordance with the ontology of the new medium, in addition to his explicit concurrence with Arnheim that the photographic medium is homogeneous in nature. In a film such as *Pleasantville*, the ontologies of differing media are aesthetically manifest, reflecting the differences between the two media—between the "analogue continuity" figured as black-and-white film and the "digital discontinuity" broken into color elements within an image.[37] To be more precise, the ontological *conceptions* are aesthetically addressed, since black-and-white portions in the film are rendered through the elimination of colors, instead of being shot on black-and-white film stock.

However, Belton falls into the same pitfall as Arnheim in his attempt to forge new media aesthetics based on its ontology. A finer distinction should be of help here, although Arnheim himself does not clearly articulate the relationship between homogeneity and its corresponding perceptual effects. He often discusses homogeneity in relation to unity or harmony, but the former is often linked to function while the latter is linked to perception as well as the formal relationships within an image. A composite or multi-media art may not be homogeneous in the functional sense of the term, since it is not interchangeable, but it may be perceived as "harmonious," when it shares a kinship of expressivity. For Arnheim, a full color shot in *Pleasantville* may be as inharmonious as a single shot composite of black-and-white and color. In fact, in some shots colors are well welded into the black-and-white. The gradual coloring of flowers and trees as Bud and Margaret drive into Lovers' Lane seems less perceptually disruptive than a shot of the "colored" townsfolk in costumes of high-contrast hues at the diner when they discuss the new bans reached at the town meeting. By equating homogeneity with harmony, Belton is unable to explain harmony achieved within a "heterogeneous" shot of black-and-white and color.

Digital effects cinema may pursue a more flamboyant mode even further, inscribing the presence of new technology more visibly by juxtaposing competing elements within a single shot. Perceptual complexity as much as perceptual unity and harmony may contribute to the expressive function of film form regardless of the Brechtian political implications often associated with it. As Aylish Wood demonstrates, however, the heterogeneity of a digital image is not distinctive to the digital medium, rather it is a potential that has existed and been explored across media including animation, live action film, and installation art.[38]

Prince takes a revisionist approach, delineating two different aesthetic modes manifest in DI color processing—a display of technology as spectacle and a controlled use of technology—and it is in the latter that he locates more artistic value.[39] Films such as *Pleasantville* (1998) showcase the use of digital technology, drawing the viewer's attention to the blending of black-and-white and color in the same frame. On the other hand, films like *O Brother, Where Art Thou?* (2000), the first Hollywood feature film digitized in its entirety for color grading and correction, makes the digital correction play a subservient role to enhancing an overall look of the film.

> The dustbowl look, the hand-tinted postcard quality of *O Brother*, are, of course, effects but they do not advertise them as such. They do not subvert a viewer's impression of the photographable character of the images. This makes a more powerful digital tool because its use does not require the filmmakers to sacrifice a relative appearance of *naturalism*, as happens in *Pleasantville* and *The Phantom Menace*.[40]
>
> (My italics)

Prince sees the DI process as an enhancement of artistic powers on the filmmakers' part, compared with more traditional or lab-based color imaging, such as silver-retention processes, flashing, and cross-processing, which does not allow selective control. For Prince, DI finally gives filmmakers the level of control that Arnheim saw in painters.

> The filmmaker here approaches the <u>painter's ability</u> to control the fine details of color, shading, contrast, filtration and other attributes of the image—*within images that can otherwise appear naturalistic*.[41]
>
> (Original italics, my underline)

Such a use of digital technology in *O Brother* may not be registered as so artificial as its more flamboyant use in other films, where digitally created images become visual spectacles in and of themselves. In *O Brother* the digital technology enables the traditional photographic medium to overcome its limitations of representation by providing tools to refine the use of color, yet it can still be conducive to traditional aesthetic norms. Prince expresses the same concern for elegant control and organization that Arnheim always endorsed and valued. Expressivity of the medium should not be sought in an ostentatious use of film technique, but a subtle, indirect use of it.

The discussions of DI advanced by both Belton and Prince, although coming to rather different conclusions on the aesthetic significance of specific films, share similar aesthetic concerns to those that had preoccupied Arnheim. It is not my intention to surmise whether Arnheim would approve of films like *Pleasantville*, or the use of digital technology for that matter. What is intriguing is the aesthetic limbo that allows an amplification and modulation of the function of a new medium, be it sound or color (for Arnheim) or DI (for Belton and Prince). The tension in creating the complete cinema lies in, as Arnheim nicely puts it, the competing desires for the mimetic as well as the expressive use of the medium.

This chapter is not about contesting medium specificity. Rather, the point has been to demonstrate how new media aesthetics—photographic and digital—in different points within the history of cinema have revolved around a similar set of aesthetic issues, and how new media conforms as well as transforms traditional aesthetic norms and conventions such as naturalism or homogeneity. The assumed trajectory of digital technology, for many (possibly including Arnheim), has always been the perfecting of photographic realism.[42] Yet, the debate about the aesthetic capacity of, and use of, DI underscores its alternate aspect: its expressive dimension. The privileged aesthetic for a new medium is often pulled back and balanced by aesthetic principles that are not medium-specific. Arnheim, perhaps unintentionally, betrays this tension, while a revisionist such as Prince more consciously demonstrates it.[43]

notes

1. A portion of this essay appears in Choi's chapter "Rudolf Arnheim," in P. Livingston and C. Plantinga eds. *The Routledge Companion to Philosophy and Film*, New York: Routledge, 2009, pp. 291–300.
2. Marc Furtenau brought my attention to this aspect.
3. J. Elster, *Ulysses Unbound: Studies in Rationality, Precommitment, and Constraints*, Cambridge: Cambridge University Press, 2000, p. 176.
4. R. Arnheim, "Film," in *Film as Art*, Berkeley: University of California Press, 1933 (1957), pp. 63–64.
5. Ibid., p. 158.
6. A. Bazin, "The Ontology of the Photographic Image," trans. H. Gray, in *What is Cinema?* Vol 1, Berkeley: University of California Press, 1945 (1967), p. 9.
7. Arnheim, "Film," p. 157.
8. Arnheim, "A New Laocoön: Artistic Composites and the Talking Film," in *Film as Art*, Berkeley: University of California Press, 1938 (1957), p. 223.
9. N. Carroll, *Philosophical Problems of Classical Film Theory*, Princeton, NJ: Princeton University Press, 1988, p. 82.
10. Arnheim, "Film," pp. 35, 57.
11. Ibid., p. 158.
12. Ibid.
13. Arnheim also discusses subtlety in performance under the notion of "naturalistic" acting. Film acting shapes and forms otherwise indeterminate

and ambiguous everyday action into clear and legible actions (what Arnheim calls "pure acting"), but also needs to develop a subtle, naturalistic acting that would convey the psychological and emotional states of characters via indirect visual methods, such as minute gestures and elements within *mise en scène* that are not typically associated with the physical manifestation of an emotion. See Arnheim, "Film," pp. 136–141.

14. Arnheim, "Film," pp. 40–41.
15. Ibid., p. 90.
16. Arnheim develops a rather peculiar theory of expression here, where expression has a structure of feeling that can be embodied through various sensory modes or between inanimate and animate beings. See Noël Carroll, *Philosophical Problems of Classical Film Theory*, pp. 70–75.
17. Arnheim, "A New Laocoön," p. 227.
18. Arnheim, "Film," pp. 19–20.
19. Ibid.
20. Ibid., p. 137.
21. Arnheim, "A New Laocoön," p. 205.
22. Ibid., p. 227.
23. R. Arnheim, "Remarks on Color Film," trans. F. G. Renier, in *Film Essays and Criticism*, Madison: University of Wisconsin Press, 1935 (1997), p. 20. Interestingly, Arnheim does not construe music as homogeneous, since each musical tone has a different value.
24. Ibid.
25. S. Prince, "The Emergence of Filmic Artifacts: Cinema and Cinematography in the Digital Era," *Film Quarterly* 57/3, 2004, p. 24.
26. Arnheim, "Remarks on Color Film," p. 21.
27. Arnheim, "A New Laocoön," p. 205; "Remarks on Color Film," p. 21.
28. Ibid., pp. 21–22.
29. Ibid.
30. Ibid., p. 156.
31. Prince, "The Emergence of Filmic Artifacts," p. 27.
32. S. Higgins, *Harnessing the Color Design in the 1930s: Technicolor Rainbow*, Austin: University of Texas Press, 2007.
33. S. Argy, "Cinematography's Computer Age," *American Cinematographer* 80/8, 1999, p. 75.
34. J. Belton, "Painting by the Numbers: The Digital Intermediate," *Film Quarterly* 61/3, 2008, p. 65.
35. Ibid.
36. Ibid., p. 61.
37. Ibid., p. 59.
38. A. Wood, *Digital Encounters*, London, New York: Routledge, p. 7.
39. Scott Higgins claims that the differing aesthetic strategies manifest in *Pleasantville* and *O Brother* do not represent two competing or alternative approaches to digital colorization, but rather two "phases" within the development of the aesthetic norms of the new technology in the film industry. It is unclear how strict a chronology Higgins assumes is operating between the two phases—whether one phase is gradually being replaced by the other—since these two modes still coexist after the later phase of *O Brother* had been introduced. See his "A New Color Consciousness: Colour in the Digital Age," *Convergence* 9/4, 2003, pp. 60–76.
40. Ibid., pp. 28–29.

41. Prince, "The Emergence of Filmic Artifacts," p. 28.
42. M. Allen, "The Impact of Digital Technologies on Film Aesthetics," in D. Harries ed. *The New Media Book*, London: BFI Publishing, 2002, p. 100.
43. I would like to thank Marc Furstenau, Vince Bohlinger, and Scott Higgins who provided me with valuable comments on the earlier version of this chapter. A further thanks goes to Federico Windhausen, who provided me with valuable documents on digital intermediates.

art, accident, and

the interpretation

of the modern world

p a t r i c k   k e a t i n g

In *Theory of Film*, Siegfried Kracauer argues that film has a unique relationship to the contingent features of the world. In some passages, Kracauer uses the example of the wind blowing through the leaves to stand for these contingencies. Since no filmmaker could possibly predict or orchestrate all the subtle movements of every rustling leaf, anyone who points a camera at a tree must accept the fact that the subject will ultimately elude the filmmaker's complete control. With this example, the contingent is presented as an inescapable fact of nature. Elsewhere, Kracauer proposes a different model of contingency—a model that places contingency at the center of modern life:

> The affinity of film for haphazard contingencies is most strikingly demonstrated by its unwavering susceptibility to the "street"—a term designed to cover not only the street, particularly the city street, in the literal sense, but also its various extensions, such as railway stations, dance and assembly halls, bars, hotel lobbies, airports, etc. [. . .] Within the present context the street, which has already been

characterized as a center of fleeting impressions, is of interest as a region where the accidental prevails over the providential, and happenings in the nature of unexpected incidents are all but the rule.[1]

Here, Kracauer returns to an idea that had originally appeared in his writings from the 1920s: the idea that chance plays a particularly significant role in the modern world, with the unpredictable masses reshaping the spaces of the city.[2]

Several contemporary film scholars, such as Mary Ann Doane and James Lastra, have taken up this idea that the study of the cinema can teach us about the modern experience of contingency.[3] In this essay, I will argue that some later essays by Rudolf Arnheim can make a valuable contribution to this discussion. At first glance, the idea that Arnheim and Kracauer have such an interest in common may seem like a surprising claim. These two giants of classical film theory are usually classified as opposites, with Arnheim representing the "formative" position, and Kracauer representing the "realist."[4] While there is certainly merit to this opposition, we should also remember that the two theorists were in dialogue with each other. By 1960, Kracauer had adopted Arnheim's passion for medium specificity. Meanwhile, several of Arnheim's writings from the 1950s and 1960s suggest that Arnheim had at least partially adopted Kracauer's idea that photography and film have a special affinity for the accidental. Taking a closer look at those writings can help us understand how Arnheim's ideas had developed in the years since he wrote *Film as Art*. More importantly, these writings propose a useful distinction between films that merely capture contingency, and films that thematize contingency. With his rare gift for stylistic analysis, Arnheim can help us see what a film about contingency might look like.

In comparison with the essays in *Film as Art*, Arnheim's post-war essays are much more explicit in their attempts to situate the analysis of film within a psychological and philosophical framework. For this reason, I want to start by summarizing his general theoretical position, as articulated in various works from this later period. The central premise of his theory is simple: "perception is the discovery of structure."[5] In an essay from 1947, he explains:

> The elementary processes of perception, far from being mere passive registration, are creative acts of grasping structure, even beyond the mere grouping and selecting of parts. What happens in perception is similar to what at a higher psychological level is described as understanding or insight. Perceiving is abstracting in that it represents individual cases through configurations of general categories.[6]

When we see an object, on this account, we do not simply see its surface appearance. We also see generalized patterns. Perhaps we see that it is a square. Perhaps we see that it is off-center. Perhaps we see that it has a diagonal orientation. The structures that we see will vary from object to object, and they may even vary from person to person, but any act of visual perception worthy of the name will involve seeing some sort of generalized structure.

Significantly, Arnheim often explains his theory of perception by contrasting it with an alternative theory: the idea that perception is a mechanical recording of the world. A mechanical recording is passive, but Arnheim insists that true perception is active. In other words, a mechanical recording simply captures the world's contingent details, whereas perception allows us to see the world's lawlike properties. We perceive a generalized structure amid a confusing mass of irrelevant particulars. As we shall see, this rejection of "mechanical recording" will shape his response to photography and film.

Arnheim's discussion of structure raises certain philosophical questions. Are these structures determined by the objective features of the world itself? Or are they imposed on the world by the perceiver? On the one hand, Arnheim insists that he is talking about perceptions. Patterns do not become structures until a perceiver sees them, and different perceivers may see different structures in the world. On the other hand, Arnheim consistently rejects absolute relativism as an option. Perception is a form of insight; seeing a pattern can give us a genuine understanding of the world. At the risk of oversimplifying Arnheim's account, we might summarize this view by saying that the world is theorized as a vast set of *potential* patterns—patterns that are more or less available to perception depending on the circumstances.[7]

Arnheim adds another layer of complexity to this model by introducing an important component: art. In a later essay, he writes:

> The organizational principles that govern perception in the nervous system are one of the three constituents of human cognition. The second is the objective structure of physical reality, as conveyed to the mind through the senses. [...] The third constituent is especially pertinent to the arts. It has to do with the properties of the media through which cognitive experience takes shape.[8]

This is an interactive model: each component can have an impact on all the others. The world has a countless number of potential patterns. A successful artwork has a form that will allow the perceiver to see a certain pattern. Because the world has so many potential patterns, Arnheim maintains that we should not measure the worth of an artwork by a single standard of realism. Instead, he celebrates a wide variety of artworks—from Tintoretto to Picasso, from museum art to children's art—because he believes that all of these forms can perform the function of discovering a potential pattern in the world. An original artwork might even allow us to see a pattern that we have never seen before.

For the purposes of clarity, it might be useful to draw a distinction between form and structure. The work of art has a *form* that allows the perceiver to discover a *structure* in the world. That form will vary from artwork to artwork, depending on the characteristics of the medium. Indeed, this explains why it is a good thing to have different media in the first place. Because each medium employs different forms, each medium allows us to perceive different structures. The fact that each artwork can reveal a different structure helps explain why Arnheim argues that the artwork *interprets* its subject. There can be many different interpretations of a subject, though some interpretations are more insightful than others. A good interpretation will look beyond the specific details of the subject and reveal a generalized structure. A bad interpretation will arbitrarily impose a structure on the subject. A work that simply records the subject's external appearance runs the risk of offering no interpretation at all.[9]

Given that film is, in some sense, a mechanical recording of the world, it was bound to occupy an ambiguous position in Arnheim's aesthetic theory. The problem is not simply that a mechanical art would fail to meet aesthetic standards of creativity or originality. The problem is even deeper. A purely mechanical art could fail to accomplish art's essential function: creating a form that helps us see structure. In *Film as Art*, Arnheim resolves this dilemma by arguing that film is not just a technique of mechanical reproduction. In a famous passage, he writes, "Art begins where mechanical reproduction leaves off, where the conditions of representation serve in some ways to mold the object."[10] If film were simply mechanical, it could not be art. Fortunately, film has other resources that give the artist the necessary tools to create meaningful form.[11]

Decades later, Arnheim looked back on this argument and admitted that he could have resolved his dilemma in a different way:

> In a sense it was a negative approach because it defended the new medium by measuring it with the standards of the traditional ones—that is, by pointing to the range of interpretation it offered the artist, very much like painting and sculpture, in spite of its mechanical nature. Only secondarily was I concerned with the positive virtues that photography derives precisely from the mechanical quality of its images.[12]

This reference to the "positive virtues" of photography's mechanical nature is surprising. Arnheim had long argued that a purely mechanical work of art would inevitably capture the contingent features of the world, failing to reveal any kind of lawful, generalized structure. In so doing, a mechanical work would simply accept the world's accidental appearances, refusing to offer a fresh interpretation. How could Arnheim find any positive virtue in such a work? Accidents obscure the orderliness of the world. An artist who relies on accident as a compositional principle may fail to provide the form that is needed for the revelation of structure.

Without ever abandoning this argument, in later essays Arnheim shows a willingness to modify his initial assessment. The idea that art must reveal structure is still the core of his aesthetic theory, but this one rule cannot explain everything that art has to offer. Instead, Arnheim proposes that the search for order must be balanced by another principle: the search for complexity. He writes, "Order and complexity are antagonistic, in that order tends to reduce complexity while complexity tends to reduce order. [. . .] Order and complexity, however, cannot exist without each other. Complexity without order produces confusion; order without complexity produces boredom."[13] It is fairly easy to create a painting with a high degree of order; all you need to do is paint a square. The problem is that such a simple painting might not produce a new way of seeing the world. By increasing the complexity of the work, the artist can refresh our experience of seeing. The trick is to increase complexity without losing the sense of order that gives art its purpose. Note that Arnheim makes this argument at a very high level of generality. The conflict between order and complexity is supposed to shape the development of all art, in all media.

In an important essay from 1957, "Accident and the Necessity of Art," Arnheim narrows down this general argument by examining a variety of ways that an artist can use "accidents" to increase or decrease the complexity of a work.[14] He begins the essay by admitting that his theory would appear to leave no place for contingency:

> Offhand, the use of accident would seem to be the very opposite of what the artist is expected to do, since one of the functions of art is that of discovering order, law, and necessity in the seemingly irrational world of our experience.[15]

Arnheim goes on to modify this observation by noting that the strategic use of accident could be one way to increase the work's complexity.

> Under the impact of reality, art, too, develops toward more and more complex patterns in order to take care of the variety of appearances and the peculiarities of the individual mind. In Western art, growing complexity takes the form of increasing realism.[16]

An interest in the surface appearance of things necessarily involves an interest in contingency: each individual person will inevitably depart from the "typical" structure of a person in various unpredictable ways. At its best, Western art uses its concern with appearances to add some refreshing complexity to its forms. At its worst, Western art treats the task of capturing appearances as an end in itself, losing sight of the fact that the artist must find a way to balance the opposing principles of order and complexity. This argument opens a space (admittedly, a rather limited space) for contingency in art. Used correctly, contingency creates complexity.

Arnheim does not fully explain why so many post-Renaissance Western artists made the mistake of thinking that the capturing of appearances was the primary function of art. However, in a few striking passages, Arnheim does suggest that the explanation has something to do with modernity. In contrast to theorists like Benjamin or Kracauer, we do not normally think of Arnheim as a thinker with much to say about modernity. As a gestalt psychologist, he was much more interested in explaining art's relationship to the universal features of the human mind. To suggest that human psychology changed substantially from epoch to epoch was antithetical to his approach. Still, Arnheim was consistently interested in the ways that different cultures produced different forms, allowing people to perceive different structures in the world. As such, he was willing to entertain the idea that we can explain certain trends in the history of Western art by seeing them as responses to modernity.[17]

Specifically, he argues that we can explain the increasing realism of Western art as a response to the increasing ephemerality of modern life. In *Art and Visual Perception*, he writes:

> The modern artist was heir to a tradition that had come to identify an object with its pictorial projection. The correctness of the projection seemed to guarantee the validity of the image. Later, in the nineteenth century, such representation was found to be one-sided, subjective, accidental—which at first occasioned applause, and then apprehension. Although the fleeting images aptly reflected the passing and superficial experiences that had come to typify the life of Western man, the world represented by these images began to look alarmingly insubstantial. Artists were exposing the fact that in relation to reality, modern man was sentenced to catching nothing but glimpses.[18]

The precise meaning of this argument is not necessarily clear. Perhaps Arnheim believes that modernity, with its insistence on newness, has encouraged people to see the world without looking for eternal structures. Or perhaps he believes that the modern environment is a complex, unpredictable space that defies our attempts to make sense of it. In any case, it is clear that Arnheim is in a dialogue with an important tradition of thinking that examines the ways that modernity has changed our experience of time and space. Drawing on this tradition, Arnheim offers a symptomatic interpretation of Western perspective: as life grows more ephemeral, artists pay more attention to the accidental surface features of the world. Realism increases the complexity of Western art, at the expense of order.

Some artists take this process a step farther, creating seemingly disorganized images that offer an insightful *interpretation* of modern life. In "Accident and the Necessity of Art," Arnheim cites Degas as a model for this approach. Analyzing Degas's 1873 painting *Cotton Market in New Orleans*, Arnheim writes, "Viewed with the eyes of the pictorial tradition, these figures may appear scattered over the canvas at random." Such disorder would normally be the mark of an unsuccessful artwork. However, Arnheim goes on, "The composition ceases to appear accidental and instead becomes compelling and unchangeable as soon as we recognize that the lack of a common purpose, the atomization of society in an age of individualism, is precisely the theme of these pictures."[19] The appearance of accident is just a strategy to reveal a deeper structure: the atomization of society. Arnheim's analysis here is historically specific; the composition looks disorganized in comparison with previous strategies of composition. A later viewer might see the painting in a different way. However, taking the historical context into account, we can see that the painting does what a painting is supposed to do, enabling viewers to see a deeper structure in the world.

After the period of Degas, many artists turned toward abstraction. In an essay on modern art, Arnheim argues that the turn to abstraction was also a symptomatic response to ephemerality. Referring to the typical abstract painter, he writes:

> His work is abstract because he has abstracted himself. His mind is not a clean slate; it is full of relinquished memories and trained in all the trickeries of the civilized intellect. Simple shapes are a refuge from unmanageable complica- tion and a barbarian refreshment to the tired Alexandrian palate. Furthermore, the artist as a sensitive observer and citizen is subject to the disorder, violence, and ghostliness of modern life, and his traumas are reflected in his work.[20]

The modern world has become so complex and disorganized that the artist must use art to restore a vanishing sense of form. Although Arnheim is usually a champion of modern art, here he criticizes modern art as an escape from an overly refined, decadent society.

Photography represents a different response to the same cultural development. Instead of rejecting the increasing ephemerality of modern life, the photographer embraces it, capturing contingent moments in all their disorganized complexity. Arnheim's account of this development is nuanced—and surprising. He explains his response most fully in the 1963 essay "Melancholy Unshaped," a review of Kracauer's *Theory of Film*.[21] We might expect Arnheim to have written a scalding review of Kracauer's theory. These two giants of classical film theory are typically classified as opposites. Even if we look beyond the traditional formative/realist split, we can find several other salient distinctions. Kracauer is far less concerned with the question of whether film is an art. If anything, he argues that film offers a mode of understanding that traditional art cannot offer.[22] Meanwhile, Arnheim's interest in the universal features of psychology would seem to be at odds with Kracauer's interest in experiences that are specific to modernity. While there is certainly merit to all of these oppositions, we find in this review that Arnheim is actually willing to adopt some of Kracauer's ideas—at least partially. In fact, Arnheim explicitly endorses Kracauer's primary argument:

> Kracauer's presentation may call for correction and clarification, but the core of his thesis is surely valid and important: The photographic medium has made its most significant contribution by depicting the world, more extremely than ever has been done before, as an unbound, loosely knit continuum.[23]

While Arnheim maintains the ambivalent stance he had outlined in *Film as Art*, the source of that ambivalence has changed. Previously, Arnheim had argued that the artist had to work against film's capacity for mechanical reproduction. Here, Arnheim argues that the artist must work with that capacity.

Now, the challenge is to use mechanical reproduction in such a way that the work makes a meaningful statement about the modern world. Unfortunately, it is all too easy to get distracted by surface appearances.

> "Modern man" is immensely better informed about the epidermis of the world at large, the appearance of what goes on; but we have good reasons to call him less wise than his counterpart of the prephotographic era. The addicts of photography seem highly distracted. They think less well. Their ever stimulated curiosity makes them lose themselves in the capillaries of the particular rather than move on the mainstream of life. Photographic information, potentially a magnificent source of knowledge, seems to serve as a powerful distraction from insight.[24]

Arnheim has certainly not accepted all of Kracauer's ideas. Arnheim scoffs at the idea of distraction, an idea that had once played a major role in Kracauer's thinking.[25] For Arnheim, the purpose of art is to produce insight, by allowing us to see orderly structures in the chaotic world of appearances.

148

When a film simply duplicates contingent appearances, it fails to fulfill art's essential function.

This is a pessimistic analysis, but Arnheim suggests that the filmmaker has another option: using the compositional resources of photography to produce an insightful *interpretation* of the increasingly disorganized state of modern life. This is not the same thing as accepting the appearance of the world. Instead, the filmmaker adopts the same strategy used by Degas, creating potentially confusing images that are actually carefully crafted to allow the spectator to see the increased complexity as an expression of the modern world's bewildering complexity. The filmmaker is still producing form—it is just a more open form that is well suited to the theme.

What would such a film look like? Unfortunately, Arnheim does not give us a detailed answer, but he does suggest that the neorealist classic *Umberto D.* (Vittorio De Sica, 1952) strikes the right balance between order and complexity. He writes:

> In De Sica's *Umberto D.*, the im-pertinence of the lonely man's environment is characterized with all the precision of aesthetic economy. Such Neorealism is profoundly different from the amorphousness of a photographic reality recorded mechanically and at random. The "open form"— to use H. Wölfflin's term—is characterized in the arts by a less direct dependence of the composition on the central theme. It works with an abundance of material rather than with scarcity, with coordination rather than subordination. However, the difference between open form and closed form—or between the epic and dramatic style—must not be misinterpreted as a difference between one kind of composition controlled by the criteria of unity and necessity and another using "free" material, undetermined by function.[26]

Borrowing the idea of "open form" from Heinrich Wölfflin, Arnheim argues that an open composition rejects the obvious hierarchies that organize all the visual elements around a central subject. Instead, an open composition emphasizes its own complexity, encouraging us to notice diversity rather than unity. The contrast between open and closed form has a structural equivalent in the contrast between epic and dramatic styles of narration. Whereas the dramatic style shows a character tackling and solving a problem, the epic style strings together a loose sequence of episodes. The former style emphasizes unity; the latter, complexity.[27] However, Arnheim does not want us to take this concern for complexity too far. We must remember that the complexity gets unified at a higher level, as an interpretation that turns the apparent disorder into a sharp critique of modern life.

Although Arnheim does not offer a detailed analysis, he does give us some suggestive hints, proposing that *Umberto D.* expresses its ideas by using compositions that lack the hierarchical structure we normally expect to find in a more conventionally organized film. Some examples from the film might suggest what Arnheim has in mind.

In Figure 8.1, Umberto and his dog Flike walk by a group of men working under scaffolding. Here, we see several familiar traits of the neorealist style: a real location, natural lighting, non-actors, and deep-focus photography. The image is packed with detail. A realist critic might say that these details force us to scan the image the way we would scan the real world, look-ing for meanings that are not pre-given. Arnheim would agree that the abundance of detail encourages us to scan the image, but he would add that this very strategy produces an important meaning. Amidst all this detail, Umberto cannot dominate the composition the way we would expect a protagonist to do. Rather, he is surrounded by a sea of details, details that have no visible relationship to his life. This is what Arnheim means when he writes that the open form "works with an abundance of material rather than with scarcity, with coordination rather than subordination." A subordinated image is a hierarchical image, allowing the most important figure to dominate the frame. A coordinated image is one where no single figure assumes a place at the top of the hierarchy. Here, Umberto must compete with the young workers for our attention, and the composition expresses his insignificance in the contemporary urban environment.

Figure 8.1 In *Umberto D.*, the "open form" expresses Umberto's insignificance in the urban environment. Frame enlargement

As Arnheim suggests, the open form is not chaotic. De Sica has not abandoned his directorial responsibilities, and we do not need to search a random array to find Umberto. He is easy to spot, isolated on the left side of the frame. We compare him with the more energetic figures on the right because the similarity in scale encourages us to make such a comparison. In short, compositional factors work to express the theme regarding Umberto's increasing irrelevance. To the extent that the image does contain accidental details, they contribute to this expressive strategy. However much the image is staged, a photograph of such a location will inevitably capture a world of contingent details. No production designer could possibly control every piece of metal and stone; no director could possibly predict each gesture of every extra in the frame. For Arnheim, these contingencies would only add to the intended effect, underlining the city's "im-pertinence," its unconcern for Umberto's human needs.

De Sica employs similar compositional strategies throughout the film, putting Umberto in positions where he cannot dominate the frame. For instance, De Sica often chooses to show Umberto in group shots, whereas another director might have preferred to use a more hierarchical close-up. After the police break up the pensioners' march, there is a three-person scene with Umberto and two other men. While one of these men is typically shown in a single, Umberto is presented in a two-shot. In the public dining hall, Umberto attempts to sell his watch to a man in glasses. The man in glasses gets his own shot, but Umberto is often shown in a wider shot, framed with the bearded man who will eventually buy the watch in the next scene. Later, Umberto goes to the pound to look for his dog Flike. The bureaucrat at the pound is shown in a single, but Umberto appears in a two-shot, next to a sad-looking man in a mustache. Of course, the film does include several singles of Umberto, but the group framing strategy is consistent enough to emerge as a motif. Even in the scene showing a solitary Umberto contemplating suicide while riding the bus, De Sica includes an image of Umberto noticing the lonely, nameless man sitting next to him.

All four scenes are about contingency. At the most basic level, each scene represents a random encounter. These random meetings underline the idea that the modern city is a space of ephemeral contact, rather than meaningful relationships. Indeed, there is a downward progression to the four scenes. In the first two examples, Umberto goes on to have a dialogue scene with the man in question. In the pound scene, Umberto barely acknowledges the man with the mustache, but we later learn that the man is facing an identical sort of crisis. On the bus, we never learn anything about the other man, who remains an anonymous member of the crowd. We have moved from two examples of ephemeral contact to a missed opportunity for contact, and then to no contact at all. At the same time, the narrative's emphasis on randomness serves to underline Umberto's powerlessness. In a classical film, character goals cause the most significant events. Here, the human agent is powerless to effect change, since so many events occur because of random chance.

More abstractly, the theme of contingency operates at the level of narration. The film tells the story of Umberto, but it constantly reminds us that it could be telling us someone else's story. He is just one of many other pensioners, each of whom could have an equally compelling tale. The opening scene hints at this idea, by picking Umberto out of a crowd. Occasionally, the film even leaves Umberto for a while to follow an alternative storyline, as in the pound scene, when the camera stays in the room with the sad-looking man after Umberto has left the screen. More famously, we spend a few minutes watching the maid Maria go about her morning routine. The idea that the film could be telling Maria's story instead—or the story of the sad-looking man with the mustache, or the story of the man on the bus—does not diminish the importance of Umberto's story. Rather, in a spirit of humanism, it reminds us that the world is full of stories worth being told. In other words, Umberto is worthy of our attention, but not because he is special. He is worthy of our attention because all people are worthy of our attention.[28]

Figure 8.2 shows an image from the pound scene, with Umberto standing in front of the sad-looking man. The composition is certainly not random: the tight framing and the simplified background ensure that we will keep our attention on the faces of the two men. At the same time, there is a certain "openness" to the composition.

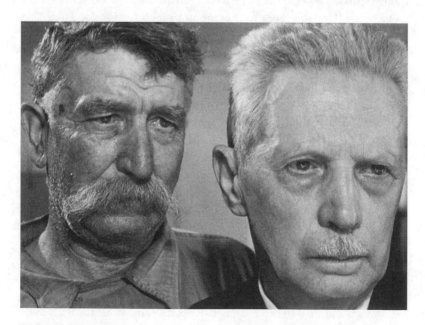

Figure 8.2 The composition gives almost equal weight to Umberto and a minor character. Frame enlargement

Umberto is a bit closer and a bit brighter, but the hierarchy is ultimately weak. Instead, the composition encourages us to look back and forth between the two men, noticing all the subtle details in their faces. We recognize that this apparently simple image contains an "abundance of detail"—from the style of their hair to the texture of their skin. Here, our awareness that the film is a neorealist film plays an important role. Without losing the thread of the story, we can appreciate that these are the faces of real people—faces that have been shaped by their own contingent experiences. This adds another layer to the film's thematization of contingency. Just as the film asks us to believe that it could be telling someone else's story, it asks us to recognize that the camera could be showing us someone else's face—perhaps the face of the sad-looking man, or perhaps any other face drawn from the contingent world beyond the frame. We should leave the theater with a newfound willingness to pay attention to people we might otherwise overlook.

The "open form" appears several times in *Umberto D*. However, this is not the only aspect of the film's compositional style that seems relevant to Arnheim's analysis. Significantly, these open compositions are often combined with closed compositions that do the reverse: taking characters whom we would not expect to be central, and allowing them to dominate the frame. The scene depicting Maria's morning routine is celebrated as the ultimate example of the neorealist urge to document the everyday, but the style of the scene is remarkably forceful. The sequence begins with a strongly hierarchical image. In Figure 8.3, the lines of perspective converge on Umberto, while the relatively wide-angle lens makes Maria look small.

Figure 8.3 A hierarchical composition with Umberto in a prominent position. Frame enlargement

Umberto exits the scene, and, to our surprise, the film stays with Maria. Some of the compositions are open, encouraging us to view Maria in the context of her environment, but many shots allow Maria to dominate the composition. One shot is a sweeping dolly move that amplifies Maria's movement to the window. A few moments later, the camera dollies in to a medium-close-up of Maria as she contemplates her pregnancy.

Figure 8.4 shows the culmination of this second dolly move. The dolly-in works together with several other strategies to draw our attention to Maria. A gentle backlight separates Maria from the background, and there is a tiny point of light adding sparkle to each eye. Maria is in crisp focus, while the background goes soft. In a reversal of Figure 8.3, the lines of perspective converge towards Maria. This is not an "open form" composition—and that is precisely the point. Figure 8.4 almost looks like a Hollywood close-up, with the significant caveat that we never lose our awareness that this is a real person placed in the center of this composition. Just as the film occasionally uses the open form to de-emphasize a character who should be the center of attention (the protagonist Umberto), the film here uses a more assertive style of composition to demand that we notice Maria, a character who would normally be marginalized on both a narrative and compositional level. This is the sort of precision that Arnheim is discussing. Rather than allow reality to unfold randomly, the film takes elements from the real world and places them within carefully crafted compositions, subtly shifting from the open form to the closed form to balance our awareness of Umberto's story with an awareness of other faces and other spaces.

Figure 8.4 Later in the sequence, the camera dollies in toward Maria, as focus and lighting separate her from the background

The fact that Arnheim has chosen a neorealist film as his example is evidence of the freshness of his approach. For many critics, there is a contradiction between the film's neorealist elements (real locations, non-actors) and its artful compositions, which seem to betray the movement's embrace of the contingent world. Arnheim argues that the skillful compositions are an important part of the film's neorealist agenda. *Umberto D.* does not just capture its real locations and non-actors for the sake of preserving their appearances. The film uses its contingent details to express a historically specific set of hopes and fears concerning the individual's place in the structure of modern life.

Before concluding, it might be useful to point to the limitations that Arnheim himself places on his own analysis. Arnheim contrasts *Umberto D.* with Antonioni's *L'Avventura* (1960). While acknowledging that Antonioni has a compelling critique of modernity, Arnheim charges that Antonioni blunts the force of his critique by getting lost in a fascination with surface appearances. Instead of expressing modernity's loss of structure as a theme, the film simply unmasks Antonioni as another modern artist succumbing to the distractions of contingent details.[29] Rather than encourage us to be more fascinated with contingencies, the true film artist must create a structural equivalence between the contingencies captured on film and a deeper theme concerning the challenges posed by the increasingly ephemeral world. According to Arnheim, De Sica accomplishes what Antonioni does not: he manages to control contingency by thematizing it fully.

This comparison raises troubling issues about the applicability of Arnheim's theory. Most critics would argue that Antonioni is a master of composition, and a serious critic of modernity. The fact that he does not meet Arnheim's criteria indicates that they are strict criteria indeed. Arnheim certainly has thoughtful things to say about film, contingency, and modernity, but it seems fair to ask if those ideas really have any kind of broad applicability.[30] After all, if we want to read thought-provoking ideas about film, contingency, and modernity, then wouldn't we be better off sticking with Kracauer, who treats the issue in a more expansive way?

I think there are two reasons why Arnheim's ideas have an enduring value. First, Arnheim has proposed a perceptive distinction between films that accidentally capture contingent details and films that actively thematize contingency. The fact that Arnheim is overly dismissive of the first category should not negate the fact that he has some insightful things to say about the second. Filmmakers can and do make use of photographic contingencies to enrich their films' themes.

More importantly, Arnheim reminds us that the analysis of contingency can and should also involve the analysis of visual style. Here, he contrasts with Kracauer in a revealing way. In *Theory of Film*, Kracauer rarely analyzes visual style; instead, he offers a complicated taxonomy explaining which kinds of films do the most justice to film's inherent affinities. Whatever the strengths of Kracauer's approach, he does not show much interest in explaining what a film really looks like. By contrast, Arnheim is always working to make us see. Like Kracauer, Arnheim believes that there is a relationship between modernity and contingency. Unlike Kracauer, Arnheim argues that certain artists have used compositional strategies to allow us to see that relationship in the visual nuances of their works. If a film has something to show us concerning the relationship between contingency and modernity, we ought to care about what that film looks like—its composition, its texture, its style.

In conclusion, I hope to have shown that Arnheim's ideas about the cinema had changed in surprising ways. Accepting Kracauer's idea that film is unusually good at capturing the accidental appearances of the world, his post-war essays argue that filmmakers can turn their medium's mechanical qualities to their advantage. Like *Umberto D.*, a film can use the open form to encourage spectators to look closely at a complex set of details, thereby making the complexity, disorder, and ephemerality of modern life newly visible. This remains a valuable lesson. Arnheim does more than just ask us to think about the relationship between contingency and modernity. He asks us to experience that relationship by seeing it.

notes

1. Siegfried Kracauer, *Theory of Film: The Redemption of Physical Reality*, Princeton: Princeton University Press, 1960, Princeton edition 1997, p. 62.
2. For more on the role of chance in Kracauer's theory of film, see Miriam Bratu Hansen, "Introduction," in Kracauer, *Theory of Film*, p. xxii.
3. See Mary Ann Doane, *The Emergence of Cinematic Time: Modernity, Contingency, the Archive*, Cambridge: Harvard University Press, 2002; and James Lastra, "From the Captured Moment to the Cinematic Image: A Transformation in Pictorial Order," in Dudley Andrew ed., *The Image in Dispute: Art and Cinema in the Age of Photography*, Austin: University of Texas Press, 1997, pp. 263–292.
4. For a classic presentation of this view, see Dudley Andrew, *The Major Film Theories: An Introduction*, New York: Oxford University Press, 1976. For a more recent discussion of the contrast between Arnheim and Kracauer, see Ara H. Merjian, "Middlebrow Modernism: Rudolf Arnheim at the Crossroads of Film Theory and the Psychology of Art," in Angela Dalle Vacche ed., *The Visual Turn: Classical Film Theory and Art History*, New Brunswick: Rutgers University Press, 2003, pp. 154–192.
5. Rudolf Arnheim, *New Essays on the Psychology of Art*, Berkeley: University of California Press, 1986, p. 253. In the original passage, the word "is" is italicized.
6. Arnheim, *Toward a Psychology of Art*, Berkeley: University of California Press, 1966, p. 33.
7. Arnheim wrestles with these difficult philosophical questions in *New Essays on the Psychology of Art*. See, in particular, "The Double-Edged Mind: Intuition and the Intellect," pp. 13–30, and "Objective Percepts, Objective Values," pp. 297–326.
8. Arnheim, *New Essays on the Psychology of Art*, p. xi.

9. For further discussion of the relationship between art and visual understanding in Arnheim's theories, see Malcolm Turvey's essay, "Arnheim and Modernism," included in this volume (Chapter 2).

10. Rudolf Arnheim, *Film as Art*, Berkeley: University of California Press, 1957, p. 57. The 1957 edition is a revised and condensed version of material originally written in the 1930s.

11. For a thorough discussion of Arnheim's theory in *Film as Art*, see Noël Carroll, *Philosophical Problems of Classical Film Theory*, Princeton: Princeton University Press, 1988.

12. Arnheim, *New Essays on the Psychology of Art*, p. 108.

13. Arnheim, *Toward a Psychology of Art*, p. 124. Although the passage is taken from an essay on landscape design, many of Arnheim's observations in this essay seem relevant to film. Maureen Turim also cites this essay in "Visual Thinking of the Avant-Garde Film," included in this volume (Chapter 9).

14. Rudolf Arnheim, "Accident and the Necessity of Art," in *Toward a Psychology of Art*, pp. 162–180.

15. Arnheim, *Toward a Psychology of Art*, p. 163.

16. Ibid.

17. Some of the other essays in this volume argue persuasively that Arnheim was always more interested in social context than is generally acknowledged. See, for instance, Eric Rentschler, "Rudolf Arnheim's Early Passage between Social and Aesthetic Film Criticism," and Shawn VanCour, "Arnheim on Radio: *Materialtheorie* and Beyond."

18. Rudolf Arnheim, *Art and Visual Perception: A Psychology of the Creative Eye*, Berkeley: University of California Press, 1954, The New Version, 1974, p. 132.

19. Arnheim, *Toward a Psychology of Art*, p. 167.

20. Ibid., p. 347.

21. Rudolf Arnheim, "Melancholy Unshaped," in *Toward a Psychology of Art*, pp. 181–191.

22. See Heide Schlüpmann, "The Subject of Survival: On Kracauer's *Theory of Film*," *New German Critique* 54, Fall 1991, p. 116.

23. Arnheim, *Toward a Psychology of Art*, p. 186.

24. Ibid., p. 187.

25. The concept of "distraction" was an important component of Kracauer's theories in the 1920s. See Siegfried Kracauer, *The Mass Ornament: Weimar Essays*, trans. and ed. Thomas Y. Levin, Cambridge: Harvard University Press, 1995. See also Heide Schlüpmann, "Phenomenology of Film: On Siegfried Kracauer's Writings of the 1920s," *New German Critique* 40, Winter 1987, pp. 97–114.

26. Arnheim, *Toward a Psychology of Art*, p. 188.

27. Drawing on an essay by Goethe, Arnheim had first proposed the distinction between epic and dramatic films in an unpublished essay from 1934. He translated the essay and published it for the first time in *Film Culture* in 1957. See Rudolf Arnheim, *Film Essays and Criticism*, trans. Brenda Benthien, Madison: University of Wisconsin Press, 1997, pp. 78–81. See also Heinrich Wölfflin, *Principles of Art History: The Problem of the Development of Style in Later Art*, trans. M. D. Hottinger, New York: Dover Publications, 1950.

28. I have discussed this aspect of *Umberto D.*'s humanism in another essay. See Patrick Keating, "The Fictional Worlds of Neorealism," *Criticism* 45.1, 2003, pp. 11–30.

29. Arnheim, *Toward a Psychology of Art*, pp. 188–189.

30. See Merjian, "Middlebrow Modernism," pp. 172–177.

visual thinking of

the avant-garde film

n i n e

m a u r e e n   t u r i m

Let me begin with the first lines of Rudolf Arnheim's "To Maya Deren," an essay first published in *Film Culture* in 1962, as a eulogy to the filmmaker he admired:

> There is a photograph of Maya Deren, so striking and so well known that some of us think of it when we think of her. It is taken from a scene of her film *Meshes of the Afternoon* and shows a girl looking out through a window. Those who knew her recognize her, and yet the image is not really she. Her face is transformed into photographic matter.[1]

This stunning opening paragraph not only mourns in elegant terms the admired film artist whom Arnheim had come to know in New York City, it does so by recalling the author's main argument in his foundational work of film theory, *Film as Art*, first published in Germany in 1932.[2] While able to appreciate film's mimesis creating the "almost physical immediacy" of the mourned artist, Arnheim argues that it is not through its representational realism that it achieves its art.[3] Rather it is in defamiliarization, abstraction, and self-aware foregrounding of film's material differences from reality that film art emerges for Arnheim.

Thus Maya Deren recorded herself with the "authenticity of a fingerprint," an invocation on Arnheim's part of the indexical sign, the "noisier and more spectacular" property of the cinema, poignantly evoked here as a "miracle" supplying "even now, after her death, . . . the figure of Maya Deren."[4] Having called to mind this image reimagined as a death mask, Arnheim will go on to speak of the "quieter, but more magical" qualities of Deren's image as art and magic, for her face yields a transparent whiteness as abstraction, her hair disappears in reflections, and her raised hand signals the window pane from its invocative absence.

It is no wonder that Arnheim, who was one of the first to highlight theoretically the abstract and expressive qualities of the film image's formal properties, should find Deren's films so important. Her vision of film, articulated in "An Anagram of Ideas on Art, Form and Film," closely corresponds in many respects to his.[5] Unlike the filmic German expressionists, whom Arnheim had long critiqued for such films as *Das Cabinet des Dr. Caligari* (*The Cabinet of Dr. Caligari*) that departed from indexical signs of the real, Deren's images depend on perception of spaces that are rendered mimetically, even while temporality, and the juxtapositioning of events unfolding in these spaces, defies the logic of physical reality.[6] As Arnheim says, Deren's delicate magic could be distinguished from both surrealism and expressionism in terms that he had long advocated:

> Of crude magicians we have had many. Some call themselves surrealists, although, instead of going beyond reality, they merely add a few tricks to it . . . Others—the expressionist kind of miracle worker—have invaded our prosaic space with wild make-up and crooked scenery. Maya Deren had little patience with either technique. She insisted that the true magic of the photograph in motion is more than a re-shuffling of raw material, more than a masquerade. And she, who could be energetic to the point of violence when she fought for her ideas, had the sensitive fingers and eyes of a surgeon when it came to shaping her photographic visions without damaging the tissues of the physical surface.[7]

160

Arnheim holds, then, to what he takes to be film's invigorating paradox, which he expresses economically in the opening paragraph of this eulogy: to be able to depict physical reality while mining the differences imposed by what he called the medium's "limitations" in reproducing reality, its formal constraints, enumerated as framing, two-dimensionality, lighting, black and white, and the cut.

When Arnheim goes on to ask "Do these pictures show us more than the alienation of the familiar?" he evokes without direct reference Viktor

Shklovsky's Russian formalist theory of defamiliarization, which often runs through his writing on the visual arts.[8] Yet here he suggests in his rhetorical question something beyond defamiliarization to be appreciated in Deren. He lauds her attention to the relationship between ritual cultures and high art interventions. Deren's "picture language," which Arnheim calls "half-shrouded in personal meanings and half-revealed by common sensation," is celebrated for its "call" to us.[9]

That this eulogy was written for *Film Culture*, the journal edited by Jonas Mekas that in the sixties heralded both the U.S. avant-garde and the European art film, indicates how Arnheim during his New York period was involved in this film scene, even while no longer often writing about film. Consider the traces of Arnheim's involvement. It is telling that Mekas, recalling his arrival in NYC from Lithuania in 1949 speaks of "the second or third evening upon arriving in New York," attending screening of *The Cabinet of Dr. Caligari* and *The Fall of the House of Usher* sponsored by the New York Film Society, "run at that time by Rudolf Arnheim," though I have been unable to verify this memory.[10]

Mekas then discusses the Cinema 16 Film Society, started in 1947 by Amos Vogel, a Viennese refugee and his wife, with screenings held at the Provincetown Playhouse in New York City, which was indeed a forum at which Arnheim would interact with the U.S. avant-garde.[11] When Vogel turned to organizing the New York Film Festival, Arnheim served on the jury for its 1960 Creative Film Awards.[12] In 1966 the special issue of *Film Culture* devoted to the New York Film Festival reprinted Arnheim's address to the festival "Art Today and the Film" that was also published in *Art Journal*, and later anthologized in *The Film Culture Reader*.[13] Further, one can see the impact of Arnheim's theories on the writing of Amos Vogel; for example, Vogel's "Thirteen Confusions," first published in *Evergreen Review* in 1976, chastises attitudes that crippled the advancement of film art and demonstrates his affinity for Arnheim.[14] Section 12 admonishes "Confusing Literary Critics with Visual Critics" while naming Arnheim as the type of visually aware critic the avant-garde film needs, as opposed to more verbally oriented critics whose sensitivities are only to language and narrative.[15] Similarly, at the 1966 New York Film Festival, Georg Amberg, who presented a talk entitled "Cinevision, the Acquired Perceptual Proficiency of Film," was asked by an audience member after his presentation what more he could recommend one read on this subject, to which Amberg replied "the most illuminating is [Arnheim's] *Art and Visual Perception*."[16]

Both Arnheim's "Art Today and the Film" and the Deren eulogy contain resonances that take us back to *Film as Art*. Consider how the earlier volume, in discussing the power of an anonymous close-up, presents similar arguments to the eulogy passage on the medium close-up of Deren:

> Consider the face of a blond [sic] woman in a film shot: the
> color of hair and complexion approximate to each other as

a curious pale white—even the blue eyes appear whitish; the velvety black bow of the mouth and the sharp dark pencil lines of the eyebrows are in marked contrast. How strange such a face is, how much more intense—because unconventional—is the expression, how much more attention it attracts to itself and to its expression.

Anyone who has noticed how unreal most film faces appear, how unearthly, how beautiful, how they often give the impression of being not so much a natural phenomenon as an artistic creation—which of course, the art of make-up helps considerably—will get the same pleasure from a good film face as from a good lithograph or woodcut.[17]

Arnheim's rhetoric here seems to foreshadow Roland Barthes's famous short essay, "The Face of Garbo," in *Mythologies*, even though his example here is not the famous Swedish star, but a non-specific, perhaps hypothetical, close-up on a blonde.[18] However, Arnheim does twice turn to Garbo for similar examples in *Film as Art*, once citing the lighting that delineates Garbo's face in her American films, saying "her skin has a subdued satiny luster, her eyes are extraordinarily piercing, and her soft silky hair seems to glow with a mysterious inner radiance," while later discussing the rhythm of her gait in *Grand Hotel*.[19] His Garbo essay of 1928, now reprinted in *Film Essays and Criticism*, offers another assessment of this actress's close-ups, gestures, and movements as embodying the power of visual thought.[20]

Let me link Arnheim's remarks on the cinematic close-up of the actress, and the face of Garbo cited above, to the haunting images of Kiki in *Ballet Mechanique* (1924), to those of the actress who lends her name to Joseph Cornell's *Rose Hobart* (1936), as well as to those of actors in Jack Smith's *Flaming Creatures* (1963) whose transvestism is as ethereal and transcendent. In fact, a Kiki close-up from *Ballet Mechanique* appears as Figure 91 in *Art and Visual Perception* as an example of a face seen from below, though she and the film remain unidentified.[21] Arnheim's writings speak to the sort of cinephilia that would bring together the love of cinematic greatness practiced in the revival palace with that extended toward the emerging avant-garde in New York City in the post-war period. The archival programming of the Museum of Modern Art and such venues as the Regency Theater brought back to urban audiences, as did university film societies, intense cinematic pleasure before such screenings were able to reach the masses via video and cable movie channels. This cinephilia could be characterized as that which highlights the abstraction within a moment of Hollywood seduction (the close-up on Garbo), then connects this to the pleasure of a Hollywood citation within a moment of avant-garde experimentation (as in *Rose Hobart*).

Another aspect of *Film as Art* that resonates with the filmic avant-garde is Arnheim's concern with the film strip. His summary section, entitled "Of the Formative Means of Camera and Film Strip," is notable for its emphasis on film material, the strip of images, particularly in his discussion of motion.[22] He uses the film strip in other passages to present the notion of framing changes across the time of a camera movement, and his discussion of Muybridge's series photographs makes it clear that he is thinking of motion as a series of framings and transformations, much in the same way avant-garde filmmakers do, as they begin to publish stills from their films as images of the film strip itself.[23]

In the introduction Arnheim added in 1957 he defends his now classic book of theory against charges of depending on dated examples by suggesting that nothing that has emerged since 1928 fundamentally differs from earlier cinematic production, except "perhaps the remarkable blossoming of the 'abstract' film—the beginning of what someday will be the great art of painting in motion."[24] This generous and optimistic statement from 1957 begs the question of the omission of this very sort of film from the original 1928 text, since Walter Ruttmann's first abstract short films, *Lichtspiel: Opus I* (1921), *Lichtspiel: Opus II* (1923), *Lichtspiel: Opus III* (1924), *Lichtspiel: Opus IV* (1925), might well have been known to Arnheim, and Viking Eggeling first showed *Symphonie Diagonale* in 1925. Still, if it took until Hans Richter began showing his films in NYC in 1957 for Arnheim to take notice, his positive appraisal in the late fifties makes his remark that would come nine years later quite telling, when in "Art Today and the Film" he says that abstract film, like abstract art in general was on the wane:

> Following the example of painting, cinema has tried the remedy of abstraction. But the experiments, from Hans Richter and Viking Eggeling, to Oskar Fischinger, Norman McClaren and Len Lye, have amounted mainly to a museum collection of venerable curiousities. This may be surprising considering the great aesthetic potential of colored shapes in motion. But since abstract painting is also on the decline, my guess is that once an artist abandons image making, he has no longer a good reason to cling to the two dimensional surface . . .[25]

Perhaps we can understand Arnheim's wild swing on film abstraction by examining how he himself tended to use the term in relation to film. Abstraction in film for Arnheim in the early writing always dealt with how abstract concepts could be addressed through the combination of concrete images of reality. Abstraction in *Film as Art* is abstract thought deriving from concrete visual representation, and for Arnheim this is a perceptual thought process. In some ways this notion draws on the Kuleshov experiments. In his essay on *The End of St. Petersburg*, Arnheim imagines the spectator walking out of Pudovkin's film continuing to see the world with the eyes of the "great film poet," forming the abstract notion "It's cold" out of hypothetical "shots" Arnheim describes in the ordinary street scene.[26] His purpose for this exercise is to prove that it is not the subject matter of revolution that lends Pudovkin his artfulness, but the carefully chosen combination of frames building towards abstract thought. In *Film as Art*, he found like means of expression in E. A. Dupont: "What is arresting, however, in Dupont's scene is that in order to symbolize the abstract it was not found necessary to interfere with reality . . ."[27] In another instance, a montage sequence is said to show the abstract substance—a cumulative tone—of scenes rather than their status as distinct events: "But superimposition is a simple way of showing the abstract substance of all of these scenes; that is, their meaning and mood rather than merely the events."[28]

It seems as if Arnheim cannot really embrace the artistry of the filmic avant-garde other than for the modes adopted by Pudovkin and Deren, the poets who imaginatively reframe and reorder realist images. Yet I find that Arnheim's later writings on art may be seen in their inspiration to an avant-garde that perhaps he should have appreciated more than he was able in the late sixties, seventies and eighties. His titles alone inspired and supported that movement, suggestive even for those who never grappled deeply with his arguments: "A psychology of the creative eye" and "visual thinking" are the types of phrases that visual artists of film found empowering. If many filmmakers of this period often eschewed a soundtrack on the grounds that visual explorations were already so complex that music or language would be interference with their purposes, and as their artwork mined the "great aesthetic potential of colored shapes in motion," Arnheim's writings on art would surely have been of interest to them.

Arnheim's gestalt art theory was first published in *Art Journal*, then reached a more general audience in 1954 with *Art and Visual Perception: A Psychology of the Creative Eye* and continued with the 1966 *Toward a Psychology of Art*.[29] Each of these was reissued in 1972 and 1974, respectively, dates that serve to remind us of the building interest of Arnheim's art theory across these decades. Through such notions as "perceptual abstraction," in which we understand space and relationships by inference, and "proportion dynamics," which describes the tensions between shapes, Arnheim teases out a theory in which art is actively perceived in time. In his essay "The Myth of a Bleeding Lamb" he briefly introduces the notion of visual thinking, as he speaks of how "perceptual abstraction lays the groundwork for perceptual thinking."[30] He then cites Einstein and Wittgenstein as support on how thoughts are not necessarily encompassed by language. Two essays in the book, "Melancholy Unshaped" and "The Holes of Henry Moore," serve to offer examples of the expression of abstract concepts indirectly, underneath language.[31] Similarly, his analysis of Picasso's "Nightfishing at Antibes" argues "The meaning of a work of visual art is contained in the property of its shapes and colors."[32] Yet he reads this painting allegorically, taking it as the "foreboding of violent, yet unknown things to come," an analysis that rests largely on the jumbled abstract shapes that comprise the less active, more contemplative of the two fishermen, whose gaze into the water speaks to unseen dangers that Arnheim links to the painting's date of August 1939. Conflict etched in space, shape, and color become useful ways of addressing Picasso, and entirely consonant with gestalt psychology, yet one senses that abstract art frees Arnheim to use other methods alongside the expressive reading of form. Besides taking into account historical context, he references other paintings (Raphael's "Mysterious Draught of the Fishes" and Piero della Francesca's "Resurrection") as well as Freudian readings of dream imagery, which here suggest for Arnheim, "the pregnancy of the water." So even as Arnheim aims, as his title announces, "toward a psychology of art," his reading practice seems to be more complexly intertexual, contextual, semiotic, and psychoanalytic in the instance in which his object departs from classical conventions of balance and order in composition.

Subsequently, reflections on shape and color take their place alongside light, form, growth, movement, tension, and expression as the elements under discussion in *Art and Visual Perception*. Filmmakers of the 1950s and 1960s who formed the avant-garde might well have read this book as confirmation of their thought processes in composing and conjoining images. Film artists were thinking about the tension between shots, the force of motion of the camera as it conjoins or detaches from the motion of the objects in the frame, the abstract configuration of wind in a window curtain's shadow, or the effect of closing down the shutter within a shot. For those for whom formal image reshapings were the means of their art, Arnheim's clear delineation of this level of formal investigation as a conduit of abstract thought could serve as affirmation. Further, they could feel that their works were learning tools, helping viewers learn to perceive and think visually, didactic purposes that align with Arnheim's writing on art education in *Art and Visual Perception*. Still, some of Arnheim's gestalt concepts might have been more ambivalently received by those of an avant-garde film aesthetic, as they invoke preferences for balance and assumptions of visual organization that were no longer the goal of innovative artists.

In that light, Arnheim's paragraph on disorder in *Toward a Psychology of Art* shows that he could voice a propensity for an orderly middle ground in art. Stronger inscriptions would lack the balance to achieve aesthetic validity:

> What is disorder? It is not the absence of all order but rather the clash of uncoordinated orders. An accumulation of pieces assumes the quality of disorder only when within each piece, or group of pieces, there appears a clearly discernible order, which however, is neither continued nor contradicted by the neighboring order but rather is ignored, denied, distorted, made incomprehensible.[33]

One wonders whether it is his immediate subject matter in this passage—landscape design—that allows him to feel so confident that the clash of

165

uncoordinated orders need be judged so definitively as negative. As complex as his notion of order might be, including as it does here order induced through the self-consciously orchestrated conflict of different orders, he seems to hold nonetheless to an ideal of harmony and balance. He seems to be quite unable to entertain a more arbitrary, random, or chaotic aesthetic at this juncture, though the entirely random and the willfully chaotic will become the pursuit of many artists, recalling similar gestures already pursued by the Dadaists. Notably, Arnheim rarely addressed Dada, so it makes sense that his address to neo-Dadaist aesthetics occurs as negative inference.

Similarly in *Art and Visual Perception* Arnheim speaks of the "order seeking mind" striving for a middle path between extremes:

> One extreme is the complete surrender on the quest for order to multiplicity . . . exemplified by illusionism. The other extreme is the complete withdrawal from multiplicity, which is defeat by the excess of order, exemplified in the empty patterns of the schizophrenic. All styles of art seem to lie somewhere between the danger zones of these two poles. A strong need for order produces the predominance of relatively simple form that is found in the classic styles. Byzantine art is an example. A leaning toward the protean variety of nature makes for the complex form found in the "romantic" styles of which projective realism is an example. Whatever the position of art between the two poles, it must draw its lifeblood from the one, and its wisdom from the other.[34]

There is a tendency on Arnheim's part to appeal to notions of balance and order, to affirm a lack of excess, even while recognizing how different historical periods tend to highlight one aspect of the structural opposition of forces, while keeping the other in check. This tendency addresses centuries prior to the twentieth better than changes that characterize the very period in which Arnheim was writing. Yet as Arnheim's notion of visual thinking continues to evolve, his task becomes less to explain the balanced aesthetics of the past. He does come to suggest that radical changes in structure and ordering principles are being thought visually.

Earlier I suggested how 1969's *Visual Thinking* lines up with the thoughts of Amos Vogel and the filmmaking of Maya Deren. We might also find correspondences to Deren's writing on film, as well as those of such filmmakers as Stan Brakhage, Paul Sharits, and Hollis Frampton, and in doing so would actually find that they tend to push Arnheim's notion of visual thinking towards a more radical proposition of thinking: the thinking of unsettling and demanding thoughts of an entirely experimental order. If the latter two examples, Sharits and Frampton, might appear to be less self-evidently

Arnheim-like in their approach, I will show how the concept of formally inspired visual thinking in all these filmmakers has a determined edge of challenge, rather than confirmation.

Deren in "An Anagram of Ideas on Art, Form and Film" emphasizes her notion of an ethics of form in which every parameter of film should be energized with thought, a process I look at in detail in an essay "The Ethics of Form: Structure and Gender in Maya Deren's Challenge to the Cinema."[35] For our purposes here, let's look at an instance in which this emphasis on form coincides with visual perception and thought. Deren, in speaking of slow motion, emphasizes enabling visual discovery particularly when the action that is subject to the slowed projection in reality had been quite rapid. She writes: "One can shake one's head from side to side at almost any speed. When a fast turning is reduced by slow motion, it still looks natural, as if it were being performed more slowly. The hair, however, moving slowly in the lifted horizontal shape possible only to rapid tempos is unnatural in quality."[36] This description evokes her slow-motion close-up in the yarn-winding scene in *Rituals in Transfigured Time* (1946), in which she, as actress, performs just such head movements. Deren wants each shot to have such visual surprises in which jarringly original combinations generate thought. So as I argue in "The Ethics of Form," "For her form constitutes those structures that take advantage of cinematic specificity and that mold reality through artifice." Another example I cite is how the woman watching over the first section of *Rituals in Transfigured Time* (Anaïs Nin) becomes an abstracted figure of triangulation, in which "The social geography of visual representation meets a geometry of form."[37] Here we are very close to Arnheim's sense in *Film as Art* that the aesthetics of the cinema rests on such manipulations of filmic parameters, and *Visual Thinking*'s attention to how spatial arrangement of objects generates thought.

Brakhage's relationship with *Visual Thinking*'s concepts is more vexed, though one associates him with highly attuned visual sensitivities. He entitled his first writing on his films *Metaphors on Vision*, presenting his films as not just the expression, but the embodiment of visual perception, as well as vision's poetic, self-conscious meta-language.[38] Yet his notion of vision is far more personally anarchic than is Arnheim's visual thought, as his famous introduction to this book incants: "Imagine an eye unruled by man-made laws of perspective, an eye unprejudiced by compositional logic, an eye which does not respond to the name of everything but which must know each object encountered in life through an adventure of perception." In seeking to make his art an analogy of vision, he explored an inner emotional darkness and haunting memories whose thoughts were also expressed visually. Still, there are ways that the rationalist visual thinker we find in Arnheim and the Romantic visual thinker we find in Brakhage intersect. Brakhage's film *The Art of Vision* (1961–1964), rather than being involved with a singular image plane, is a fugue in which superimposed layers, visual traces of his earlier film *Dog Star Man* meet in recombinatory collage. Recall Arnheim's remark on superimposition that I quoted earlier: "superimposition is a simple way of showing the abstract substance of all of these scenes; that is, their meaning and mood rather than merely the events." This points to the type of abstract poetics Brakhage engages in in *The Art of Vision*. In addressing his work with pulsing colored light in *23rd Psalm Branch: Part I* and *Part II and Coda* (1966/78) at the premiere of those films at the Filmmaker's Cinematheque in 1967, Brakhage speaks of seeking to reconstruct his memories of the World War II footage: the film serves as metaphor on memory, not simply a metaphor on visual perception, but vision construed as subjectivity, consciousness, emotions, memories, and dreams.[39] Yet paradoxically, as I have shown in discussing Arnheim's analysis of Picasso, Arnheim himself often broadens visual thinking and artistic perception in similar encompassing ways. Let me suggest that it is Arnheim's work on Picasso that would serve best as a model for how he might address Brakhage's notion of vision as inner, poetic vision able to transform the rendering of spatial and temporal visual representation.

Surprisingly, perhaps, it is Sharits who comes closer to seeking an analogue of visual thinking in his filmic practice. In speaking of the final section of *T,O,U,C,H,I,N,G* (1969) he says:

> I wanted to visualize "inverse pain" as a kind of imploding reverberation of the picture edge—the screen appears to collapse, in rhythmic pulses, into itself. This latter mode— of introducing shapes that were reflective of the film frame's perimeter shape and which acted as a commentary on the state of consciousness of the film's protagonist at that stage of the backward narrative—struck me later as being somewhat too related to the strategies of painting.[40]

Let me suggest that Arnheim is the type of thinker about the strategies of painting that seems to be informing Sharits's goal in his film. Sharits continues in this essay to talk about needing next to remove narrative representation, to have the film shapes in time become the sole form of expression in his films.

As for Frampton, in his famous essay, "A Pentagram for Conjuring the Narrative?" he asks a question reminiscent of *Visual Thinking*: "What are the irreducible axioms to that part of thought we call the art of film?"[41] His answer is threefold, culminating in his argument that due to temporal change, the film image is always narrative, in his expanded sense of that term. Before this, though, his first two points echo Arnheim, as when he says:

> The first is the visible limit of the projected image itself, the frame . . . The second is the plausibility of the photographic

illusion, since the photographic record proves to be, on examination, an extreme abstraction from its pretext, arbitrarily mapping values from a long sensory spectrum on a nominal surface.[42]

The kind of intertextuality I am formulating here may have had other causal circuits, including a body of visual works and writing about them that address such issues as the function of the frame in thought, and the thinking that enters into the discernment of pictorial space. Sharits's "imploding reverberation of the picture edge" might be the combustion of many traces of Clement Greenberg, or perhaps more graphically of Kasimir Malevich and Aleksandra Ekster. Certainly, thoughts about art and film, about visual thinking, were freely circulating, often with source citations, but just as often without.

One film that directly cited a pictorial analysis of a picture plane, albeit by another author, by framing an open book and thus displaying diagrammatic explanations of image structures, is Larry Gottheim's *Four Shadows* (1978). Chosen for this close-up is Erle Loran's *Cézanne's Composition: Analysis of his Form with Diagrams and Photographs of his Motifs*, a text that in many ways prefigures Arnheim's later work on artistic composition.[43] Loran, a painter, analyzes Cézanne's compositions, including sketching them to demonstrate their treatment of spatial planes. Gottheim's shot from the book lasts a full four minutes in each of its four iterations, becoming one of the insistent images in this highly structured film that plays with the repetition of image segments with different sound segments associated with them. The page from the book is itself photographed in bright sun that casts the shadows of leaves that move subtly in a breeze. The first image in the shot is of Cézanne's painting *House and Tree at Pontoise, 1873–74*, then the shot segments in two, temporally, as the page is turned; on the second page, Cézanne's drawn harlequin walks forward on the stage that surrounds him, out of the picture frame. This diagram of motion is the echo of the motion of the actual page of the book turning in the light and shadow.

Four Shadows performs a comparative analysis of the formal structures of the image—four sets of four-minute image segments are repeated against four sets of soundtracks, one of which is silence, creating sixteen variations in all for its sixty-four-minute duration. Gottheim asks the viewer to compare the types of thoughts that occur within the film frame for these slices of time. Gottheim asks what is a visual event, and what are the parameters of its unfolding?

We might take this film as a response to Arnheim's *Visual Thinking*, as well as an auditory retort to those who would argue against troubling visual thoughts by sound juxtapositions, as it is precisely the shifting conjunctions and disjunctions that compel both visual and auditory thought in this highly conceptual framework.

Arnheim's later work itself brings a new emphasis to structure, corresponding to a moment in art and filmmaking that, like *Four Shadows*, is increasingly self-conscious about structure. Arnheim introduces entropy and conflict as defining principles. His 1971 *Entropy and Art: An Essay on Disorder and Order* may be read as reacting to a political atmosphere of upheaval, including protests against racial discrimination and the war in Vietnam, for he prefaces the book by talking about it as a reaction to strife in the world.[44]

"Why would experiments in perception show that the mind organizes visual patterns spontaneously in such a way that the simplest available structure results?"[45] Arnheim asks, entertaining some far-reaching gestalt-oriented speculation on human preference for order. Still, he complicates this argument by turning to physics:

> The vision of such harmonious striving for order throughout nature is disturbingly contradicted by one of the most influential statements on the behavior of physical forces, namely, the Second Law of Thermodynamics. The most general account physicists are willing to give of changes in time is often formulated to mean that the material world moves from orderly states to an ever-increasing disorder and that the final situation of the universe will be one of maximal disorder.[46]

Arnheim thus will juxtapose the two discourses:

> Physicists speak of entropy as a tendency towards disorder when they have their minds set on the catabolic destruction of form. Gestalt theorists, on the other hand, concentrate on situations in which a disorderly or relatively less orderly constellation of forces is free and indeed compelled to become more orderly.[47]

Grappling with tendencies in modern art that subvert conventional notions of order, Arnheim turns to the writing of Jean Arp:

> In a crucial period of his life Arp found himself moving from the extreme of "impersonal, severe structures," intended to eliminate the burden of personal experience, to the forsaking of defined form and the acceptance of dissolution ... It was the work of a fellow-artist, his wife Sophie Taeuber, that showed him "the fine balance between Above and Below, light and darkness, eternity and transitoriness." And he concluded: "Today even more than in my youth I believe that a return to an essential order, to a harmony, is necessary to save the world from boundless confusion."[48]

Clearly the filmic avant-garde would find this writing speaking to their struggle with new forms of expression and yet the embracing of unifying principles of order.

Frampton's *Zorns Lemma* (1970) takes on slight variations within predictable repetitions of images to create out of the random series many structural principles that unify. *Entropy and Art*'s "call for structure" finds an answer in such self-consciously structured films as Gottheim's *Four Shadows* and Frampton's *Zorns Lemma*.

Arnheim asks:

> Is the modern world socially, cognitively, perceptually devoid of the kind of high order needed to generate similarly organized form in the minds of artists? Or is the order of our world so pernicious as to prevent the artist from responding to it?

On one hand, Arnheim posits "an almost desperate need to wrest order from a chaotic environment," yet on the other, a more symptomatic artistic response, "the frank exhibition of bankruptcy and sterility wrought by that same environment."[49]

As provocative as this book may have been in its context, its tendency to polarize order and disorder still reiterates the longstanding tendency in Arnheim's thoughts that I discussed earlier in relationship to *Art and Visual Perception* to present the classical solution to order as fundamental, with aesthetic departures from order being symptoms of sociopolitical stress. These symptoms, while they bring necessary complexity and development, nonetheless never are granted as fundamental and satisfactory an aesthetic *raison d'être*.

Yet, Arnheim seemingly cannot rest with order, even though his next book, *The Dynamics of Architectural Form*, revisits the order and disorder opposition in Chapter VI in a manner largely familiar by now.[50] For here, dynamics increasingly becomes his interest, as he celebrates dynamics even in classical architecture, tracing viewer perceptions of architecture in space. Instead of speaking of architecture from the perspective of drawn plans and cross-sections, he thinks about moving through architectural spaces, developing temporally changing perspectives, relative to the movement of the human body, and its manner of visual perception. Besides order and disorder, other structural oppositions obtain, such as horizontality and verticality, solids and hollows, and most intriguingly, as specific in his implicit debate with international modernism, expression and function, displacing the expression vs. realism opposition in the other visual arts. The implications of this work for art filmmaking lie in the degree to which a camera vision of architecture departs from human visual movement through architectural spaces; some avant-garde filmmakers, such as Michael Snow in *Wavelength* (1967) and ⟷ (Back and Forth) (1969) or Ernie Gehr in

Serene Velocity (1970), seek various non-anthropomorphic camera visions, generating abstract expression from nondescript functionalist architecture, something I explore in the chapter "Scanning Landscapes and Collapsing Architectures: Shattering the Grounding of the Subject/Eye" in *Abstraction in Avant-Garde Films.*[51]

Let me note here that in that book, I was proposing an entirely different model. I did not trace the history nor do the analysis I trace here, as I had other concerns. Arnheim was not a theoretical tool of choice for me at that juncture; instead, a combination of semiotics, psychoanalysis, and philosophy forged a new way of looking at force and signification. To Arnheim, I preferred Anton Ehrenzweig's *The Hidden Order of Art* for its connection of dynamic complexity in art with a theory of the unconscious.[52]

As regards my discussion of the films of Snow and Gehr, the phenomenological architectural theory of Christian Norberg-Schulz's *Existence, Space and Architecture* serves as point of departure, but ultimately my philosophical stake was more deconstructive, examining the ways these filmmakers call into question, rather than merely affirm, the phenomenological subject. In contrast, Arnheim centers on the psychological perceptions such a subject might have, with oppositions structuring his understandings of that subject in space. Despite the expressionist rendering of architecture that graces the book's cover which might hint at how deconstructive architecture to come would introduce new dynamics, Arnheim's structuring oppositions and his architectural examples do not address the most adventurous architectural examples, such as constructivist models whose rendering of mass and void presents a more disorienting architectonics.

Yet the "Vectors and Nodes" section of Arnheim's next book, 1982 *The Power of the Center: A Study of Composition in the Visual Arts*, considers a constructivism that was largely missing in *Dynamics.*[53] Even so, the structural opposition of centricity and eccentricity is the preoccupation here, and centricity is privileged. One of Arnheim's main arguments is that the center of a circular frame corresponds to the human viewer's centrality, and that the mandala has a privileged place within design due to the centrality of mind within perception. The work on mandalas might be brought into conjunction with films such as *Allures* (1961) and *Samadhi* (1967) by Jordan Belson. Belson creates an entirely abstract contemporary visual image training light sources through masks cut as stencils to mandala shapes, on a unique rotating animation stand.[54] The resulting images evoke Eastern traditions of meditation, in which staring at a mandala correlates to experiencing circles of energy connecting mind to body, and further accomplishes a "centering."

In a quite different way, *Zorns Lemma* intersperses segments dominated by circular motifs with those organized by contrasting, eccentric vectors, and those whose overall design flattens the picture plane abstractly. Many of the images—the progress of the star cookie cutter marking the dough, or the meat grinder churning its product, or the egg frying—exhibit marked centrality, while others, such as the figure walking through the city, play on constructivist vectors. Image segments conceptually build on these structural contrasts; one way to view this film is as a play with ways in which a single shot can be completed as a miniature visual narrative, laced as a series of repetitions of its fragments. Since temporal change enters these miniature narratives, an image may transform itself from one type of visual organization to another, as when the more vectoral collection of falling balls becomes an overall pattern of circles at the film's end. So the opposition between centrality or eccentrality cedes to another principle which unifies actions, that is the notion of a complete set of actions constituted as a series of additions, subtractions, or movements with an implicit logic.

Centrality can be combined with a radical eccentricity, as in Michael Snow's *La Region Centrale* (1970), whose specially constructed rotating camera platform rotated the lens a full 360 degrees shifting the direction of the arching pans at the remote Quebec landscape. In other words, the formal and structural experiments of the sixties and seventies might be seen collectively as an exploration of the paradigm of centricity and eccentricity in its most abstract terms, even those which supersede psychological norms of visual thinking for structural deviations that ask the human subject to rethink her own assumptions about vision and subjectivity.

Thus Arnheim's later writings on art offer new connections to be made between visual thinking and film, through exploring how forces of centering, balancing, and structure work to compensate for dynamic discontinuities and decentering. In this light, Arnheim's 1996 *The Split and the Structure* groups essays that reiterate the role structure plays in conjoining elements that were otherwise disjunct.[55] After the flowering of structuralism as a theory, and its coincidence with attention to structure in minimalism, culminating in P. Adams Sitney's coining of the category of "structuralist film," Arnheim's book title reminds us that he had long been speaking of structures that create ties across splits and fragments; commonly this would be called unifying form, but Arnheim's formulation had the advantage of recognizing the split, the fragment, or eccentricity as fundamental.

So as we return to Arnheim as historical figure, this essay paints him as a figure who saw and thought about visual form in art in ways that have been useful historically for art filmmaking, and that we can still use today, to elucidate artwork that challenges us the most, art which presents something conceptually new. This chase towards the conceptually new itself may have waned in recent years, as art film and video makers engage postmodern play on one hand, or more direct social commentary or inscription of the sexual body on the other. Still, images in Su Friedrich's *Damned if You Don't* (1987) will allow us to juxtapose Arnheim to a filmmaker who is a contemporary inheritor of Deren's legacy, in her concern with narrative, the representation of desire, and cinematography and editing that suggestively evoke the mental states of her protagonists through imagery. *Damned if You Don't* has what I have termed an installation aesthetic in several scenes, most notably the scene of a young woman in bed, framed by a fishtank on the left and a television on the right, and of a Nun at an aquarium, observing both dolphins and jellyfish. The tanks of aquatic creatures link these scenes. Let me suggest that Friedrich is going night fishing at Antibes, here, constructing through montage, visual thoughts of our best sexual nature. That visual thinking should be so linked to the exploration of desire, particularly contemporary lesbian desire in art, is usually beyond the way Arnheim's psychology of the visual has been framed. Yet, as I discussed earlier, his essay on this Picasso painting shows that his visual thought would go precisely in different directions when the object he was addressing did as well. I want to end then suggesting that we open Arnheim's writings on visual thinking, as one way of exploring the dynamics of creative filmmaking.

notes

1. Rudolf Arnheim, "To Maya Deren," in *Film Essays and Criticism*, Madison, Wisconsin: University of Wisconsin Press, 1997, pp. 227–230. Appeared originally in *Film Culture*, No. 24, Spring 1962.
2. Rudolf Arnheim, *Film as Art*, Berkeley: University of California Press, 1957. First published in Germany in 1932 as *Film als Kunst*, Berlin: Ernst Rowohlt, revised ed.
3. Arnheim, "To Maya Deren," p. 227.
4. Ibid.
5. Maya Deren, "An Anagram of Ideas on Art, Form and Film," in Bill Nichols and Maya Deren, *Maya Deren and the American Avant-Garde*, Berkeley: University of California Press, 2001.
6. See Rudolf Arnheim, "Dr. Calgari Redivivus (1925)," and "Expressionist Film," in *Film Essays and Criticism*, pp. 84–85, 111.
7. Arnheim, "To Maya Deren," p. 227.
8. Viktor Shklovsky, "Art as Technique," in Julie Rivkin and Michael Ryan eds. *Literary Theory: An Anthology*, Malden: Blackwell Publishing Ltd, 1998, pp. 17–23.
9. Arnheim, "To Maya Deren," p. 228.
10. Scott MacDonald, *A Critical Cinema: Interviews with Independent Filmmakers*, Berkeley: University of California Press, 1988, p. 86.
11. Scott MacDonald and Amos Vogel, *Cinema 16: Documents Toward a History of the Film Society*, Philadelphia: Temple University Press, 2002.
12. Ibid., p. 383.
13. Rudolf Arnheim, "Art Today and the Film," *Film Culture*, No. 42, Fall 1966, pp. 43–45. It was also published in *Art Journal*, Vol. XXV, No. 3, 1966 and later anthologized in P. Adams Sitney, *Film Culture Reader*, New York: Praeger Publishers, 1970.
14. Amos Vogel, "Thirteen Confusions," in MacDonald and Vogel, *Cinema 16*, pp. 428–435.
15. Ibid., p. 434.

16. Georg Amberg, "Cinevision," *Film Culture*, No. 42, Fall 1966, pp. 25–28.
17. Arnheim, *Film as Art*, p. 68.
18. Roland Barthes, "The Face of Garbo," in *Mythologies*, New York: Hill and Wang, 1972, pp. 56–57.
19. Arnheim, *Film as Art*, pp. 70, 183.
20. Arnheim, *Film Essays and Criticism*, pp. 216–218.
21. Rudolf Arnheim, *Art and Visual Perception*, Berkeley: University of California Press, 1954, plate 91 between pages 78–79.
22. Arnheim, *Film as Art*, p. 127.
23. Ibid., pp. 174–175.
24. Ibid., pp. 4–5.
25. Arnheim, *Film Essays and Criticism*, p. 26.
26. Ibid., pp. 130–134.
27. Arnheim, *Film as Art*, p. 37.
28. Ibid., p. 121.
29. Rudolf Arnheim, *Toward a Psychology of Art*: Collected Essays. Berkeley: University of California Press, 1966, and Arnheim, *Art and Visual Perception: A Psychology of the Creative Eye*, Berkeley: University of California Press, 1974 (first 1954).
30. Rudolf Arnheim, "The Myth of a Bleeding Lamb," in *Toward a Psychology of Art*, pp. 136–150.
31. Rudolf Arnheim, "Melancholy Unshaped" and "The Holes of Henry Moore," in *Toward a Psychology of Art*, pp. 181–191, 245–255.
32. Rudolf Arnheim, "Nightfishing at Antibes," in *Toward a Psychology of Art*, pp. 258–260.
33. Arnheim, *Toward a Psychology of Art*, p. 125.
34. Arnheim, *Art and Visual Perception*, 1954, p. 113.
35. Deren, "An Anagram of Ideas on Art, Form and Film"; Maureen Turim, "The Ethics of Form: Structure and Gender in Maya Deren's Challenge to the Cinema," in Nichols and Deren, *Maya Deren and the American Avant-Garde*, pp. 77–102.
36. Nichols and Deren, *Maya Deren and the American Avant-Garde*, p. 47.
37. Ibid., pp. 77 and 97.
38. Stan Brakhage, "Metaphors on Vision," *Film Culture*, No. 30, 1963, p. 25.
39. Stan Brakhage and Robert A. Haller, "23rd Psalm Branch," in *Brakhage Scrapbook: Collected Writings, 1964–1980*, New Paltz, NY: Documentext, 1982.
40. Paul Sharits, "Hearing: Seeing," *Film Culture*, Nos. 65–66, 1978, p. 72.
41. Hollis Frampton, "A Pentagram for Conjuring the Narrative?" in *Circles of Confusion: Film/Photography/Video Texts 1968–1981*, Rochester, NY: Visual Studies Workshop Press, 1983, pp. 59–68.
42. Ibid., p. 63.
43. Erle Loran, *Cézanne's Composition: Analysis of his Form with Diagrams and Photographs of his Motifs*, Berkeley: University of California Press, 1943.
44. Arnheim, *Entropy and Art: An Essay on Disorder and Order*, Berkeley: University of California Press, 1971.
45. Ibid., p. 3.
46. Ibid., p. 7.
47. Ibid., p. 29.
48. Ibid., p. 28.
49. Ibid., p. 55.
50. Rudolf Arnheim, *The Dynamics of Architectural Form*, Berkeley: University of California Press, 1978, pp. 162–204.

175

51. Maureen Turim, *Abstraction in Avant-Garde Films*, Ann Arbor: UMI Research Press, 1985.

52. David Bordwell at the time urged some consideration of Arnheim in my dissertation, and trying to accommodate, I added a few paragraphs noting his relevance, but noted my dissatisfaction with the gestalt predilection for order and harmony that I have been discussing here, and that I found then to be dominant in his writings. When I edited the dissertation as a book, these paragraphs were ones I excised. I was worried that my comments were too cursory and that I couldn't do justice to Arnheim while aiming elsewhere, hence this return in homage now.

53. Rudolf Arnheim, *The Power of the Center: A Study of Composition in the Visual Arts*, Berkeley: University of California Press, 1982.

54. Scott MacDonald, "Jordan Belson (and collaborator Stephen Beck)," in *A Critical Cinema 3: Interviews with Independent Filmmakers*, Berkeley: University of California Press, 1998, pp. 64–92.

55. Rudolf Arnheim, *The Split and the Structure: Twenty-Eight Essays*, Berkeley: University of California Press, 1996.

arnheim on radio

materialtheorie and beyond

ten

s h a w n   v a n c o u r

Reflecting on his seminal 1932 *Film as Art* in the oft-cited introduction to his revised 1957 English edition, Rudolf Arnheim explained the guiding concern of this early work as what he called *Materialtheorie*: "a theory meant to show that artistic and scientific descriptions of reality are cast in molds that derive not so much from the subject matter itself as from the properties of the medium—or *Material*—employed."[1] The goal of *Film as Art*, as he elaborated in a later article, was "to show that the very deficiency of the screen image, its lack of sound, its flatness, its confined space, its reduction to black and white, was [a] means of interpreting the sensory world" that provided the foundation for a distinctive visual art form.[2] This same method, he continued, had been used in his lesser-known 1936 book, *Radio*: "as the countermedium of the silent film, radio offered ways of interpreting the world by sound alone," existing solely in "the realm of speech and the realm of noises" with "all sorts of possibilities which weren't possible in visual space."[3] While in Arnheim's view, "[the] two books complemented each other" as two sides of the same analytical coin, his radio work had never gained the same recognition as his film writings; whereas *Film as Art* was published in multiple translations throughout the world, *Radio*, he lamented, remained largely unread, " 'surviv[ing]' as a sleeper or more exactly in a state of comatose slumber."[4]

While Arnheim's radio writings were never wholly neglected, it is true that these have yet to receive the same attention as his work on film, owing in part to their relative scarcity within Arnheim's overall scholarly output. Beyond *Film as Art*, Arnheim's film writings include over 100 reviews for the satirical *Das Stachelschwein* and left-wing *Die Weltbühne*, written before Arnheim's expatriation from Germany in 1933; his celebrated "New Laocoön" essay and articles for the *Enciclopedia del cinema*, *Intercine*, and *Cinema* composed at the League of Nations International Institute for Educational Film in Italy from the mid- to late 1930s; and a long list of articles completed after his emigration to America in 1940.[5] Beyond his 1936 book, Arnheim's remarks on radio were, by contrast, limited to a few short essays and reviews from 1927 to 1933, some brief passages in his 1932 film book and 1935 essay, "Forecast of Television," and two studies for Columbia University's Radio Research Office in 1941–1942. Though numbering far fewer than his film writings, these radio writings have not lain wholly comatose, thanks to Arnheim's inclusion of his television essay in the 1957 edition of *Film as Art*, recent publication of his once-scattered radio essays in Germany, and several successive reprintings of *Radio* in German, Italian, and English.[6] Nonetheless, readership for this work has been limited primarily to radio scholars, and little effort has been made to connect these writings to Arnheim's broader research agenda. The present essay thus aims, first, to illuminate this neglected area of Arnheim's media scholarship and argue its importance for any consideration of his larger scholarly legacy.

At the same time, however, this essay also challenges Arnheim's own, retrospective reflections on the nature and goals of these radio writings. As Sabine Hake has observed in her thoughtful reassessment of Arnheim's Weimar film writings, "The 1957 American edition [of *Film as Art*] eliminated all traces of a political consciousness" that pervaded the 1932 original, deleting any references to what Arnheim referred to in a revised 1974 German edition as "the ideological-political nature of film production," i.e., film's relation to the broader spheres of economics, society, and politics. Thus, in place of what were initially "two strands of thought in Arnheim's work," explains Hake, only the single, "formalist tendency" was preserved.[7]

Arnheim's radio work was likewise by no means restricted to the *Materialtheorie* to which he later sought to confine it. "If wireless [radio] claims the whole attention of the theorist of art . . . it is a no less enthralling phenomenon for the sociologist," he explained in *Radio*, which, as Arnheim's definitive account of the medium, itself moved beyond strictly aesthetic matters to take up many decidedly extratextual issues. Examining the effects of policy regulations, industry structure, and audience demographics on preferred forms of program content, and the impact of domestic reception conditions on the experience of radio artworks, this study like most of Arnheim's radio scholarship far exceeds any straightforward application of *Materialtheorie* in its method and scope.[8]

By no means an incidental detour or analytical dead end, extra-formalist considerations held an important place in Arnheim's radio writings. Figuring prominently in the 1927–1933 Weimar essays that provided a foundation for his subsequent explorations of the medium, this sociological/contextual line of inquiry was dramatically expanded in Arnheim's 1936 book and dominated his 1940s Columbia studies, which in keeping with the research group's focus devoted themselves to radio's industrial logics, ideological distortions, and sociocultural impact. Representing important and recurring strands in Arnheim's scholarship, these investigations moved Arnheim well beyond the *Materialtheorie* to which he restricted subsequent accounts of his work, suggesting critical concerns not only with the material properties and possibilities of radio and film, but also with their social effects and the external determinants that converged to shape their form and content. Revealing a more complex and nuanced understanding than is commonly acknowledged, these writings offer a multifaceted model of media analysis with continued relevance today.

toward a theory of radio: material properties and possibilities of sound art

To the reader of *Radio*, Arnheim offered the warning that the work might prove "harder than my previous one dealing with the film," since "acoustic effects are more difficult to describe than visual ones," and "far less is known to-day [about the subject] than was known about film at the time my book on film appeared." Being "followed with much less attention than the film was in its time," radio had suffered scholarly neglect, presenting the theorist who attempted "an analysis of the conditions of the material" and "expressive potentialities of the art" with an imposing task.[9] Arnheim himself did not fully embrace this medium as a legitimate art form and object of sustained inquiry until his 1936 book. Nonetheless, many of the ideas advanced here may be traced back to earlier journal essays and little-remarked passages in *Film*, which together established important parameters for Arnheim's later *Radio* investigations.

Arnheim's journalistic discussions of radio date back to the late 1920s and grew in number during the early 1930s, as *Film as Art* first entered publication in Germany. Among the first of these radio pieces was a 1927 review for *Die Weltbühne*, in which Arnheim lamented the poor quality of period radio plays and called for more care in program arrangement to avoid the "shoddy broadcasts without cohesion" that assaulted listeners at every turn.[10] By 1932, Arnheim was publishing a series of radio articles in *Die Weltbühne* and other journals, ranging from acerbic send-ups of tech-obsessed radio hobbyists and dimwitted novices, to reviews of recent radio scholarship, and production tips for radio sound men.[11] While describing radio in 1932 as an art still "in search of its form," by 1933 Arnheim was prepared to defend both film and radio as subclasses of a larger category of "reproductive art" that was not limited to the mere mechanical reproduction of reality but rather bore the imprint of a genuinely "creative labor." However, all reproductive arts were not evenly matched: radio's limited sensory appeals made it a decidedly poor cousin of the photographic art of cinema, as a medium of "impoverished artistic means," "unable to achieve the richness and character of the visual arts."[12]

While Arnheim would not fully endorse the new medium until his 1936 volume, he worked in his film book and several essays from the early years of the decade to delineate the precise nature of the methods available to practitioners of this struggling sound art. As Nora M. Alter notes elsewhere in this volume (Chapter 4), Arnheim's original 1932 version of *Film as Art* included considerable discussion of radio. Exploring the aesthetic potentialities of a sound film that included not just a musical score but also dialogue and sound effects, Arnheim turned to radio as "a very obvious opportunity for dealing ... with the acoustic factor of sound film" and model for cinematic practice. Unfortunately, he observed, radio plays of his time were limited in their technique, "developing dramatic action purely from the dialogue" and "[using] sounds other than speech ... as sparingly as possible." However, a second, more pertinent type of radio play was also conceivable, one "constructed as a unity of speech and sound such that the spoken part alone would be quite incomplete and meaningless." This imagined "sound drama" suggested the possibility of a compelling aural art form drawn from the materials of radio but with broader applicability for film, as well.[13]

As "sight and hearing are such very different things," Arnheim explained here, the *Material* of the coming sound art and methods available to its practitioners were distinct from their visual counterparts. Though they revealed "nothing corresponding to the space dimensions of visible objects," radio and film sound were nonetheless "indicative of position" within space, and sound artists possessed numerous means of manipulating these spatial cues for aesthetic effect.[14] While monaural microphone technologies limited the effectiveness of experiments with "microphone angle" and directional sound sources, Arnheim noted that microphone distance could still be effectively manipulated to indicate spatial proximity, sound could be passed through materials with varying "transparency" for changes in clarity or texture, and acoustic reverberation could be altered to simulate particular surroundings—ideas treated more systematically in a separate 1933 essay under the headings of "Directionality," "Movement," "Distance," "Sound Quality," and "Room Tone."[15] Expressing frustration in his 1935 television essay at radio producers' tendency to ignore entire categories in this list (e.g., needlessly limiting their art by "eliminat[ing] the resonance that gives information about space"), Arnheim again reiterated the virtue of these techniques in the pages of his 1936 book, devoting entire chapters to "Spatial Resonance" and "Direction and Distance" that offered an even more elaborate treatment of these ideas.[16]

In addition to manipulations of sound's spatial qualities, Arnheim also saw significant aesthetic possibilities in temporal manipulations. As early as *Film as Art*, Arnheim suggested that radio producers should "give up . . . performances directly in front of the microphone" in favor of editable sound recordings. In his 1933 essay on the reproductive arts, Arnheim again championed the use of sound film to capture a scene and break it down into "different 'shots' " that could, as in the cinema, be carefully trimmed and ordered for maximum aesthetic effect.[17] While Arnheim continued to sing the praises of "sound montage" in *Radio* chapters on "Sequence and Juxtaposition" and "The Use of Recording," here he offered a slight qualification. Some forms such as musical presentations could indeed benefit, he conceded, from "allowing the listener to participate in events *in statu nascendi*" and "watch the present taking shape."[18] Nonetheless, live broadcasting too often reduced radio to a mere "relaying apparatus" that left it chained to externally occurring events, whereas the aesthetically sound radio art succeeded in "creating an entire world complete in itself out of the sensory materials at its disposal."[19] "Careful montage work" remained essential for achieving aesthetic autonomy for forms such as radio drama, Arnheim explained, where sound effects or music cued at precisely the right moment and properly mixed could create the illusion of a larger, self-contained world freed from its studio origin. For this reason, montage was without question "the right policy for the future" and had an important place within the radio artist's battery of techniques.[20]

Based on the strength of his described methods of spatial and temporal manipulation, Arnheim was by 1936 prepared to accord radio full legitimacy as a distinct and valued art form—one with its own aesthetic properties and possibilities, and the capacity to provide listeners with experiences as compelling as any derived from the visual arts. "Broadcasting," he explained, "has constituted a new experience for the artist, his audience and the theoretician: for the first time it makes use of the aural only, without the almost invariable accompaniment of the visual which we find in nature as well as in art."[21] If this lack of a visual channel had initially seemed to condemn radio to second-class status next to the more sensory-rich art of film, Arnheim's 1936 book now offered an entire chapter "In Praise of Blindness" and repeatedly stressed the medium's aurality as its defining virtue and source of expressive potential. As Noël Carroll and commentators within this volume explain, expressivism is central to Arnheim's theory of art, with his reproductive arts enjoying a distance from reality that lets them draw out expressive qualities of the world overlooked in regular, everyday perception.[22] Working within an isolated sphere of sound, Arnheim's radio artist could use his described methods of spatial and temporal manipulation to foreground the expressive qualities of the music, speech, and noises that formed the raw materials of radio, thus providing listeners with profoundly satisfying forms of aesthetic experience. "The 'expressive characteristics' of sound affect us in a far more direct way . . . which [has] very little to do with the objective meaning of the word or sound," Arnheim explained, and radio placed its listener in direct touch with this elemental force at the center of sound.[23] In this, radio not only matched film but had a decided advantage: since "the wireless is not, like the sound-film, tied to naturalistic pictures," Arnheim concluded, it could more easily free itself from mere imitation to exploit "the direct expressive power" of sound, and so achieve its rightful place within the pantheon of the arts.[24]

If Arnheim's thinking on radio in his initial 1927–1933 Weimar essays proved at times ambivalent, his position in his 1936 book was clear. No longer a subject of sideline investigation or poor cousin to film, radio was embraced as an independent object of study and autonomous art form that created its own "world of sound differentiated from reality by its own formal laws."[25] However, elaborating the material conditions and possibilities of this new art of sound proved but one strand of Arnheim's early radio scholarship, which moved beyond the strictly formalist considerations of *Materialtheorie* to explore a series of external determinants on practices of radio artmaking and situate this medium within its broader sociohistorical context.

beyond *materialtheorie*: external determinants on aural artmaking

While *Radio*'s primary goal was to pursue the same mode of material analysis that Arnheim had followed in his previous book on film, his investigations ended on a markedly different note. Having established the material properties of the medium and advocated specific sets of aesthetic techniques that could exploit its capacities to full effect, Arnheim devoted *Radio*'s final chapters to consideration of extratextual factors affecting the technical quality, content, and reception of radio artworks. Building on ideas that may be traced back to some of his earliest Weimar writings, Arnheim's analysis here turned to questions of regulatory policy and control of production, cultural differences among competing audience demographics, and the effects of reception conditions on the psychology of radio listening. By supplementing and enriching the formalist method of *Materialtheorie* through this second, contextualist framework, *Radio* raised critical questions concerning the role of external determinants in enabling or limiting particular forms of aesthetic expression.

Radio regulation, Arnheim explained, was motivated by specifically nationalist concerns that had profound effects on both the technical quality of radio reproduction and the types of content pursued. In a chapter on "Wireless and the Nations," Arnheim explained that whereas "film, although a social problem of enormous significance," remained a private industry which "the State has never found the proper occasion to lay hands on," radio "proved from the day of its birth to be so obviously a monopoly instrument concerning the whole of the community that in most countries it immediately came under the direct influence of the State."[26] In Europe, each state's desire for its own national service produced a system of international frequency allocation with considerable compromises in sound quality. While Arnheim saw a frequency range of 10,000 Hz as the minimum needed for quality radio reproduction, standard bandwidths were much narrower to permit more broadcasters in Europe's crowded spectrum space. Worse still, these broadcasters often strayed from their assigned frequencies and ignored international limits on transmitting power, resulting in "a medley of voices screaming together in a long distance set," with "each country strengthening its own transmissions so as to drown the disturbance of foreign stations." This competition between broadcasters created an ever-escalating wireless war, with Arnheim's desired art of sound all but lost to the resulting noise.[27]

At the level of content, Arnheim's concern shifted from international competition to struggles over control of production within the state itself. In the final pages of *Film*, Arnheim insisted that monopoly control by a centralized state agency had a detrimental impact on national culture, limiting the creative talent pool and creating a "thoroughgoing standardisation of all forms of culture." "Centralization is in many respects certainly not in the interests of art," he explained, and broadcasting's own growth and success would require "a multiplicity of local and provincial stimuli and opportunities for evolution."[28] Yet, some degree of centralization was still required to resolve this multiplicity into a broader national unity and ensure that all parts of the country enjoyed access to the very best works. Celebrating radio's nation-binding potential in two separate 1932 essays, Arnheim lauded its capacity for "bridging the opposition between cultured and uncultured peoples" and breaking down the "walls that currently segregate political and ideological groups, social, educational, and economic classes, and geographical regions" in Germany.[29] This cultural unification, he explained, required a balance between local and state control:

> Just as in the ideal state individualities are not effaced, yet are subordinated to a central authority, in wireless, too, a monopoly control and unified transmission will be rejected, but a central transmitting station will be employed to emphasize all that the regions have in common, thus bringing about a unity.

Whether using this central broadcaster to create a full schedule of programming from across the country for mandatory distribution by stations

183

in all regions, or giving regional stations more autonomy and requiring only partial carriage of official state and outside programs, the national character of radio could be maintained while preserving a diverse pool of creative talent. The goal, Arnheim explained, was "not systematic uniformity but 'unity in multiplicity' as they say in esthetics," with "everyone contribut[ing] to the whole what is his own and his best" and so raising the nation's culture to its highest possible level.[30]

Given radio's status as a mass medium, Arnheim maintained that broad appeal was essential for successful programming. Refuting suggestions by his contemporaries that producers pursue specialized content targeted at narrow demographics, Arnheim declared in 1932 that "all stratification within special spheres . . . is, in radio, extremely objectionable."[31] Revisiting the point in 1936, he explained that the successful program could err neither on the side of high culture nor the popular taste: "Wireless is not well administered if it gives very learned specialties or highly complicated works of art which make the average man despair," no more than "if [its] 'popular' entertainment is so inferior that it turns the stomach of educated people."[32] Successful radio art achieved universal appeal, but without devolving into meaningless diversion; and, in Arnheim's view, it was only by maintaining its social relevance that radio achieved this popularity. Well-crafted programming possessed what Arnheim in 1932 called a "folkloric" quality, tapping into the broader cultural currents of its time and presenting material that was universally accessible but deeply meaningful.[33] The task of radio art, he affirmed in 1936, was "to select from existing art what is simple enough to be felt by everyone—which is precisely the quality of great art—and to get down to the root problems of the cultural life of the period."[34] A medium that "can excellently teach our musicians, poets and speakers of all sorts to be simple in content-rich ways," radio would avoid the dangers of both "bleak esoterica on the one hand and shallow amusement on the other."[35]

Unfortunately, reception conditions created a psychology of listening that compromised the effectiveness of even the most carefully crafted content. Arnheim had already raised concerns in 1932 essays about "those who, to distract themselves evenings, turn the receiver on without reading through the schedule," or "the passive listener, who recklessly flicks the tuning knob around, grazing at bits of every program, desiring only to be somehow diverted."[36] The sheer availability of programming was largely to blame, he concluded in his 1936 study, requiring special care in selection of programs and strict appointment listening to stimulate the proper "activity of the mind":

> Even if wireless offers a programme entirely made up of
> what deserves by its beauty and value to be made accessible
> to everyone, good can only come of it if the listener does not

let one broadcast after another pour out on him quite mechanically, but selects when and to what he shall listen.[37]

The larger problem, however, was the domestic reception environment itself. "The wireless performance," he explained, "does not stand outside the rest of life as the concert does. One does not need to make a pilgrimage to it, but finds it at home."[38] Domestic listening made lapses in discipline easy, as "no one can find out whether you tune in to Bach or musical comedies at home, nor whether you listen devoutly until the end or leave off in the middle and do other things."[39] Even the most devout listener could fall prey to distraction in this environment:

> The daily life in the home makes all sorts of demands, so the listener never sits "idly" in front of the loudspeaker, but does all sorts of useful and useless things at the same time ... The concentration which is enhanced in church or concert-hall ... must be fought for by the listener *against* his surroundings, and he rarely succeeds in doing this.[40]

Thus, apart from a grasp of the material possibilities available to the radio artist and techniques for effectively mobilizing these, successful radio art depended on several critical external factors: 1) a regulatory environment that secured satisfactory technical reproduction, enabled deserving artists to gain airtime, and encouraged a sufficient state presence to counter tendencies toward fragmentation into competing subnational constituencies; 2) effective program selection that secured mass appeal through universally accessible and socially meaningful content; and 3) audiences who could resist domestic distractions and pursue a disciplined "art of listening-in."[41] Attention to these external determinants pervaded much of Arnheim's early radio writings, moving these studies well beyond his initial formalist goals. A prominent line of inquiry from the start, these contextualist concerns would persist in Arnheim's 1940s Columbia research and figure even more centrally in his thinking than before.

the columbia era: extra-aesthetic considerations in arnheim's later radio writings

While Arnheim remained in Italy for some months after its withdrawal from the League of Nations in 1938, at the official outbreak of war he took a job with the BBC in London and in 1940 joined Paul Lazarsfeld's Rockefeller-funded Office of Radio Research in the U.S.[42] Though it had relocated from Newark to Princeton, and then to Columbia the year Arnheim joined it, the Radio Office's mission remained the same: close empirical analysis of program content and audience response. As Lazarsfeld put it, "Radio reaches more people than do the movies, newspapers, books, pamphlets, or the stage, and its effects are problems of increasing importance to the sociologist."[43] Within this context, it is not surprising that Arnheim's own writings emphasized the broader socioeconomic and political dimensions of radio. However, such concerns were by no means absent from Arnheim's earlier work, with his Columbia-era writings representing not a new or foreign line of inquiry, but rather an intensification of an enduring strand of Arnheim's media scholarship that extends as far back as his earliest Weimar writings, echoing nearly point for point not only his early radio essays but also his remarks on film.

As Hake notes, a significant portion of the original *Film as Art* was devoted to a lengthy content analysis in which Arnheim sought to trouble traditional distinctions between film form and thematic content.[44] "From the fundamental choice of the theme up to the most subtle and specialised detail," Arnheim insisted,

> there is but one formative process . . . Understanding of art
> will be achieved neither by him who is too ready to call that
> which is actually already moulded "only material," "only
> theme," nor by him who avoids all questions of . . . artistic
> construction in favour of a non-artistic interest in the story
> alone.[45]

Studying this material shaped by the artist took the theorist on a "foray into extra-aesthetic areas," requiring critical consideration of the socioeconomic conditions within which this subject matter was formed and its ideological implications as superstructural manifestation of the same.[46] While Arnheim strategically omitted these sections from the revised 1957 edition and instead stressed the contributions of his *Materialtheorie*, these "extra-aesthetic" concerns pervaded his early media criticism and resurfaced with full force again in his 1940s Columbia writings.[47]

A concern with the industrial exigencies informing processes of media production is evident in both Arnheim's writings for *Die Weltbühne* and his original film book. In a 1929 *Weltbühne* column on "Professional Film Criticism," Arnheim had already complained that "All too many film critics see, like the public at large, not much more in the film than the contents," with no knowledge of underlying conditions of production, or how a film is "brought to the screen."[48] *Film* continued to stress the importance of the mode of production, putting a particularly fine point on industry economics. "In film the work is done on the economic principle that the cost of production must be kept as low as possible . . . Therefore movie men must not experiment, must not wait for inspiration, must not 'fritter away' material." Even if costs could be kept low, the limited public appeal of these works made them distinct liabilities within a commercially driven system: "as a general rule, there would not be a sufficiently large public for really good works of art, and if there were such a public it would be *in spite* of and not *because* of the artistic appeal."[49] To truly understand the "how" and the "what" of film form and film content thus required an industrially savvy grasp of the financial "why" behind them.

In addition to economic motivations, the sociopolitical dimensions of film content also proved of direct concern to Arnheim in his early media scholarship. Taking up the question of film censorship in *Die Weltbühne*, for instance, Arnheim expressed particular dismay at a 1929 law that gave censors expanded authority not only to ban the exhibition of films, but also to "precensor" them during production; now, not only would "the repertoire that Pensioner Kruger and Mother Woffen get to see in the cinema . . . depend on what Head Official Fightingcock thinks of Pudovkin and Stroheim," but government officials could review and demand changes at the levels of scripts and shooting.[50] Arnheim continued to lament in his 1932 book that German film had "much of politics and little of art," with stories presenting "ridiculously false descriptions" of a "princely state of imaginary millionaires and of exquisites in evening dress" that served as empty distractions from the nation's real economic hardships.[51] As Hake explains, Arnheim saw popular film as "exploit[ing] the hopes and fears of average people," while "offering individual solutions" to problems that required collective social action; creating false resolution "through simplistic oppositions of good and evil"; and restoring faith in flawed "bourgeois values" and "social institutions like the state."[52] However, such stories remained undeniably popular with audiences, and producers could scarcely be blamed for pursuing them; rather, Arnheim explained, "Anyone who wishes to improve film must first improve social conditions," with better art hinging on solutions to the deeper structural problems that motivated these ideological distortions in the first place.[53]

While Arnheim's Weimar radio essays and 1936 book continued this effort to place the reproductive arts within their broader socioeconomic and political context, his most forceful articulation of these concerns came in his subsequent Columbia studies. His first study, published in 1941, documented foreign language broadcasts on local stations throughout the United States, with careful attention to sponsorship and the "national appeals" embedded in both programs and advertising content. Motivated by concerns over how "to conciliate the public service character of broadcasts and the commercial requirements of their sponsors," the study sought to address fears that targeting "the largest possible audience" might lead to "neglect of minorities who call for special interest programs without furnishing the large market to which the advertiser feels he is entitled."[54] Luckily, foreign language broadcasts seemed to thrive on local stations. But unhappily, "At a time when the solidarity of the people of this country must be considered a matter of vital interest," both programming and advertising appeals showed a "tendency to maintain the status quo of the listener's stage of assimilation or even to drive him back to a setting of life which he left beyond the ocean many years ago," offering idealized and anachronistic images of the home country instead of adjusting listeners to demands of life in America.[55] As with film, these programs presented "superstructural" manifestations of problems whose solution required deeper social change: "finding for [immigrants] a better place in the mechanism of production of the country and ... conveying to them the feeling of being welcomed as equal members."[56]

Arnheim's second essay, published in 1942, continued this sociological line of investigation with a detailed content analysis of forty-three American soap operas that echoed nearly point for point his assessment of German film a decade earlier. Soap operas made frequent displays of wealthy "society characters," showed a world "continuously threatened by catastrophe" that exploited listener fears, and presented these problems as being "caused by individuals, by their shortcomings or corruption, rather than by any general social, economical, or political conditions."[57] Sharp moral contrasts were drawn in these stories, confirming the listener "in her belief that her suffering is caused not by herself, but by the imperfection and villainy of others," and enabling solutions through punishment of individual offenders without addressing underlying social causes.[58] Ending on a familiar refrain, Arnheim affirmed radio's powerful capacity for community building and stressed that, while "radio programs by themselves do not have the power to bring about a change in the social situation of women," they could play a progressive role in society by presenting problems with "roots . . . in human nature and social institutions," and offering solutions that demonstrated "the mutual dependence of community and individual."[59] "There is no entertainment that has nothing to do with art or education," Arnheim concluded, and even the soap opera could, with critical guidance, offer its entertainment in an aesthetically sound and socially uplifting manner.[60]

While Arnheim left Lazarsfeld's organization in 1942 with a Guggenheim grant to pursue his work on art and visual perception, his Columbia essays remain a significant part of his early scholarship that speak to persistent concerns in both his film and radio writings.[61] Throughout his work, Arnheim showed a remarkable sensitivity to external factors shaping mass media production and the specific social, political, and economic demands to which these media responded. However, Columbia provided an environment in which these concerns could rise to the fore and receive more focused and sustained attention than at any other point in Arnheim's career. Advocating a firm knowledge of modes of media production and their effects on style and content, and insisting on ideological analysis of media texts as an important complement to formalist studies, Arnheim pursued a multipronged critical approach that positioned the artwork as the product of a particular medium with its own *Material* and methods, while remaining fully cognizant of the social effects of that medium and the complex convergence of broader industrial and contextual forces that shaped its dominant forms of expression.

conclusion

If Arnheim later in life stressed the formalist contributions of his early media scholarship over its extra-aesthetic lines of inquiry, he returned to the question of contextualism one last time in his 1981 essay, "Style as a Gestalt Problem." His own analysis of style, Arnheim noted, had begun with the essentially "deductive procedure" of *Materialtheorie*, attempting "to derive the possibilities of the new media of film, radio, and television . . . from an analysis of their technical characteristics" and so "predict the kinds of style a medium could develop." Typically, however, styles were "derived from inductive observation," employing an art historical method that linked particular groups of works to the "broader political or cultural periods in which these are at home," i.e., their larger sociohistorical context.[62] The task here, as Colin Burnett has noted in his own analysis of this essay, was to develop a method that could preserve the respective insights of these two approaches without limiting the analyst to a reductive either/or account that could at best tell only half the story. Instead, Arnheim advocated a view of style as a complex "gestalt" formed from multiple, intertwining elements (both medium-specific and sociohistorical), preferring an account that recognized the importance of both the particular *Material* in question and the broader historical influences that acted on different artists.

For present purposes it remains only to be stated that in overcoming the apparent opposition between the inductive and deductive methods, Arnheim's preferred approach to style would likewise seem to dissolve any unresolved tension between the formalist and sociological/contextualist dimensions of aesthetic analysis. Though by no means negating the importance of the technical characteristics of a medium, understanding their mobilization by an artist required consideration of the specific sociohistorical environment within which he operated and to which his art responded. Just as the *Material* of the medium presented certain possibilities and constraints for artmaking, the individual artist brought to that medium a particular set of sensibilities and personal predilections, which were in turn shaped by a larger set of specific sociocultural influences: "an individual is created by nothing but . . . determining factors, hereditary, environmental, or whatever," and "the arts, of course, are basically . . . a means of coping with the[ir] environment."[63] Aesthetic form, in short, arose at the dynamic intersection of medium, artist, and social context, as a "gestalt" formed in and through their interaction that was irreducible to any one part.

Though re-inflected to address contemporary debates within the field of art history, this later work remains wholly consistent with tendencies seen throughout Arnheim's earlier scholarship, suggesting the resurgence of longstanding concerns over the relationship between formalism and contextualism in film and media studies. While insisting that each medium introduced particular limitations and possibilities of its own, Arnheim's early

189

writings also moved beyond *Materialtheorie* to address a wide range of external determinants on media artmaking, drawing connections between aesthetic form and the myriad extra-aesthetic exigencies to which it responded. In his radio book, Arnheim built on the foundation laid in his initial Weimar writings and pursued an inquiry into the effects of regulatory policy, control of production, audience demographics, and listening environment on the production, content, and reception of radio artworks. His subsequent Columbia research raised related questions concerning radio's industrial logics, ideological distortions, and sociocultural impact. These remarks on the economic, political, and sociological dimensions of radio were by no means isolated, but closely paralleled many points in Arnheim's early film writings. While Arnheim himself emphasized the formalist elements of his work, any effort to assess his scholarly legacy must engage with the full range of analytical methods employed in these writings. To do so is to recognize not one but multiple, intertwining strands of thought: to see in Arnheim, beyond *Materialtheorie*, a rich and multidimensional theory of aesthetic form whose methods and insights hold continued promise for media scholarship today.

notes

1. Rudolf Arnheim, *Film as Art*, Berkeley: University of California Press, 1957, p. 2. The original 1932 edition was published in Germany as *Film als Kunst*, Berlin: Ernst Rowohlt. The first English translation was published in 1933 as *Film*, trans. L. M. Sieveking and Ian F. D. Morrow, London: Faber and Faber.
2. Rudolf Arnheim, "Confessions of a Maverick," *Salmagundi* Nos. 78/79, Spring/Summer 1988, p. 50. As Noël Carroll and David Bordwell explain, Arnheim embraced an expressive (vs. imitative) theory of art, stressed film reproduction's divergence from the reality reproduced, and claimed these divergences as medium-specific properties to be embraced and exploited by film artists. See Noël Carroll, *Philosophical Problems of Classical Film Theory*, Princeton: Princeton University Press, 1988, pp. 17–91, and *Theorizing the Moving Image*, New York: Cambridge, 1996, pp. 3–36; David Bordwell, *On the History of Film Style*, Cambridge: Harvard University Press, 1997, pp. 27–35.
3. For "countermedium" and "realm," see "Confessions of a Maverick," p. 50; for "possibilities," see "Vincent Scully and Rudolf Arnheim—Dialogue," in Kent Kleinman and Leslie Van Duzer, eds., *Rudolf Arnheim: Revealing Vision*, Ann Arbor: University of Michigan Press, 1997, p. 124. *Radio* was first published in an English translation by Faber and Faber, 1936.
4. For "complemented," see "Vincent Scully and Rudolf Arnheim," p. 122; for international translation, see *Film as Art*, 1957, p. 5; for "sleeper," see "Confessions of a Maverick," p. 50.
5. For full details on Arnheim's scholarship and career, see Helmut H. Diederichs, "Complete Bibliography of Writings on Film by Rudolf Arnheim," in Rudolf Arnheim, *Film Essays and Criticism*, trans. Brenda Benthien, Madison: University of Wisconsin Press, 1997, pp. 233–248; Diederichs, "Gesamtverzeichnis der Schriften zu Film, Photo, Presse und

Rundfunk/Grammophon von Rudolf Arnheim," available online at
<http://www.soziales.fh-dortmund.de/diederichs/arnforum/ragesv1.htm>;
Ralph A. Smith, "Rudolf Arnheim: An International Bibliography of his
Writings," *Journal of Aesthetic Education*, Vol. 27 No. 4, Winter 1993, pp. 165–189;
Roy R. Behrens, "Rudolf Arnheim: The Little Owl on the Shoulder of
Athene," *Leonardo*, Vol. 31 No. 3, June/July 1998, pp. 231–233.

6. For discussion of radio in *Film*, 1933, see pp. 214–227, 294–296; for "A Forecast
of Television," see *Film as Art* (1957), pp. 188–193. For Columbia studies, see
Rudolf Arnheim and Martha Collins Bayne, "Foreign Language Broadcasts
over Local American Stations: A Study of a Special Interest Program," in
Paul F. Lazarsfeld and Frank N. Stanton eds., *Radio Research, 1941*, New York:
Duell, Sloan and Pearce, 1941, pp. 3–64, and Rudolf Arnheim, "The World
of the Daytime Serial," in Paul F. Lazarsfeld and Frank N. Stanton eds., *Radio
Research, 1942–1943*, New York: Duell, Sloan and Pearce, 1944, pp. 34–85,
reprinted by Arno Press, New York, 1979. *Radio* was first published in
German as *Rundfunk als Hörkunst*, München: Hansen, 1979, then reissued with
a collection of early essays as *Rundfunk als Hörkunst und weitere Aufsätze zum Hörfunk*,
Frankfurt: Suhrkamp, 2001. An Italian edition was published in 1937, with
1987 and 1993 reissues; see *La radio cerca la sua forma*, Milano: Ulrico Hoepli,
1937; and, *La radio: l'arte dell'ascolto*, Rome: Riuniti, 1987, 1993. For English
reprints, see *Radio*, Arno, 1971, and Ayer, 1986, and *Radio: An Art of Sound*, De
Capo, 1972. Thanks to Doron Galili for helping to secure the Suhrkamp
essays, and for Hannah Goodwin for her invaluable assistance translating
these. All other quotes are taken from existing English translations.

7. Sabine Hake, *The Cinema's Third Machine: Writing on Film in Germany, 1907–1933*,
Lincoln: University of Nebraska Press, 1993, p. 290. For additional comment
on the 1974 introduction, see Gertrud Koch, "Rudolf Arnheim: The
Materialist of Aesthetic Illusion—Gestalt and Reviewer's Practice," *New
German Critique*, 51, Autumn 1990, p. 168.

8. *Radio*, 1986, p. 226.

9. Ibid., pp. 17–18.

10. "Hörspiele" (1927), in *Rundfunk als Hörkunst*, 2001, p. 182.

11. See, respectively, "Kiebitz, Fachmann, Lautsprecher" (orig. published in *Der
Querschnitt*, 1932), "Funkliteratur" (*Die Weltbühne*, 1932), and "Fragen an den
Tonmeister" (*Filmtechnik*, 1933), in *Rundfunk als Hörkunst*, 2001, pp. 203–206,
194–197, 207–210.

12. For "in search of," see "Der Rundfunk sucht seine Form" (*Die Weltbühne*,
1932), in *Rundfunk als Hörkunst*, 2001, pp. 185–189. For remaining quotes, see
"Film und Funk," *Neue Zürcher Zeitung*, 1933, in ibid., pp. 211–213. While
expressing reservations about radio's ability to attain the same heights as
the photographic arts, Arnheim was nonetheless hopeful that it might
someday "bring forth an important and enjoyable audio culture" of its own
(p. 213).

13. Arnheim, *Film*, 1933, pp. 215–216.

14. Ibid., p. 218.

15. For Arnheim's discussion of microphone distance, transparency, and
reverberation see *Film*, 1933, pp. 221–222, and "Film und Funk," pp. 213–214.
For "Directionality," etc., see "Fragen an den Tonmeister," pp. 207–210.

16. "A Forecast of Television," p. 190, and *Radio*, 1986, pp. 95–104 and 57–94.

17. For "give up," see *Film*, 1933, p. 232. For "shots" [*Einstellungen*], see "Film und
Funk," p. 213.

18. *Radio*, 1986, p. 127.

19. For "relaying apparatus," see ibid., p. 141; for "creating," ibid., pp. 137–138.
20. Ibid., p. 132.
21. Ibid., p. 14.
22. For a later, more extensive discussion of the expressive qualities of art, see Rudolf Arnheim, *Art and Visual Perception: A Psychology of the Creative Eye*, The New Version, Berkeley: University of California Press, 1974, pp. 444–461. Comparing this chapter of *Art and Visual Perception* with ideas developed in the original film book, Carroll rightly notes several important shifts in Arnheim's views on expressivity; see Carroll, *Philosophical Problems*, pp. 58–75. Nonetheless, Arnheim held to the view that projection of expressive, emotional qualities was a defining goal of art throughout his career.
23. *Radio*, 1986, p. 28.
24. Ibid., pp. 30, 42. As with his earlier *Film* chapter, Arnheim argued that sound cinema could benefit from studying methods used in radio. While filmmakers had much to learn in this department, Arnheim approvingly noted a small number of "experimental films" that treated the "sound-strip" as not merely an illustration of the "image-strip" but separately, in a "kind of isolation [that] arrives quite logically at wireless-forms" (p. 16).
25. Ibid., p. 141.
26. Ibid., p. 285.
27. Ibid., p. 237.
28. *Film*, 1933, pp. 294–295.
29. For "bridging," see "Der Rundfunk sucht seine Forme," p. 187. For remaining quotes, see "Funkliteratur," p. 196.
30. *Radio*, 1986, pp. 252–253, 257.
31. See "Funkliteratur," p. 196. Arnheim was responding in particular to calls for specialized programming by contemporary radio scholar Ernst Jolowicz; see Jolowicz, *Der Rundfunk: Eine psychologische Untersuchung*, Berlin: Verlag, 1932.
32. *Radio*, 1986, p. 249.
33. As models for this type of aesthetic practice, Arnheim cited Jack London novels or plays by Bertolt Brecht; see "Der Rundfunk sucht seine Form," p. 187.
34. *Radio*, 1986, p. 249.
35. For "excellently teach," see "Der Rundfunk sucht seine Form," pp. 187–188. For "bleak esoterica," see "Funkliteratur," p. 196.
36. For "distract themselves," see "Der Rundfunk sucht seine Form," p. 187. For "passive listener," see "Funkliteratur," p. 195. Arnheim hastened to add that, "It is important not to accept the wild listening practices of the average radio listener . . . as standard and given, but as a sign of the necessity to educate the listener."
37. *Radio*, 1986, p. 260–261.
38. Ibid., p. 265. Productive comparisons might be drawn between Arnheim's views and Walter Benjamin's discussion of the "withering" of the artwork's "aura" through technological reproduction. "Technical reproduction," Benjamin explains, "can put a copy of the original into situations which would be out of reach for the original itself." As a result, "the quality of [the artwork's] presence is always depreciated," and audiences no longer engage it with the same degree of attention or devotion as the original. See Walter Benjamin, "The Work of Art in the Era of Mechanical Reproduction," trans. Harry Zohn, in Hannah Arendt ed., *Illuminations: Essays and Reflections*, New York: Schocken, 1968, pp. 220–221.
39. *Radio*, 1986, p. 269.

40. Ibid., p. 274 (orig. emphasis).
41. Ibid., p. 268.
42. Behrens, "The Little Owl," p. 232.
43. Marjorie Fiske and Paul Lazarsfeld, "The Columbia Office of Radio Research," *Hollywood Quarterly*, Vol. 1 No. 1, October 1945, p. 51. On the history of the Radio Office, see David Morrison, "The Beginnings of Modern Mass Communication Research," *European Journal of Sociology*, 19, 1978, pp. 347–359; Daniel Czitrom, *Media and the American Mind: From Morse to McLuhan*, Chapel Hill: University of North Carolina, 1982, pp. 122–146; Paddy Scannell, *Media and Communication*, Sage: Thousand Oaks, 2007, pp. 63–90.
44. Hake, *The Cinema's Third Machine*, p. 290.
45. *Film*, 1933, p. 141.
46. Quoted in Hake, *The Cinema's Third Machine*, p. 292. Hake is working here from the 1974 German edition of *Film als Kunst*, Munich: Hanser.
47. Arnheim, *Film as Art*, 1957, p. 4. "I have omitted . . . the chapters tangled with tasks for which respectable techniques are now available," Arnheim explained, citing what he referred to as his "sketchy 'content analysis' of the standard movie ideology," in particular. As Hake notes in her discussion of the 1974 introduction, Arnheim did not necessarily seek to repudiate this aspect of his scholarship. However, as he himself explained it, "analysis of the formal means [of film production] . . . must necessarily precede any ideological analysis," and it was thus this element that he chose to emphasize in the revised editions. Hake, *The Cinema's Third Machine*, p. 290.
48. "Professional Film Criticism," in Arnheim, *Film Essays and Criticism*, p. 105. For further discussion of this article, see Koch, "The Materialist of Aesthetic Illusion," p. 169. David Bordwell has also called attention to this concern with trade practices in Arnheim's criticism, citing Arnheim's admonition in the 1974 edition of *Art and Visual Perception* that "Good art theory must smell of the studio." See this volume, Bordwell, "Rudolf Arnheim: Clarity, Simplicity, Balance" (Chapter 1).
49. Arnheim, *Film*, 1933, p. 293 (orig. emphasis). This 1933 edition was prefaced with an introduction by British film critic Paul Rotha, who cast Arnheim's industry analysis as a defining aspect of his critical project. Rotha himself disagreed with Arnheim's conclusion in this edition "that 'artistic films are films produced without regard to the general public' "; nonetheless, he affirmed that the dominant commercial production system had created conditions inimical to art, it being "clear from precedent that a creative mentality cannot flourish under factory conditions such as those which most trade executives have chosen to enforce in the past." Arnheim, *Film*, 1933, pp. x–xi.
50. Arnheim, "Film and the State," in *Film Essays and Criticism*, p. 89.
51. *Film*, 1933, p. 165.
52. Hake, *The Cinema's Third Machine*, p. 293.
53. Arnheim, *Film*, 1933, p. 293. Arnheim raised a similar point with regard to radio in a 1932 essay, remarking that it was to be fully expected "that the ruling social class would . . . use such an important tool of power" to its advantage, and that any meaningful change in form and content would require more fundamental changes in "politics-at-large"; see "Der Rundfunk sucht seine Form," p. 186.
54. Arnheim and Bayne, "Foreign Language Broadcasts," p. 3.
55. Ibid., pp. 13, 58.
56. Ibid., p. 61.

57. Arnheim, "The World of the Daytime Serial," pp. 41, 44, 48.
58. Ibid., pp. 72–76, 78.
59. Ibid., pp. 79, 81–82.
60. Ibid., p. 85. "It is time to realize that art, education, and entertainment are not . . . neatly separated from each other," he explained. "Art that fails to entertain and that misleads instead of educating" was no better than "entertainment that detracts from the aims and real satisfactions of life," and "unsatisfactory entertainment can be defeated . . . only if we believe that art, now largely reserved to the 'happy few' can be restored in its full meaning to the many who created it wherever it has existed."
61. For additional information on the Guggenheim study, see Behrens, "The Little Owl," p. 232.
62. Rudolf Arnheim, "Style as a Gestalt Problem," *Journal of Aesthetics and Art Criticism*, Vol. 39 No. 3, Spring 1981, p. 283.
63. Ibid., pp. 286, 288.

television from afar

arnheim's understanding of media

d o r o n g a l i l i

Rudolf Arnheim's essay, "A Forecast of Television," became well known in film studies following its inclusion in *Film as Art* more than twenty years after its original version appeared in Italy in 1935. As its title suggests, the essay offers a speculative theorization about television. It was written during the period when television was not yet put into practice as a mass medium, but was no longer a matter of science fiction, having been tested successfully in numerous laboratories and stations around the world. However, despite its inclusion in the canonical volume of Arnheim's writings and its unusual status as a remarkably early theoretical consideration of television, the essay has not inspired a great deal of scholarly debate or enduring influence on subsequent media studies.

To a great extent, it is possible to argue that within the context of *Film as Art*'s focus on the question of what could qualify cinema as an artistic form, "A Forecast of Television" indeed adds little to the understanding of Arnheim's aesthetic theory. The essay's discussion of media in relation to human sense perception, insistence on the use of medium-specific expressive means, and rejection of combinations of media, are very much in line with the parameters Arnheim established earlier with respect to cinema, and developed further in his more influential essay, "A New Laocoön" (which also mentions television in passing).[1] Television, in Arnheim's view, exemplifies a hybrid medium. Mixing sound and moving images–two means of expression that were already manifested in their pure forms in radio and silent film–television could not develop its own new artistic devices; thus, it had to rely on the dramaturgic principle of other media forms. Additionally, Arnheim feared that television's reliance on direct and continuous "live" transmission would sacrifice its ability to utilize montage techniques (with the exception of broadcasts of pre-recorded footage), since live transmission could not enable the selection of the best shots and their arrangement in an artistically meaningful order. For these reasons, Arnheim did not foresee television possessing any aesthetic value, and did not regard it as an art form. "It is a mere instrument of transmission," he writes, "which does not offer new means for the artistic interpretation of reality—as radio and film did."[2]

However, Arnheim's early engagement with television is interesting not only as an example of putting yet another object under the scrutiny of his familiar aesthetic theory. The assertion that television does not qualify as an art form allowed Arnheim to theorize on aspects that go beyond his typical concern with artistic values, and elaborate on the new technology's relations to other media and its anticipated social and political impact. As he admitted years later, his attempts to foresee the future of the technology, in "A Forecast of Television" and a number of other texts, were for Arnheim a way to lose himself in "futuristic fantasy."[3]

Given proper and overdue attention, those futuristic fantasies reveal a little-known aspect of Arnheim's work. In the following pages, I revisit Arnheim's under-explored writings on television from throughout the 1930s in order to demonstrate how this key thinker, who is best known for his commitment to concepts of medium specificity and interest in aspects that distinguish media from one another, was also attentive to questions of intermedial relationships. Arnheim conceives of television as a technology that combined and extended the capacities of film and radio, and in turn threatened to replace them altogether. In this respect, his strikingly early attempts at theorizing television have much in common with current studies of new media devices and practices. The ideas he expresses in his 1930s writings on television are thus of particular relevance to today's speculations on the implications of the convergence of distinct media, the future developments of new digital media, and the links between technological changes and new economic and cultural conditions.

This examination of Arnheim's writing on television also allows an assessment of his work—which has traditionally been discussed in the contexts of film studies, art theory and gestalt psychology—in the context of media studies, which reveals how his observations prefigure central concepts from later media theory. Particularly, Arnheim's concern with how television would absorb or replace film demonstrates how he never considered film's history, technology, and social impact as distinct from those of television. In this sense, a better familiarity with his early theorization on television complements our understanding of his well-known observations on specificity with a view on his approach to matters of intermedial relations and media convergence, and sheds new light on his classical writings on film. Arnheim's thought on the coming of television presents conceptions of media specificity and of distinctions between media that are fundamentally different from the concepts most commonly related to his film theory. This more flexible and dynamic understanding of media may prove to be of particular relevance to today's study of new media forms.

rudolf arnheim, television, and media convergence

By 1935, the mode of forecasting was not new to Arnheim. Neither was the interest in television. As a number of commentators note, a great part of his theoretical work is invested in speculating on the future of cinema (or, for that matter, radio) and prescribing proper aesthetic principles for it.[4] The emergence of television, at once a new moving-image medium and a new form of broadcasting, attracted Arnheim's critical attention as a natural extension of his studies of both media. In various writings from throughout the 1930s, Arnheim referred to the emerging medium as "Radio-Film," as both "a marriage" and "struggle" between radio and film, and as "a hybrid creature, born of the movies, the radio, and the theater."[5] Tellingly, he chose to conclude his first two major theoretical books, *Film* (*Film als Kunst*, 1932) and *Radio* (1936), with chapters about the coming of television. In these speculations about the advent of television from an intermedial perspective, Arnheim remarks that television is not only lacking in aesthetic value, but may also have the power to corrupt the artistic potential of other media.

Arguments about the coming of television appeared in Arnheim's writings about the future of cinema starting as early as 1930, alongside the objections to sound and color films that became fundamental in the reception of his film theory.[6] Whereas for Arnheim sound and color films threatened the medium's aesthetics by bringing it closer to a mechanical recording of reality, he hoped silent black-and-white film could coexist alongside them. The coming of television, conversely, was in his view a threat to the very existence of film. "Within measurable time," he writes, "films will be broadcast from a central projecting station by wireless, so that the same film will be performed in hundreds of theatres simultaneously, or may even be listened-in to in private houses."[7] According to this prediction, once television technology became available to producers, the traditional method of filming, printing, and distributing reels of film would become economically unviable compared with the transmission of a single live performance from a studio to millions of receivers at once. Under such conditions, Arnheim warned, the film industry would cease. The motivation of television broadcasters to cater to as broad an audience as possible would then lead them to aim at lower artistic standards than those of film, in order to satisfy viewers uninterested in art who would seek "distraction and amusement" in the form of "raw, pointless viewing."[8]

Radio aesthetics, according to Arnheim, was facing a similar fate in its competition with television. In many ways, Arnheim's turn from the study of film aesthetics to the study of radio (which he undertook the year *Film* was published) may be seen as motivated by his disappointment with the way the pure visual form of silent cinema was ruined with the coming of sound. Radio signified a new, exciting medium that could realize Arnheim's aesthetic ideals by purely aural means. However, Arnheim doubted that radio could exist in its pure form for much longer. He anticipated that television would take over broadcasting, and that the audiovisual trans-missions—which, like the sound film, were closer to a concrete and factual depiction of reality—would destroy radio's pure aesthetic character "even more radically than the sound film destroyed silent film."[9]

In the terms of today's discourse on media, those forecasts suggest that Arnheim thought of television as a product of technological and economic media convergence.[10] Television, in this view, is a hybrid not only of different aesthetic means, but also of various technologies and institutions. Arnheim foresaw the integration of sound broadcasting and moving image media into the new all-encompassing televisual technology. Accordingly, he antici-pated that television's economic potential would attract film producers and radio broadcasters to the new medium. What is at stake in this case, therefore, goes beyond matters of elitist taste; in Arnheim's account, such convergence of media could profoundly impact not just aesthetic standards, but the very nature of cultural production.

In a section titled "Radio Film," which concludes his book *Film* (and was excluded from its later shortened version, *Film as Art*), Arnheim discusses the appearance of television in a manner which resembles the remarks made by media theorist Friedrich Kittler decades later about digital technology's creation of a single converged and standardized "information channel that can be used for any medium."[11] As Arnheim predicted, technological advances would make it possible to broadcast sounds and images to the entire country from a single television transmitter. The new technology, he claims, would not only put an end to the prolific and diverse film and radio industries, but also eliminate the need for multiple television broadcasting stations. Moreover, Arnheim predicts that when all audiovisual media content would derive from a single televisual "central-monopoly-station," all decision-making "would lie with *one* person."[12]

For Arnheim, the convergence of media technologies and institutions into a single transmission station meant "dire uniformity." In his view, the cultural development of the nation depended on "a multiplicity of local and provincial stimuli and opportunities for evolution."[13] The monopolization of television broadcasts and its assimilation of other technological media marked for him the beginning of a "thoroughgoing standardization of all forms of culture."[14] This assertion demonstrates the extent to which the political currents of the late Weimar period influenced Arnheim, as it describes a situation analogous to that of totalitarian government control over media institutions. Arnheim's concerns regarding the impending centralization of power, silencing of creative voices, and standardization of culture in the political realm are thus projected in this text onto his account of the concurrent process of technological media change. When the Nazi party came to power in Germany and banned Arnheim's book just months after its publication, this anxiety proved justified. Soon after, as part of the efforts towards the centralization of culture, the Nazi government launched the first regular television service in the world. It is very appropriate, therefore, that Arnheim concludes *Film* with the statement "The future of film depends on the future of economics and politics . . . what will happen to film depends upon what happens to ourselves."[15]

In the summer of 1933 Arnheim left Germany and spent the next six years in Italy, where he continued writing about television on occasion. Upon his arrival in Rome, he received an appointment as a researcher, translator, and editor at the International Institution of Educational Cinematography. The Institution was founded in Italy by the League of Nations in order to promote international political communication through the study and the making of educational films.[16] In February 1935, the Institute's official journal, *Intercine*, dedicated a special volume to television. That volume featured Arnheim's essay "Seeing Afar Off," which later appeared in an abbreviated English version as "A Forecast of Television." As opposed to the fear of the monopolization of media that Arnheim expresses in his writing in Germany, "Seeing Afar Off" concludes with a plea to the modern state to exercise its authority and put television to positive use. As Arnheim remarks in this essay, the "monopolization of intellectual life" could mean standardization not only in a negative sense; it could also "assist at the same time that unification of popular culture which today is so much desired by every government capable of interpreting the spirit of the times."[17] The essay's conclusion suggests that the state utilize the advantages of television in order to reawaken communal feelings and to save the creative powers of the individual from being "irrevocably atrophied by the division of labor." In accordance with the Institute's stated purpose, Arnheim calls for a productive use of television, saying, "The state might allocate the beautiful new reception apparatus to its proper place, to convert passivity to activity, so that what treasures the electric wave brings into the house don't rot like dead capital but are made useful."[18]

"Seeing Afar Off" puts its faith in state administration of media not only due to renewed political optimism, but also as a result of what Arnheim observed regarding the control of radio and cinema in the 1930s. According to him, radio programs have greater intellectual and education value than the cinema. While in his view the film studios were managed by profit-driven producers "of execrable taste and minimum culture," radio services in most countries are under the influence of governments who use it for educational ends rather than give in to public taste. For Arnheim, the cultural significance of television was going to be determined by the outcome of the struggle between values it inherited from cinema and values it inherited from radio. The possibility that the new medium would follow the model of radio and be under the control of the state was therefore preferable in his view to television being privately owned and becoming an arm of what we might call today "the culture industry." Nonetheless, as the exclusion of the essay's concluding section from its 1957 republication indicates, the hope that television could offer an alternative to mindless entertainment media was not realized even long after the appearance of television.

between medium specificity and intermediality

The notions of hybridity and convergence that initially drew Arnheim's interest to television remained central in a number of his essays on the new technology throughout the 1930s. In those essays, Arnheim revises some of the notions regarding media specificity that he articulates in his film theory. *Film as Art*'s insistence that the unique formal properties and physical structure of the cinematic apparatus must dictate the proper aesthetic use of film has been criticized as essentialist, for it assumes the existence of a fixed inherent nature of each medium.[19] However, in his writings on television's relationships with other media, Arnheim puts forth a more dynamic and flexible conception of what constitutes a medium, which goes beyond reliance on the material characteristics and distinctions among media.

Arnheim's revised notion about media becomes apparent in his discussion of television in the concluding chapter of *Radio*, where he claims that, "With the addition of picture, radio loses its peculiarity as a new medium of expression and becomes purely a medium of dissemination."[20] Put differently, Arnheim indicates in this claim that although television is a new technology, and although it has novel aural and visual methods of representation, it is not a medium in its own right but merely a new variation of radio. This claim conflicts with the common understanding of what constitutes a medium; despite the fundamental material differences between the technologies of radio and television, it refers to them as different manifestations of the same medium.

Arnheim introduced the notion that a single medium may exist in different material variations earlier on in his writings on sound films, where he questions whether or not sound cinema is a new medium governed by its own aesthetic laws. Instead of an essentialist, fixed notion of what constitutes a medium, he provides a spatial analogy according to which every artistic medium is a sphere consisting of a center, periphery, and outer boundaries. Commenting on the hybridization of moving images and recorded sound, Arnheim writes that "At its edges," a medium may indeed "encroach upon other domains." However, he adds, "[i]t is not the boundaries of a sphere of art that are important, but its center . . . Great artists strive towards the center of their subject . . . they work in perfectly clean media."[21] According to this view, silent film is the center, that is, the purest form of the sphere of cinema, while sound films are closer to its boundaries—where cinema overlaps with the sphere of theater.

This formulation also sheds light on Arnheim's view of television. It suggests that the differences between the material properties of radio and television do not make them distinct media. Rather, the two technologies appear to be two manifestations of what Arnheim sees as the medium of broadcasting.[22] Broadcasting may take the form of aural, visual, or audio-visual technology, while still remaining the same medium; like all media, it is neither coherent nor fixed. Within the sphere of broadcasting, radio defines the center due to its reliance on pure aural means of expression. The hybrid form of television, on the other hand, is considered to be farther away in the periphery of broadcasting, where its overlap with the boundaries of cinema brings together moving images with sound.

Like other classical film theorists, Arnheim elaborated in his canonical writings about the factors that distinguish film from theater. He points out, for instance, that as opposed to the effect of the actual space and the presence of real flesh-and-blood performers in the theater, cinema only involves a two-dimensional, colorless representation of performers and spaces, bound in the limits of the film frame. In addition, he singles out the device of cinematic montage, which grants film a greater degree of temporal and spatial liberty than that of the theater.[23] The encounter with television, however, prompted Arnheim to present a different view on the distinction between a live performance and its presentation in a technological medium. Writing about NBC's multi-camera television studio in New York in a 1937 article, Arnheim elaborated on television's new ability to emulate (to a degree) the possibilities of filmic montage by shifting between the points of view of several cameras during a live transmission. Arnheim greatly valued this technique. For him, the "simple transmission" of a performance, deprived of the ability to shift between different points of view, "would not be enough to distinguish a television show from a normal theatrical production." As he remarks, "It would be theater electrically transmitted through space, but still theater!"[24]

By stating that a theatrical performance could be represented on the small electronic screen, apart from its actual space and flesh-and-blood presence, and yet remain "still theater," Arnheim clearly devalues the extent to which material properties distinguish between media. As film theorist Mary Ann Doane noted in her recent exploration of the concept of medium specificity in film, "Despite its essentialist connotations, medium specificity is a resolutely historical notion, its definition incessantly mutating in various sociohistorical contexts."[25] The historical moment of the technological realization of television brought such change in context. It required Arnheim to rearticulate his view regarding specificity and distinctions among media, because of the way television's direct transmission could, in his view, deliver films and theatrical productions while fully adopting (or mediating) their respective dramaturgies. The notion that televised films or theater performances retain all the expressive means and dramaturgical principles of their original media suggests that, for Arnheim, the artistic significance of a medium may in fact be manifested autonomously from its original material support.

Arnheim's view of television as a new platform that would absorb existing forms such as film and theater and would function as "a lecturer's desk, a concert platform, and a pulpit" anticipates Jay Bolter and Richard Grusin's influential concept of remediation. Bolter and Grusin define remediation as "the representation of one medium in another," and consider it a "defining characteristic of the new digital media" that absorb and re-appropriate former media forms.[26] They provide a description and analysis of a "spectrum of ways in which digital media remediate their predecessors," which they define according to the "degree of perceived competition or rivalry between the new media and the old." Since Arnheim argues that films and theater performances may retain their expressive qualities while being transmitted on television, it is possible to claim that in Bolter and Grusin's terms he sees televisual remediation as an extreme case where the essential characteristics of older media are represented by a new technology "without apparent irony and critique."[27] For Arnheim, in other words, television's act of mediation is transparent.

Similar arguments about the ability of a new technological medium to adopt the formal characteristics of other media and by that to challenge the accepted distinctions between the media have been made by theorist Lev Manovich with respect to digital technology. Discussing the capacity of various digital devices to simulate works that originated on different material bases, Manovich argues that once it is possible to "make radically different versions of the same art object . . . the traditional strong link between the identity of an art object and its medium becomes broken." For Manovich, this is one of the motivations to develop "a new conceptual system which would replace the old discourse of mediums," given that the "traditional concept of medium does not work in relation to post-digital, post-net culture."[28] Conversely, Arnheim's discussion of television comes to a diametrically opposed conclusion precisely because television is able to adopt seamlessly the forms of other media. Arnheim writes that on the television screen, the differences between film and theater would either appear non-existent, or would "have to be founded on more essential and inner differences."[29] In other words, instead of discarding the theoretical category of medium altogether, Arnheim insists that television may bring to light finer diagnoses regarding the specific features of each medium. As he argues, while the distinction between theater and film is traditionally related to the fact that the former involves "an actual flesh and blood performance" and the latter "a projected representation," the televisual transmission of films or stage performances proves these physical qualities to be mere "external facts." For Arnheim, the fact that filmic and theatrical works may both be televised as electronic images indicates that it is rather the dramaturgic principles that are important as the "essential and inner" characteristics that define the specificity of film and theater. This way, the spatiotemporal continuity and the centrality that are given to the spoken word may be seen as the essential qualities of theater, while the shifts between different points of view, times, and spaces may typify film more accurately than its material basis. In Arnheim's view, therefore, television's ability to transmit films and stage performances would enable the inspection of the aesthetic characteristics of cinema and theater separately from their respective material bases. This way, their truly essential artistic qualities could more fully reveal themselves. The appearance of television thus challenged Arnheim's existing ideas of medium specificity, but at the same time allowed him to articulate a new insight about the qualities that define and distinguish various media.

foreseeing the future television spectator

The assertion that television is a hybrid medium with no particular aesthetic value of its own also influenced the way Arnheim theorized the issue of television spectatorship. In his film theory, Arnheim is interested in the perception of formal and compositional qualities, as he explores the ways spectators engage with filmic images by recognizing patterns, creating expectations, and making new observations. His discussion of television spectatorship, conversely, does not revolve around the questions of visual perception. The significant novelty in the coming of television was for Arnheim not a matter of new aesthetic characteristics or possibilities, since he regarded the visual aspect of television as not different from that of film. According to him, the new and unique aspects of television were rather its temporal nature and the new contexts of reception it introduced by transmitting pictures into the home.[30]

Arnheim finds that television's "live" simultaneous transmission makes its impact on viewers distinct from that of cinema. As he writes, "Television will not only portray the world as the film does . . . but it will make this portrayal all the more fascinating because instead of seeing the mere records, we shall be able to participate in distant events the moment of their happening."[31] Arnheim does not find that the way television allows "to perceive *immediately* what is visible in far off places" has an aesthetic significance in and of itself. Yet, he claims that the "liveness" of television affects not only the spectators' relation towards the transmitted images, but also their attitude towards reality.[32]

From a strictly aesthetic perspective, Arnheim claimed that live transmission is one of the chief factors that impair television's expressive possibilities, because it does not allow selecting and organizing materials by means of montage. However, he also notes that since live transmission of images and sounds does not represent events in a false artificial succession, it could enable viewers to "feel the multiplicity of everything that happens simultaneously" and be aware that they are "only one point among many." Such realization, according to Arnheim, would make the television viewer of the future "more modest and less egocentric."[33] This utopian prediction bears striking resemblance to Marshall McLuhan's concept of "the global village," according to which the decentralizing effect of electronic media would ultimately create a universal collective consciousness and restore the universal feeling of tribalism that modern life annihilated. Furthermore, by focusing on television's potential effect on its viewers' worldviews not through the contents of the programs, but through the very experience of the technological capacities of the apparatus itself, Arnheim also anticipates by several decades McLuhan's famous assertion that "the medium is the message."[34]

Based on this conception of the new technology, Arnheim considers the social implications of the coming of television as twofold. The positive social effects of television, in his view, derive from its ability to facilitate a rich cultural exchange between nations, and grant access to visual information in a faster, finer, and more concrete fashion than other media allow. With television, as he states, "the world in all its vastness comes to our room."[35] Arnheim goes as far as describing television, put to proper use, as an embodiment of a democratic ideal that provides a new technological manner to bypass opaque and indirect government systems and grant the public a greater involvement in state affairs.

However, although Arnheim finds utopian potential in instantaneous television transmission, he is not a proponent of technological determinism. He insists that while television enhances the human sensory capacity, it would be the viewers' responsibility to interpret adequately the new information it would make available. Arnheim considers television as a new instrument of "the cult of sensory perception"—a social tendency he observed as typical for the era of technological media.[36] "The easier and more accessible the means of perception become," he notes, "the firmer becomes fixed in us the dangerous illusion that seeing means knowing."[37] According to Arnheim, true knowledge of "the character of the present world situation, of the crisis, of the form of a modern state is not immediately recognizable by means for the senses." Rather, "If anyone wants to understand the present epoch, he should speak with the people, the businessman; he should read the memoirs of diplomats." In Arnheim's view, true understanding depends on grasping general concepts, whereas television can only present its audience with images of particular cases. Since concrete and raw visual sensation requires analysis and interpretation, television would be beneficial only to viewers who are accustomed to independent and critical thought, unless its programs are accompanied by a commentary track that provides the voice of "an invisible commentator." Contrary to his rejection of the addition of sound to moving images in the cinema, Arnheim argues that in television a voice-over narration and interpretation could complement the presentation of particular images with the introduction of general, abstract concepts. As he puts it, the spoken words may introduce the causes, while the images merely present the effects.

Well aware of the fact that television broadcasts inevitably address a broader audience than that of critically reflective spectators, Arnheim also pointed out their potential negative social effects. He argued that by offering an appealing substitute for intellectual means of acquiring concepts such as conversing and reading, television threatens to weaken those capabilities for communication and education. Arnheim's view of human faculties is similar in this sense to his view of media technologies and art forms, where the more convenient and immediately available means supersede and marginalize their rivals. As he writes, "when it becomes sufficient to move the finger in order to indicate, it may come about that the lips will grow mute, the hand that writes or draws will be arrested, and the spirit will perish."[38] Accordingly, Arnheim predicts that the television viewer of the future may become a culturally impoverished and anti-social being. Whereas spectators in a theatrical setting partake in a genuinely collective experience and have the ability to respond actively to the film or the performance by cheering, laughing, weeping, or booing, this has no equivalent in Arnheim's description of the domestic television spectator. For him, television allows its viewers to be merely passive consumers of spectacles, isolated from society since they are content with the televisual simulation of the presence of others.[39]

Recognizing a utopian potential, as well as possible negative psychological and social effects of television, Arnheim's perspective on the new technology is highly ambivalent. As "A Forecast of Television" states, "Television is a new, hard test of our wisdom. If we succeed in mastering the new medium it will enrich us. But it can also put our mind to sleep."[40] The meaning of "enrich" in this context is relatively clear: television's ability to function as an educational device, provide documentary information, facilitate global exchange of cultural products, and allow an understanding of the complexity of the world, are all valued by Arnheim as enlightening effects.

Conversely, the meaning of Arnheim's assertion that television could also "put our mind to sleep" is not made clear in the essay. Arnheim states, however, that the ease of communication by modern means may weaken the human powers of expression and creativity. It is worth paying attention to how this concept corresponds to Arnheim's views about the role of art and its relation to the mind, as expressed in his writings in the fields of psychology and aesthetics. As Ara Merjian notes in his insightful discussion of Arnheim's film and art theory, for Arnheim "art is a tool, a method of learning about the world so as to more easily inhabit it . . . viewing art is a form of necessary mental and perceptual exercise."[41] To briefly recap Arnheim's position, visual perception involves interpretation and organization of raw sensory material into meaningful forms.[42] Works of art, similarly, embody a procedure of interpretation of raw materials from reality, although on a higher order. Artists express and organize their work's particular subject matters in a manner that captures something universally significant about reality. The encounter with such works of visual art thus demands from the viewer an intensified act of interpretation. This way, art challenges and coaches the viewer's mental capacities by making perceivable principles of organization and meaning of reality that the viewer otherwise remains unaware of. Experiencing art, therefore, actively and productively intensifies the capacities of the mind. In other words, it is the opposite of putting the mind to sleep.

In this light, it is possible to argue that Arnheim considers television not only as lacking artistic means of expression, but also as countering the effects of art in a manner that might numb the mind. This is not to say, of course, that every non-artistic object has such an effect. The dichotomy between "enrich" and "put us to sleep" does not correspond to the dichotomy between aesthetic and not-aesthetic. Even at its best, Arnheim would argue, television cannot acquire a medium-specific artistic value of its own, but it still may have positive social and educational effects. However, since Arnheim believed that "without the flourishing of visual expression no culture can function productively," television's power to supersede other media appeared to him as a threat to the mental capacities of individuals as well as to culture as a whole.[43] He feared that the ubiquitous audiovisual offering of the impure medium of television, administered by profit-driven producers who aim at cheap amusement entertainment, would replace the artistic products of radio and film with mere entertainment that does not enrich the mind. According to Arnheim's formulation, therefore, the future of television is still to be determined; but the potential loss it involves is far greater than the possible gain.

In the 1937 magazine article "Discipline of the Record Player, the Radio, the Telephone and Television," Arnheim suggests that the way to remedy or avoid the possible numbing effect of television is not by evading the medium altogether, but rather by carefully regimenting and measuring the manner of engaging with it. The term "Discipline" in the article's title refers to self-control and the restriction of the use of new devices, which Arnheim sees as the key to heightening their positive effects and eliminating their negative ones. For Arnheim, the danger the new devices introduce is not in the devices themselves, but rather in the uncontrolled tendency to see new technologies capable of answering every need. He invokes the figure of the Sorcerer's Apprentice to argue that the modern user of technology "risks his sovereignty over the spirits that he has called to his service" by not exercising discipline against the seduction of passivity.[44] In Arnheim's view, the efficiency of modern communication technologies "is tied to the economy—understood in the broad sense—of their use."[45] Therefore, new technologies are appropriate only when traditional means—human or technological—prove insufficient. Although the article deals with a large group of new technological devices, Arnheim clearly presents this etiquette of new technologies with the coming of television in mind—attempting to make use of the few years left before it becomes publicly available in order to advocate for the need to discipline the use of the new technology before its negative consequences take effect.

the shared concerns of classical film theory and new media studies

Arnheim's early writings on television reveal the extent to which his theoretical project shares similar concerns with current debates in film studies. Both the coming of television in the 1930s and the present increasing impact of digital technologies raise parallel questions about media convergence, obsolescence, and advent of new media, in a manner that challenges existing theoretical conceptions. Notably, many of today's debates on the impact of new media technologies on cinema revolve around questions of materiality. Numerous commentators have manifested particular concern with the way in which the transition from photochemical media to digital formats changes cinema's relation to history and reality, for it allegedly annihilates the indexical nature of photographic based filmic images.[46] Such views, in turn, have been criticized for allowing the material aspects to over-determine our understanding of media change, and for considering the emergence of digital media as a utopian "historic break in the nature of media and representation" rather than as a transformation that occurs within the existing context of media technology and practice.[47]

The dynamic and flexible conceptions of media that Arnheim puts forth in his writings about the coming of television seem particularly instructive for such theoretical debates on new media. Arnheim's early writings on media change demonstrate how the characteristics of each medium are

207

determined not only by its material structure, but also in accordance with shifting political and economic situations, patterns of reception, and inter- actions with other media. Undermining the centrality of the materiality in the understanding of media change, these writings point out how different media have different essential and inner aesthetic significance outside of their material bases, and that the same medium may even exist in several distinct material variations. Arnheim's view of media as spheres with "pure" centers and outer boundaries also allows the examination of media hybridization and convergence without sacrificing a positive notion of specificity. If, as he claims, the boundaries between media are fluid, then the appearance of each new technology also introduces multiple possibilities of combinations and overlaps with all other media. In this sense, each new media technology is not a distinct entity, for it may also be seen as impacting the entirety of the mediascape. This notion allows accounting for transformations in the mediascape by examining new particular configurations of existing forms— that is, to examine continuities rather than proclaimed historical breaks.

According to this view, film and new media belong together as parts of a unified discourse, which retains the sensitivity to distinctions between media without determining them solely according to their material bases. Whether or not we choose to hold to Arnheim's ideas of aesthetic evaluation, and whether or not we are interested in identifying what would be the "purest" form of digital media (if such exists), there is value in understanding digital moving image forms in relation to concepts of the theoretical paradigm of film, rather than as a radically new condition that requires a break from the existing notions of film or media theory.

Moreover, Arnheim's early writings on television also demonstrate how in a deeper sense, classical film theory and current film studies share a similar attitude towards cinema as their object of study. The body of works that constitutes classical film theory is often viewed as an historical attempt to come to terms with the new phenomenon of cinema by isolating it from other art forms and proposing fixed notions about its nature. Arnheim's legacy within this tradition is most strongly associated with a rigorous, essentialist insistence on medium-specificity principles. By contrast, con- temporary film scholarship is preoccupied with notions of crisis and radical transformations in the nature of the moving image. A number of theorists have argued recently that film theory must account for the ontological uncertainty that typifies the present state of film, and reconsider classical theory's fundamental inquiries regarding "what is cinema?" in light of film's impending disappearance, or convergence with new technologies.[48] As Mary Ann Doane remarked, "It is as though the object of theory were to delineate more precisely the contours of an object at the moment of its historical demise."[49]

But as Arnheim's writings of the 1930s demonstrate, despite his insistent position regarding the aesthetic possibilities of cinema, in his view film was never an isolated media phenomenon with fixed essential characteristics, for it continuously responded to changes in the modern mediascape. Given how the specters of the advent of television and the consequent threat to the future of film loom over Arnheim's major works on cinema, it could be argued that his theoretical project was motivated not by a will to provide fixed notions regarding the nature of film, but by a concern with the dynamics of its transformation, and, indeed, disappearance. Arnheim's classical theory, similar to many contemporary writings on film and new media, speculated on the cinema's possible futures in moments when the cinema appeared to change its cultural significance, and to converge with, or be entirely eclipsed by, other media forms. As Arnheim best described it in a retrospective observation he made in 1987, "When the silent film was replaced by the talkies and radio had to defend itself against television, I clung to those early media with a zoologist's love for endangered species."[50]

acknowledgments

I want to thank Chiara Montanari, Katharina Loew and Inga Pollmann for their invaluable help with translation during the research for this essay, and Julie Turnock, Jason Paul, Scott Richmond, Ariella Sidelsky and Renée Melton for their careful readings of previous versions of it. I am also indebted to the generous help and advice of Joshua Yumibe and Tom Gunning.

notes

1. For further discussion of "A New Laocoön" and the concept of medium hybridity, see Jinhee Choi's and Greg Smith's contributions to this volume (Chapters 7 and 12).
2. Rudolf Arnheim, "A Forecast of Television," in *Film as Art*, Berkeley: University of California Press, 1966, p. 194.
3. Rudolf Arnheim, "Immagine-avvenimento e durata," *Cinema Nuovo* No. 305, Jan.–Feb. 1987, p. 22 (translated by Bobby Baird).
4. See, for instance, Gertrud Koch's discussion of Arnheim's film criticism as "pre-construction" of film art in "Rudolf Arnheim: The Materialist of Aesthetic Illusion—Gestalt Theory and Reviewer's Practice," *New German Critique* No. 51, Fall 1990, pp. 164–178.
5. See Rudolf Arnheim, *Film*, London: Faber and Faber, 1933, p. 294; *Radio*, London, Faber and Faber, 1936, p. 286; and in "Televisione, Domani sarà così," *Cinema* No. 20, Apr. 1937, pp. 337–338 (translated by Bobby Baird).
6. See, for instance, "Die traurige Zukunft des Films," *Die Weltbühne* No. 37, 9 Sept. 1930, pp. 402–404 (translated as "The Sad Future of Film," in *Film Essays and Criticism*, Madison: University of Wisconsin Press, 1997, pp. 11–13) and "Die Zukunft des Tonfilms," 1934, reprinted in *Montage A/V* Vol. 9 No. 2, 2000, pp. 19–32.
7. Arnheim, *Film*, p. 294.
8. Arnheim, "The Sad Future of Film," p. 11.
9. Arnheim, *Radio*, p. 16.

10. See, for instance, Henry Jenkins, "Quentin Tarantino's Star Wars? Digital Cinema, Media Convergence, and Participatory Culture," in David Thorburn and Henry Jenkins (eds.), *Rethinking Media Change*, Cambridge: MIT Press, 2003, pp. 281–312, and "Convergence? I Diverge," *Technology Review*, June 2001, as well as Aril Fetveid, "Convergence by Means of Globalized Remediation," *Northern Lights* Vol. 5 No. 1, Sept. 2007, pp. 57–74.

11. F. A. Kittler, *Gramophone, Film, Typewriter*, Stanford: Stanford University Press, 1999, p. 1.

12. Arnheim, *Film*, p. 295 (emphasis in the original).

13. Ibid.

14. Ibid.

15. Ibid., p. 296.

16. For a history of the Institute, its studies and the methodologies it promoted see Jürgen Wilke, "Cinematography as a Medium of Communication: The Promotion of Research by the League of Nations and the Role of Rudolf Arnheim," *European Journal of Communication* No. 6, 1991, pp. 337–353.

17. Rudolf Arnheim, "Seeing Afar Off," *Intercine* Vol. 7 No. 2, Feb. 1935, p. 80 (revised translation by W. Martin).

18. Ibid., p. 82 (revised translation by W. Martin).

19. See the discussions of Arnheim's work in Noël Carroll, *Philosophical Problems of Classical Film Theory*, Princeton: Princeton University Press, 1988 and Dudley Andrew, *The Major Film Theories*, London: Oxford University Press, 1976.

20. Arnheim, *Radio*, p. 277 (translation modified; the word in the German origin "Rundfunk," means both radio and broadcasting. In this instance "radio" seems to be indicated, as Arnheim discusses earlier in the paragraph "blind broadcasting" ("blinde Rundfunk") reffering to the aural medium of radio. My modification is also consistent with the translation of "A Forecast of Television.")

21. Arnheim, *Film*, p. 209.

22. As noted above, "Rundfunk" means both radio and broadcasting.

23. See Arnheim, *Film as Art*, especially pp. 24–29.

24. Arnheim, "Televisione, Domani sarà così."

25. Mary Ann Doane, "The Indexical and the Concept of Medium Specificity," *Differences* Vol. 18 No.1, 2007, p. 129.

26. Jay David Bolter and Richard Grusin, *Remediation: Understanding New Media*, Cambridge: MIT Press, 1999, p. 45.

27. Ibid.

28. Lev Manovich, "Post-media aesthetics," 2001. Available online at http://www.manovich.net/ (accessed 29 January, 2009).

29. Arnheim, *Radio*, p. 277.

30. Arnheim, "Seeing Afar Off," p. 75.

31. Arnheim, *Radio*, p. 278.

32. Arnheim, "Seeing Afar Off," p. 75 (emphasis added).

33. Ibid., p. 77.

34. See Marshall McLuhan, *Understanding Media: The Extensions of Man*, Cambridge: MIT Press, 1994.

35. Arnheim, "Seeing Afar Off," p. 77.

36. Ibid. (Translation modified. The word "Anschauung" from the German original appeared as "apperception through sensory channels" in the 1935 translation, and as "sensory stimulation" in the version published in *Film as Art*.)

37. Ibid., p. 78.
38. Ibid.
39. Ibid., p. 81.
40. Arnheim, "A Forecast of Television," p. 195.
41. Ara Merjian, "Middlebrow Modernism: Rudolf Arnheim at the Crossroads of Film Theory and the Psychology of Art" in Angela Dalle Vacche (ed.), *The Visual Turn: Classical Film Theory and Art History*, New Brunswick: Rutgers University Press, 2003, p. 162.
42. See Andrew, *The Major Film Theories*, pp. 35–41.
43. Rudolf Arnheim, "Introduction," in *Film Essays and Criticism*, p. 3.
44. Rudolf Arnheim, "Disciplina del grammofono, della radio, del telefono e della televisione," *Sapere* Vol. 6 No. 71, 15 Dec. 1937, pp. 415–417 (translated by Bobby Baird). An English version of this text, translated by Christy Wampole, was published in *Modernism/Modernity* Vol. 16 No. 2, April 2009, pp. 422–426.
45. Arnheim, "Disciplina del grammofono."
46. See, for instance, comments on the topic in Doane, "The Indexical and the Concept of Medium Specificity" (especially pp. 130–132); Lev Manovich, *The Language of New Media*, Cambridge: MIT Press, 2001, pp. 293–296; and D. N. Rodowick, *The Virtual Life of Film*, Cambridge and London: Harvard University Press, 2007.
47. Philip Rosen, "Old and New: Image, Indexicality and Historicity in the Digital Utopia," in *Change Mummified: Cinema, Historicity, Theory*, Minneapolis: University of Minnesota Press, 2001, p. 302. Rosen offers an in-depth discussion of the concern regarding the question of indexicality in film and digital media. See also Tom Gunning's "What's the Point of an Index? Or, Faking Photographs," *Nordicom Review* Vol. 25 Nos 1–2, Sept. 2004, pp. 39–50.
48. See D. N. Rodowick, "An Elegy for Theory," *October* No. 122, Fall 2007, pp. 91–109.
49. Mary Ann Doane, "The Object of Theory", in Ivone Margulies (ed.), *Rites of Realism: Essays on Corporeal Cinema*, Durham: Duke University Press, 2003, p. 85.
50. Rudolf Arnheim, "A Maverick in Art History," in *The Split and the Structure: Twenty-Eight Essays*, Berkeley: University of California Press, 1996, p. 109.

arnheim and comics

t w e l v e

g r e g   m .   s m i t h

More than perhaps any other major theorist, Rudolf Arnheim wrote extensively about film and painting/drawing, the art forms most often compared to comics. And yet comics never received more than passing mention in his writings. This is not surprising, given comics' low cultural status and Arnheim's emphasis on art with a capital A. Art critics in Arnheim's day would occasionally become enamored with individual exceptional comics, but there was probably little in the Sunday funnies that would catch the eye of a critic who dealt with El Greco and convince him that this medium was worthy of serious, extended aesthetic consideration.[1] The understanding of what constitutes "art" has loosened in the academy, and the cultural cachet of comics has improved in recent decades, particularly as comics are packaged into "graphic novels." Critics and scholars have also begun to study comics with more close attention, and so the time is ripe for a new consideration of how Arnheim's thinking on film and art might be productively applied to this increasingly complex visual storytelling medium.

This essay begins by considering Arnheim's stance on composite media. He famously disapproved of the coming of sound in film, arguing that sound and the image pull the audience in contradictory directions, denying sound film the aesthetic unity (and validity) of silent film. How, then, can we use Arnheim's concepts to think about a medium that is usually composed of two quite different forms of expression: words and pictures? This essay asserts that we may need to separate Arnheim's prescriptive ideas from his pro-cessual concepts about art, and in the latter portion of this essay I discuss how the non-prescriptive Arnheim can shed light on the expressive capac-ities of comics. To provide illustrations of how these concepts might be applied, I will make reference to Alan Moore's and Brian Bolland's elegant portrait of the relationship between Batman and the Joker in *Batman: The Killing Joke*.[2]

comics as a composite medium

Arnheim's 1938 essay "A New Laocoön: Artistic Composites and the Talking Film" presents his most extended discussion on hybrid media.[3] Many such media, he argues, are fatally misconceived, dooming them to wrestle over the audience, much as the two serpents depicted in Greek mythology intertwined to take Laocoön's life. Like Lessing before him, Arnheim argued that each medium has unique capacities for expression, and that artists should focus on the things that the medium does best. Each medium, therefore, has an essence that defines it and determines its preferred aesthetic course. The talking film combines two different expressive registers, each one with its own essence. This creates an irreconcilable tension in the sound film, according to Arnheim, with dialogue and image struggling for dominance. Arnheim maintained his preference for the silent film throughout his life, never backing down from his argument that sound film was fundamentally compromised as a hybrid medium trying to serve two masters.[4]

The "Laocoön" essay considers at some length the conditions under which composite media can be aesthetically unified, and so we will examine these criteria to see if comics fit. Partly the reason that Arnheim opposes composite media is because they violate the gestalt principles at the center of his conception of art. Gestalt theories are grounded in the understanding that there are strong continuities between how we perceive art and how we make sense out of the real world. Both art and the real world call on the same perceptual capacities, and we apply similar principles in each realm to find simplicity, coherence, and stability. Art provides a kind of aesthetic exercise for those real world capacities, but art is different from reality because it provides a clarity of experience that real life cannot. One reason that we value art is that it is unified in its intent and content, unlike reality. Art is characterized by a formal precision that makes it expressive, and without such precision, art is as unclear and cluttered as reality itself. The argument that sound film is more like the real world (in which we both watch and listen to people simultaneously) is not convincing to Arnheim. By combining media, the sound film may more closely resemble reality, but that added realism is gained by losing a coherence that art requires and that the real world does not. If a composite medium is going to be viable as art, Arnheim asserts that it must maintain an Aristotelian unity that provides coherence.

One way for a hybrid art form to maintain this unity is by ensuring that one medium is clearly dominant. Opera, for instance, integrates words and music, but Arnheim recognizes opera as a unified artistic medium because the music so obviously outweighs the words. No one goes to an opera to hear the libretto, and so the music's primacy is never threatened. The intermixing of words and music in opera is comparable to the use of intertitles in silent film. The picture component of silent film is so clearly the dominant that the intertitles never threaten to take control, preserving the unity required for artistic expression.

Another possibility for mixing two media is for both to express the unified theme of the work in parallel. Songs, for instance, integrate words and music with both tracks expressing the overall tone of the song in different registers. In a song, the music and lyrics are clearly separable, and each can be appreciated on their own terms (as in an instrumental version of a popular song, or in a published lyric sheet). Together they make an integrated presentation with each one maintaining its own integrity, as Arnheim notes:

> Their combination resembles a successful marriage, where similarity and adaptation make for unity but where the personality of the two partners remains intact, nevertheless. It does *not* resemble the child that springs from such a marriage, in whom both components are inseparably mixed.[5]

Each form expresses the total subject in different ways, taking advantage of its unique properties, completing each other instead of duplicating the other track's efforts. Arnheim notes that it may be easier for one representational element and one non-representational element to combine in this way, so that music and lyrics in a song do not interfere with each other as they present the song's theme in clearly distinct registers.[6] Similarly, the non-representational music and the representational image work together in a silent film, each one being complete but each one separable from the other. If either the image or the music halts, then the audience senses that something is wrong, that one of the two intertwined partners has disappeared.

Sound film does not satisfy this criterion of parallel, complete component media because dialogue is intermittent, not uninterrupted. Thus a halt in the dialogue is perceived as "silence," as an expressive presence

215

akin to the background of a painting. But if the picture goes black while the dialogue continues, this feels like an absence of the depicted world. The two component forms, therefore, are not parallel; dialogue weaves in and out of the film and merely "enlarges" (according to Arnheim) what already exists in the continuous moving image.[7] The dialogue film obviously fails to satisfy this criterion for an aesthetically justified composite medium because both component media do not make complete parallel presentations of the subject matter.

But shouldn't the sound film qualify as a hybrid medium with one component (images) remaining dominant? Isn't the dialogue component of a film somewhat comparable to the libretto of an opera? No, because although the dialogue track interrupts the continuous, complete image component (somewhat like an operatic libretto), it then hijacks control of the film away from the dominant component in ways that never happen in opera. The compunction to show the actors speaking in film is so strong that it ties down the rich visual potential of the images. For Arnheim, this is the worst possible compromise: a component medium that is not only inter-mittent but also wrests control from the dominant medium.

Comics appear to be a composite medium composed of pictures and words. Yet various writers attempting to define comics have struggled with the extent to which the combination of the two forms is a necessary condition for the medium. Will Eisner's attempt to re-label comics as "sequential art" is both an attempt to distance the medium from its devalued past and an acknowledgment that comics are primarily pictures (art).[8] Scott McCloud in *Understanding Comics* also foregrounds the image in his definition (comics are "juxtaposed pictorial and other images in deliberate sequence, intended to convey information and/or to produce an aesthetic response in the viewer").[9] Both recognize that comics are still comics even when they are wordless, but there is no such thing as comics without pictures. Mila Bongco, on the other hand, makes words part of her definition of comics, acknowledging their importance in most comics' practice.[10] In most instances, comics act as a composite medium intertwining words and pictures.

In their composite form, comics greatly resemble the dialogue film, as many have noted. They clearly do not qualify under Arnheim's criterion that a hybrid medium be composed of parallel, continuous expressive tracks. Words in comics can disappear for periods of time, but this simply makes them "silent" or "wordless" comics; this does not disqualify them as part of the comics medium. For instance, the opening pages of *The Killing Joke* show Batman and Commissioner Gordon as they enter Arkham Asylum to interrogate the Joker.[11] The comic leaves behind dialogue or verbal narration, making this a "silent" sequence of comics. If a pictorial/language combination abandons *pictures* for any length of time, however, the result begins to move the narrative form away from "comics" toward something like "book illustrations" (such as Cruikshank's drawings in Dickens's novels).

Judging from the definitions above, it seems apparent that pictures are the dominant partner in comics, but are they dominant in ways that more closely resemble the unified opera or the fatally compromised sound film? Scenes with considerable dialogue often pose problems for comics. Comics artists must find ways to make naturalistic conversations visually interesting, and so they shift figure positions and vary the angle or apparent "shot distance" from panel to panel. For instance, in the abovementioned interrogation scene in *The Killing Joke*, Batman and the Joker are seated at a table, facing each other. To provide visual variety while also satisfying the compunction to display the dialogue speaker, Bolland not only alternates between straight-on images of the two conversationalists but also interjects a high angle view of the table, a panel showing Gordon's face framed through the cell door window, a panel showing Gordon's point of view, a close-up of Batman's gloved hand grabbing the Joker's hand, a silhouetted view of Batman, and so on.[12] Bolland here works hard (and elegantly) to overcome the dialogue's tendency to tie down the visual signification of comics. Comics, therefore, are a composite medium that functions comparably to the sound film with one component (pictures) dominant except when another intermittent element (words) struggles for control. Although Arnheim loved the two media closest to comics (drawing and film), the combination of media in comics would likely displease him. To view comics productively through Arnheim's lens, we need a reconceptualization of his writings.

From the perspective of contemporary film studies, Arnheim's work appears both oddly archaic and interestingly prescient. On the one hand, his stubborn refusal to accept color and sound in film isolates him as a theorist of limited modern utility. On the other hand, his emphasis on the continuity between everyday processes and artistic perception, along with his consistent grounding in psychological experimentation, anticipates the rise of cognitive film theory. A contemporary film cognitivist would recognize the form of argumentation in much of Arnheim's writing as he justifies his assertions about art by citing empirical research. Viewed in this manner, Arnheim's famous "Laocoön" essay is somewhat of an anomaly. He makes minimal reference to empirically grounded psychological theories to justify his argument that a mixed medium is less suited for aesthetic expression.[13] Here (as in other points in *Film as Art*) we see Arnheim defining what a medium *should* be, rather than describing how artworks function by balancing intensification and simplification or complexity and order. Here we have the prescriptive Arnheim, not the processual.

In order to make Arnheim's ideas more broadly useful, I suggest parsing his thought into these two separate camps: the prescriptive and the processual. As a film cognitivist I believe the latter to be more useful than the former because the processual Arnheim tends to be grounded in systematic empirical observation, not a mythic transhistorical understanding of a medium's "essence." I recognize that to split Arnheim's theory apart does considerable violence to his system, and Arnheim is a systematic thinker. His preference for silent film is not idiosyncratic; it makes sense given his fascinating, productive notion that a medium is shaped by its limitations more than its capabilities. The limited palette of silent film makes greater artistic expression possible within the gestalt system of expression.

To make Arnheim's insights useful for today, I believe we need to bracket off the prescriptive assertions that have been thoroughly challenged.[14] A comprehensive re-evaluation of the processual Arnheim's fascinating assertions, evaluating them in light of contemporary research into the perception of art, is beyond the scope of this article. Instead I will suggest how insights from Arnheim's less prescriptive discussions of media can help us understand comics better. Comics do behave at times like film and at other times like drawing, and so Arnheim's thoughts on the limitations and advantages of each are instructive. Although I believe the prescriptive Arnheim would have significant difficulty in accepting the composite medium of comics, I also assert that the non-prescriptive Arnheim provides instructive hints into the distinctive capacities of comics.

the limitation and expressivity of comics

Comics use pictures, and so these pictures have all of the qualities that Arnheim and other gestalt theorists notice in painting and drawing. They cue our perception through line, balance, shape, space, and the other primary qualities that Arnheim uses to organize his landmark *Art and Visual Perception*.[15] Thus any individual comic panel can be analyzed very much like any other drawn composition. Such analysis, however, does not emphasize what distinguishes comics as a medium.

Comic panels are distinct from most drawing or painting because they are arranged into a sequence. Unlike freestanding drawings, comics depend much more on the juxtaposition of panels against each other to achieve their artistic effects, and accordingly they act much more like film. Juxtaposition is not one of the primary qualities studied in *Art and Visual Perception* (which deals mostly with painting, drawing, and sculpture), but it is much more central to Arnheim's discussion of film. He spends many pages elaborating a system of the many ways that film segments may be combined through montage.[16] The shot is a unit that has its own integrity and coherence, which then may be juxtaposed with another such unit that follows the first. Such juxtapositions emphasize certain parameters, which artists can manipulate for aesthetic purposes. For instance, when the failed stand-up comedian who will eventually become the Joker has a conversation with his pregnant wife, each of the panels in the scene is composed mostly of muted blues and grays. Certain elements of each panel, however, are colored in vivid yellows and oranges (a light bulb, the characters' faces, the comedian's back, the wife's belly), which make that element stand out from the rest of the panel.[17] Considering the page as a whole involves juxtaposing these panels, thus focusing our attention on these bright splashes of color, which lead our eye from panel to panel. The yellows and oranges would be striking enough in a single composition; looked at in juxtaposition to each other on a page, these colorful elements become even more important than they do in any individual panel.

A neo-Arnheimian approach to comics would then take his emphasis on dynamic spatial relations in art and translate that from single compositions into juxtaposed panels. "Not only the shape of objects, but also that of the intervals between them is dynamic,"[18] Arnheim says. When two objects are placed into a composition with each other, they necessarily establish an interrelationship, and that relationship changes how each object is perceived. If this gestalt principle is true for individual compositions, it also functions across comic panels on a page.

Because single comic panels do not operate independently of each other, they are particularly open to analysis according to gestalt principles. A comic book page, therefore, is a system composed of panels, each one being a systematic composition of line, shade, and light. Each of these pages can use cues to prepare the reader for the pages that are later in the sequence, and so pages become units in a higher order system (the entire comic or graphic novel). This comics reader (and gestalt critic) examines a more complex, nested system of resonances and contrasts than those viewing non-sequential drawings. They find connections at three separate levels: within the panel, across panels on a page, and among pages in the entire work. Although comics panels may be fruitfully analyzed like any other drawing to tease out their artistic expression, critics also need to examine the way they function within the whole as components within a narrative system.

For Arnheim, film is different from painting and drawing not only because it juxtaposes images but also mostly because film can capture the image of reality so readily. For film to become art, it must fight against film's automatic tendency toward realistic representation. To show the imprint of an artist, film must lean toward the expressivity that comes easily to painting and drawing. Expression is built into every line that an artist makes; representation is the difficult task in painting/drawing. Although the live action filmmaker can never escape representation at some level (a camera always takes a picture of *something*), she must emphasize the ways that film is unlike the real world in order to show the artist's reshaping of the world. Film's flatness, its frame, its singular perspectival viewpoint: these are the qualities that the filmmaker must emphasize to transform film's representation into art. Drawn or painted comics images obviously do not have the same automatic ties to representation that film and photography do, and so they attain expression much more easily. Comics, therefore, have much of the same expressive capacities that drawing does, combined with the sequential capacities of the cinema.

One obvious drawback that comics have in relation to film in presenting a sequential action is that comics images do not move. For Arnheim, apparent limitations are the keys to a medium's capacities. A medium becomes art when it embraces the ways that it is unlike reality. An Arnheimian approach to comics would emphasize the ways that comics foreground their own stillness. Because comics cannot capture real motion, they must work to overcome this limitation, and this work creates the potential for art. Of course almost all painting and drawing is still, but this feature only rarely attracts notice. Since comics juxtapose images, this accentuates the differences between still frames, making immobility a more privileged and expressive property in comics' narrative system. In a neo-Arnheimian approach to comics, stillness becomes a distinguishing characteristic of the medium. This falls somewhat short of a pure comics "essence." Instead, stillness functions more as a dominant practice that can be used for distinctive expressive and storytelling purposes. Comics can pause motion in interesting positions, such as when Batman breaks through a funhouse mirror to attack the Joker, and Bolland arranges the flying shards of glass into an aesthetically pleasing composition.[19] *The Killing Joke* begins and ends with the same image, that of raindrops spattering on a puddle, causing stilled ripples to appear on its surface.[20] Comics deliver an image reminiscent of what Henri Cartier-Bresson calls the "decisive moment" in photography, reminding us of the capacity of comics and still photography to capture a heightened, well-chosen moment of evanescent stillness that we cannot perceive in the moving world.

Media have different proclivities for stillness and motion, between what Arnheim calls "things" and "happenings."[21] We live in a world of objects, of a universe of things that we perceive to be stable entities. These things engage in actions which we can label as separate concepts, as "happenings." Thus we can distinguish between a dancer and the dance he does, between a lobster and the act of its being cooked. A happening necessarily occurs over time, while a thing may be considered without reference to time. The immobile arts (statuary, painting, drawing) excel at presenting things, while film and theater can more readily present things in a time sequence (happenings). In a rare mention of comics, Arnheim notes that they help us to distinguish sequentiality from mobility, noting that comics (like the small subset of narrative paintings) use an immobile signifier to convey succession.[22] Borrowing from Lessing, Arnheim says "whereas narrative painting or sculpture presents action by means of objects, the dramatist or novelist uses actions to present states of affairs."[23] Comics present happenings/actions as do other sequential media, but they do so using things/objects, as other immobile media do. Obviously comics cannot literally show the full action when the Joker shoots and cripples Barbara Gordon in *The Killing Joke*. Instead we see panels showing us a pistol; a close-up of Barbara's startled face; the bullet trace connecting the gun to a bloodstain on her gut; Barbara's body in mid-plunge and her spilled coffee, both frozen in time.[24] When the artist places these things into a sequence in a comic, the things become narrativized. They can be used to present happenings in ways that make us simultaneously aware of their stillness, their "thingness."

In this way the still images of comics function much like close-ups do in film (the example above is almost a textbook example of the Kuleshov effect). Close-ups are one of the formal features that Arnheim emphasizes as a distinct parameter for cinematic expression. They emphasize the difference between the film medium and reality by manipulating apparent size. We don't encounter any twenty-foot-high pistols in the real world, but a close-up can create such an unrealistic view of the object, detaching it from its real world context in a way that foregrounds the filmmaker's artistry: "The delimitation of the [film] image is as much a formative tool as perspective, for it allows some particular detail being brought out and given special significance . . ."[25] For Arnheim, the close-up takes fullest advantage of this cinematic capability to select objects through framing, allowing the artist to choose a particularly characteristic detail to stand in for the whole.[26] The film artist's job is to select and present the "essentials" of an action, and if those essentials are well chosen, the audience accepts the story's illusion. Similarly, the comics artist must choose objects/things that convey the essentials of an action/happening. In this way comics greatly resemble one of Arnheim's metaphoric descriptions of the cinema, that looking at a film is like looking at a "collection of picture post cards," with the distinction that comics (and film) arrange those post card views into a sequence that the viewer assembles into complete actions.[27] Comics are a narrative form and thus present happenings in time (as film does), but they do so by presenting objects (as drawing does).

Comics help us to see the unvoiced emphasis that Arnheim places on film as narrative. *Film as Art* spends most of its time discussing film aesthetics, not film as narrative per se. He does, however, focus on how the medium manipulates time (encouraging filmmakers to use slow motion, reverse motion, and various forms of montage). The presentation of space and time by an artist constitutes narration, not simply expressivity, and so this is the fundamental connection between comics and film from Arnheim's perspective. Both arrange pictures into a sequence in which reading/viewing time is translated into diegetic time, unlike painting and drawing, where the time spent perceiving the image becomes contemplation, not narrative. Films and comics both use line, light, shade, and so on, but their juxtaposition in time distinguish them from being purely expressive arts. A good comic panel points us toward the next panel in the sequence, moving the reader's eye from one space/time to another.

Movement (the closest concept to timing in Arnheim's discussion of art) becomes even more crucial for comics, therefore. Arnheim devotes a chapter of *Art and Visual Perception* to the topic, discussing how the perceiver's eye is moved across an artistic composition.[28] The comics artist must not only manage the way a reader traverses a single panel, but she also tries to control how the reader works her way down the comics page. In this way comics resemble traditional drawing and painting more than film, because the filmmaker has direct control of the pacing of shots. The comics artist and the traditional painter/draftsman can only encourage the perceiver's eye to linger longer in one spot than another, or to move from one point to another in sequence. In comics the movement of the reader's eye across the page has direct bearing on her perception of the story's pace, and so Arnheim's concept of movement has additional functionality when applied to comics. Comics theorist/practitioner Scott McCloud has asserted that "In comics, space *is* time!" This catchy phrase captures an intuitively productive insight that opens up the possibility of a new link between Arnheim's theory of art and his theory of film. It may be fruitful to elaborate a system of principles for how movement across still images can lead us to linger on certain objects while speeding past others; how those movements can guide us through a spatial arrangement of pictures; and how these cues can be interpreted as different narrative times and spaces.

Let us summarize the Arnheimian connections and differences among film, drawing, and comics thus far. The dynamic relationship among panels on a comic page has consequences, both spatially (between objects on a page) and narratively (between happenings in the story). Spatial cues in comics lead the reader across the page, using line, color, and other properties to make dynamic connections between panels. Because comics cannot directly present events, the artist is limited to portraying things, but for an Arnheimian approach, this limitation creates artistic possibilities. Comics' stillness and juxtapositions create the capacity for an enormous range of interconnections. The juxtapositions are potentially richer in comics than with film because comics panels are presented together on a page, but in film the connections between shots must be made when at least one shot is in memory. Just as a traditional artist may create dynamic relations between objects within a composition, the comics artist can use the expressive capacities of the immobile arts to move the reader across the page. The job for a neo-Arnheimian approach to comics would be a systematic laying out of the ways that the medium creates distinctive possibilities for using the spatial portrayal of things to influence two forms of "time": the reader's time in parsing the panels and the story time depicted by those panels. In the interest of my reader's time (and of demonstrating the usefulness of Arnheim's thought to comics study), I will discuss selected techniques that both showcase comics' distinctive potential and elaborate on insights Arnheim has voiced.

Not surprisingly for a theorist who examines light and shade in art, Arnheim discusses the artistic possibilities of lighting in film. Through lighting, the filmmaker can work against the medium's tendency to reproduce the image of reality, thus encouraging the viewer to consider the formal properties of the objects being filmed. The "lighting" in comics differs from film because there is no actual light falling on real surfaces, and so comics are not bound to representation in the way that live action film is. Comics, therefore, are capable of impossible lighting effects in the way that painting is. Paintings that mix representation with showy unmotivated plays of light tend to do so in somewhat subtle fashion, as do the Flemish still lifes. Comics are mass-reproduced objects, so they tend not to use light as subtly as original painting does because reproduction loses some of the nuance of light. The nature of shadow and line encourages comics artists to explore shadow effects. In comics, making a shadow can be as simple as drawing a line, and no real light can make a line that is as sharp as the one made by an artist's pencil. When the Batmobile pulls into the old amusement park in *The Killing Joke*, the light spilling from the headlights creates starry, artfully crisscrossing beams that are sharper than they could be in real life.[29] As Batman and the detective visit Barbara's hospital bedside, their figures become graphically flattened against the noirer-than-noir sharp shadows from window blinds.[30] We see the figure of the man who will soon become the Joker reflected in a rain-specked puddle that still is clear enough to display the sign for "Ace Chemical Processes."[31] Because shadows, light, and reflections are more easily created through the expressive line of drawing in comics, comics are distinctly capable of using impossible shadow and light for dramatic purposes.

Comics also can vary the level of detail of their presentation, which is much more difficult to do using live action film. By varying lenses, lighting, and film stock, the cinematographer can decide which planes of focus in front of the camera will be sharply delineated and which will remain less clear. There are always practical limits to how much a cinematographer can vary the level of detail within a single shot. In comics, however, the artist has more control over the level of detail in a single panel since she is not bound by using real light on real objects. Faraway and near objects can be in the same panel, as when Bolland depicts butler Alfred walking down the stairs of the Batcave in the same "shot" as Batman doing research on a computer a great distance away.[32] Even if objects are in the same plane, an artist can portray the more narratively significant one in lush detail, leaving other objects relatively sketchy. One can arrange dark silhouettes and brightly lit backgrounds, or place objects in the foreground with only vague cross-hatching in the background. Comics artists vary the level of detail in order to provide narrative emphasis, but they also do so to help control the reader's pace. The reigning assumption is that the more details shown on an object/image, the longer the reader's eye lingers over those details. A comics author can lessen the level of details in an image to encourage a faster pace, or pack the panel with detail to slow the reading pace down. In real life the level of detail in an environment remains constant, but in comics an environment only exists to the extent that the artist draws it. This gives the artist an expressive parameter that cinematographers almost never manipulate: an environment that changes on a shot-by-shot level to convey the specific narrative purposes of the moment.

In *The Killing Joke* Bolland depicts a conversation between the stand-up comedian and some hardened criminals in a seedy seafood restaurant/bar. The bar is lushly detailed: menu items scrawled on a blackboard, various lowlife characters packing the room in multiple planes of depth. The level of detail helps slow down the reader as she takes in the dialogue in which the goons spell out the details of the caper. At times the background detail disappears entirely for a moment of dramatic emphasis. When one of the criminals removes the legs from a crayfish in the foreground, the black background (in contrast to the busy backdrops for the other panels on the page) gives this simple, small action more foreboding importance.[33] Contrast this busy scene with a montage that cuts between Batman's roving pursuit of clues to the kidnapped Commissioner Gordon's whereabouts and Gordon's mad ride through the funhouse. When we see Batman and other figures in various locales, they are often depicted as outlines (Batman and a policeman in silhouettes, women reduced to foregrounded legs in miniskirts). This relatively wordless page (the only "sound" is the "Bdump" of Gordon's funhouse car bumping repeatedly into a door) is narratively much more complex than the bar scene, with two different narrative lines (Gordon's ride, Batman's interrogation), the latter taking place in a variety of locales (an alley, Arkham Asylum, a street, a mansion, a building roof). And yet the page "scans" quickly like a film montage.[34] Varying detail can emphasize a particular object in a panel (the crayfish) or can influence the reader's overall pace in parsing a page.

Most artists consider words in comics as a means to slow down the reading pace, just as increasing the level of detail does. When Batman traverses the booby-trapped funhouse in *The Killing Joke*, this scene could be consumed quite quickly by the reader who is simply noting the sequence of actions: Batman running past mirrors, falling into a pit of sharp stakes, climbing out, and so on. The comic scatters word balloons across the panels as the Joker's video image delivers a soliloquy.[35] The Joker's words do not have much direct bearing on the current action, but they ask the reader to linger longer over Bolland's artfully configured action compositions. The words here connect to the larger themes of the comic, but they also provide a significant additional spatial element in a composition, needing additional attention and time.

As Arnheim noted with the intervention of dialogue into film, the verbal track has the tendency to root the visual in place, keeping the images focused on the speaker. In comics, the order of speakers is so important in a panel that it even governs the placement of human figures in the composition. In film, the continuity system manages the arrangement of actors in the frame, keeping the camera on one side of the 180-degree line that connects two conversationalists, thus guaranteeing that the speakers remain in consistent screen position from shot to shot. This rule exists because the filmmaker is concerned about the spectator getting disoriented in the scene's space. Comics do not seem to feel the same fear because comics regularly ignore the 180-degree rule, seemingly unconcerned about the reader's losing track of its non-moving characters. Instead comics regularly arrange figures from left to right (in the assumed Western reading order) depending on who is speaking first. When the Joker meets the seller of a ramshackle carnival, the first panel frames the seller at the left as he delivers a greeting. When the Joker replies in the next panel, the comics "camera" has "crossed the line," placing the first speaker (the Joker) at the left and the subsequent speaker at the right.[36] During the scene between the stand-up comedian and his pregnant wife, the figures switch sides at almost every change of panels, depending on who says the first line.[37] Here Arnheim's assessment of the sound film is borne out in comics, with the verbal component determining the spatial orientation of the image. The practice of rearranging figures to match speaking order lends further credence to the notion that comics are *read*, that the emphasis is less on presenting a continuous diegetic space (as film does) and more on promoting an unproblematic parsing of the scene's dialogue.

Comics, as we have noted, almost always combine words with pictures, but these two component media are not on parallel tracks, such as the music and the image in a silent film. Words in comics occupy space within the panel, and as such they function within the composition instead of providing a separate channel for artistic expression. Therefore words in comics are not purely a transparent conveyor of meaning; they are physically present, just as any graphic element in the picture. In comics, words and pictures are both representational and spatial, lending words a design function that they rarely have in literature. When the Joker emerges from his accidental fall into chemicals and he sees his own disfigured face for the first time, the panel is filled with a repeated purple disjointed "HAHAHA" that becomes a wallpaper-like background to the figure.[38]

Words' connotative meanings depend on their lettering and arrangement (more like advertising than literature), but the integration of the words into the pictorial composition is so crucial in comics that the medium has added a distinctive design element to the "language" of comics. The word balloon does more than delimit a space for spoken words and thoughts. Like any design element in a picture, it establishes dynamic relations with other objects. The shape, color, and line of the balloon give it expressive capacities. When the man-who-will-be-the-Joker flees the gunfire at the chemical plant caper in *The Killing Joke*, he screams so loudly that his word balloon takes on the contour of the letters, with the peaks of the "AAAAAAAA" making a jagged edge at the top of the otherwise rounded word balloon.[39] The outline of the word balloon helps narratively to distinguish among voices emanating from a video monitor (a spiky word balloon outline), a sobbing plea (in a wobbly outline), or a vocal flashback (enclosed in rectangles). In Arnheimian fashion, the limitation of the medium (comics' inability to reproduce sound) becomes an expressive element in its own right.

Like the sound film, comics mix two representational forms, but in this case the words actually intrude into the visual register, becoming a component of the image track. Comics, however, represent a visual synthesis of two different registers that Arnheim did not quite anticipate in his landmark "Laocoön" essay. Words certainly ground the visual play of images in comics, but because they are a graphic element within the image track, they become a parameter that comics artists can use for expressive, narrative, and compositional functions.

The tricky part in analyzing comics is handling the sheer variability of their aesthetics. At times comics rely on the expressive capacities of paintings and drawings: line, color, balance, shape (including the size and shape of the frame itself). At other times they behave more like film and television, using juxtapositions to create narratives and to compare/contrast compositional elements. Comics also integrate verbal narration into their storytelling in ways that film and drawings rarely do: the actual lettering becomes part of the visual composition, spatially interacting with the pictorial elements. In addition, comics' nested units of signification (panel, page, graphic novel) give the medium the capacity to make connections among all these levels, yielding a huge number of possible permutations within the space of a few pages. The critic needs to be able to discuss the full range of comics' expression, noting how various elements have different functions when placed within a system without reducing their signification to a series of rules. Rudolf Arnheim's gestalt criticism gives us ways to discuss the "painterly" and "cinematic" aspects of comics, while also presenting broad principles (grounded in empirical processes) that can examine aspects of comics' expression that neither film nor drawings typically manipulate. Although the prescriptive Arnheim would likely find comics' combination of words and images to be a troubling composite, the less prescriptive, more processual Arnheim points the way toward intriguing possibilities to investigate in comics.

226

notes

1. Gilbert Seldes, *The Seven Lively Arts*, New York: Harper, 1957, pp. 231–245.
2. Alan Moore and Brian Bolland, *The Killing Joke*, New York: DC Comics, 1988. *The Killing Joke* allegedly served as an important influence on the portrayal of the Joker in the 2008 film *The Dark Knight*.

3. Rudolf Arnheim, "A New Laocoön: Artistic Composites and the Talking Film," in *Film as Art*, Berkeley: University of California Press, 1957, pp. 199–230.

4. In the introduction to the 1957 edition of *Film as Art*, he said, "I still believe what I believed then [in the 1930s] . . . [t]he talking film is still a hybrid medium," p. 5.

5. Arnheim, "Laocoön", pp. 207–208 (emphasis in original).

6. Ibid., p. 216.

7. Ibid., p. 225.

8. Will Eisner, *Comics and Sequential Art*, expanded ed., Tamarac, FL: Poorhouse Press, 1985.

9. Scott McCloud, *Understanding Comics: The Invisible Art*, Northampton, MA: Tundra, 1993, p. 20. McCloud's definition excludes single panel images (such as most political cartoons and Gary Larson's *The Far Side*). In his terms, such images are "cartoons" but not "comics."

10. Mila Bongco, *Reading Comics: Language, Culture, and the Concept of the Superhero in Comic Books*, New York: Garland, 2000, p. 49.

11. Moore and Bolland, *The Killing Joke*, pp. 2–3.

12. Ibid.

13. There are no fun doodles in the essay either!

14. Noël Carroll, "Medium Specificity Arguments and the Self-Consciously Invented Arts: Film, Photography, Video," *Millennium Film Journal* 14/15, 1984–1985, pp. 127–153.

15. Rudolf Arnheim, *Art and Visual Perception: A Psychology of the Creative Eye*, rev. ed., Berkeley: University of California Press, 1974.

16. Arnheim, *Film as Art*, pp. 87–102.

17. Moore and Bolland, *The Killing Joke*, p. 8.

18. Arnheim, *Art and Visual Perception*, p. 429.

19. Moore and Bolland, *The Killing Joke*, p. 41.

20. Ibid., pp. 1, 48.

21. Arnheim, *Art and Visual Perception*, pp. 372–373.

22. Ibid., pp. 375–376.

23. Ibid., p. 377.

24. Moore and Bolland, *The Killing Joke*, p. 14.

25. Arnheim, *Film as Art*, p. 73.

26. Ibid., p. 79.

27. Ibid., p. 28.

28. Ibid., pp. 372–409.

29. Moore and Bolland, *The Killing Joke*, p. 35.

30. Ibid., p. 18.

31. Ibid., p. 30.

32. Ibid., p. 12.

33. Ibid., pp. 16–17.

34. Ibid., p. 27.

35. Ibid., p. 39.

36. Ibid., p. 7.

37. Ibid., p. 8.

38. Ibid., p. 33.

39. Ibid., p. 31.

arnheim on style history

c o l i n   b u r n e t t

How a historian defines a style class depends upon the proximate mecha-nisms the historian privileges.[1] From these mechanisms, a style's qualitative parameters or constituent elements, and historical beginnings and endings, are accounted for. Identifying a style depends on a series of complex con-siderations relating to the nature of artistic intention and agency. Other factors that allow for explanation and periodization include "external," that is, social, institutional, economic, and technological levers, and "internal" traditions, techniques, and subjects. Remaining only with film, these factors have helped define large-scale group classes like Hollywood classicism, as well as more localized designations like cinema of attractions, Italian neorealism, and the *cinéma du look*, and individual entities like "early Godard," "1930s Mizoguchi," and "Griffith at Biograph." Each is a style or an episode in a style with distinguishing features and framing dates that are often the subject of principled debate regarding the pertinence of specific kinds of evidence and the appropriate interpretation of this evidence.

Perhaps due to the delicacy of these considerations, and for fear that theorizing about them could only take place at too high an altitude to adjudicate focused historical questions and stalemates both old and new, direct theoretical inquiry about the concept of style qua historical class is rarely undertaken in contemporary film studies. Many basic questions therefore remain to be asked. For instance, how exactly does the historian infer a style class from these various considerations?

This chapter draws on Rudolf Arnheim's approach to style history in order to answer this question. In doing so, my hope is that it will bring to the media scholar's attention, and solve, a number of until now unacknowledged problems in the commonplace film studies conception of style classes as *those techniques or devices exemplified by a set of films of a particular place and time.* This conception shares much with that of *Film Art,* one of the field's standard textbooks, where style is defined as "the repeated and salient uses of film techniques characteristic of a single film or a group of films (for example a filmmaker's work or a national movement)."[2] The implication of these conceptions is that a style class is delineated by listing the class's stylistic devices.[3] I will argue that this position does not hold. It rests on an unsubstantiated amalgamation of the notions of style as devices or techniques and style as historical classes; style at one level (devices) is believed to establish style at another (classes). It also permits a degree of arbitrariness in the application of style terms like "baroque" and "naturalism." A commonplace approach assumes that style class identification is an inductive procedure of technique collection, thus ignoring the conceptual inferences, based on observable features, that lead the historian of styles from features to style class concepts.

Ultimately, these common conceptions result from, or cannot solve, three problems, which I call the naturalization problem, the class-device relation problem and (after Arnheim's phrasing) the atomization problem. These problems are discussed in this chapter's first section. The second section argues that the first two find solutions in Arnheim's theory of style historiography and his distinction between devices and styles. In the third section, case studies of the classical Hollywood and Robert Bresson styles demonstrate the practical benefits of Arnheim's handling of the atomization and class-device relation issues. The penultimate section considers two formulations central to Arnheim's theory—"ways of making" and "structures"—in order to show how his theory is separable from a thick gestaltism.[4] And the final one proposes that Arnheim's model addresses limitations in the most widely accepted film studies approach to style, the functional theory of style, specifically in terms of atomization and class-device relations.

three problems for a theory of film style

In "Style as a Gestalt Problem" Arnheim replies to ten lectures on the subject of style delivered at the 1977 Summer Institute in Aesthetics in Boulder,

Colorado.[5] He uncovers a set of difficulties in the idea of style held by many art historians and aestheticians. The only way to avoid the "hopeless complexity" and "intolerable complications" that plague scholarly discussions is to conceive of style as a gestalt structure.[6] While this assertion has an air of inevitability to it coming from a lifelong advocate of gestalt psychology, Arnheim's reasoning is not so easily dismissed because of three major problems it permits film scholars to solve in their concept of style. This section will show how the naturalization problem, the class-device relation problem and the atomization problem undermine a number of prevalent conceptions of style in film studies.

Naturalization is the process whereby an idea is accepted in the absence of a deliberate weighing of options. Common usage promotes naturalization by concealing the process of the idea's development and acceptance. The absence of a rigorous examination of alternatives—as Meyer Schapiro and James Ackerman provide the art historian—has exacerbated the situation in film studies.[7] Beyond the functional model, few fully formed theories about the nature of style classes have been developed in film, and media, studies.[8] As a result, film studies' version continues to circulate without the benefit of sustained critical scrutiny and in the absence of a nuanced sense of the role of empirical investigation, low- to mid-level theoretical reasoning, and intricate argument and counter-argument in shaping the colloquial and functional conceptions.[9]

A point lost in this naturalization process is that a colloquial notion of "film style" proposes a theoretical amalgamation of what have historically been two separate conceptions: style as a historical class and style as those devices characteristic of the individual work.[10] The first is an art historical concept of style, as in the expression "X film participates in Y style." The second, a linguistic or rhetorical concept of style, is seen in the expression "X film uses the stylistic device Y." Although a colloquial amalgamation of "style" concepts has facilitated much research, it risks becoming a source of major and minor confusions by sliding over the intellectual process implicated in defining a style.

If film scholarship can address the related class-device relation problem, it will promote much more plainness about the theoretical assumptions underpinning "film style." Not inconsequential is the tendency for contemporary scholars to mention "filmmaker X's style" or "use of style" while leaving unacknowledged the distinction implied in these formulations given the concept's composite nature. Are scholars referring to the devices the filmmaker wields or to the historical category to which the filmmaker's works belong? The concept in its informal guise allows in a confusing manner for the simultaneous reference to both meanings, thus hiding the theoretical amalgamation it proposes. Some might argue that the territory of a style qua historical class is identical with those devices the films within the class wield. But this point does not receive due consideration in the film style literature. A sustained argument demonstrating that devices are sufficient to draw the boundaries of a historical class is still needed, at least because its absence perpetuates a terminological ambiguity between the two kinds of "style."

One way to evade the ambiguity might be to develop a cluster account of "style," where the array of overlapping and competing usages at play at any moment is considered. But whether or not style can be usefully examined as a cluster concept—a point that cannot be settled here— theorists like Arnheim who defend a particular "style" have some utility, setting up standards of evaluation amongst competing models. As we will see, Arnheim proposes a disaggregation of the two "styles," thus rejecting the view that devices are a sufficient condition for isolating styles.

Finally, Arnheim suggests ways to identify the atomization problem. He finds fault in the art historian's penchant for viewing style classes as "monoliths," as "compact, unitary entities," or as mere "labels" for "a sorting box" of works or artists dropped into the container.[11] This observation extends to works themselves; all notions of style that propose an atomistic conception of phenomena like films and classes are exposed as fraught. Arnheim does not advocate a traditional style-class approach—one that entails slotting works into arbitrarily demarcated categories—because style class designations become empty under this model. If "classicism" and "impressionism" are mere labels for sorting boxes, then they are divorced from what gives them use value—their role in naming the historian's concept for a way of using artistic means and materials. As an alternative to presenting works and classes as self-contained units of analysis or cate- gorization, Arnheim recommends that historians of style study individual and groups of works as "fields of forces."[12]

The three problems facing a theory of style classes present a set of corresponding questions:

1. How do competing approaches explain the historian's thought process in defining style classes, and on what theoretical bases should they be evaluated?
2. What is the relation between style as devices and style as historical classes?
3. How can style classes maintain their use value as classificatory concepts while still respecting the complexity of individual works, focusing on practical artistic goals and revealing how similar goals motivate works in series?

"Style as a Gestalt Problem" provides answers, beginning with the separation of two areas of inquiry: composition and style.

compositional devices and style classes: an arnheimian distinction

A critical difference between a commonplace film studies conception of style and Arnheim's is the former's attention to rhetorical components of style (i.e., the techniques used by one work or many) and the latter's emphasis on the historical class forged conceptually from heterogeneous products. Arnheim's object of study is the historian's thought process as it relates to style classes. With this unique angle on the problem of style, he addresses the shortcomings in the commonly held view that a style is a label for a sum of observable formal features and patterned techniques that dominate for a given period. He instead underscores the conceptual work that goes into perceiving style classes. "Cubism," for instance, is

> a name for *a way of making art*, defined by a particular use of the medium, the subject matter, etc. Such a style can be traced and isolated as a component in the work of one artist or several, in one period or place or several, and it can show up as dominant or secondary, persistent or temporary. Cézanne is neither an Impressionist nor a Cubist; but the individual nature of his work can be described as a unique gestalt structure composed of these and other stylistic constituents.[13]

A gestalt structure is usually understood as two related things. It refers to a perceptual or intellectual structure or unity that is functionally greater than the sum of its parts. It follows that a structure cannot be understood by analyzing its constituent elements alone. Let us focus on the second aspect because it seems most foreign to the historian of style. Arnheim does not consider cinematic examples, but if the implication is that scholars should not research jump cuts in early Godard, perspectivally skewed sets in German expressionism, or, in the case of other media, Shigeru Miyamoto's lateral scroll design for NES's *Super Mario Bros.* (1985), and Robert Altman's deep staging and deep focus in his episodes of *Troubleshooters* (1959–1960), then what does Arnheim's theory propose for the historian of moving image styles?[14]

Arnheim does not discuss "rhetorical" techniques like these as "style" because he distinguishes between style and composition. In other words, as he translates "style" into the terms of a gestalt perceptual problem, he will take it as something other than a series of perceptual cues in artworks. Perceptual cues are the purview of a theory of composition, which attempts to explain the beholder's perception of a work's compositional organization. A theory of style, however, tries to explain the historian's task of conceptualizing historical classes of art.

This distinction between compositional devices or techniques and style classes has logical implications for film scholarship. For instance, the *Film Art* definition of style holds that attributes like matches on action, three-point lighting, and shot/reverse shot editing are representative of the "classical Hollywood style."[15] Films belong to the style by virtue of the qualitative similarities the historian observes. By contrast, Arnheim defines style as "an intellectual concept derived from myriad perceptual observations."[16] He later calls style a "mental" or "intellectual construct."[17] He clarifies this by arguing that we must distinguish between the concept ("style" itself, or any given style concept, like "French Impressionism") and its "perceptual sources," that is, a set of works or attributes of works.[18] This is so because although "[m]ore commonly, concepts of styles are derived from inductive observation," Arnheim hopes that we will avoid the problems of the inductive approach, which sees the concept as the sum total of observable attributes.[19]

Arnheim's argument against a strictly inductive model for defining style classes goes something like this. Just as we need to know what the color red is in order to describe cherries for their redness, we need to know what the concept "calligraphic style" means in order to see it in Japanese films of the 1920s. The trap of the inductive model is circular reasoning; defining redness by what cherries are, or the calligraphic style by what its films display, offers no concept because the concept is already assumed in the process of noticing the traits. With inductively prescribed styles, we are left instead with a casually ascribed label for a cluster of features.

The logical consequences of the distinction between devices and classes are clear, but what does it do for the film scholar in practical terms?

two cases: hybridity in classical hollywood and in the cinema of robert bresson

Examining two cases will allow us to further clarify Arnheim's solution to the class-device relation problem. The styles of classical Hollywood and Robert Bresson will also show how this paradigm resolves complicated problems of description and analysis, particularly with films that register more than one style. This is a central consideration in Arnheim's solution to the atomization problem, or the question of whether "style" must study works, classes, or periods as self-contained units.

For Arnheim, the theory that styles are gestalts eludes the confusion in the language of art historians between "historically and geographically confined" styles and the "timeless types of style" that take the same name.[20] Consider the concept "classical Hollywood style." Some scholars use it to refer to a self-contained period style (lasting from c.1917 to 1960), while others use it to designate a style that dominated in this period but that is now portable.[21] At stake here is whether a style must be tied to a time and place. Arnheim argues that the mode of thinking that ties styles to periods, with each period possessing its own style(s), operates along the lines of a

234

phenotype in biology, which views species as independent entities given their external qualities. His theory of style history instead proposes the study of *genotypes*, a "decisive turn" in the biological sciences in which organisms are taken as "confluences of underlying structural properties or groups of properties, so that the taxonomic system must now be based on the underlying strands rather than on external appearance."[22] This reframing of the issue suggests that historians of film style distinguish between a period named "classical Hollywood" and the "classical continuity style" that characterized it, with only the latter seen as a structuring property or stylistic genotype.

Furthermore, Arnheim's genotype model argues that periods of filmmaking will show a confluence of styles: "[a] plurality of styles will be recognized as the rule rather than a bothersome obstacle to conceptualization, and homogeneity or constancy will be shown as what it is, namely a rare exception."[23] Periods, styles, and works, the theory claims, are complexes rather than compact, unitary entities.[24] Both this view and Arnheim's solution to the atomization problem rest on a stratification thesis, which claims that history, diachronically and synchronically, is a field of forces. The study of stylistic atoms stems from the false traditional impression that style history moves along like a sequence of integral beads or boxes. Arnheim argues that an atomistic picture is ill-suited to describe how structures of intentional and situated art-making interact or compete with one another in given periods and works, even ones taken as relatively unified. One implication of this is that works that exemplify a style will have a different make-up at higher and lower levels of magnification.[25] At a high level of magnification, a given period or selection of ostensibly related works, no matter how apparently unified, has constituent parts that exemplify other styles—other ways of making. What might have been taken at one point as stylistic monoliths are "revealed as complex combinations of strata."[26] Arnheim crystallizes his conception of style history in a "droodle"—halfway between a drawing and a doodle (Figure 13.1). Rather than present a style or period as a discrete unit comprised of a series of works or their distinguishing features as we find in droodle A, Arnheim favors the conception in droodle C, where a style or period of related works is a weave of components unified by the way of making that structures it. In his view style classes form a twisting multi-strand rope moving through time.

235

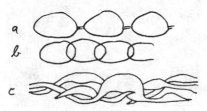

Figure 13.1
Arnheim's droodle of three conceptions of style history

Droodle C also has the benefit of shedding light on how such a field of forces weaves its way through individual works; any single work may have two or more strands winding through it.

This is a particularly persuasive point with regards to a complex art—an art made of other arts—like cinema. For example, Juan Antonio Ramírez's study of the styles of film architecture in classical Hollywood reveals that, although many of a classical film's parameters follow the higher order goal of creating an intelligible and coherent story world, at a lower level of description the classical genotype is porous, consisting of different architectural looks stitched into the films by set designers. *The Bride of Frankenstein* (1935) and *Camille* (1937) rely upon the continuity storytelling style, but their architectural styles range respectively from a "historically impossible" Gothicism, with the set of the baronial palace characterized by "a great medieval vestibule with oppressive, mysteriously low ceilings,"[27] to what the author dubs "Bourgeois Baroque," an "a-temporal" style typically reliant upon "decorative overload" to "denote wealth, distinction, power."[28] *Camille's* "otiose and exaggerated curved moldings" in Figure 13.2 point to this style's presence in the work.[29]

The result is not a conception of style history that sunders the classical period into many; it rather denies that the "classical" elements of the period at the higher level of description—continuity storytelling principles—exhaustively describe the look and goals of Hollywood films.[30] If the classical period were identified with a monolithic style, then a dimension of classical Hollywood art would be lost, namely how set designers repurposed architectural styles of the past and created their own style, which Ramírez dubs "Eclecticism."[31]

Arnheim models his theory after just such an approach, showing how the historian can perceive a variety of styles sitting beside one another in a set of works, and how certain style classes—in this case eclecticism—reflect a way of making movie sets that is itself a hybrid of previous styles. Supported by Arnheim's theory, Ramírez's findings also suggest that a comprehensive description of a period must consider its films as a weave of artistic impulses and not as unified phenomena. But of the two stylistic genotypes considered, one is cinematic (classical continuity) and the other

Figure 13.2
Camille frame enlargement

is architectural (eclecticism). Can Arnheim's model help us see a series of works as a weave of two *cinematic* styles?

A common assumption about Robert Bresson's style is that it is unified by either a worldview, described as Jansenist for the aesthetic and moral austerity of the films, or a penchant for certain techniques, like offscreen sound, elliptical narration, and dispassionate acting styles.[32] Whichever traits are viewed as essentially Bressonian, Arnheim's theory predicts that the films will include elements that are qualitatively or structurally different from the Bresson genotype. In other words, not all aspects of Bresson's films will exemplify the Bresson "way of making."

Arnheim's theory proves useful here as well. If one assumes that Bresson's films are a field of disparate forces rather than an aesthetic atom, and if one takes the style to be different at different scales of magnification, then one has a better means for making sense of *Diary of a Country Priest* (1951). While at the one level of description the film presents a pared-down narration devoid of visual depictions of characters' inner states like dream and hallucinatory sequences—a key touchstone of Bresson's "austere" style—at another level its cinematography is expressionist. The soft-edged chiaroscuro and high contrast lighting of Figure 13.3 captures the emotional gravitas of a "confession" scene involving the titular priest and Chantal, the estranged daughter of the film's adulterous Count and aloof Countess. The cinematography expresses the scene's caliginous atmosphere, as the priest confronts the embittered child for slandering her parents, especially her mother, grief-stricken by the loss of another child. After convincing her to hand over what would have been her suicide note, the priest is accused of being the devil for his meddling.

Léonce-Henri Burel's cinematography recalls the expressionist effects he created for Abel Gance; he weaves into the film a stylistic purpose distinct from Bresson's anti-expressionist asceticism. With Burel as *opérateur*, Gance's *Le droit à la vie* (1917) uses sidelighting and key spot lighting against black backgrounds, "not only to model characters in a three-dimensional space, but also to heighten their emotional expressiveness," as one historian comments.[33] Bresson sheds this expressionist "way" for a coarser, less atmospheric approach in *A Man Escaped* (1956) and *Pickpocket* (1959). What is

237

Figure 13.3
Diary of a Country Priest's
expressionism.
Frame enlargement

important is that Arnheim presents an alternative to categorically dismissing *Diary*'s cinematography as a momentary lapse on Bresson's part, promoting a means to explain this aspect of his moviemaking as the revival of a venerable solution.

This alternative shows that movies need not be completely unified in order for the historian of style classes to account for them. Moreover, it provides theoretical justification for the analysis of apparently self-contained oeuvres as exemplars of more than one stylistic gestalt. It now remains to be seen how an artistic "way"—whatever this constitutes—structures a work's features. Must one adhere to a thick gestaltism to accept Arnheim's theory of style?

the nature of style as structure

Arnheim believes that if historians of style view works or periods as stylistic atoms (the atomization problem) defined by empirically observed surface traits (the class-device relation problem), then they will become bogged down with difficulties, particularly as it relates to the complexity of works and the necessary conceptual basis of style class identification. But if Arnheim wants to claim that "ways of making" "structure" the intellectual constructs of historians, then these two ideas require clarification. It is based on such clarifications that historians of media styles can decide whether Arnheim's solutions can be retained despite their gestaltist embryo. This section will argue that, although Arnheim's theory of style as structure depends upon gestaltist logic, it offers a sound explanation for the relation between style class concepts, on the one hand, and practical artistic goals and devices, on the other. How then do historians infer style class concepts?

The gestaltist theory about the nature of structures is not presented in "Style as a Gestalt Problem," so we must look to other sources.[34] Arnheim believes that works relate to one another through that which structures them. In *Visual Thinking*, he argues that relations depend upon structure: "to see is to see in relation, and the relations encountered in percepts are not simple."[35] He follows with a perceptual example.

> The seven brightest stars of the Ursa Major are seen as a quadrilateral with a stem attached to one of its corners. Here the perceptual relations go much beyond connection by similarity. What is seen is indeed a constellation, in which each item has a definite and unique role. Because of its graspable shape, the constellation can also be compared to familiar objects of similar visual structure, such as a dipper, a wagon, or a plough, or an animal with a tail. Its relation to neighboring constellations is established by further structural connections, since two of its stars point to Polaris and its "tail" leads to Arcturus, the bear-watcher.[36]

Let the visual field of stars from which the Ursa Major constellation is derived stand for an array of works under the historian's consideration—let us say, French films of the late 1930s. Then let the stars or items in the visual field stand for works with similar qualities. What unites works as instantiations of a style is similar to what unites a group of stars in a constellation: that is, the pattern of relations that orders or structures them. In the case of a constellation, the structuring pattern is visual. In the case of a style, the structuring pattern is conceptual. Combined, the stars have a definite shape, and each star plays a unique role in the constellation as a pattern. Without the stars that form the tail, Ursa Major would not be a candidate for comparison with objects of comparable visual structure, like a dipper.

The stars that form the tail are therefore linked through a relation of shape that ties them to the total structure. Works of art also share traits. But what relates works for the historian of style are qualities in time. The foggy cinematography of *Jour se lève* (1939) and *Quai des brumes* (1938) links these films, suggests a similarity. Yet, just as stars in a constellation need to be connected by more than mere resemblance, so what makes these films "poetic realist" is what ties these qualities to something more—an aesthetic target concept that combines the "poetic" and the "realist," resulting in a stylized handling of social, working class, and psychological problems. It is the governing style concept (akin to the pattern of the stars) that unites these lower order qualitative relations (akin to local relations that make some of the stars play the role of a tail) into a stylistic structure (akin to the constellation). Without the overall visual pattern of the constellation, there would be no link between these stars; likewise, without the guiding style concept "poetic realism," tenebrous visual technique would be insufficient to link these films as a historical stylistic classification. To deny this by claiming that poetic realism is unified by the qualities poetic realist films show is to beg the question.

The implication is that the ties that bind films to a style are irreducible to a technique or a cluster of techniques; these merely suggest a relation. The linchpin is the presence of a guiding principle behind the techniques. Poetic realist films have an overarching purpose, and in the process of realizing this purpose, a series of techniques and subjects are brought to bear. A style, then, is a particular way of achieving a particular kind of aesthetic purpose. A historian of style infers the "way" that structures the style by considering the features of works, the purposes of features, and the processes of making. Should this way of making, which registers itself concretely in works as features, and the goals this "way" aims to achieve carry over a series of works, then a style presents itself. If in other words smoky cinematography weaves its way through a body of films towards the goal of giving a stylized handling to working-class dilemmas, then the historian of style is justified in claiming (as many have) that a historical aesthetic class dubbed "poetic realism" snakes its way through 1930s France.

I will call this Arnheim's guided process principle of style history. Arnheim proposes that the historian of styles do more than enumerate devices; more important is that she study how these same devices are used. This "how" becomes a separable consideration from the devices themselves—a quality irreducible to the devices. His point is that works need to be explored for this "how." Returning to our Bresson example, an analysis that notes offscreen sound, elliptical narration, and dispassionate acting styles would fail to capture the Bresson genotype. The important step would be to distill the style concept called "Bressonian" from these observable traits. The Bressonian style qualifies as a style because the term Bressonian reveals a unique way of using filmic devices and subjects towards certain goals. Devices, after all, can be made more or less prominent, components can be shuffled and altered, and solutions can be embraced or rejected. Our newly minted Arnheimian approach to film style argues that whether a given film shows an elliptical narration or linear storytelling with few temporal gaps, it could still be Bressonian because "Bressonian" names a register of stylistic minimalism, a certain attitude toward the medium that advocates restraint and indirect expressivity rather than a set of techniques. A wide range of divergent techniques could conceivably achieve these ends. Bresson's cinema yields a style qua genotype because it proffers a unique conception of what film art can achieve—it sees a particular set of ends for the medium that other styles do not—which is different from and lies beneath the various devices that Bresson wields like an armature below overlaying membranes of skin.

arnheim and the functional theory of style

By examining Arnheim's research principles through numerous examples, they have shown themselves to be useful and logical, dependent upon a rather "thin" gestaltist analysis one could accept without becoming a gestaltist oneself. But how does Arnheim's theory of style fare next to a competing model, the functional theory of style? This final section will claim that a new definition of film style classes based on Arnheim's paradigm completes Noël Carroll's functionalism and proposes revisions to David Bordwell's. Previous sections have prepared the way: Arnheim's solutions to the atomization and the class-device relation problems serve as points of comparison.

On first glance these models appear to compete for different terrain. Arnheim's theory of style sees style as relating a body of works. Carroll's functionalist theory sees style as the "*ensemble of choices intended to realize the point or the purpose of the [individual] film.*"[37] While Arnheim's offers a multi-work theory, Carroll's claims that "style" is most useful and rigorous if applied to the single film. Despite this, both seek relations: in Arnheim's case, between the qualities in works that point to structural relations; in Carroll's case, between film form and underlying motivations in the individual work. Why does Carroll narrow his concept to the individual film?

Carroll designs his concept so as to evade deficiencies in multi-work approaches to style. His criticism of multi-work approaches argues that they "[leave] a large number of a given film's stylistic features unaccounted for."[38] Carroll's functionalist alternative would, unlike most concepts of historical style, be able to account for the expressionist cinematography of *Diary of a Country Priest* because it is not restricted to the process of simply forcing the film into the Bresson sorting box. Instead it would analyze the functions of this choice in the context of the film's overall purpose. Carroll views style classes as an impediment to this kind of fine-grained analysis and explanation of an individual film's characteristics.

But Carroll's model remains silent about how links between films made over time could be established so as to define style classes. Perhaps the theory is not designed for this purpose. But let us assume that it could be used to define a group style. Presumably the functionalist theory would group together those films that are similar in their reliance upon the same set of choices used to achieve the same purpose(s). It has already been established that concepts of style based on a principle of surface similarity rather than underlying structure fall prey to circular reasoning. Revealing that poetic realist films use similar devices stops short of delivering a style concept. But Carroll's model is different because it claims that by linking a film's form to its purposes the guiding principle behind the work can be accessed. If the functionalist model can accept that style concepts must be derived from a series of observations so as to name the underlying generative purposes of the works' features, then on this point Arnheim's theory completes Carroll's.

Arnheim's theory supplements Carroll's in other ways that point to further provisos in a functionalist-Arnheimian alliance. Arnheim's historical classes approach shows that the rejection of multi-work conceptions of style on the basis of a lack of comprehensiveness depends upon three related misunderstandings. First, Carroll's model stipulates that the concept of style best equipped to explain a film's style exhaustively must take the film as an atom or unit. That is, relating a film's form to its own function is a necessary and sufficient analytical means to explain the film, conceived as a self-contained entity. Second, it argues that a multi-work conception of style by necessity leaves a greater quantity of formal features unaccounted for. Finally, it suggests that a multi-work conception is a non-generative conception of style. While not stated directly, this point is implied in the characterization of the style qua historical classes approach as limited by virtue of its narrow preoccupation with films as "unalloyed exemplars of their period, movement or school."[39] These are presented as grounds for a functionalist theory of style in the individual film.

These ideas hold only if the multi-work conception adopted is identical to the one Arnheim rejects, namely the conception that styles are sorting

241

boxes for groups of works, or phenotypes. Indeed, this conception leaves many features unexamined. Unlike the multi-work approach criticized by Carroll, Arnheim's is designed to account for features that appear to be at odds with the style the work is generally taken to exemplify, as the *Diary of a Country Priest* case showed. Finally, on the generative point, Arnheim's "style" is by nature a concept derived from the processes and target ideas from which the work sprang. Carroll is correct to claim that the reproduction of a style's conventions tends to include some measure of invention. One consequence is that traditional style-class models invariably pigeonhole artworks, unable to account for fine creative variations on established traditions. But this criticism is anticipated in Arnheim's position that film-makers often make creative choices dependent upon the guiding principles of style classes. In this way, styles become woven into their works. A basic component of Arnheim's dynamic model of style history is the ways of making that filmmakers actively inherit or alter for their own purposes. Arnheim need not distort works to make them fit.

David Bordwell's functionalist theory of style is animated like Arnheim's by a focus on works in series.[40] He presents a multi-layered conception that integrates stylistic devices and style classes (or traditions).[41] (See Figure 13.4.) The theory demonstrates how film historians should conceive of change and stasis in cinema's aesthetic history. Genres and styles tend to change at a slower rate than, say, devices. The ramification is that styles are not defined by devices alone. The theory also shows that because traditions remain relatively stable, unified by verifiable continuities across a series of films, the diversity of devices wielded even in a single style can be explained by reference to the functional equivalency of the devices. For instance, films manifesting the classical style might favor one in a variety of devices to depict a character's mental or optical perception. In terms of camerawork and editing alone, such techniques as point-of-view (POV) shots, superimpositions, split screens, and flashbacks punctuated by dissolves or fades are all part of the classical filmmaker's toolkit to introduce intelligible dramatic

Technical or stylistic devices

Spatial and temporal systems
recruiting these devices

Figure 13.4
Bordwell's functionalist
theory of style

Genres and traditions (or styles)
recruiting these systems

information about a character's inner world. This information will tend to advance the plot, motivating the character's behavior in a later scene, for example. Films using one or the other device can display "classical" qualities because of the devices' functional aims. If styles qua classes are said to change with the recruitment of new devices, argues Bordwell, then our model of style history would be unable to account for the constancies that remain despite apparently radical shifts in technique. The history of styles would devolve into the history of fashions.

This position raises a number of questions. First, do these continuities unify at the highest level of description to form a concept that defines the class? Elsewhere Bordwell and two colleagues explain how the technical features of studio era films are unified by a quality captured in a concept that describes the films' common purposes: "the label 'classicism' serves [us] well because it swiftly conveys distinct aesthetic qualities (elegance, unity, rule-governed craftsmanship) and historical functions (Hollywood's role as the world's mainstream film style)."[42] An Arnheimian theory of film styles would embrace this particular yield of the functionalist theory: a conceptual unity for the class derived from a way of making. But this unity has limits. Recall that Arnheim's paradigm requires that the historian respect the diversity of goals that films of the classical style pursue; there will be a plurality of styles at a lower level of description. The studio era was a period of nesting styles, one of which was architectural eclecticism.

Second, are stylistic devices or techniques the only necessary constituent elements of styles? Like Carroll, Arnheim does not limit the study of styles to the study of devices or techniques. Rather, Carroll (who looks to "choices" or "features") and Arnheim (who looks to "perceptual observations") are willing to entertain any observable element as a candidate for a deposit of a style category. Because the aim of style historiography is to examine the ways of making that shape historical time, and because ways of making involve drawing upon artistic materials like techniques *and* narrative subjects and themes, the focus on stylistic devices and techniques lacks theoretical justification, at least as far as the delineation of styles qua classes is concerned.

Finally, the Arnheimian theory of styles would ask whether "functions" are simply another approach to the "ways of making" that structure stylistic genotypes. In Bordwell's elaboration of the functionalist theory, certain aims must remain stable enough for a style to be discovered, so the theories of Arnheim and Bordwell are in agreement on this front. But this raises another question: why present style as "the repeated and salient uses of film techniques characteristic of a single film or a group of films" (as *Film Art* does) when the three-layered theory appears to make functions an essential condition for delineating a style class?[43]

Here it must be granted that *Film Art* is a textbook designed for use in undergraduate courses aimed at training students in film analysis. So, its

243

definition of style may appear justified in this context. Yet, even with this concession, its conception is misleading, and this, on functionalist and Arnheimian grounds. Not only does the *Film Art* concept conceal its fusion of art historical and rhetorical concepts of style, but it fails to reflect the intricacies of the functionalist theory that ostensibly motivates it. An Arnheimian theory of style history offers an alternative conception more appropriate to style research than the *Film Art* reduction or the commonplace model. A film style qua historical class is (i) *the class concept that refers to* (ii) *the quality that is exhibited by* (iii) *the structurally related functions that are inferred from* (iv) *the technical and non-technical features of a group of films.* The crucial point is that the phenomenon that (i) names—that is, (ii)—is distilled from (iii), which in turn is extracted from (iv). There must, in other words, be something "classical" about the functions to which choices in Hollywood films aim in order for them to exhibit "classicism." In this way, the manner in which the historian processes raw data is incorporated into the definition. Furthermore, it would argue that, given this new definition, devices and techniques do not merit the name "style"; rather they are best described as compositional "choices" or "features" that are stylistic only to the extent that they participate in a style class.

conclusion

This chapter has called upon Arnheim's "Style as a Gestalt Problem" to argue that the work of style history includes but is not limited to the tabulation of devices if a style qua historical class is to be identified. In this way, a colloquial conception of style as those techniques or devices exemplified by a set of films of a particular place and time proves inadequate. Style classes, as Arnheim and the functionalists demonstrate, fall beneath one's radar if the only means of detection remains the "look-a-like" test that a colloquial conception allows. An Arnheimian model also shows, particularly given the film studies consensus on "style," that the style theorist must focus on three problems—naturalization, class-device relation and atomization—in order to develop a sounder conception of style history research. We have seen how approaches to style classes must be evaluated for a reliance on inductive circularity; how the relation between devices and classes is structured by the way of making inferred; and how, via a stratification theory of historical phenomena, style terms can retain their use value in classification while still registering the diversity of goals in works and periods.

These findings raise questions that future theories of style might address. Are features limitable to technical devices? Is "style" a cluster concept that includes both "devices" and "classes"? Can the use of designations like "Hollywood classicism" as labels, and the related inductive study of devices, survive the criticism of circularity? Finally, can style theory account for three approaches to works in series: the study of continuities among devices, the study of geographically and temporally contained style classes, and the study of migratory style classes not limited by place and time (like "naturalism," "mannerism," "expressionism," and so on)? These questions show that style is an area deserving of its own theory, one with historiographic utility.

notes

1. I thank Dave Resha, Jonah Horwitz, Scott Higgins and especially Brian Crane for their comments on previous versions of this essay.
2. David Bordwell and Kristin Thompson, *Film Art*, 8th ed., New York: McGraw-Hill, 2005, p. 481. I would like to clarify two points. First, as a textbook for undergraduate courses, *Film Art*'s simplification of "style" might seem justified for some. Still, the fact that the authors do not make this point explicit either here or elsewhere, that the textbook is so widely used and cited, and that its definition overlaps with the colloquial conception in film scholarship mean that a consideration of it in this context is warranted. Second, *Film Art* does at times rely upon a properly functional approach to style. (See below for what I mean by a "properly functional approach.") Cf. for instance page 446, where classical continuity technique is discussed in the context of narrative motivation (i.e., there is a governing purpose for technique). Yet, consider page 304, where a group style is defined as "the consistent use of techniques across the work of several filmmakers." As conceived, a style becomes a set of technical continuities; no reference is made to the consistency of artistic purposes in defining styles. My point is that simplifications like this can be misleading in their suggestion that the regular use of devices by a filmmaker or group of filmmakers is sufficient to define a style.
3. I lack the space for a balanced and extensive list of works attesting to this usage. Before citing examples, I would like to underscore that I refer to a general phenomenon evident in many written and oral communications. One can observe a consistent or intermittent identification of "style" as historical class (including group and individual styles) with "style" as a set of devices—that is, a given style is defined by a "look-a-like" examination of observable stylistic techniques—in this random sample of recent articles: Laszlo Strausz, "The Politics of Style in Miklós Jancsó's *The Red and the White* and *The Lord's Lantern in Budapest*," in *Film Quarterly* 62.3, Spring 2009, pp. 41–47; Jurica Pavicic, " 'Lemons in Siberia': A New Approach to the Study of the Yugoslav Cinema of the 1950s," in *New Review of Film and Television Studies* 6.1, April 2008, pp. 19–39; Jean-Pierre Geuens, "The Grand Style," in *Film Quarterly* 58.4, Summer 2005, pp. 27–38; and Brian O'Leary, "Hollywood Camera Movements and the Films of Howard Hawks: A Functional Semiotic Approach," in *New Review of Film and Television Studies* 1.1, November 2003, pp. 7–30 (especially p. 24).
4. By "thick gestaltism" I mean 1) the theory that, in principle, entities perceived as wholes cannot be deduced from parts considered in isolation; and 2) the research by gestalt psychologists into perception that supports this theory. While the concept of style offered in the closing sections of this chapter betrays a gestaltist pattern of thinking (namely, that a style class concept cannot be reduced to the collection of stylistic devices a set of films

uses), I do not defend this alternative concept of style on these gestaltist grounds alone. In fact, one can reject the general principle that wholes are greater than the sum of their parts and still accept the notion that if the names of style classes are to appear motivated, then they must name something other than a set of observable traits in works of art. For this reason, this chapter argues for a "thin" gestaltist logic that applies not to all cases but rather to *the particular case* of style class concepts. Whether or not the blanket claim that wholes are irreducible to their parts is true matters less than the specific claim that if style class terms ("classicism," "realism," "baroque," etc.) are to have meaning then they cannot refer to a cluster of traits alone. An analysis of what makes the use of these traits "classical" or "baroque" would be lacking. I therefore propose that style class concepts must refer to the quality exhibited by the goals that are inferred from the use of these traits.

5. R. Arnheim, "Style as a Gestalt Problem" (1981), in *New Essays on the Psychology of Art*, Berkeley: University of California Press, 1986, pp. 261–273. The essays of the Summer Institute are collected in Berel Lang, *The Concept of Style*, Ithaca, NY: Cornell University Press, 1987.

6. Arnheim, "Style as a Gestalt Problem," p. 266.

7. M. Schapiro, "Style" (1953), in *Theory and Philosophy of Art: Style, Artist, and Society*, New York: George Braziller, 1994, pp. 51–102; and J. Ackerman, "A Theory of Style," in *Journal of Aesthetics and Art Criticism* 20.3, 1962, pp. 227–237.

8. Cf. Jeremy Butler, *Television Style*, New York, NY: Routledge, 2009, influenced by Bordwell's functional approach, which is examined below.

9. I sketch some of these developments in Colin Burnett, "A New Look at the Concept of Style in Film: The Origins and Development of the Problem-Solution Model," in *New Review of Television and Film Studies* 6.2, August 2008, pp. 127–149.

10. Cf. András Bálint Kovács, *Screening Modernism: European Art Cinema, 1950–1980*, Chicago: University of Chicago Press, 2007, p. 51. Kovács acknowledges these two concepts of style. Cf. also S. Alpers and Paul Alpers, "*Ut Pictura Noesis?* Criticism in Literary and Art History," in *New Literary History* 3.3, Spring 1972, pp. 437–458, where a distinction is made between a historical and a literary-critical concept of style.

11. Arnheim, "Style as a Gestalt Problem," pp. 266, 268.

12. Ibid., p. 267.

13. Ibid., p. 268 (emphasis added).

14. Mark Minett, "Investigating Style and Authorship: Robert Altman, *Troubleshooters*, and *Combat!*," unpublished manuscript, 2007.

15. Bordwell and Thompson, p. 446.

16. Arnheim, "Style as a Gestalt Problem," p. 263.

17. Ibid., pp. 263–264.

18. Ibid., p. 263.

19. Ibid., p. 265. Arnheim re-reads his *Film as Art* as a deductive approach to style determining the stylistic possibilities of a medium based on its perceived nature.

20. Ibid., p. 265, n.1.

21. As instances of the former, cf. Peter Kramer, "Post-Classical Hollywood," in *The Oxford Guide to Film Studies*, New York: Oxford University Press, 1998, pp. 289–309 (especially pp. 306–307); and Angela Ndalianis, *Neo-Baroque Aesthetics and Contemporary Entertainment*, Cambridge, MA: MIT Press, 2004 (especially pp. 3–5).

22. Arnheim, "Style as a Gestalt Problem," p. 268.

23. Ibid., p. 269.

24. Ibid., p. 266.

25. Ibid., p. 266.

26. Ibid., p. 266.

27. Juan Antonio Ramírez, *Architecture for the Screen: A Critical Study of Set Design in Hollywood's Golden Age*, Jefferson, NC: McFarlane, 2004, p. 139.

28. Ibid., p. 168.

29. Ibid., p. 168.

30. Cf. D. Bordwell, Janet Staiger, and K. Thompson, *Classical Hollywood Cinema: Film Style and Mode of Production to 1960*, New York: Columbia University Press, 1985.

31. Ramírez, *Architecture for the Screen*, p. 114.

32. Kovács, *Screening Modernism*, p. 141.

33. Richard Abel, *The First Wave, 1915–1929*, Princeton, NJ: Princeton University Press, 1984, p. 87.

34. This reasoning is analogical in nature (i.e., "styles work the way gestalts work"). I will leave it to others to level the charge at Arnheim that in order for his reasoning to avoid the fallacy of indigent analogy, we must know more about the term in the analogy that is meant to clarify. The argument would go like this: we would have to know more about gestalts to clarify what "style" is, and since this is not the case, Arnheim's reasoning falters. What interests me here is whether the results of his reasoning are detachable from his theoretical commitments.

35. R. Arnheim, *Visual Thinking*, Berkeley: University of California Press, 1969, p. 54.

36. Ibid., p. 55.

37. Noël Carroll, "Film Form: An Argument for a Functional Theory of Style in the Individual Film," in *Engaging the Moving Image*, New Haven: Yale University Press, 2003, p. 141, italics in source.

38. Ibid., p. 130.

39. Ibid., p. 130.

40. I owe much here to an email correspondence with Ian Verstegen, February 2009. While I present Bordwell's "style" as a theory, it is best described as an approach aimed at facilitating results in a practical research program. In this way, his writings on "style" differ from those of Arnheim and Carroll, who explicitly aim to solve theoretical problems. Still, for all the ways my transformation of Bordwell's approach into a theory disregard its original purpose, I feel compelled to include it in order to offer as comprehensive a discussion I can of the dominant concept of style in the field.

41. D. Bordwell, *On the History of Film Style*, Cambridge, MA: Harvard University Press, 1997, p. 44.

42. Bordwell *et al.*, *Classical Hollywood Cinema*, p. 4. One gathers that a non-classical style would be inelegant, lacking in unity, non-rule-governed, and so forth.

43. Cf. note 2 above.

arnheim on the

ontology of the

photographic image

v i n c e n t   b o h l i n g e r

In the early 1990s, Rudolf Arnheim published his article "The Two Authenticities of the Photographic Media" as a response, of sorts, to the Rodney King trial.[1] Many people—intellectuals, laypeople, and rioters alike—were aghast that four Los Angeles police officers could have been acquitted of using excessive force when videotape documenting the seeming brutality was exhibited extensively during the trial. The footage came from George Holliday, who was able to film the beating on his Sony Handycam because he just happened to be awakened at the incident's precise time (a little after midnight on 3 March 1991) and exact place (on a balcony from across the street).[2] Holliday's presence with his camera at the profilmic event and his arguable status as an unbiased third party made the trial more than just a case of King's word versus the word of four policemen. Moreover, the very content of the footage seemed to guarantee the lopsidedness of the violence. In the video, King was shown being continually beaten after he was already incapacitated and writhing on the ground, something that perhaps neither testimony nor medical records alone would be able to prove as overtly. When the officers' acquittal was handed down from the jury, among the many complaints were cries that the defense had manipulated the content of the footage through the form of its presentation. For example, in an Op-Ed piece for *The New York Times*, psychology professor Patricia Greenfield and aikido expert Paul Kibbey together claimed that the video footage in the trial was often "distorted or misused."[3] They argued that the defense's screening of the footage via slow motion and still images mitigated the forcefulness—and even changed the nature—of the content itself, so that the beating looked "less real and more fantastic."[4]

For Arnheim, the ways in which the screening methods of the beating footage were criticized and discredited demonstrate what he considers to be a longstanding tension within the aesthetic principles of the figurative arts. This tension, he argues, is situated between two authenticities, the authenticity of realistic representation versus the authenticity of human experience and expression. To explain these two authenticities, Arnheim sketches a broad history of art, in which photographic media have inherited and intensified this tension from earlier figurative art forms. In drawing from centuries of artwork and seeking to explain their foundational qualities, Arnheim essentially presents an ontology of the photographic media, very much in the same spirit and approach as André Bazin in his famous essay "The Ontology of the Photographic Image," though with differing conclusions.[5] Significantly, it is within this ontological discussion that Arnheim revisits and slightly amends the well-known claims that he had made six decades earlier in his seminal work *Film as Art*.[6]

In this essay, I aim to contextualize Arnheim's notion of these two authenticities within his conception of the history of photography. Since Arnheim and Bazin are often framed in opposition to each other within the field of film studies, I compare their competing notions concerning the place of photography within the broader overall function or "calling" of art. Both consider the advent of photography highly significant, though Bazin considers it a major turning point in the ontology of art whereas Arnheim simply views it as having intensified an ongoing ontological unease. I then discuss the issue of manipulation, as the accusations that the King beating footage had been unfairly manipulated were what inspired Arnheim's article in the first place. I explore Arnheim's contention that certain types of photographic manipulation are not only still indeed authentic, but also actually necessary and to be expected. Arnheim concludes his article with concerns about digital image-making and manipulation. Such concerns seem fairly widespread among film theorists, so I end with an application of Arnheim's two authenticities to another recent scandal concerning photographic evidence of excessive force and brutality: the digital photographs of seeming prisoner abuse and torture at Abu Ghraib. I believe that Arnheim's notion of the two authenticities can be very helpful in understanding how these photographs elicit strong, unsettling emotional responses from us in large part because they seem to embody intensely the very tension that Arnheim has identified between these two authenticities.

the two authenticities

Arnheim posits an oppositional nature between the two authenticities, labeling it "a compromise," "dilemma," and "ambiguity that has plagued the aesthetic and epistemological theory of the figurative arts."[7] On one hand, there is the drive toward an authenticity with respect to, as Arnheim writes, "a faithful rendering of the facts of reality."[8] This authenticity "offers recognizable images of creatures and objects."[9] We understand what an image represents by virtue of the similarity of that image's component parts to the thing or things it represents in phenomenological reality. To be gauged authentic in this first sense, an image must simply look to some degree like what it is. On the other hand, there is the drive toward "expressing the qualities of human experience."[10] This second authenticity is indeed much more vague, and the standards by which such authenticity is measured are rather indefinite. In characterizing this indeterminacy, Arnheim allows for the authenticity of expression to be achieved "by any means suitable to that purpose."[11] There is, then, no baseline determinant for the second authenticity. Furthermore, Arnheim argues that this second authenticity "hampers" the first authenticity: "the fancies and liberties of the human imagination are anything but authentic when taken as documents of physical reality."[12]

Arnheim suggests that the opposition between the two authenticities arises from their interdependence. In writing of the relationship between reality, art, and artists, he writes, "in order to make their images comprehensible to the human mind they had to select and shape and organize the material taken from reality—they had to find and impose form."[13] For Arnheim, reality must be manipulated to some degree, as form must be imposed, in order for us to understand it. Human experience, which leads to recognized and understood forms, determines recognized and understood reality. The second authenticity does not simply mitigate the first authenticity; rather, the second seems to help guarantee the first. Arnheim contends that the distortion inherent in the second authenticity is necessary in order to achieve the first. He argues that it is necessary "to partially reshape the facts of nature" in order for it to be "perceived by the eyes."[14] We can certainly judge the first type of authenticity in an image by virtue of how accurately it represents reality, but, Arnheim claims, some means of manipulation had to have already occurred in order for us even to begin to recognize what the image is supposed to represent in the first place.

Arnheim's beliefs concerning the necessity of imposing form signal his longstanding allegiance to the principles of gestalt psychology. In his *Principles of Gestalt Psychology*, Kurt Koffka discusses "external organizing forces," in

251

which the mind of the viewer actively works to organize and shape an image in order to comprehend it.[15] Koffka argues that the viewer imposes form to "constrain" the image; there is a "stress toward simplification."[16] The mind engages in a process of simplifying and reducing the image so that the very image itself can be recognized. Max Wertheimer, Arnheim's teacher at the University of Berlin, explains the factors involved in this process: "operations come into the picture externally: on the basis of recall, of some previous knowledge, general or analogical, of associations in connection with some items."[17] For Arnheim, these prior associations and connections are fundamental to the imposition of form, which in turn is crucial to the legibility of the image. The second authenticity therefore not only involves the mere expressiveness and formal patterning necessary for perception, but also draws from our previous outside knowledge and associations about that which we are perceiving.

At issue is Arnheim's supposition that phenomenological reality is too vast, too grand for instant and singular comprehension. Arnheim understands ambiguity to be an essential aspect of reality, a notion presupposed by Bazin as well. However, Arnheim and Bazin differ in how they conceive of art functioning in relationship to this ambiguity. Both recognize dueling oppositions with respect to reality, authenticity, and art. Arnheim describes a "competition between the two aspirations of authenticity," while Bazin characterizes art as "torn between two ambitions."[18] In Bazin's conception of art history, the drive toward realistic representation—what Arnheim considers to be the first authenticity—arises from what Bazin famously calls the "mummy complex," alongside a "proclivity of the mind towards magic."[19] Claiming to put the representational arts "under psychoanalysis," Bazin contends that the longstanding desire for realistic representation was perhaps illustrated earliest by the ancient Egyptian practice of embalming a corpse as a means to preserve the body and hence defy death.[20] What is achieved in the substitution of the preserved body for the dead person is "the preservation of life by a representation of life."[21] Similarly, Bazin considers a clay bear in a prehistoric cave "a magical identity-substitute for the living animal," in which representation again equals preservation.[22] Arnheim meanwhile ventures forth no claim as to the origins of the first authenticity; he simply presumes that this first authenticity has always existed.

Bazin's second "ambition" for art differs significantly from Arnheim's second authenticity. Bazin describes the second ambition as "symbolic" and "namely the expression of spiritual reality."[23] With some interpretive finesse, such similarly vague terminology might initially make this second ambition compatible with Arnheim's second authenticity for "expressing the qualities of human experience," but such a correlation is precluded when Bazin further elaborates on this second ambition in stipulating the place and role of photographic media within the history of art. For Bazin, the two ambitions of art—the realist ambition and the expressive ambition—coexisted together in "a varied balance" in all representational art up until the Renaissance, when the camera obscura began to be seen as an instrument useful for more precise, realistic drawing.[24] Bazin argues that it was only after the possibility of greater illusions of three-dimensional space that the two ambitions became oppositional. He writes, "perspective was the original sin."[25] Although Bazin concedes that "the great artists" were still able to "combine the two tendencies," he contends that with the development of linear perspective, greater attention was given to the "purely psychological" ambition for reproducing reality, "the duplication of the world outside."[26] This increased focus came at the expense of the "primarily aesthetic" ambition of expressing spiritual reality. He writes, "the satisfaction of this appetite for illusion merely served to increase it till, bit by bit, it consumed the plastic arts" and "seriously upset the equilibrium of the plastic arts."[27] For Arnheim, it bears noting, the oppositional and balanced relationship between the two authenticities has existed "ever since antiquity" because of their mutual reliance.[28]

The invention of photographic media figures differently in Bazin's and Arnheim's accounts of art history. For Bazin, art was "redeemed from sin by Niepce and Lumière."[29] He cites these pioneers of photography and film and argues that "photography has freed the plastic arts from their obsession with likeness."[30] Bazin claims photography ended the oppositional nature between the two ambitions of art because it "freed" artists from the constraints of the first ambition toward greater realism, "the 'resemblance complex.' "[31] He references Picasso and suggests that the increasing abstraction found in late-nineteenth- and twentieth-century art is evidence of this liberation. Arnheim, however, contends that the "dilemma" between the two authenticities was not at all resolved, but rather "was sharpened by the advent of photography."[32] For Arnheim, the ambiguity of reality poses greater difficulties when less overt subjectivity is involved in its reproduction. He argues that "the confusing untidiness of the sights projected by the camera lens tended to make images unreadable."[33] Arnheim seems largely in step with Bazin's assertion of "the essentially objective character of photography."[34] Bazin signals the importance of photography in that "for the first time an image of the world is formed automatically, without the creative intervention of man."[35] Allowing for some measure of subjectivity for the photographer, Bazin admits that "the final result may reflect something of his personality," but what matters most is the decreased significance of the photographer's hand in photography.[36] Perhaps deliberately overstating his case, he proclaims that "all the arts are based on the presence of man, only photography derives an advantage from his absence."[37]

For Arnheim, photography is perhaps in and of itself objective, but that objectivity demands human intervention in order to rein in the ambiguity of reality for the sake of the viewer. It is for this very reason that the opposition between the two authenticities is exacerbated by photographic media.

He argues, "no image conveys its meaning and expression readably without being carefully composed."[38] The process is mutually reinforcing: we recognize an image and understand its meaning and expression because it adheres to forms with which we are already familiar. Human intervention therefore is needed to guarantee the comprehensibility of an objective image.

In the quest to locate recognizable form within a vast and shifting reality, Arnheim designates the photographer as "a vigilant hunter" who searches for the "momentary revelation."[39] The photographers Arnheim references all help to reinforce his emphasis on human intervention and the importance of either composed or found form. He first describes the mid-nineteenth-century Scottish photographers David Octavius Hill and Robert Adamson, who in a four-year partnership managed over 3,000 calotype photographs, predominantly portraiture. Arnheim emphasizes that these portrait photographers were necessarily involved in "the proper selection and arrangement of subjects"—a clear example of form being imposed by the artist in the reproduction of reality.[40] In an 1848 letter, Hill himself references his own sculpting presence in his photographs: "they look like the imperfect work of man—and not the much diminished perfect work of God."[41] Hill claims authorship of his images and manages both boldly and modestly to suggest that his work is not just the reproduction of a fragment of the vast reality created by God, but something altogether that he himself has created. Arnheim emphasizes the second authenticity in his admiration of how Hill and Adamson "captured the lasting character and super-individual beauty of their sitters."[42] Arnheim then moves to Henri Cartier-Bresson, whom he labels as "the most gifted" of "the best photographers."[43] Cartier-Bresson is a particularly useful reference for Arnheim, as he was a painter (note that Hill was a painter as well), and he is famous for having used a viewfinder to compose his photographs carefully—with both painting and the use of viewfinders being self-evident examples of human intervention. Arnheim acknowledges that the first authenticity is certainly easier in photography, but he argues that the "finest results" come from "the deliberate display of the fleeting moment."[44] Cartier-Bresson's photography epitomizes for Arnheim "the skillful union of the two authenticities" in that his images look entirely fortuitous while simultaneously managing to be instantly readable and highly expressive.[45] Cartier-Bresson was widely regarded as a master of contemplated happenstance, or intended chance, and the fact that his work spans painting, photography, and film helps Arnheim both to link and maintain his argument of the two authenticities across the technological developments within art history.

Like Bazin, Arnheim considers film to extend further the characteristics and principles of photography, with the important inclusion of a new temporal dimension. Arnheim seemingly is in agreement with Bazin's assertion that with film "for the first time, the image of things is likewise the image of their duration, change mummified as it were."[46] Arnheim writes that film's "interest in the dimension of time" expands "enormously the range of phenomena accessible to visual art and thereby broaden[s] the medium's authenticity of the first kind."[47] Film has more extended and sustained access to reality in its ability to record across time. Although that portion of reality captured by film is just an infinitesimal fragment, it can be exponentially greater than a mere snapshot. Arnheim claims that film also "enriched authenticity of the second kind by focusing on action."[48] On one hand, there are so many more forms to be found and imposed within any duration of time. On the other hand, this seems an implicit recognition in the rise and dominance of fiction film, which easily can be aligned and measured according to the authenticity of human expression.

Interestingly, despite their many seeming points of congruence and departure, Arnheim does not openly address Bazin's arguments anywhere in his article. He instead briefly critiques his fellow countryman Siegfried Kracauer, but it is worth noting that the specific issue that Arnheim contests with Kracauer is one point of alignment between Kracauer and Bazin. Arnheim contends that Kracauer's *Theory of Film* "stressed the affinity of the photographic medium with the transitory, the indefinite, the fortuitous and the indeterminate."[49] Such a summary of Kracauer makes his work comparable to Bazin's notion of "change mummified," as well as Bazin's interest in film's exploitation of the ambiguity of reality. In his criticism of *Theory of Film*, Arnheim finds Kracauer's position "one-sided in that it neglected the indispensible contribution of interpretive form."[50] Bazin, like Kracauer, undervalues aspects of Arnheim's second authenticity by focusing only on aspects of the first authenticity.

Perhaps part of the contention is that Bazin premises that there is aesthetic value in the inherent ambiguity of reality. His discussions of filmmakers such as Orson Welles, William Wyler, and Jean Renoir all emphasize cinematic techniques such as long takes and deep focus cinematography, which he believes best reflect the ambiguity of reality.[51] For Arnheim, however, ambiguity interferes with comprehensibility. If a film is truly ambiguous like reality, then it cannot be readable. In his oft-cited discussion of Charlie Chaplin's *The Immigrant* (1917) in *Film as Art*, Arnheim describes the opening scene in which we see Chaplin's backside as he leans over the rail of a ship and twitches spasmodically, presumably seasick.[52] Chaplin then stands and turns to reveal that he was in fact fishing as he smiles and shows off his catch. Although we made an incorrect assumption about what we saw, there was nothing ambiguous in the scene and getting the joke is predicated on an intended misunderstanding. The shot was designed so as initially to showcase a recognized form of expression (seasickness) that would be counter to the form of expression next revealed (fishing). Ambiguity for Arnheim simply cannot be a component of the first authenticity. Importantly, in taking time to critique Kracauer, Arnheim revisits *Film as Art* and surmises that in his book he "all but neglected the 'documentary' aspects emphasized by Kracauer."[53] While Kracauer and, by default, Bazin disregard the importance of the second authenticity in their works, Arnheim admits that he himself downplayed the significance of the first authenticity. He concedes that "in practice, any photograph or film partakes of both authenticities."[54] Arnheim's qualification of his position in *Film as Art* is rather significant, even if he presents this qualification in terse understatement.

manipulation, authenticity, and troubling images

The history of art presented by Arnheim ends with a brief discussion concerning the two authenticities in the age of digital media. Like so very many critics and scholars of visual culture, Arnheim displays some concern over the digital image's increased ease of mutability. At stake are "the accidental, fugitive qualities recognized and appreciated as specifically photographic."[55] The first authenticity, then, is seemingly endangered. He writes that "the digitalization of the photographic image will increase the distrust of the information offered by still photography and film."[56] To explain this potentially increased distrust, he cites William J. Mitchell's characterization of the technical similarities and differences between paintings, photographs, and digital images.

> Here photography and digital imaging diverge strikingly, for the stored array of integers has none of the fragility and recalcitrance of the photograph's emulsion-coated surface ... [T]he essential characteristic of digital information is that it *can* be manipulated easily and very rapidly by computer. It is simply a matter of substituting new digits for old. Digital images are, in fact, much more susceptible to alteration than photographs, drawings, paintings, or *any* other kinds of images. So the art of the digital image cannot adequately be understood as primarily a matter of capture and printing ... intermediate *processing* of images plays a central role. Computational tools for transforming, combining, altering, and analyzing images are as essential to the digital artist as brushes and pigments are to a painter, and an understanding of them is the foundation of the craft of digital imaging.[57]

Mitchell, however, essentially goes on to question why we ever granted authenticity to the photographic image (Arnheim's first authenticity) in the first place. Arnheim seems to take solace in his own theory of the two authenticities, which provides a useful corrective to worries such as those offered by Mitchell.[58]

Crucial is Arnheim's contention that the first authenticity has never been exclusive to the photographic image. Moreover, Arnheim conceives of human intervention as an essential component of authenticity. Therefore, because manipulation necessarily exists in every recorded image, authenticity for Arnheim is always a measure of degree rather than kind. Digital images, then, promise at least not entirely to do away with the first authenticity, just as painting never has. Recent history seems to bear out Arnheim's inference, as digital images have proven to be quite powerful reminders of our faith in their two authenticities. YouTube, for example, holds a wealth of footage documenting seeming police abuses with tasers upon victims of varying degrees of haplessness, from the unrepentant chubby nudist to the bellicose blue-haired grandma. More tragic and unforgettable are the video footage of a very small teenage girl in Matta, Pakistan being brutally beaten by the Taliban as punishment for being accused of adultery and the shocking on-camera death of Neda Agha-Soltan in Tehran from Basij militia gunfire during the protests over the 2009 Iranian presidential election. Notoriously, the digital images from Abu Ghraib have shocked people the world over. In writing of these latter examples, David Rodowick notes, "the immediate cultural impact of these images has shown that our belief in the documentary powers of digital capture is undiminished."[59] Although Rodowick argues that digital imaging is accelerating "the waning of indexicality," he admits that "this does not mean that faith in such images as historical 'documents' has been lost or that we necessarily approach them with increased skepticism."[60] No one contests that these images are fictional, and the strength and earnestness of our response—be it laughter, disquiet, outrage, or tears—is testament to our belief in the authenticities of these digital images. Arnheim suggests that digital images will simply carry on the same ontological tension that has always existed in figurative art, regardless of medium. Because manipulation has always been a fundamental component of representational image-making, any increased skepticism toward digital images will have to arise from context and experience. He advises, "the more the photochemical material of photography and film becomes subject to surreptitious modification, the more its consumers will learn to be on their guard."[61] The above examples, despite being digital, do not test our expectations through any suggestion of surreptitious modification and therefore maintain their unquestioned authenticities.

Authenticity for Arnheim will always be determined by the extent of the manipulation, and he is willing to allow a rather high degree of intervention in deeming an image authentic. The often criticized process of retouching does not automatically preclude authenticity. He finds "more objectionable" retouching to achieve "the cheap effects of prettiness and false perfection," but he does find the elimination of "accidental flaws" for the sake of clarity to be "legitimate."[62] He cautiously proposes that "digitalization will amount

257

simply to a more refined procedure of traditional retouching."[63] He concedes that there is an overabundance of detail provided by reality and that there is an "inherent imperfection of physical appearance."[64] Retouching is necessary, as strict adherence to the first authenticity with such "inherent imperfection" would then diminish the second authenticity. Arnheim writes, "The accidental shape of individual specimens interfered with the search for canonic perfection and beauty."[65] Art, for Arnheim, clarifies and expresses, and these processes are dependent on recognized forms.[66] In support of such an assertion, it is telling that even in an age of more convenient and less expensive printing of photographic reproductions, many major field guides for birds—including Peterson, National Geographic, Sibley, and Kaufman—still favor illustrations over photographs. An individual specimen of a particular species being represented via an unadulterated photograph would seemingly best preserve the first authenticity, yet such an image might be neither as effective nor as efficient in presenting the identifying markers—the characterizing forms—of a species. Hand-drawn images, then, seem to best represent the formal distinctions between similar species, be they variations in beak size, wing shape, color accents, and the like. A more subjective illustration (emphasizing the second authenticity) is vital for achieving an idealized—in this case, most generic—representation, yet the use value of these guidebooks reveals our trust in the first authenticity offered therein.

Arnheim even considers composite images capable of both authenticities. He references photographer Jerry Uelsmann's works, which he characterizes as "mysterious fairy worlds" and "dream kingdoms."[67] Arnheim finds Uelsmann's photographs "perfectly convincing" and admires how "positive and negative material, giant size and miniatures fuse seamlessly."[68] Consider Uelsmann's *Apocalypse II* (1967), in which a group of people standing on the beach stare off into the distance at a massive lightning-inspired tree arising from the water in front of mountains on a not-too-distant shore.[69] Immediately one is seized by the great sense of balance within the image. The seemingly lone male stands in the middle of the group, nearly centered at the bottom third of the picture with two people to his left and three people—one being virtually hidden—to his right. He stands out from the others with his white shorts and dark shirt with white collar, while they all wear dresses with strong black-and-white vertical stripes. The tree that rises just above his head has an exacting bilateral symmetry, and even the splash caused by the seeming surge upward is perfectly symmetrical. The mountains in the distance likewise share the bilateral symmetry of the tree on the very same axis. The mountains are shaded differently to suggest differing atmospheric or geological conditions, and the water stretching between the people and the tree shines with a greater luminosity presumably stemming from the tree's explosion upward. There may be ambiguity to the overall meaning or interpretation of this image, but each of its component parts is instantly readable and identifiable. Arnheim writes that such images "look entirely trustworthy, and only the better knowledge of the viewers discloses that they are not."[70] The assumption is that the first authenticity is assured—despite all the obvious manipulation to the image—because of the very fact that the manipulation is so obvious. Viewer knowledge of both the outside world and the creative possibilities of photography help to assure the clarity and expressiveness of forms offered by the second authenticity. We may be unable to determine the exact seams for the extensively composite tree, but it is clear to us that it is both a composite and a negative image. For another example, the photographer Joseph D. Jachna at times will either use lenses with extremely short focal lengths or incorporate mirrors to create distorted landscapes.[71] For Arnheim, then, the test of whether or not Jachna's images are authentic resides in the relationship between the presentation of his images and our understanding of them, in terms of both what they are and how they were constructed. As long as we already comprehend that image distortion can occur from such creative decisions as lens choice and the use of mirrors, we can grant his images authenticity.

Arnheim follows this same reasoning in his determination of whether or not the footage used in the Rodney King trial was excessively manipulated. Patricia Greenfield and Paul Kibbey argue that "slow motion minimizes the violence . . . a slower blow is softer. In the tape, slow motion makes the blows appear less harmful than they really were."[72] For Arnheim, the purpose for this kind of manipulation was an attempt to single out specific forms in order to elucidate their precise nature (i.e., let us watch the blows in painstaking clarity, whereby we can contemplate every millisecond of the action in order to determine for ourselves whether or not the blows were excessive). Arnheim asserts that this manipulation went too far because "those video shots also modified certain other aspects of the scene, which interfered with the material's authenticity of the first kind."[73] The slow motion and still-frame images violated the distant framing, long-take aesthetic of Holliday's footage, not to mention the accompanying recorded sound. The forms under this kind of scrutiny basically changed; the expressions themselves were so altered as to ultimately express something altogether different. Greenfield and Kibbey cite one observer's remarks that the slow-motion footage " 'looks like a ballet.' "[74] Once the second authenticity was manipulated to this great extent, the first authenticity was imperiled. The jurors ended up repeatedly seeing a reality in slow motion and still frames that was markedly different than the reality the rest of us thought we saw.

Arnheim's distinction between the two authenticities offers a valuable model for thinking about troubling images that seem to present a reality that we may wish to deny because they do not conform to our understanding of that reality. Such images are the result, I would argue, of our wish for a potentially accidental manipulation of form, so that we might contest the second authenticity in light of the seeming strength of the first authenticity. For example, consider a photograph taken near Auschwitz in 1944 (see Figure 14.1). This image comes from an album of photographs owned by and featuring Karl Höcker, an SS officer who worked for about half a year (1944–1945) as the adjutant to Richard Baer, the commandant of Auschwitz.[75] Höcker stands among a row of SS Helferinnen—female auxiliaries who worked at the camps—posed and seated on a wooden fence. This picture is part of a series of photographs in the album concerning the theme of blueberries. We are to understand that these women here have all finished their respective shares of blueberries, as they each display an overturned empty bowl and smile for the camera. One woman at the center of the frame amuses the woman beside her with an exaggerated anguished face that mockingly cries, presumably over the fact that all her blueberries are gone. There is no question as to the first authenticity of this image since this image is entirely believable as what it is. At the same time, however, I find this image unsettling, and in the back of my mind I am constantly thinking that it just does not seem right. A description of the overall album given in *The New Yorker* seems fitting for this particular photograph: "the people it depicts are engaged in the greatest mass murder ever committed, yet its principal impression is one of pleasure. The people portrayed do not look like villains."[76] Researchers at the U.S. Holocaust Memorial Museum have been able to determine that on the very day that this photograph was taken, over one hundred people were executed upon their arrival at Auschwitz just a few miles away. Of course, this photograph does not assume to be art, so aesthetic issues need not apply. But Arnheim deems that the two authenticities figure in all photographic media, be they "aesthetic or merely informational."[77]

For me, as well as the writer for *The New Yorker*, this photograph seems— but only seems—partially inauthentic in the second sense. The expressive

Figure 14.1 "Here there are blueberries" (22 July 1944) from the Karl Höcker album. Image courtesy of the United States Holocaust Memorial Museum

qualities of the image—the playfulness and pleasure of these women—is authentic if it is an accurate portrayal of these women at that very moment. As Arnheim finds our understanding of expressive forms to be based on recognition and, therefore, context outside of the image, we cannot help but bring our foreknowledge of historical events and personal evaluative judgment to bear upon this photograph. The image does not seem to properly convey the form or expression that I and others recognize as the reality that it should be. Put most simply, this image looks like it should represent something else; the problem, however, is that it does not. With the Rodney King video, the obvious manipulation of the footage changed its form from what many, if not most, people would likely deem a brutal beating (at regular speed) to what was considered "ballet" (in slow motion). With the SS Helferinnen photograph, there is no alternative version, so it is much more difficult to pursue the question of manipulation in order to prove the image inauthentic. What we are left with is merely the feeling that the image is inauthentic due to the disparity between the expressive forms found within the image and the expressive forms that we otherwise would expect to see.

A perhaps more complicated example is the infamous image from Abu Ghraib of U.S. Army Specialist Sabrina Harman beside the corpse of Manadel al-Jamadi (see Figure 14.2).[78] Dressed completely in brown with antiseptic sea-foam-colored latex gloves, Harman smiles and gives a thumbs up as she leans over a seemingly dead but definitely bruised body draped in bags of ice. Julia Lesage's description of her initial response to the Abu Ghraib images seems particularly apt for this picture: "when I first saw the photos from Iraq's Abu Ghraib prison, showing U.S. military abusing detainees, I was both shocked by them and found them strangely familiar, like travel pictures, trophy photos."[79] Indeed, the expressivity of this image suggests that it is a "trophy photo," in which the proud individual broadly smiles in self-congratulation while displaying a freshly caught big fish now resting dead on ice. Harman herself insists that she had this picture taken in order to document al-Jamadi's abuse under so-called enhanced interrogation techniques at the hands of others. Her words, however, fall far short in mitigating the forms and expressions contained within the image. Lesage

261

Figure 14.2
Sabrina Harman with the corpse of Manadel al-Jamadi (4 November 2003)

describes this image as possibly having had "hidden or bypassed the social reality beyond and behind the frame."[80] Harman's grin and pose in this photo are immediately and intensely recognizable as being expressive forms for a trophy photo. We as viewers are so powerfully persuaded by this second authenticity that the image's first authenticity has been locked into a seemingly stable and understood representation of a highly damning reality. In the SS Helferinnen photograph, the expressivity of the image confirmed a profilmic event that simply did not conform to our preconceived notions. In the King video, the profilmic event seemed to change with the manipulation of the expressive forms that represented it. With the Harman photograph, the profilmic event is being contested not through the manipulation of its expressive forms, but through the re-evaluation of the outside knowledge that greatly determines our reading of these forms.

Errol Morris has written extensively about this last image in both his book and his blog for *The New York Times*, and he features it at length in his film *Standard Operating Procedure* (2008). He examines personal letters and military documents, as well as other images, in order to claim that such an image reveals an altogether different reality from that which is otherwise so strongly portrayed. Morris contends that Harman gives a thumbs-up pose in many pictures, so much so that the gesture is not committed consciously. A similar line of reasoning explains why Harman is smiling: she smiles because she is getting her picture taken and everyone smiles when getting a picture taken. Moreover, supported with the testimony of an expert in facial expressions and the evidence of doctored photographs, Morris explains how Harman's smile is not even genuine in the first place.[81] If we are to believe Harman and Morris, then what we have here is an image that is markedly and truly inauthentic in the second sense, since the expressivity it conveys so clearly to so many of us supposedly betrays a false reality. Morris's aim is to show that Harman is guilty of neither abuse nor cruel glee, despite the dead body and smile. His strategy is to raise doubts about the second authenticity of the image through a systematic explication of the false forms by which the image is constructed. Perhaps Morris's arguments are convincing, but the strength of that second authenticity still lingers (and he certainly must recognize this authenticity as well if he is to undertake so lengthy a process of invalidating it).

It seems that Arnheim was not just being glib when he claimed, "it took training to read photographs."[82] With such images as the video footage of Rodney King and the picture of Sabrina Harman, there are extremely high stakes for a "correct" reading, as that which seems obviously authentic can be undermined and proven otherwise, for better or worse. The King and Harman examples perhaps demonstrate that our "training" to read images is not quite done. Philip Gourevitch, Errol Morris's partner in much of his Abu Ghraib work, argues that "photographs cannot tell stories. They can only provide evidence of stories, and evidence is mute; it demands investigation and interpretation."[83] Gourevitch is in part justifying the elaborate project set out by Morris and him to investigate and interpret beyond the reality that the images of Abu Ghraib seemingly reveal, but of course his point is well taken. Arnheim's theory of the two authenticities can help us better understand and be more attentive to our emotional responses to images, particularly those that evoke strong reactions due to a contestable featured reality.

notes

1. Rudolf Arnheim, "The Two Authenticities of the Photographic Media," *The Journal of Aesthetics and Art Criticism* 51.4, Fall 1993, pp. 537–540. Slightly expanded and reprinted in Rudolf Arnheim, *The Split and the Structure*, Berkeley: University of California Press, 1996, pp. 24–30. All citations for this article will refer to the version anthologized in *The Split and the Structure*.
2. For Holliday's recollections on his recording of the King beating and the aftermath, see Michael Goldstein, "The Other Beating," *Los Angeles Times*, 19 Feb. 2006, p. 128.
3. Patricia Greenfield and Paul Kibbey, "Picture Imperfect," *The New York Times*, 1 Apr. 1993, p. A19. Arnheim himself cites this essay in his article.
4. Ibid.
5. André Bazin, "The Ontology of the Photographic Image," *What is Cinema?* vol. 1, ed. and trans. Hugh Gray, Berkeley: University of California Press, 2005, pp. 9–16.
6. Rudolf Arnheim, *Film as Art*, Berkeley: University of California Press, 1957.
7. Arnheim, "The Two Authenticities," pp. 24–25.
8. Ibid., p. 24.
9. Ibid., p. 25.
10. Ibid.
11. Ibid.
12. Ibid.
13. Ibid., p. 24.
14. Ibid.
15. Kurt Koffka, "The Environmental Field: Visual Organization and its Laws," in *Principles of Gestalt Psychology*, New York: Harcourt, Brace & World, 1963, p. 138. This book was originally published in 1935.
16. Ibid.
17. Max Wertheimer, "Dynamics and Logic of Productive Thinking," in *Productive Thinking*, New York: Harper & Brothers, 1959, p. 237. This book was published posthumously in 1945.
18. Arnheim, "The Two Authenticities," p. 25; Bazin, "Ontology of the Photographic Image," p. 11.
19. Ibid., pp. 9 and 11.
20. Ibid.
21. Ibid., p. 10.
22. Ibid.
23. Ibid., pp. 10–11.
24. Ibid., p. 10.
25. Ibid., p. 12.
26. Ibid., p. 11.

263

27. Ibid.
28. Arnheim, "The Two Authenticities," p. 25.
29. Bazin, "Ontology of the Photographic Image," p. 12.
30. Ibid.
31. Ibid., p. 13.
32. Arnheim, "The Two Authenticities," p. 25.
33. Ibid.
34. Bazin, "Ontology of the Photographic Image," p. 13.
35. Ibid.
36. Ibid.
37. Ibid.
38. Arnheim, "The Two Authenticities," p. 26.
39. Ibid.
40. Ibid., p. 25.
41. David Octavius Hill, letter to Mr. Bicknell, 17 January 1848, George Eastman House, Rochester, New York. Quoted in Beaumont Newhall, *The History of Photography, From 1839 to the Present*, New York: Museum of Modern Art, 1982, p. 48.
42. Arnheim, "The Two Authenticities," p. 26.
43. Ibid.
44. Ibid.
45. Ibid.
46. Bazin, "Ontology of the Photographic Image," p. 15.
47. Arnheim, "The Two Authenticities," p. 26.
48. Ibid.
49. Ibid.
50. Ibid.
51. See, for example, André Bazin, "The Evolution of the Language of Cinema," in *What is Cinema?* vol. 1, pp. 23–40; or, André Bazin, *Jean Renoir*, ed. François Truffaut, New York: Da Capo Press, 1992.
52. Arnheim, *Film as Art*, pp. 36–37.
53. Arnheim, "The Two Authenticities," p. 27.
54. Ibid.
55. Ibid., p. 29.
56. Ibid.
57. William J. Mitchell, *The Reconfigured Eye: Visual Truth in the Post-Photographic Era*, Cambridge: MIT Press, 1992, p. 7.
58. For an interesting use of Bazin's theories to counter worries concerning the ontology of digital images, see Daniel Morgan, "Rethinking Bazin: Ontology and Realist Aesthetics," *Critical Inquiry* 32, Spring 2006, pp. 443–481.
59. D. N. Rodowick, *The Virtual Life of Film*, Cambridge: Harvard University Press, 2007, p. 146.
60. Ibid., p. 145.
61. Arnheim, "The Two Authenticities," p. 29.
62. Ibid., p. 28.
63. Ibid., p. 29.
64. Ibid., p. 25.
65. Ibid.
66. See, for example, Arnheim's discussion of facial expression in *Film as Art*, pp. 134–143.
67. Arnheim, "The Two Authenticities," pp. 27–28.

68. Ibid.
69. Uelsmann's *Apocalypse II*, along with many other Uelsmann photographs, can be found online either via ARTstor or on the website for the Art Institute for Chicago (artic.edu/aic).
70. Arnheim, "The Two Authenticities," p. 28.
71. For examples of Jachna's photography, see *Light Touching Silver: Photographs by Joseph D. Jachna*, Chicago: Congress Printing, 1980.
72. Greenfield and Kibbey, "Picture Imperfect," p. A19.
73. Arnheim, "The Two Authenticities," p. 28.
74. Greenfield and Kibbey, "Picture Imperfect," p. A19.
75. There are 116 photographs in the Höcker album, which was anonymously donated in 2007 to the United States Holocaust Memorial Museum by a retired U.S. Army officer who discovered the album in Germany in 1946. The images can be accessed via the online exhibit "Auschwitz through the Lens of the SS: Photos of Nazi Leadership at the Camps" at the website for the Holocaust Memorial Museum (ushmm.org).
76. Alec Wilkinson, "A Reporter at Large: Picturing Auschwitz," *The New Yorker*, 17 Mar. 2008, p. 48.
77. Arnheim, "The Two Authenticities," p. 27.
78. 279 photographs, plus 19 video files, can be found in the Abu Ghraib files posted online since 2006 at Salon.com.
79. Julia Lesage, "Abu Ghraib and Images of Abuse and Torture," *Jump Cut: A Review of Contemporary Media* 47, Winter 2005.
80. Julia Lesage, "Torture Documentaries," *Jump Cut: A Review of Contemporary Media* 51, Spring 2009.
81. Errol Morris, "The Most Curious Thing," *The New York Times*, 19 May 2008, available online at <http://morris.blogs.nytimes.com/2008/05/19/the-most-curious-thing/>
82. Arnheim, "The Two Authenticities," p. 25.
83. Philip Gourevitch, "The Abu Ghraib We Cannot See," *The New York Times*, 24 May 2009, late ed., p. WK10.

bibliography

works on rudolf arnheim cited in this book

Andrew, Dudley, *The Major Film Theories*, London: Oxford University Press, 1976.

Bordwell, David, *On the History of Film Style*, Cambridge: Harvard University Press, 1997.

Carroll, Noël, *Philosophical Problems of Classical Film Theory*, Princeton: Princeton University Press, 1988.

Hake, Sabine, *The Cinema's Third Machine: Writing on Film in Germany 1907–1933*, Lincoln: University of Nebraska Press, 1993.

Kleinman, Kent and Leslie Van Duzer (eds.), *Rudolf Arnheim: Revealing Vision*, Ann Arbor: University of Michigan Press, 1997.

Koch, Gertrud, "Rudolf Arnheim: The Materialist of Aesthetic Illusion," *New German Critique* 51, Fall 1990, pp. 164–178.

Merjian, Ara H., "Middlebrow Modernism: Rudolf Arnheim at the Crossroads of Film Theory and the Psychology of Art," in Angela Dalle Vacche (ed.), *The Visual Turn: Classical Film Theory and Art*, New Brunswick, NJ: Rutgers University Press, 2003.

Verstegen, I., *Arnheim, Gestalt, and Art: A Psychological Theory*, Austria: Springer-Verlag Wien, 2005.

Wilke, Jürgen, "Cinematography as a Medium of Communication: The Promotion of Research by the League of Nations and the Role of Rudolf Arnheim," *European Journal of Communication* No. 6, 1991, pp. 337–353.

works by rudolf arnheim cited in this book

Arnheim, Rudolf, *Stimme von der Galerie*, Berlin: Benary, 1928.

—— *Film als Kunst*, Berlin: Rowohlt, 1932.

—— *Film*, trans. L. M. Sieveking and Ian F. D. Morrow, London: Faber and Faber, 1933.

—— "Die Zukunft des Tonfilms," 1934, reprinted in *Montage A/V* Vol. 9 No. 2, 2000, pp. 19–32.

—— "Seeing Afar Off," *Intercine* Vol. 7 No. 2, Feb. 1935, pp. 71–82.

—— "Remarks on the Colour Film," *Sight and Sound* Vol. 4, Winter 1935/36, pp. 160–162.

—— *Radio*, London: Faber and Faber, 1936, reprinted New York, Ayer, 1986.

—— "Televisione, Domani sarà così," *Cinema* No. 20 Apr. 1937, pp. 337–338.

—— "Disciplina del grammofono, della radio, del telefono e della televisione," *Sapere* Vol. 71 No. 6, 15 Dec. 1937, pp. 415–417; English version translated by Christy Wampole, *Modernism/Modernity* Vol. 16 No. 2 Apr. 2009, pp. 422–426.

—— and Martha Collins Bayne, "Foreign Language Broadcasts over Local American Stations: A Study of a Special Interest Program," in Paul F. Lazarsfeld and Frank N. Stanton (eds.), *Radio Research, 1941*, New York: Duell, Sloan and Pearce, 1941, pp. 3–64.

—— "The World of the Daytime Serial," in Lazarsfeld and Stanton (eds.), *Radio Research, 1942–1943*, New York: Duell, Sloan and Pearce, 1944, pp. 34–85. Reprinted by Arno Press, New York, 1979.

—— *Art and Visual Perception*, Berkeley: University of California Press, 1954, The New Version, 1974.

—— *Film as Art*, Berkeley: University of California Press, 1957.

—— "Melancholy Unshaped," *Journal of Aesthetics and Art Criticism* Vol. 21 No. 3, Spring 1963, pp. 291–297.

—— *Toward a Psychology of Art*, Berkeley: University of California Press, 1966.

—— "Art Today and the Film," *Film Culture* No. 42, Fall 1966, pp. 43–45.

—— *Visual Thinking*, London: Faber and Faber, 1969.

—— *Entropy and Art: An Essay on Disorder and Order*, Berkeley: University of California Press, 1971.

—— "Colors Irrational and Rational," *The Journal of Aesthetics and Art Criticism* Vol. 33 No. 2, 1974.

—— *The Dynamics of Architectural Form*, Berkeley: University of California Press, 1978.

—— "Style as a Gestalt Problem," *Journal of Aesthetics and Art Criticism* Vol. 39 No. 3, Spring 1981, pp. 281–289.

—— "Perceiving and Portraying," *Times Literary Supplement*, 29 Oct. 1982, p. 1180.

—— *New Essays on the Psychology of Art*, Berkeley: University of California Press, 1986.

—— "Immagine-avvenimento e durata," *Cinema Nuovo* No. 305 Jan.–Feb. 1987, p. 22.

—— *The Power of the Center: A Study of Composition in the Visual Arts*, The New Version, Berkeley: University of California Press, 1988.

—— "Foreword" in Agusto Garau, *Color Harmonies*, trans. Nicola Bruno, Chicago: University of Chicago Press, 1993.

—— *The Split and the Structure: Twenty-Eight Essays*, Berkeley: University of California Press, 1996.

—— *Film Essays and Criticism*, trans. Brenda Benthien, Madison: University of Wisconsin Press, 1997.

—— "Composites of Media: The History of an Idea," *Michigan Quarterly Review* Vol. 38 No. 4, Fall 1999, pp. 558–561.

—— *Rundfunk als Hörkunst und weitere Aufsätze zum Hörfunk*, Frankfurt: Suhrkamp, 2001.

—— *Die Seele in der Silbersicht: Medientheoretische Texte. Photographie—Film—Rundfunk*, Baden Baden: Suhrkamp, Carl Hanser Verlag, 2004.

bibliographies of arnheim's work

Arnheim, Mary, *Rudolf Arnheim: Bibliography of his Writings, 1928–1982*, Ann Arbor: Self-published, 1983.

Behrens, Roy R., "Rudolf Arnheim: The Little Owl on the Shoulder of Athene," *Leonardo* Vol. 31 No. 3, June/July 1998, pp. 231–233.

Diederichs, Helmut H., "Complete Bibliography of Writings on Film by Rudolf Arnheim," in Rudolf Arnheim, *Film Essays and Criticism*, trans. Brenda Benthien, Madison: University of Wisconsin Press, 1997, pp. 233–248.

—— "Gesamtverzeichnis der Schriften zu Film, Photo, Presse und Rundfunk/ Grammophon von Rudolf Arnheim," available online at <http://www.soziales.fhdortmund.de/diederichs/arnforum/ragesv1.htm>.

Smith, Ralph A., "Rudolf Arnheim: An International Bibliography of his Writings," *Journal of Aesthetic Education*, Vol. 27 No. 4, Winter 1993, pp. 165–189.

contributors

Nora M. Alter is Professor and Chair of Film and Media Arts at Temple School of Communications, Temple University, Philadelphia, Pennsylvania. She is author of *Vietnam Protest Theatre: The Television War on Stage* (1996), *Projecting History: Non-Fiction German Film* (2002), *Chris Marker* (2006), and co-editor of *Sound Matters: Essays on the Acoustics of Modern German Culture* (2004).

Dudley Andrew is the R. Selden Rose Professor of Film and Comparative Literature and serves as Director of Graduate Studies in the Film Studies Program at Yale University. He has authored and edited some ten books on the history, theory, and aesthetics of cinema.

Vincent Bohlinger is an Assistant Professor of Film Studies in the Department of English at Rhode Island College. He is working on a book on Soviet socialist realist film style.

David Bordwell is the Jacques Ledoux Professor Emeritus of Film Studies at the University of Wisconsin–Madison. He has authored and edited some seventeen books on the history, theory, and aesthetics of cinema. He is recently retired from teaching and maintains a website at www.david bordwell.net.

Colin Burnett is a PhD candidate in Film at the University of Wisconsin–Madison. He was recently awarded a Social Sciences and Humanities Research Council of Canada fellowship to pursue his research on a dissertation tentatively titled "The Invention of Robert Bresson: Market, Process, Film Style."

Jinhee Choi is Lecturer in Film at the University of Kent, UK. She is the co-editor of *Philosophy of Film and Motion Picture* with Noël Carroll (2005) and author of *The South Korean Film Renaissance: Local Hitmakers, Global Provocateurs* (2010).

Meraj Dhir is a PhD candidate in History of Art and Architecture at Harvard University. His thesis is on performance, stylistic composition and emotion in the films of Robert Bresson.

Doron Galili is a PhD candidate in the Committee on Cinema and Media Studies at the University of Chicago. His research deals with the early phases of the relationship between film and television.

Patrick Keating is an Assistant Professor of Communication at Trinity University, San Antonio, Texas. He is author of *Hollywood Lighting from the Silent Era to Film Noir* (2010). He has published on Hollywood narrative, Italian neorealism, and the film theory of Pasolini.

Eric Rentschler is the Arthur Kingsley Porter Professor of Germanic Languages and Literatures at Harvard University where he chairs the German Department and also teaches in the Department of Visual and Environmental Studies. He has authored and edited a number of books on German film history, including *The Ministry of Illusion* (1996). He is presently working on two book projects: *The Enduring Allure of Nazi Attractions* and *Courses in Time: Film in the Federal Republic of Germany, 1962–1989.*

Greg M. Smith is Professor of Moving Image Studies in the Department of Communication at Georgia State University. His books include *Beautiful TV: The Art and Argument of Ally McBeal* (2007), *Film Structure and the Emotion System* (2003), and *Passionate Views: Film, Cognition, and Emotion* (1999).

Maureen Turim is Professor of English and Film and Media Studies at the University of Florida. She is author of *Abstraction in Avant-Garde Films* (1985), *Flashbacks in Film: Memory and History* (1989), and *The Films of Oshima Nagisa: Images of a Japanese Iconoclast* (1998). Her current book project is entitled *Desire and its Ends: The Driving Forces of Recent Cinema, Literature and Art.*

Malcolm Turvey teaches Film Studies at Sarah Lawrence College. He has published widely on film theory and avant-garde film. He is an editor of *October* and author of *Doubting Vision: Film and the Revelationist Tradition* (2008).

Shawn VanCour is a Visiting Assistant Professor of Cinema and Media Studies at Carleton College, Northfield, Minnesota. He has published on the rise of contemporary media historiography and on debates over musical form for early radio presentations. He is currently completing a larger study on the aesthetics of 1920s American broadcasting.

contributors

index

index